173668

BIOLOGY
OF THE
REPTILIA

BIOLOGY OF THE REPTILIA

Edited by

CARL GANS

*State University of New York at Buffalo
Buffalo, N.Y., U.S.A.*

VOLUME 2

MORPHOLOGY B

Coeditor for this volume

THOMAS S. PARSONS

*University of Toronto
Toronto, Ontario
Canada*

1970

ACADEMIC PRESS
LONDON AND NEW YORK

ACADEMIC PRESS INC. (LONDON) LTD
Berkeley Square House
Berkeley Square
London, W1X 6BA

U.S. Edition published by

ACADEMIC PRESS INC.
111 Fifth Avenue
New York, New York 10003

Library of Congress Catalog Card Number: 68-9113

SBN: 12-274602-3

PRINTED IN GREAT BRITAIN BY
W. S. COWELL LTD
IPSWICH, SUFFOLK

Contributors to Volume 2

Irwin L. Baird, *Department of Anatomy, The Milton S. Hershey Medical Center, Pennsylvania State University, Hershey, Pennsylvania 17003, U.S.A.*

Robert Barrett, *Department of Zoology, University of California, Los Angeles, California 90024, U.S.A.*

Carl Gans, *Department of Biology, State University of New York at Buffalo, Buffalo, New York 14214, U.S.A.*

Paul F. A. Maderson, *Department of Biology, Brooklyn College of the City University of New York, Brooklyn, New York 11210, U.S.A.*

Richard M. Meszler*, *Department of Anatomy, University of Louisville School of Medicine, Louisville, Kentucky 40202, U.S.A.*

Thomas S. Parsons, *Department of Zoology, University of Toronto, Toronto 5, Ontario, Canada.*

Garth L. Underwood, *Department of Botany and Zoology, Sir John Cass College, London E.C.3, England.*

*Present address: Department of Anatomy, Albert Einstein College of Medicine, Bronx, New York 10461, U.S.A.

Preface

This volume presents chapters summarizing information on the morphology of four major sense organs of Recent reptiles. It also continues the pattern established in the first volume. Structure is emphasized, in the expectation that the physiology of these organs will be treated in subsequent volumes. The chapters furthermore reflect the very uneven level of information available for each system. They clearly demonstrate areas on which additional information is required.

Only for temperature receptors have structure and function been combined. since the subject seemed sufficiently restricted. This chapter has been supplemented by two appendices, the first indicating the distribution of these organs in different species and the second dealing with the functional changes in the ultrastructural arrangement of the sensory endings. The latter appendix results from work carried out while this chapter was being written.

The contents of these chapters document the extent to which the sense organs of the various reptiles differ. These structures obviously reflect the striking effects of phylogeny and of ecological influences, though the difference between the two is often unclear. For this reason we have encouraged the authors to provide a fairly detailed treatment of structural variation down to the familial and even the generic level. It is our hope that the basis thus presented will lead to a better understanding of the function of these systems in terms both of sensory physiology and of its utilization in the animals' behavioral sequences.

This volume also contains a chapter by the editors, designed as an introduction to the literature in reptilian taxonomy. This is not addressed to the specialist and is far from exhaustive. Rather, it is conceived as a review of journals and references that may facilitate identification of material collected from one or another region or obtained from dealers. We have, therefore, emphasized recent work and statements that were sufficiently well illustrated and clearly written to permit their use by the non-specialist.

I wish to thank the authors, who agreed to repeated and major changes in the nature of the required contributions. Drs. I. L. Baird, A. d'A. Bellairs, F. Crescitelli, C. O. Diefenbach, W. D. Elliot, G. Haas, D. W. Hamilton, J. E. Heath, A. G. Kluge, A. E. Leviton, W. G. Lynn, C. J. McCoy, S. B. McDowell, Jr., R. Mertens, M. R. Miller, S. A. Minton, Jr., P. J. Regal, D. B. Webster, H. Wermuth, E. G. Wever, and E. E. Williams reviewed individual manuscripts, and Mrs. Gloria Griffin and my wife provided extensive editorial assistance. My coeditor, Dr. Thomas S. Parsons shared all aspects of the work and was instrumental in seeing much of this volume through the press during my absence. Drs. James A. Peters and Heinz Wermuth critically read the proofs for usage and accuracy of the Latin names employed. National Science Foundation Grants GB 3881 and GN 815 provided for some financial assistance and the Department of Biology of my University paid the considerable bills for postage and copying.

September, 1969   Carl Gans

Contents

2. The Nose and Jacobson's Organ

Thomas S. Parsons

3. The Anatomy of the Reptilian Ear
Irwin L. Baird

4. The Pit Organs of Snakes
Robert Barrett
with appendices by P. F. A. Maderson and Richard M. Meszler

Errata for Volume 1.

	Instead of	To read
p. 208, line 3, from bottom	it is never complete	it is not always complete
p. 209, line 9	posterodorsally or dorsoventrally	in a posterodorsal-anteroventral direction
p. 233, line 20	intervertebral central in position	intervertebral in position
p. 269, line 9	seventh or ninth caudal	seventh to ninth caudal
p. 286, last line	(Fig. 77 D)	(Fig. 82 D)
p. 303, lines 5, 6, 8 10	Baur, G. von	Baur, G.

The cover photograph on the dust jacket of volume 1 shows several specimens of *Boiga dendrophila*. It was taken in the Buffalo Zoological Gardens.

CHAPTER 1

The Eye

GARTH UNDERWOOD

Principal Research Fellow, British Museum (Natural History),* London, England

I. Introduction

The classical approach to the reptilian eye tends to be that of comparative anatomy as it has grown out of medical anatomy. There is a good deal of detailed and accurate information about the eye as a whole and its adnexae but, unlike that of the ear, the study of reptilian eyes never contributed to any triumph of classical morphology. Indeed the classical duplicity theory was never clearly applied to reptiles, and the older literature, surveyed by Franz (1934) who gives an extensive guide to the literature, contains relatively little useful information about the visual cells. Rochon-Duvigneaud (1943) gives the results of his extensive personal studies and a wealth of illustrations of various parts of the eye; only the visual cells are not treated in much detail. Walls (1942), who added much to our knowledge of reptile eyes, provides the first comprehensive interpretation; his work is the first important contribution of comparative ophthalmology to reptilian biology.

The eye clearly shows how species have modified their basic equipment to current conditions and evolutionary opportunities. Study of the eye may contribute to reconstruction of the group's phylogeny. The morphological changes at the level of gross anatomy are paralleled by changes at the cellular level in the retina, and biochemical studies are now extending our knowledge of further changes down to the molecular level.

This chapter contains a detailed survey of the eyes and their adnexae. The other structures of the orbit are considered sufficiently to place the eyes in their anatomical context, and the developmental concepts are included to provide the background to some morphological interpretations.

The formal treatment thus begins with embryology. This is followed by the description of the eye in a diurnal lizard, a member of the best known

---

* Now at Sir John Cass College, Jewry St., London, England.

group of reptiles. Each part of the eye and its associated structures is treated in detail and followed by a survey of the conditions in other lizards and amphisbaenians. To complete the account of a diurnal lizard it was necessary to combine observations from several species and even so it was barely possible to make it reasonably complete. The condition in lizards then serves as a basis for comparison with that in other groups of Recent reptiles. An attempt is also made to review the inferences that a paleontologist may draw. A discussion of the various parts of the eye and their adaptive modifications is followed by a review of what the eye can tell us about the various groups of reptiles. I hope that readers will accept the more extended flights of speculation as intended to provoke discussion rather than to state positions firmly held.

The eye, which offers an exceptionally difficult combination of hard and soft tissues, presents some special technical difficulties that influence the reliability and interpretation of results. The soft lens of a turtle or lizard undergoes shrinkage and distortion on fixation and dehydration and loses contact with the ciliary body. Thus it is probable that no published figure (including Fig. 4) shows the lens in a natural relationship with the rest of the eye. The older literature abounds in inaccuracies and omissions concerning the visual cells; Walls (1938) has stressed the importance of good fixation and careful observation. I endorse Walls' recommendation of Kolmer's fluid as a fixative; it penetrates well, decalcifies scleral ossicles where present, and gives the tissues good staining properties. Bouin's fluid, which has often been used, gives rather poor results with reptilian material. A particularly common artifact of poor fixation is the formation of vacuoles; these have sometimes been mistaken for oil-droplets. Either the microtome knife or distortion due to poor fixation may separate the two members of a double cell thus producing artifacts. The plane of section is important because double cells tend to be oriented vertically and can be properly seen only in vertical sections. Tangential sections are valuable; they permit a check on the distribution and relative frequency of visual cell types and, in particular, facilitate recognition of rare cell types. Indeed the orientation and structure of double cells cannot be fully discerned without study of tangential sections.

The topography of the eye can easily give rise to confusion. Some of this derives from the transfer of terms from human anatomy, for what is anterior in the human eye is lateral in that of most other vertebrates. Another source of confusion arises from the fact that the terms "external" and "internal" do not mean the same thing when the eye is considered in the head and when the eye is considered alone. Dorsal and ventral are, fortunately, unequivocal terms. I use the terms "nasal" and "temporal" as they have the same meaning whatever the direction of the optical axes. I propose to distinguish the opposite ends of the optical axis as "corneal" and "orbital"; between these poles lies the equator of the globe, lines running from pole to pole are meridional. Radially within the eye we may distinguish scleral and vitreal directions. Sections are usually cut in radial or tangential planes in relation to the spherical curvature of the eyeball.

Visual pigments are classed as scotopic, those that function under conditions of dim illumination, and photopic, those that function in bright light. The individual visual pigments are nowadays defined by their absorbance spectra. There are, however, a number of older reports of scotopic pigments seen by inspection of the dark adapted retina; I have referred to these imprecisely defined pigments as "visual purple". These old reports do at least indicate the occurrence of pigment in sufficient quantity probably to repay spectrophotometric study.

I have recently made some suggestions concerning the nomenclature of visual cell types (Underwood, 1968). The members of the type B double cells of tetrapods and snakes (see pp. 34 and 58) are here termed "axial" and "peripheral". The axial cell, as I call it, has been known as "accessory" in tetrapods and "chief" in snakes and the peripheral as "chief" in tetrapods and "accessory" in snakes. I term the larger member of the type C double cell, peculiar to geckos (see p. 42), the "major" and the smaller the "minor".

The classification of lizards and turtles follows that of Romer (1956). Some years ago I put forward some proposals concerning the classification of geckos (Underwood, 1951b) based largely on characters of the eyes. Kluge (1967), studying a wider variety of characters, has made some amendments that I fully accept and I here follow his scheme. I find the classification of snakes more difficult. It is widely agreed that existing schemes of classification of snakes are artificial. I have recently made a new attack upon the problem drawing on a wide variety of evidence and giving prominence to the retina (Underwood, 1967a). My suggestions were intended to be provocative rather than definitive; indeed the scheme proposed is already undergoing revision in my own mind as a direct result of further studies of the retina. I here present the data within the framework of my 1967 arrangement whilst pointing out that some of these same data indicate the need for amendment.

II. Embryology

A general account of the development of the vertebrate eye is given by Walls (1942). There does not appear to be any general account of the development of the eye of a reptile, but there are two studies of certain aspects that are important for the interpretation of the morphology of reptile eyes. Jokl (1923) studied the closure of the embryonic fissure and development of the optic papilla and associated structures, and Leplat (1921, 1922) studied the development of the musculature of the eye and of the conus. This brief account is drawn from these sources.

The first rudiments of the paired retinae are recognizable in the embryonic forebrain before closure of the neural tube; when closure occurs the retinal rudiments expand to form the optic vesicles and make contact with the ectoderm. The optic vesicle invaginates to form the two-layered optic cup, and at the same time the overlying ectoderm invaginates and pinches off to form the lens vesicle. The optic vesicle extends largely dorsal to the level of the hollow optic stalk, so that on invagination it forms what is more precisely a dorsal half-cup; at the same time the ventral surface of the optic stalk invaginates so that it forms a dorsal crescent in cross section. The ventral edges of the half-cup grow downwards and approach one another until an approximately circular cup is formed with an open slot, known as the embryonic fissure, on the ventral side.

The optic cup now has two layers and the space between them is in virtual continuity with the ventricles of the brain which later become lined by flagellated ependymal cells. Once the optic cup is formed, further growth takes place at the rim which eventually becomes the pupillary margin of the iris. The outer layer of the optic cup differentiates as pigment epithelium. The inner layer develops into the nervous retina. The differentiation starts at the orbital pole and advances towards the corneal pole. As seen by light microscopy, differentiation begins on the vitreal surface with the development of the ganglion cells. Olney (1968) has however recently shown that in the mouse, as seen by electron microscopy, the synapses of the outer plexiform layer differentiate *before* those of the inner plexiform layer. Interpretations of the pattern of development based on observations by light microscopy are therefore open to revision. Svanidze (1959) finds, by light microscopy, that in the "rock lizard" (*Lacerta*) the first ganglion cells to differentiate are in the posterodorsal region of the retina, in the position of the presumptive fovea. The axons of the ganglion cells grow across the vitreal surface of the retina and towards the brain between the cells of (not within the lumen of) the optic stalk. From the vitreal face, cells proliferate in a scleral direction to give rise to the other nervous layers. As seen by light microscopy the visual cells are the last to differentiate.

The lens vesicle meanwhile differentiates by the thickening of its orbital wall, the cells of which become columnar and transform into lens fibres. The rest of the lens vesicle becomes the lens capsule investing the lens proper. The cells of the lens capsule undergo some further differentiation, differently in different reptile groups.

The hyaloid circulation develops from an artery running along the ventral groove of the optic stalk to the optic cup. It enters the optic cup through the fissure and spreads over the vitreal face of the retina. The fissure starts closing about the middle of its length and closure proceeds in both corneal and orbital directions, thus embracing the hyaloid vessels within the optic cup. The vessels extend by following mesoderm cells that spread across the inside of the optic cup, but do not reach its corneal margin. As closure approaches the optic stalk, the fissure becomes reduced orbitally to a small aperture through which enter the hyaloid vessel and mesodermal tissue. Corneally the fissure forms a large notch in the ventral margin of the pupil, and its edges meet and fuse reducing this part of the fissure to a tiny distal opening by which the hyaloid vessels leave the cup. By this time the hyaloid vessels pass across the floor of the optic cup on a crest of tissue, leave by the distal opening, and join a vessel on the corneal face of the iris (Jokl, 1923).

By this stage the rudiments of the conus have begun to appear in lizards, dorsal to the entry of the optic nerve, arising from ependymal (glia) cells of the optic stalk. The middle region of the hyaloid vessel atrophies. With closure of the proximal aperture the proximal portion of the hyaloid vessel disappears. The distal part of the vessel remains filled with blood for a while. Leplat (1922) is emphatic that the blood supply of the conus derives from a vessel that enters the eye separately from the hyaloid vessel and runs in the axis of the nerve. By the time that the conus is vascular the hyaloid artery has atrophied, and both apertures of the fissure have closed.

The vitreous humour is formed initially by contributions from glial cells of the retina and mesodermal cells that enter with the hyaloid circulation. With the disappearance of the hyaloid vessels the remaining, secondary, vitreous is formed by glial cells. As the outer layer of the optic cup develops pigment, the mesoderm surrounding the eye develops a capillary network. Further mesoderm condenses to form the connective tissue of the chorioid and sclera. At first these two layers are one, but later are separated by the development of the epichorioidal lymph spaces.

The anterior chamber of the eye is formed early as a split in the mesoderm separating iris mesoderm from corneal mesoderm. The rim of the optic cup resumes growth in a corneal direction as a simple double layer between the iris mesoderm and the lens. The ciliary and transversalis muscles of lizards differentiate solely from iris mesoderm. The outer layer of the iris develops pigment that spreads from the pupillary margin to the inner layer. The outer layer then develops striated muscle fibres that form the sphincter in lizards. The suspensory fibres of the lens develop from the ciliary epithelium in the same way as do the other fibres of the vitreous body.

In Testudines the formation and closure of the embryonic fissure occur very much as in lizards, accompanied by formation and atrophy of the hyaloid circulation. There is no trace of a conus (Jokl, 1923).

In *Alligator* the hyaloid vessel, richly invested with mesoderm, ends blindly while the embryonic fissure is still open. As the fissure closes, a proximal aperture remains but no distal aperture forms. As the distal part of the blind hyaloid vessel and its associated mesoderm atrophies, the proximal part gives rise to a mesodermal conus that reaches nearly to the lens (Jokl, 1923). This later atrophies leaving almost no trace.

The history of the mesodermal tissues is rather different in snakes. With closure of the optic fissure a large, richly vascular strand of mesoderm passes across the floor of the optic cup to emerge by a notch in the pupillary margin and join the circulation of the surrounding mesoderm. Later the distal portion of the mesodermal ridge atrophies along with its blood vessels. The proximal portion builds up into a conus that eventually reaches almost to the lens. At the same time the mesoderm spreads on the vitreal face of the retina. By the time of hatching, in *Natrix*, a vascular sheet of mesoderm extends across the whole of the inner face of the retina and drains into a ringvein (the orbicular vein) between the ora serrata and the ciliary roll. The conus is by now dwindling, but in a few snakes, such as *Vipera*, it persists in the adult. The optic nerve becomes divided into bundles by septa of connective tissue. Leplat's (1921) account implies that the powerful sphincter muscles at the root of the iris of snakes have the same (mesodermal?) origin as the few fibres in the ciliary roll. Unlike lizards, snakes develop radial iris muscle fibres.

III. Lacertilia and Amphisbaenia

A. Orbit and Adnexae of a Diurnal Lizard

The account is based upon Oelrich's (1956) detailed study of the iguanid *Ctenosaura pectinata*, supplemented by dissection of the related form *Cyclura carinata*.

The large orbits are separated in the sagittal plane by a thin interorbital septum (Fig. 1). This septum consists of a sheet of cartilage with three membrane-filled fenestrae. The two trabeculae cranii emerge from the basisphenoid and unite to form the trabecula communis from which rises the septum; the slender parasphenoid rostrum of the basisphenoid lies ventral to the trabecula. Dorsally the septum passes into the planum supraseptale which meets the frontal bones and forms a trough supporting the olfactory tracts and bulbs. The large superior orbital fenestra occupies the dorsal half of the septum; the tendon of the nictitating membrane arises from the anterodorsal border of this fenestra. Posteroventrally the optic fenestra is largely filled by membrane, but is pierced by the large optic foramen posteriorly. Below the optic fenestra is the small triangular supratrabecular fenestra. Posterior to the septum the paired orbital cartilages and membranes enclose the forebrain. The paired orbitosphenoid bones lie posterior to the optic fenestrae, meet the planum supraseptale dorsally, and pass into the hypochiasmatic cartilage ventrally. Behind the planum supraseptale are the epioptic membranes which are bordered posteriorly by the pilae accessoriae. Ventral to these pilae and the more ventral pilae antoticae are the metoptic membranes which extend posterior to the orbitosphenoid bones and are separated from the supratrabecular membrane by the subiculum infundibuli cartilage and the foramen for the anastomotic vein.

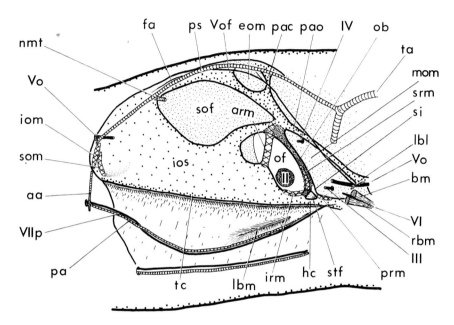

Fig. 1. The left orbit of *Cyclura carinata* with the eye and muscles removed. aa, Anastomotic artery; arm, origin of anterior rectus muscle; bm, bursalis muscle; eom, epioptic membrane; fa, frontal artery; hc, hypochiasmatic cartilage; iom, origin of inferior oblique muscle; ios, interorbital septum; irm, origin of inferior rectus muscle; lbl, ligament of levator bulbi muscle; lbm, levator bulbi muscle; mom, metoptic membrane; nmt, tendon of nictitating membrane; ob, orbitosphenoid bone; of, optic fenestra; pa, palatine artery; pac, pila accessoria; pao, pila antotica; prm, origin of posterior rectus muscle; ps, planum supraseptale; rbm, retractor bulbi muscle; si, subiculum infundibuli; sof, supraorbital fenestra; som, origin of superior oblique muscle; srm, origin of superior rectus muscle; stf, supratrabecular fenestra; ta, temporal artery; tc, trabecula communis; II, optic nerve; III, oculomotor nerve; IV, trochlear nerve; Vo, ophthalmic nerve; Vof, frontal nerve; VI, abducens nerve; VIIp, palatine nerve.

The oblique muscles arise at the anterior margin of the interorbital septum, the superior somewhat posteroventral to the inferior; they insert respectively on the dorsal and ventral sides of the eyeball (Fig. 2). The anterior rectus muscle arises from the posterior margin of the orbital membrane, passes over the optic nerve, and inserts on the anterior face of the eyeball.

The superior rectus muscle arises from the lower part of the orbitosphenoid and (in *Ctenosaura*, but apparently not in *Cyclura*) upper subiculum infundibuli, and inserts on the dorsal side of the eyeball overlying the superior oblique. The inferior rectus muscle arises mainly from the hypochiasmatic and trabecular cartilages and inserts on the ventral face of the eyeball inside the inferior oblique. The posterior rectus originates from the posterior tip of the subiculum infundibuli and from the trabecular cartilage;

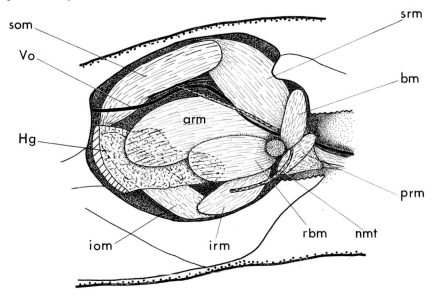

Fig. 2. The left orbit of *Cyclura carinata* with the eye removed. arm, Anterior rectus muscle; bm, bursalis muscle; Hg, Harder's gland; iom, inferior oblique muscle; irm, inferior rectus muscle; nmt, tendon of nictitating membrane; prm, posterior rectus muscle; rbm, retractor bulbi muscle; som, superior oblique muscle; srm, superior rectus muscle; Vo, ophthalmic nerve.

it passes laterally to insert on the posterior face of the eyeball. The retractor bulbi and bursalis muscles arise from a pit in the basisphenoid dorsolateral to the pituitary fossa. The origin of the bursalis is more lateral, surrounding the abducens foramen and extending down medial to the Vidian canal. The bursalis passes anteriorly and turns laterally to insert on the eyeball dorsal to the posterior rectus. The tendon of the nictitating membrane passes posteriorly above the optic nerve and around the bursalis muscle to the external face of the eyeball. The retractor bulbi muscle arises medial to the bursalis and passes forwards ventral to the optic nerve to insert on the ventral face of the eyeball where it is embraced by the inferior rectus. The levator bulbi muscles, which lie partly outside the orbital membranes, arise from a ligament (lbl in Fig. 1) which extends anteroventrally from the pila antotica below the eyeball. The levator bulbi proper arises from the length of this ligament, passes dorsal to the pyriform recess between the orbitotemporal and periorbital membranes, and inserts on the membrane of the palate. A second ligament passes anteriorly from the trabecula communis to join the first ligament and arises from the depressor palpebrae inferioris. Most fibres of this muscle pass laterally to insert in the lower lid, but some pass forwards to insert by a tendon onto the anterior part of the pterygoid bone.

The roof of the orbit is formed by the thick skin of the upper surface of the head. Along the lateral border there is a strand of particularly thick dermis which fills the gap between the prefrontal and postfrontal bones. The anterior wall of the orbit is formed by the prefrontal bone and by the orbito-nasal membrane which extends laterally from the anterior margin of the interorbital septum, between the frontal and palatine, to join the prefrontal. The largely bony floor of the orbit is formed by the palatine, pterygoid, ectopterygoid, and jugal; the participation of the maxilla is small, but the inferior orbital fenestra lies between it and the palatine, pterygoid, and ecto-pterygoid. The posterior wall of the orbit is formed by the orbitotemporal membrane which covers the mass of temporal muscles. The membrane is supported by the frontal, postorbital, ectopterygoid, and pterygoid bones and extends posteriorly to embrace the posterior rectus, bursalis, and retractor bulbi muscles. It attaches along a line from the pila accessoria and down the edge of the pituitary fossa to the anterior margin of the basiptery-goid process. The periorbital membrane lines the bony surfaces of the orbit and the interorbital septum; internally it fuses with the other orbital membranes and externally it attaches to the upper and lower eyelids well short of their free margins.

Inside the periorbital membrane and surrounding the contents of the orbit is the orbital fascia. It attaches to the first fold of the upper and lower lids and to the superior and inferior fornices. The tarsus of the lower lid lies in its fascia. Internally the fasciae fuse with the periorbital membrane; anteriorly they are free and posteriorly they follow the orbitotemporal membrane and attach to the basisphenoid.

The eye is covered by two unequal lids. The upper lid contains smooth muscle fibres but has little mobility. The lower lid, when closed, covers the greater part of the outer face of the eye. It contains a cartilaginous plate, the tarsus, which slides over the surface of the eye (Fig. 3). The eye is opened largely by depression of the lower lid which then forms a loose fold of skin to which the depressor palpebralis inferior muscles attach. The epidermis is continued on the inner faces of the lids as the palpebral conjunctiva which lines the space enclosed between the lids and the eyeball. The conjunctival spaces behind the upper and lower lids are known as the superior and inferior fornices respectively. On the nasal side of the eye, covered by the lids, is a fold of conjunctiva known as the nictitating membrane which extends between the fornices (Fig. 3). The nictitans contains three vertical crescents of cartilage. The posterior two are narrow and join at their ventral ends. From them a tendon passes posteriorly, ventral to the level of the cornea and around the temporal side of the eyeball and of the bursalis muscle and then anteriorly to the interorbital septum. The anterior cartilage is wider and extends farther around the nasal side of the eyeball. There are three vertical folds on the outer face of the nictitans which serve to catch particles of dirt. Contraction of the bursalis muscle pulls on the tendon and draws the nictitating membrane over the cornea.

The two lachrymal canaliculi arise on the anteromedial margin of the lower lid (Fig. 3). They pass forwards through the lachrymal foramen between the small lachrymal bone and the prefrontal, and join to form the lachrymal duct which runs anteriorly to open on the palate.

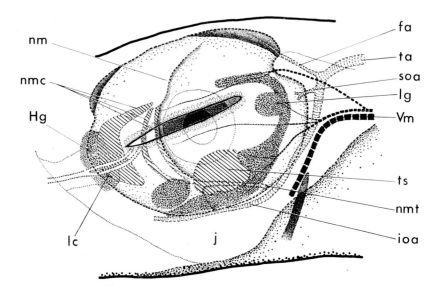

Fig. 3. Superficial structures of the orbit of *Cyclura carinata*. fa, Frontal artery; Hg, Harder's gland; ioa, inferior orbital artery; j, jugal bone; lc, lachrymal canaliculus; lg, lachrymal gland; nm, nictitating membrane; nmc, cartilage of nictitating membrane; nmt, tendon of nictitating membrane; soa, superior orbital artery; ta, temporal artery; ts, tarsus; Vm, maxillary nerve.

Much glandular tissue, both scattered cells and discrete glands, opens into the conjunctival space. The largest gland is Harder's which is mixed serous and mucous and opens on the inner face of the nictitating membrane (Figs 2 and 3). The head of the gland is overlaid by the anterior cartilage of the nictitating membrane, the body of the gland lies free in the orbit between the oblique muscles, and the tail extends back medial to the anterior rectus muscle; when the nictitating membrane is drawn back, Harder's gland follows it around the eyeball. The free part of the gland is largely surrounded by the orbital sinus. A compact, round, muco-serous gland opens on the outer face of the nictitans and partly overlies the insertion of its tendon. Scattered mucous tissue is concentrated on the nasal fold of the nictitating membrane.

There is a mucous glandular strip along the inner margin of both lids and similar lengthwise strips opening on the palpebral conjunctivae of both fornices. The lachrymal gland is a rounded concentration of tissue opening into the posterior side of the conjunctival space.

The oculomotor nerve (III) emerges from the braincase through the metoptic membrane (Fig. 1) and passes dorsal to the retractor muscles. It gives off a dorsal ramus which passes beneath the trochlear nerve to the superior rectus muscle. The main branch passes lateral to the superior rectus, where it gives off the ciliary root, and then continues forward to supply the anterior and inferior recti and inferior oblique muscles. The trochlear nerve (IV) passes through the metoptic membrane (Fig. 1) and dorsal to the superior rectus to reach the superior oblique muscle. The abducens nerve (VI) emerges within the origin of the bursalis muscle (Fig. 1) where it gives branches to the bursalis and retractor bulbi muscles; the main branch emerges from the ventral side of the bursalis to supply the posterior rectus.

Before entering the orbit the maxillary division of the trigeminal nerve (V) sends fibres to the lachrymal gland, lower lid, conjunctiva, inferior orbital artery, and orbital sinus (Fig. 3). The nerve then passes through the orbital fascia and descends to the lateral floor of the orbit over the levator bulbi muscle. It sends fibres to the orbital plexus and inferior fornix before leaving the orbit through the inferior orbital foramen in the palatine bone.

The ophthalmic division of the trigeminal nerve passes into the orbit medial to the origin of the levator bulbi muscle and divides into frontal and nasal rami (Fig. 1). The frontal ramus passes dorsally posterior to the level of the pila accessoria and bifurcates, one branch joining the lateral cranial sympathetic to serve the serous glands in the posterodorsal quadrant of the orbit and the other branch sending fibres to the upper lid.

The larger nasal ramus passes lateral to the superior rectus and gives off a long ciliary branch. It then passes forwards lateral to the superior oblique muscle. Before passing through the orbitonasal membrane, it is joined by the medial palatine ramus of the facial nerve (VII) and sends fibres to Harder's gland and the serous glands of the anterior angle of the eye.

The palatine division of the facial nerve enters the orbit from the Vidian canal below the depressor palpebralis inferior muscle and bears the palatine ganglion. The nerve passes anteriorly into the inferior orbital plexus, some fibres from which anastomose with the maxillary nerve and others run to the levator bulbi muscles. Anterior to the plexus and lateral to the origins of the oblique muscles rises a ramus communicans; this ramus bears the spheneth-moid ganglion and joins the ophthalmic nerve.

Three arteries carry blood to the orbit: the temporal artery, a branch of the stapedial, approaches the dorsolateral corner of the orbit; the palatine artery, a branch of the internal carotid, emerges from the Vidian canal at the ventromedial corner of the orbit; and the ophthalmic artery, a branch of the intracranial carotid system, enters the orbit with the optic nerve (Fig. 1).

Just behind the orbit the temporal artery gives off a medial branch, the frontal artery. This artery anastomoses with the palatine and ophthalmic arteries on the anterior face of the orbit and then passes anteriorly accompanying the frontal ramus of the ophthalmic nerve. Just above the superior oblique muscle, it gives off the anterior orbital artery to Harder's gland, the superior fornix, and the serous glands of this area. The frontal artery then descends the anterior face of the orbit and divides into the superior nasal artery, which leaves the orbit with the ophthalmic nerve, and the inferior nasal artery. Just below the level of the ophthalmic nerve the latter artery branches to supply the two oblique muscles. At the level of the palate it gives off a medial branch which joins the palatine artery. Two other branches leave the orbit.

The temporal artery descends the posterior face of the orbit and gives off the superior orbital artery. As the latter artery passes through the orbito-temporal membrane it gives off a branch which divides to supply the conjunctiva and lachrymal gland. The superior orbital artery then supplies the bursalis and posterior rectus muscles and continues forwards internal to the superior rectus which it supplies. At the level of the optic nerve the superior orbital artery gives off a ventral branch which passes posterior to the optic nerve and gives rise to the ciliary artery and branches to the retractor bulbi muscle, the optic nerve, and the posterodorsal side of the eyeball. The superior orbital artery then passes dorsal to the optic nerve and gives off the ophthalmic artery which goes under the ophthalmic nerve into the cranial cavity. Its terminal branches go to the eyeball and the anterior rectus muscle. The temporal artery continues as the inferior orbital artery accompanied by a branch of the cranial sympathetic nerve; it passes through the orbital fascia and accompanies the maxillary nerve across the floor of the orbit giving off some small orbital branches which extend dorsally (Fig. 1). The inferior orbital artery gives off the anterior orbital artery to the anterior angle of the eye and the lachrymal duct and then leaves the orbit through the infraorbital foramen.

The orbital sinus lies within the orbital fascia and occupies the greater part of the space between the eyeball and the bony wall of the orbit. In the floor of the sinus there is a sheet of smooth muscle. The sinus covers the floor of the orbit back to the orbitotemporal membrane and extends the full height of the interorbital septum reaching the roof of the orbit posteriorly. It follows the depressor palpebralis inferior muscle as far as the tarsal plate. Anteriorly it communicates with the sinus in the nictitating membrane which surrounds the free part of Harder's gland. It surrounds the optic nerve and, at the level of the chiasma, passes back into the vena cerebralis media, which anastomoses with its partner behind the supratrabecular membrane and continues back into the internal jugular vein.

Several veins and sinuses drain into the orbital sinus. Anteriorly the dorsal nasal vein connects to it from the nasal capsule, and the subseptal vein connects via the orbitonasal fissure. The frontal vein and superior palpebral vein pass posteriorly and the superior temporal vein passes anteriorly to enter the posterodorsal part of the sinus. The inferior palpebral vein extends posteriorly from the lachrymal duct to enter the sinus of the lower eyelid, and the maxillary vein discharges into the posterolateral corner of the sinus.

B. Orbit and Adnexae of other Lizards and Amphisbaenians

Large eyed lizards may have one or two more fenestrae in the anterior part of the interorbital septum in addition to those described for *Ctenosaura* (Bellairs, 1949a, b). In most burrowing lizards with reduced eyes (*Anniella*, *Acontias*, *Nessia*, *Ophiomorus*), the interorbital septum is still present although reduced in height; the orbit is thus deep in relation to the size of the eye. In *Aprasia* the anterior part of the braincase is bound to the trabecula communis by dense connective tissue so that the interorbital septum is virtually lost (Underwood, 1957). From examination of the skull it seems unlikely that *Dibamus* would have an interorbital septum. *Voeltzkowia* has probably lost the interorbital septum; the orbits are separated only by the trabecula communis (Winckels, 1914). In the Amphisbaenia there is no interorbital septum, and the frontals rest on the orbitosphenoid which in turn rests on the trabecula communis. The orbit is secondarily roofed by osteoderms in lacertids, scincids, cordylids, anguids, xenosaurids, helodermatids, and some gekkonids, including *Aristelliger*, *Teratoscincus*, *Geckolepis*, and *Tarentola*.

Most lizards have both levator bulbi and depressor palpebralis inferior muscles (Lakjer, 1926). In *Chamaeleo* the levator bulbi is absent, but the depressor palpebralis inferior is present. Chameleons are remarkable for the great mobility of the eyes; they are probably the only reptiles which achieve binocular fixation with a central fovea. The nictitating membrane is lost and the palpebral aperture is reduced, no doubt in association with the ocular mobility.

Some lizards have a transparent window in the lower eyelid, presumably permitting some vision when the eye is closed. All stages in the development of such a window are found in skinks such as *Mabuya* and in lacertids such as *Eremias* and *Cabrita*; *Lanthanotus* (McDowell and Bogert, 1954) and the iguanid *Anolis lucius* (Williams and Hecht, 1955) also have such windows. Williams and Hecht suggest that the transparent window serves as a filter to reduce dazzlement of the shade loving *Anolis lucius* when it comes into sunlight.

Several families of lizards include forms in which the eye is covered by a fixed transparent window or spectacle. Studies of development show that this spectacle is formed by fusion of the eyelids with closure of the palpebral aperture (Schwartz-Karsten, 1933). The spectacle is thus a fixed window in the lower lid covered by the stratum corneum of the epidermis which is shed with the rest of the skin. Forms with spectacles include the Pygopodidae, spectacled geckos, *Ophisops*, *Gymnophthalmus*, *Ablepharus*, *Typhlacontias*, Feyliniidae, Dibamidae, and the Amphisbaenia. In some geckos (e.g., *Ptenopus* and *Teratoscincus*) there is a fold of skin above the spectacle forming a secondary eyelid which has some mobility. Notwithstanding the possession of a spectacle, *Ablepharus* and *Ophisops* have a depressor palpebralis inferioris muscle inserting on the lower border of the spectacle.

In some forms with a spectacle the depressor palpebralis inferior is absent (Pygopodidae, Gekkonidae, Amphisbaenia); in *Pygopus* the levator bulbi is also absent (Lakjer, 1926). In lizards with a spectacle and without a nictitating membrane the bursalis muscle is absent. The burrowing *Anniella* retains a retractor bulbi muscle which takes its origin from the trabecula communis (Bellairs, 1949a). Most lizards have mobile eyelids, nictitating membranes, and eye muscles much as in *Ctenosaura*. In *Anniella* and *Coleonyx* the nictitating membrane is reduced and there is no tendon or bursalis muscle. The membrane is less reduced in *Eublepharis* and *Holodactylus* and quite well developed in *Aeluroscalabotes* and *Hemitheconyx*.

The condition of Harder's gland is usually as described for *Ctenosaura*. In *Anguis* and *Varanus* the portion of the gland internal to the eyeball is continued backwards as a tail which expands posterior to the eye. A lachrymal gland is present in most lizards including the spectacled *Ablepharus*, but is small in some such as *Scincus*, *Chalcides*, and *Mabuya*. It is absent from *Pygopus*, *Hemidactylus*, *Tarentola*, *Calotes*, *Chamaeleo*, *Ophisops*, and the Amphisbaenia (Bellairs and Boyd, 1947).

The lachrymal ducts are usually as described for *Ctenosaura*. In *Varanus* (and presumably *Lanthanotus*) the two canaliculi pass out of the orbit through two separate foramina and do not unite. In most lizards with a spectacle (geckos, *Ablepharus*, *Ophisops*) the lachrymal duct arises by two canaliculi in the usual way on the lower posterior side of the spectacle, and Harder's gland discharges into the space beneath the spectacle. In the Amphisbaenidae the lachrymal duct has a wide simple origin from the sub-brillar space. Harder's gland surrounds the optic nerve and occupies most of the orbit. Some of its ducts discharge into the sub-brillar space and some directly into the lachrymal duct. In the Pygopodidae the lachrymal duct arises by two canaliculi; in *Pygopus* and *Lialis* Harder's gland discharges into the lower lachrymal canaliculus, which in *Lialis* has only a very narrow opening into the sub-brillar space. In *Aprasia* Harder's gland discharges directly into the lachrymal duct which still communicates with the sub-brillar space by two narrow canaliculi. In *Voeltzkowia* there is a small lachrymal gland, opening into the anterior part of the conjunctival space, and a very large Harder's gland occupying most of the orbit and surrounding the eyeball, but there are no eye muscles. The lachrymal duct arises from the two lachrymal canaliculi, and the ducts of Harder's gland open into the larger dorsal canaliculus as it leaves the conjunctival space (Bellairs and Boyd, 1947).

C. The Eyeball of a Diurnal Lizard

This section is based on literature reports on *Lacerta* (Läsker, 1934) and on personal observations on *Anolis*.

Externally a corneal and an orbital segment of the eyeball are clearly recognizable. The orbital segment is approximately hemispherical but its horizontal diameter is greater than the vertical. The corneal segment, which is marked off from the orbital by a sharp change of curvature (Fig. 4), includes the cornea and has a radius of curvature about half that of the inner segment. The cornea is surrounded by a circular depression, the sulcus. The scleral ossicles lie in the sulcus and maintain its concavity against the intraocular pressure. They extend from the corneal margin to overlap slightly the orbital segment. In *Anolis* the cornea lies towards the nasal side of the eyeball and inclines between 5° and 10° nasally to the optical axis. The position of the central fovea of *Anolis* is visible externally as a slight "pimple" a little temporal to the orbital pole of the eye. The optic nerve emerges temporoventral to the central fovea. The sclera is partly fibrous and partly cartilaginous. The cup-shaped scleral cartilage reaches approximately to the equator of the eyeball and is external to the bulk of the fibrous tissue. The fourteen scleral ossicles are also external to most of the fibrous sclera and to the cartilage in the zone of overlap.

The substantia propria of the cornea is relatively thin (as compared with that of mammals), but its outer, non-cellular Bowman's layer is thick. This is covered by a thin conjunctival epithelium. Between the substantia propria and the inner mesothelium is a thin, non-cellular Descemet's layer.

The pectinate ligament lies at the sclero-corneal junction and occupies the

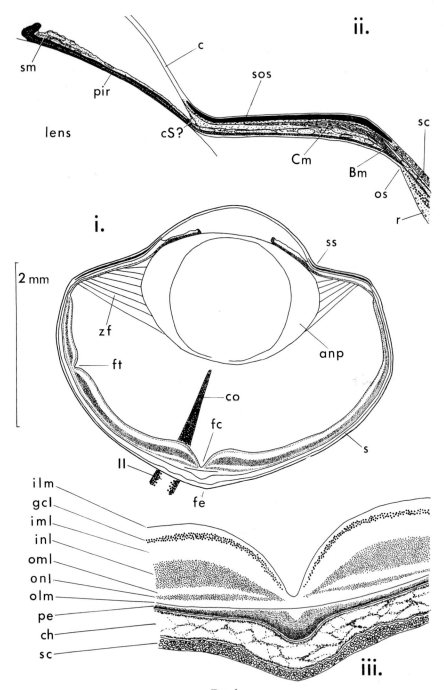

FIG. 4.

angle between the cornea and the iris (Fig. 4). It is poorly developed around most of the circumference, but is slightly more pronounced in the neighbourhood of the transversalis muscle. The canal of Schlemm, presumed to drain the intraocular fluid as in mammals, is said to lie in the tissue in the angle between the iris and the cornea in lizards (Walls, 1942), but it is poorly defined in *Anolis*.

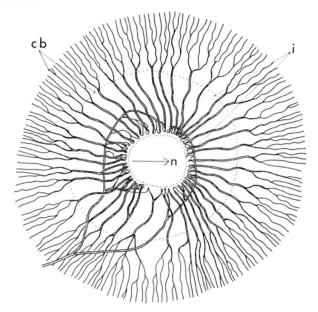

FIG. 5. Blood vessels of the iris of *Lacerta sicula*, after Läsker (1934). The number of capillaries is much greater, especially at the pupillary margin. cb, Ciliary body; i, iris; n, nasal direction.

The individual scleral ossicles have a sigmoid flexure as they pass from the concavity of the sulcus to the convexity of the sclera. They show a fairly regular pattern of overlap. Ossicles which overlap both neighbours are designated plus (+) and ossicles which are overlapped by both neighbours are designated minus (− or 0). The + plate which lies temporal to the mid-ventral plate is numbered 1 and the others are counted from there temporo-dorsally (clockwise on the right side). In *Lacerta* there are almost invariably

FIG. 4. Eye of *Anolis lineatopus*. i, Attempted reconstruction of horizontal section; ii, corneal segment of Fig. 4i enlarged 3×; iii, fovea centralis of Fig. 4i enlarged 4×. anp, Annular pad; Bm, Brücke's muscle; c, cornea; ch, chorioid plexus; Cm, Crampton's muscle; co, conus; cS?, presumed canal of Schlemm; fc, fovea centralis; fe, "fovea externa"; ft, fovea temporalis; gcl, ganglion cell layer; ilm, inner limiting membrane; iml, inner molecular layer; inl, inner nuclear layer; olm, outer limiting membrane; oml, outer molecular layer; onl, outer nuclear layer; os, ora serrata; pe, pigment epithelium; pir, pars iridiaca retinae; r, retina; s, sclera; sc, scleral cartilage; sm, sphincter muscle; sos, scleral ossicles; ss, sulcus; zf, zonula fibres; II, optic nerve.

14 ossicles (Gugg, 1939). There are three plus plates (1, 6, and 8) and three minus plates (4, 7, and 10); plates 6 and 8 meet across plate 7 to overlap slightly one way or the other. Plates 1 and 8 are opposite. The ossicles overlap at their corneal ends; there are gaps between their centres, and they just meet again at their scleral ends (Fig. 7).

The ciliary body is an annular structure lying within the eyeball internal to the ring of scleral ossicles. It is broadest ventrally and narrower on the nasal and temporal sides. The ciliary body embraces the equator of the lens (Figs 4 and 6). Between the ciliary body and the sclera, Crampton's muscle and Brücke's muscle can be distinguished but they are not sharply separated. Brücke's muscle consists of radially arranged fibres passing medially from the sclera to the pars ciliaris retinae. The fibres of Crampton's muscle pass orbitally from the scleral ossicles at the level of the sulcus to the ciliary body (Fig. 4). On the nasal side the fibres are radial, but over the temporal half of the ciliary body they are more or less vertical. In the lower part of the naso-ventral quadrant, the fibres of Crampton's muscle turn from a vertical to a circular direction. From this point a separate bundle of horizontal fibres, the transversalis muscle, passes from the sclera through the chorioid fissure to a ligament which inserts on the ventral side of the lens (Fig. 6).

The ciliary body is covered by a double epithelium, the pars ciliaris retinae, which is continuous with the two layers of the retina. The radially disposed zonula fibres arise from the ciliary body and attach to the lens (Fig. 4). The

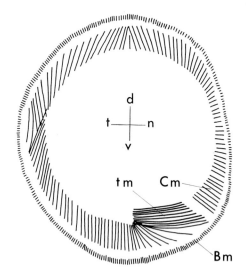

FIG. 6. Course of muscle fibres in the ciliary body of *Lacerta sicula*, after Läsker (1934). Bm Brücke's muscle; Cm, Crampton's muscle; d, dorsal; n, nasal; t, temporal; tm, transversalis muscle; v, ventral.

outer fibres are closely spaced and attach to the lens towards its corneal face. The tendon of the transversalis muscle lies orbital to the outer zonula fibres. The fine intermediate zonula fibres spread out to attach to the equatorial zone of the lens. There is then a ring of stout inner zonula fibres which attach to the inner face of the lens.

The lens is fairly soft. Its fibres run in a spiral course around the axis. An equatorial section of the lens shows the fibres in radially disposed columns, 94 in *Lacerta sicula*, 107 in *L. muralis*, and 139 in *L. viridis* (Läsker, 1934). The lens epithelium is very thick around the equator where it forms an annular pad or "Ringwulst" that brings the lens into contact with the ciliary body; the columnar epithelial cells of the annular pad are radially disposed and about 30 times as high as wide (Fig. 4). The lens of *L. sicula* is 1·6 mm in diameter and shows a ratio of diameter: (axial) thickness: thickness of annular pad of 14:11:2.

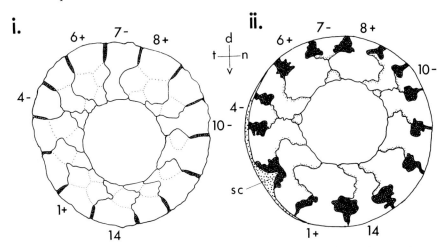

FIG. 7. Scleral ossicles of lizards. i, *Anolis lineatopus*; ii, *Lacerta lepida*. d, Dorsal; n, nasal; sc, scleral cartilage; t, temporal; v, ventral. Plus (+) and minus (−) ossicles are indicated.

Contraction of the ciliary (Crampton's) muscle draws the ciliary body corneally into the corneal segment of the eye, pressing the ciliary body against the annular pad of the lens which is thus squeezed; the increased curvature of the lens shortens its focal length. A muscular effort is thus required in accommodation as in birds, mammals, amphibians, and elasmobranchs. Deformation of the lens is shared only with the first two groups and deformation by squeezing only with birds.

The iris is a forward continuation of the ciliary body (Fig. 4), and the double layered epithelium of the pars ciliaris retinae is continued as the pars iridiaca retinae. The pupil of diurnal lizards is round with a small notch on

B

its dorsal and ventral sides. The root of the iris is anchored to the sclera by the pectinate ligament. The outer layer of the epithelium is more heavily pigmented than the inner. The iris mesoderm consists of blood vessels, pigment cells, and muscle fibres; peripherally it is thin but it thickens considerably towards the margin of the pupil. The iris sphincter muscle consists of circular fibres which are gathered together at the chorioid fissure on the ventral side of the pupil. On the dorsal side a few fibres turn radially outwards. Most of the dilator fibres, which lie internal to the sphincter, run radially inwards from the ciliary body to the pupillary margin; some of these fibres bend in a circular direction at the level of the sphincter.

D. The Eyeball of other Lizards and Amphisbaenians

Those Iguanidae, Agamidae, non-fossorial Scincidae, Teiidae, Lacertidae, Anguidae, and Varanidae which have been studied have eyes generally similar to those of *Anolis* and *Lacerta*. The conus of *Lygosoma* is in the form of a triangle with the base aligned with the fovea, in *Tupinambis* it is triangular in cross section, and in *Cyclura, Iguana, Uromastix, Shinisaurus,* and *Varanus* it has three radiating fins (Franz, 1934). Thus the surface area of the conus is increased in these large-eyed forms. In some lizards Schlemm's canal is far more prominent than in *Anolis*, but it does not appear to form a complete ring at the level of the iris root. Chameleons have a small cornea subtending an angle of only about 35°; the scleral cartilage is confined to the orbital hemisphere of the eyeball. The lens is rather convex with a thick annular pad. The ora serrata lies rather far on the orbital side of the ciliary body, extending only a little beyond the equator (Rochon-Duvigneaud, 1943). The limited field of the view of the eye is clearly related to the great ocular mobility.

Heloderma has lost the ciliary muscle and fovea, and does not show ocular movements; visual performance is evidently diminished in this nocturnal form (Walls, 1942). Three families of lizards show visual adaptation to nocturnal habits: the Pygopodidae, Gekkonidae and Xantusiidae. In the Pygopodidae the sulcus is reduced in *Delma* and *Lialis* and lost in *Aprasia* (Underwood, 1957). The lens has lost its annular pad in *Delma* and *Aprasia*. *Delma* retains some ciliary muscle, but this is lost in *Aprasia*. The scleral cartilage is fenestrated in *Delma* and lost in *Aprasia*; all three genera however retain scleral ossicles and a vascular conus. A fovea is lacking in all, and the pupil is a simple vertical slit. In view of these fairly extensive modifications it was an unexpected finding that some pygopods are, at least in part, diurnal. Dr A. Kluge (*personal communication*) reports that *Lialis* may be active in direct sunlight at midday, and Dr R. Bustard informs me that *Aprasia* is diurnal in its above ground activity.

The eublepharine gecko *Coleonyx* has a pronounced sulcus; the cornea is

proportionately somewhat larger than in *Anolis* (54% of the horizontal diameter of the eye vs. 43%) and shows a strong (14°) nasal inclination. This
inclination presumably increases the binocular field of view. The vertical
pupil aperture lies slightly toward the nasal side of the iris; there are four
lobes on its anterior margin that meet a single large lobe on the posterior
margin. There is no fovea. Lobes are not visible on the pupillary margins
of living *Eublepharis* and *Hemitheconyx*.

Of the spectacled geckos, the sphaerodactylines most resemble diurnal
lizards in the proportions of the eye. The cornea is somewhat enlarged, but
the sulcus remains pronounced. The lens is fairly flat, and the ciliary muscles
are quite well developed. There is a fovea on the temporal side of the retina.
The pupil closes to a broad vertical ellipse in most *Gonatodes* and *Sphaerodactylus*, but in *G. antillensis*, *S. parkeri*, *S. richardsonii*, *S. anthracinus*, and
a number of other species it closes to a simple vertical slit. A notable feature

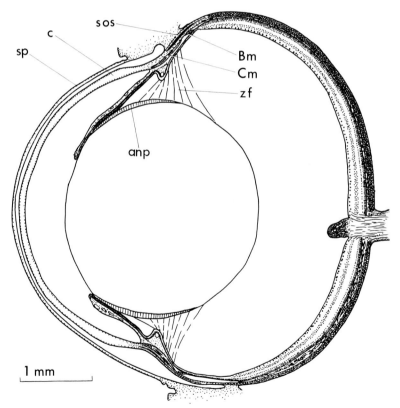

FIG. 8. Vertical section of the eye of *Tarentola mauritanica*, after Rochon-Duvigneaud (1943);
anp, Annular pad; Bm, Brücke's muscle; c, cornea; Cm, Crampton's muscle; sos, scleral ossicles.
sp, spectacle; zf, zonula fibres.

is the high degree of coordinated mobility of the eyes. *Sphaerodactylus* shows binocular following of the movements of objects, in front of, above, and even *beneath* the head. Sphaerodactyline geckos are active by day in the open shade; probably none of them is nocturnal.

The nocturnal and crepuscular spectacled geckos have a very large cornea (subtending 135° in *Tarentola*) and a reduced sulcus (Fig. 8). Descemet's membrane and the mesothelium are very thin or absent. The ciliary body forms a ring which is triangular in section; a ring vessel lies inside the apex of the triangle. Brücke's and Crampton's muscles have a disposition of fibres similar to that of *Lacerta*. The transversalis muscle arises from the sclera and passes nasally through the chorioid fissure to a fibrous insertion partly on the lens and partly in the connective tissue of the ciliary body. The lens is nearly spherical, but has a slightly flattened external face; the annular pad is proportionately much thinner than in *Lacerta*. *Tarentola* has approximately 230 radial lamellae. The mechanism of accommodation in such geckos remains uncertain; Läsker (1934) was unable to see the outer face of the lens due to the closure of the pupil and unable to observe the ciliary body from within due to the large size of the lens. Except in *Aristelliger cochranae* no trace of a fovea has been found amongst these nocturnal and crepuscular forms. Little is known about the eye of the secondarily diurnal forms; *Lygodactylus* and *Phelsuma* have a yellow lens and the latter a temporal fovea.

The pupils of nocturnal Diplodactylinae close to a vertical slit. In some the pupillary margins remain straight on closure (photograph in Kluge, 1967), but commonly each pupillary margin puckers to form five lobes (photographs in Kluge). Preserved material does not always give a reliable indication of pupil shape in these forms. The New Zealand *Naultinus* is diurnal and has a circular pupil.

The nocturnal Gekkoninae also have vertical pupils. In *Aristelliger* and *Teratoscincus scincus* (photograph in Kluge, 1967), they close to straight-edged slits. The South African genera *Chondrodactylus, Colopus, Palmato-gecko, Ptenopus,* and *Rhoptropus* show a variant of the vertical pupil; in preserved specimens there is a single lobe on each pupillary margin suggesting that on closure a small aperture would be left at each apex (Fig. 9).

FIG. 9. Pupils of geckos, with the nasal direction to the right. i, *Aristelliger praesignis*, nearly closed; ii, *Palmatogecko rangei*, nearly closed (preserved); iii to v, *Tarentola mauritanica* (after Läsker, 1934), iii, half open, iv, nearly closed, and v, fully closed.

Some of the more primitive Gekkoninae are believed to have reverted to diurnal habits and to have reacquired a circular pupil. This is most clearly suggested by the Malagasy genus *Phelsuma*; two species, *P. newtonii* and *P. guentheri*, have simple vertical pupils and all the remaining species have circular pupils. *Lygodactylus*, *Pristurus*, and *Quedenfeldtia* have circular pupils, and *Cnemaspis* and *Saurodactylus* have pupils closing to broad vertical ellipses.

The advanced Gekkoninae have a vertical pupil bearing three lobes on each margin. The lobes disappear only when, in dim illumination, the pupil is extended to a full circle. The lobes on the temporal border are slightly more prominent than those on the nasal border (Fig. 9). At maximum closure the lobes overlap, the central temporal lobe over and the upper and lower temporal lobes under the corresponding nasal lobes. The size of the pupillary aperture is thus capable of a great range, from a full circle to four pinholes. The lobes of the iris consist almost wholly of the double epithelium of the pars iridiaca retinae with very little mesodermal tissue. The sphincter fibres occupy the greater part of the width of the iris, but fall short of both the pupillary margin and the root of the iris; none of them bends radially. There are three groups of sphincter fibres distinguished by their courses at the pupillary apices. First, fibres in contact with the epithelium do not pass the apex of the pupil but turn back on the same side; the second, more superficial, group cross one another at the pupillary apices as they pass from a course nearer the pupillary margin on one side to a course nearer the iris root on the other side. The third and most superficial fibres follow symmetrical courses about the pupillary aperture. Deep to the sphincter fibres are the fine dilatator fibres which originate from the connective tissue of the ciliary body and from the basal membrane of the pars ciliaris retinae. Fibres from the vertical borders of the pupil criss-cross towards the nasal or temporal sides of the iris. Towards the apices the fibres follow a vertical course before turning nasally or temporally. The pupil opens without a diminution of its vertical height; the iris margin is therefore stretched and the lobes disappear. As in diurnal lizards (Fig. 5) the ciliary artery divides, near the root of the iris, into nasal and temporal branches which run dorsally on each side of the pupil and give off fine branches (Mann, 1929). The latter run centripetally towards the margin of the pupil, anastomose, and send off centrifugal vessels which pass to the ciliary body where they join two superficial semicircular vessels which arise from the nasal branch of the ciliary artery. From these semicircular vessels fine capillaries pass through the ciliary body to the chorioid plexus.

Many burrowing forms show reduction of the palpebral aperture and reduction of the size of the eye without much structural change. *Anniella* retains scleral cartilage and ossicles, a ciliary body with muscles, a lens with annular pad, and a vascular conus; it has, however, lost the fovea (Walls, 1942).

Voeltzkowia retains scleral ossicles which overlap the scleral cartilage (Winckels, 1914). It has no ciliary body, and the spherical lens fills the inner chamber of the eye. There is a thin chorioid with a few vessels and the iris has no mesodermal tissue. There is no conus and the retina is avascular. *Dibamus* lacks scleral ossicles and cartilage, lens, vitreous humour, iris, and chorioid plexus (Fig. 10). There is a very thin, fibrous, unpigmented sclera

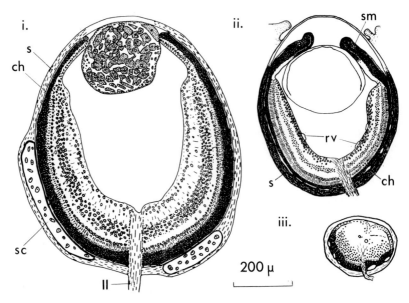

Fig. 10. Eyes of burrowing reptiles. i, *Amphisbaena fuliginosa*; ii, *Typhlops jamaicensis*; iii, *Dibamus novaeguineae*. ch, Chorioid plexus; rv, retinal vessels; s, sclera; sc, scleral cartilage; sm, sphincter muscle; II, optic nerve.

enclosing the cup of the retina which is without conus or blood-vessels. Between the sclera and the retina are some vessels which fail to form a layer (chorioid plexus). Corneally the pigment epithelium continues into an unpigmented epithelium which covers the outer face of the optic cup; at the margin of the optic cup it is reflected to continue into the retina, but there is no aperture and the inner face of the "iris" is in contact with the vitreal face of the retina.

Scleral ossicles appear to be variable in the Amphisbaenia. They were found in *Amphisbaena* (Angel and Rochon-Duvigneaud in Rochon-Duvigneaud, 1943) and *Trogonophis* (Bellairs, *personal communication*), but I have not found them in the same forms; however *Amphisbaena* (Fig. 10), *Blanus*, *Cadea*, and *Rhineura* appear regularly to retain some scleral cartilage (Franz, 1934; Hanke, 1912). This cartilage is quite extensive in *Agamodon* (Bonin, 1965) and *Trogonophis*. There is no ciliary body. The pars iridiaca retinae has the outer layer pigmented and the inner unpigmented. The chorioid is thin and has relatively few blood vessels; it is unpigmented in *Agamodon* and *Amphisbaena*, an unusual condition. The iris mesoderm is thin, no more than 4μ thick in *Amphisbaena*. There is probably always a lens; there is doubt (Gans, *personal communication*) about its alleged absence from *Rhineura* (Eigenmann, 1909). The lens of most forms has regular fibres and a thin capsule, but in *Amphisbaena* the lens is an undifferentiated mass of cells (Fig. 10). There is no vascular conus and no vascularization of the retina.

The scleral ossicles of lizards have been extensively surveyed by Gugg (1939). As in *Anolis* and *Lacerta*, so in other lizards there is almost invariably a plus plate (see p. 17) on the temporal side of the midventral line; this is scored as number one. In many lizards two plates may overlap one another across an intervening plate (Übergreifen). In many also, though not in lacertids, two adjacent plates have "S" shaped margins and overlap mutually (Verzahnung). In the accompanying table (Table I) I give data on the scleral ossicles of *Sphenodon* and lizards, mostly taken from Gugg; I have, however, revised some of Gugg's scoring. Plus plates are here scored solely by their relations with the immediately adjacent plates. Thus, if plate 6 overlaps plates 5 and 7 it is scored as plus although plate 8 may overlap 6 across 7.

Where there is mutual overlap scoring is complicated; I have found however that consistent results are obtained if the overlap nearer the corneal border is scored. Thus, for example, in *Leiolepis belliana* there is mutual overlap between plates 4 and 5, and the lobe of 5 over 4 is considerably larger than the lobe of 4 over 5, but the latter is next to the corneal border; if, therefore, we score plate 4 as plus we find exact agreement with all the other agamid lizards examined. At each plus or minus plate there is a reversal of the pattern of overlap; it is therefore a theoretical necessity that there be an even number of reversals in a complete ring. Besides the ventral plus plate (No. 1) there are nearly always two minus plates, one on the temporal side and one on the nasal side of the ring.

In *Sphenodon* and most lizards there is a plus-minus-plus sequence of plates on the dorsal side of the ring making a total of six reversals for the whole ring. There are nearly always two (Fig. 7) or three (Fig. 22) plates between number one and the temporal minus plate, and three (Fig. 11, ii) or four (Fig. 7) between number one and the nasal minus plate. Where, as in some geckos, there is a total of more than six reversals, an additional pair, or even two pairs, are added to the ventral series, generally in the nasal quadrant. In these forms the overlap pattern is generally somewhat irregular.

The dorsal series between the temporal minus plate and the nasal minus plate is subject to more regular variation than the ventral series. Usually, in the order in which the plates are numbered, there is a sequence of five: i, +, −, +, i (i = imbricating plate). The sceloporine iguanids (Etheridge,

TABLE I

The Scleral Ossicles of Lizards and *Sphenodon*

Group or genus and number of species where more than one	No. of plates	Plus plates	Minus plates	No. of eyes	Fide
Sphenodon	16	1, 8, 10	5, 9, 12	2	G
Pygopodidae					
Aprasia	13, 14	—	—	3	S, U_1
Delma, Lialis, Pygopus	14–17	—	—	9	S, U_1
Lialis	16	1, 5, 9, 14	4, 6, 13, 15	2	U_2
	17	1, 5, 9, 12, 14	4, 6, 10, 13, 15		
Eublepharinae (10 species)	13–25	—	—	111	K, U_2
Diplodactylinae (43 species)	21–40	—	—	259	K, SS, U_2
Rhacodactylus	27	1, 6, 10, 15	2, 9, 11, 20	2	U
	26	1, 13	8, 18		
Gekkoninae: Group I (185 species)	13–16	—	—	508	K, SS, U_2
Dravidogecko, Geckonia, Gehyra,					
Ptychozoon, Tarentola	14	1, 6, 8	4, 7, 10	30	G, U_2
Homonota, Pristurus	14	1, 6	4, 10	2	U_2
Aristelliger, Bogertia	14	1, 6, 11	4, 10, 12	3	U_2
Pachydactylus, Phyllopezus	14	1, 6, 8, 11	4, 7, 10, 12	2	U_2
Gekko	14	1, 6, 8, 13	4, 7, 10, 14	2	G
Gekko	14	3, 6, 8, 12	4, 7, 10, 14	2	U_2
		1, 3, 6, 8, 12	2, 4, 7, 10, 14		
Geckolepis	14	1, 6, 8, 11, 13	4, 7, 10, 12, 14	1	U_2
Uroplatus	15	1, 3, 6, 9	2, 5, 8, 15	2	G
	16	1, 4, 8, 10	2, 9, 12, 16		
Blaesodactylus	14	1, 6, 10, 13	3, 9, 11, 14	1	U_2
Thecadactylus	14	1, 5/6, 8, 11	3, 7, 10, 12	2	U_2
Hemidactylus (5 species)	14	1, 6, 8	4, 7, 11	16	G
Gehyra, Hemidactylus	14	1, 6	4, 11	10	G
Ptyodactylus	14/15	1, 6/8	4, 11/12	2	U_2
Calodactylodes	14	1, 5, 10	3, 9, 11	1	U_2
Cnemaspis	14	1, 5	3, 10	3	G
Ailuronyx	14	1, 4	3, 10	1	U_2
Gekkoninae: Group II					
Teratoscincus (2 species)	15–21	—	—	16	K, U_2
Stenodactylus (9 species)	20–28	—	—	26	K, U_2
Sphaerodactylinae (10 species)	12–15	—	—	67	K
Xantusiidae					
Xantusia	14	—	—	2	U_2
Lepidophyma	14	1, 7, 9	5, 8, 11	1	U_2
Iguanidae					
Holbrookia (2 species),					
Phrynosoma (2 species)	12	1, 5, 7	4, 6, 8	8	G, U_2
Corytophanes	13	1, 6, 8	4, 7, 9	2	U_2
Anolis, Aptycholaemus, Basiliscus,					
Callisaurus, Chalarodon,					
Crotaphytus, Cyclura,					
Holbrookia (2 species), *Iguana,*					
Laemanctus, Liolaemus,					
Oplurus, Petrosaurus,					
Phymaturus, Sceloporus (2					
species), *Urosaurus* (2 species),					
Uta	14	1, 6, 8	4, 7, 10	27	G, U_2
Polychrus	15	1, 7, 9	5, 8, 11	2	G

TABLE 1—*continued*   The Scleral Ossicles of Lizards and *Sphenodon*

Group or genus and number of species where more than one	No. of plates	Plus plates	Minus plates	No. of eyes	Fide
Agamidae					
Agama (3 species), *Amphibolurus*, *Calotes* (7 species), *Ceratophora*, *Cophotis, Draco, Leiolepis*, *Lophura, Lyriocephalus, Moloch*, *Otocryptis, Physignathus*,					
Uromastix	12(11)	1, 6	4, 9(8)	99	G, U$_2$
Phrynocephalus	11	1, 6	4, 8	4	G
Chamaeleonidae					
Chamaeleo (3 species)	11	1, 5, 7	4, 6, 8	10	G
Teiidae					
Ameiva, Neusticurus, Tupinambis	14	1, 6, 8	4, 7, 10	6	G
Scincidae					
Chalcides, Eumeces (2 species), *Mabuya* (3 species), *Sphenomorphus* (11 species),					
Tiliqua	14	1, 6, 8	4, 7, 10	59	G
Ablepharus, Scincus	14	1, 6	4, 10	4	G
Ablepharus (2 species), *Tiliqua*	13	1, 6	4, 9	5	G
Chalcides	14	1, 6	4, 9	1	G
Nessia	10	1, 3, 6	2, 4, 10	4	G
Ophiomorus	8/10	—	—	2	U$_2$
Ophioscincus	10	—	—	2	U$_2$
Lacertidae					
Lacerta (6 species), *Ophisops*	14	1, 6, 8	4, 7, 10	16	G
Acanthodactylus	14	1, 6, 8	4, 7, 11	2	G
Holaspis	11	—	—	2	U$_2$
Cordylidae					
Cordylus	14	1, 6, 8	4, 7, 10	4	G
Platysaurus	12	1, 6	4, 8	1	U$_2$
Gerrhosaurus, Zonosaurus	14	1, 6, 8	4, 7, 10	6	G
Anguidae					
Anguis	12–14	1, 5/6	4, 8/9/10	8	G
	8	1, 5	2, 7	1	
Anniellidae					
Anniella	8	c. 3	c. 7	1	U$_2$
Xenosauridae					
Shinisaurus	14	1, 6, 8	4, 7, 10	1	U$_2$
Xenosaurus newmanorum	14	1, 6, 8	4, 7, 10	1	U$_2$
Xenosaurus grandis	c. 20	—	—	1	B&S
Helodermatidae					
Heloderma	10, 12	—	—	2	G, U$_2$
Lanthanotidae					
Lanthanotus	6	—	—	1	U$_2$
Varanidae					
Varanus (4 species)	15	1, 7, 9	5, 8, 11	12	G

The number of scleral ossicles in a ring is indicated in the first column. A stroke separates counts on opposite sides of the same specimen. The second column indicates the plus ossicles and the third column the minus ossicles; alternatives are separated by a stroke, rare conditions are in parentheses. The fourth column indicates the number of eyes examined. The last column indicates the source of the data: B&S, Barrows and Smith (1947); G, Gugg (1939); K, Kluge (1967); S, Stephenson (1960); SS, Stephenson and Stephenson (1956); U$_1$, Underwood (1957); U$_2$, Underwood, recent observations.

1964) indicate how simplification of the dorsal series may occur. In *Petrosaurus* plates 5 to 9 follow the i, +, −, +, i sequence, and the plus plates are 6 and 8. Beneath plate 8 plate 9 overlaps the minus plate 7. The two plus plates lie superficial to plates 5 and 9, and plate 8 is reduced in size so that it does not reach the corneal margin. If plate 8 were lost then 9 would be scored as a plus plate and we would have the sequence found in *Corytophanes*: i, +, −, +. In *Callisaurus, Holbrookia texana, Sceloporus, Urosaurus*, and *Uta* plate 5 as well as plate 9 overlaps the minus plate 7. The two plus plates 6 and 8, show various degrees of reduction and do not always reach the corneal margin. In *Holbrookia maculata* and *H. propinqua* these plates are missing, and 5 and 9 are scored as plus so that the dorsal series is reduced to +, −, + as in *Phrynosoma* and *Chamaeleo* (Fig. 11, ii). If plate 7 were to overlap plate 9 beneath plate 8 and then plate 8 were lost, we would have the agamid sequence i, +, i, i. No such "pre-agamid" has yet been found however. One of two specimens of *Sceloporus clarkii* had supernumerary ossicles superficial to plates 6 and 8, one on the left and two on the right. It is not clear, however, whether plates can be added to the dorsal series in this way.

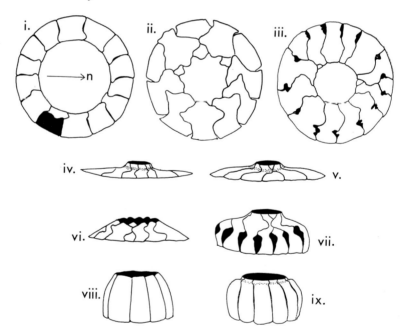

FIG. 11. Scleral ossicles of lizards, after Gugg (1939). i to iii, Corneal views, and iv to ix, equatorial views, with n indicating the nasal direction. i, *Hemidactylus frenatus*; ii, *Chamaeleo basiliscus*; iii, *Cordylus giganteus*; iv, *Calotes jubatus*; v, *Varanus niloticus*; vi, *Chamaeleo basiliscus*; vii, *Lacerta viridis*; viii, *Heloderma suspectum*; ix, *Gehyra mutilata*.

In a number of stocks the number of reversals is reduced from six to four; this always occurs by the loss of the second and third reversals in the dorsal series so that, for example, i, $+$, $-$, $+$, i becomes i, $+$, i, i, i (Fig. 11, i). The variations found in geckos, including intraspecific variation in *Gehyra mutilata*, suggest that an imbricating plate may be added to the dorsal series by a shift one place ventrally of the nasal or temporal plate that develops as a minus. Correspondingly in skinks the dorsal series may be reduced by a shift dorsally of a minus plate.

Some forms, particularly those with reduced eyes, have overlaps so poorly defined that scoring of plus and minus plates is not possible. In some forms the ring of ossicles is reduced in width on the dorsal and ventral sides. In lacertids and gerrhosaurs this phenomenon is probably associated with the habit of squeezing into crevices with consequent deformation of the eyeball (Mr. E. N. Arnold, *personal communication*). The same interpretation may hold for some geckos too. In Table II the principal variations of the dorsal series of plates are interpreted together with an indication of the numbers in the ventral series.

In the Pygopodidae the scleral plates are rectangular and, except in *Aprasia*, have their corneal ends expanded and overlapping; they extend to about the equator of the eyeball (Stephenson, 1960). The scleral plates of the Gekkonidae resemble those of the Pygopodidae. A common peculiarity of geckos is that a single ventral plate is reduced at its orbital margin whilst maintaining normal overlap relations at its corneal margin (Fig. 11, i). Sometimes several ventral or several dorsal plates are so reduced that they no longer make contact with one another at all. This contrasts with the corresponding reduction in lacertids in which the ring is always continuous around the corneal margin; it is presumably related to the reduction of the sulcus in geckos.

Kluge (1967) has published a table of counts of scleral ossicles in about 250 species of geckos. In the Eublepharinae, Diplodactylinae and Group II of the Gekkoninae there is considerable intraspecific variation in the number of ossicles; in Group I and in the Sphaerodactylinae nearly all species show a high level of constancy.

In the Eublepharinae scleral ossicle counts are high. *Aeluroscalabotes* and *Hemitheconyx* have subequal ossicles, but in *Coleonyx*, *Eublepharis*, and *Holodactylus* the ventral ossicles are reduced (Kluge, 1962).

The Diplodactylinae show the highest numbers of scleral ossicles of any vertebrates; indeed the maximum count of 40 is more than double the highest number known in any other Recent group. In one pair scored in detail there was gross asymmetry in the overlap pattern. The Gekkoninae of Group II also have high counts.

All but three genera of the Group I Gekkoninae have mean counts below 15; 562 eyes showed a total range of only 13–16. Twenty eyes of one species,

Gehyra punctata, matched this total range for the group. Of the genera with "*Rhoptropus* type" pupil shape, *Chondrodactylus*, *Colopus*, and *Ptenopus* have mean counts above 14·5; these are matched by one species of *Hemiphyllodactylus* and by *Uroplatus*. Probably most of the Group I Gekkoninae show reduction of one ossicle on the ventral side of the ring. A few, including three of the *Rhoptropus* group, show reduction of dorsal as well as ventral ossicles. Several genera, including a number of Malagasy endemics, have a ring of subequal ossicles without any marked reductions.

TABLE II

An Interpretation of Some of the Scleral Ossicle Patterns of Lizards and *Sphenodon*

	Total plates	Dorsal series	Ventral plates T	Ventral plates N	Reversals: Total	Reversals: Ventral
Sphenodon	16	i i + − + i	3	4	6	0
Polychrus, Varanus	15	i + − + i	3	4	6	0
Many gekkonids, iguanids, teiids, scincids, lacertids, cordylids, and xenosaurids	14	i + − + i	2	4	6	0
Lepidophyma	14	i + − + i	3	3	6	0
Gekko, Pachydactylus, Phyllopezus	14	i + − + i	2	4	8	2
Geckolepis	14	i + − + i	2	4	10	4
Corytophanes	13	i + − . +	2	4	4	0
Holbrookia, Phrynosoma	12	+ . − . +	2	4	6	0
Chamaeleo	11	+ . − . +	2	3	6	0
Acanthodactylus, Hemidactylus	14	i + − + i i	2	3	6	0
Gehyra, Hemidactylus	14	i + i i i i	2	3	4	0
Aristelliger	14	i + i i i	2	4	6	2
Ablepharus, Scincus	14	i + i i i	2	4	4	0
Most agamids	12	i + i . i	2	3	4	0
Phrynocephalus	11	i + i . .	2	3	4	0

In the dorsal series "i" indicates an imbricating plate and a dot indicates presumed loss of a plate. The ventral plates counted are those between plate No. 1 and the temporal minus plate (T) on one side and the nasal minus plate (N) on the other.

The patterns of overlap in the Gekkoninae are very varied and, in some cases, subject to individual variation and asymmetry. In *Ebenavia* the overlaps are so poorly defined that precise scoring is not possible. The largest cluster of genera has the standard i, +, −, +, i sequence of the dorsal series; these also have one ventral plate reduced. Several species add one or two dorsal plates to the series and some may further modify this by losing two dorsal reversals. To the standard dorsal sequence several genera add two ventral reversals and *Geckolepis* adds four. *Aristelliger* and *Bogertia* lose two dorsal reversals and add two ventral. Other patterns are not obviously simple

modifications of the standard sequence. It may be noted that there is a group
of genera in which the patterns are variable, most of which do not show
reduction of a ventral plate and some of which are known to share an
imperforate stapes (*Ailuronyx, Calodactylodes, Gekko, Ptyodactylus, Thecadactylus, Uroplatus*).

The Sphaerodactylinae have numbers of plates that are close to 14. In
Gonatodes and *Sphaerodactylus* the plates are not of uniform width, but no
single ossicle is much smaller than its immediate neighbours.

The Xantusiidae have 14 rectangular plates. In *Lepidophyma* the corneal
overlaps are large, while in *Xantusia* the overlaps are smaller.

The Iguanidae have a fairly flat ring of ossicles that scarcely pass to the
orbital side of the inflexion of the sclera. There are several regular patterns.
The largest number of forms, including representatives of the anoline,
iguanine, tropidurine, sceloporine, and Malagasy genera (Etheridge, 1964)
show the standard dorsal sequence. *Polychrus*, like *Varanus*, has 15 plates,
and the others have the usual 14 plates. *Corytophanes* has dropped one plate,
and *Phrynosoma* and some *Holbrookia* two plates from the dorsal series. The
Chamaeleonidae are just like *Phrynosoma* but with one less plate in the
ventral series; the ring of ossicles however has a conical form. A good series
of Agamidae shows a distinctive pattern with one plate and two reversals
lost from the dorsal series; *Phrynocephalus* goes a step further with two
plates lost.

The teiids, lacertids, and most of the skinks with large eyes have plates
that extend to the orbital side of the inflexion of the sclera and approach the
equator; the plates have narrow "waists" with gaps between. The gerr-
hosaurids are similar but the "waists" are formed by small notches in the
margins of the plates. Most of these have the standard dorsal sequence with
a total of 14 plates. In some skinks, however, a pair of dorsal reversals is lost.
In general the skinks with reduced eyes show reduced numbers of ossicles
that tend to be rectangular but continue to extend towards the equator of the
eyeball; the overlap patterns are simplified, but four eyes of *Nessia* (Gugg,
1939) are remarkable for their constant and peculiar pattern. In crevice
dwelling species of *Lacerta* the ring of ossicles is emarginated dorsally and
ventrally on its orbital border but remains complete in the sulcus. *Holaspis*
and *Platysaurus* are similar but the number of ossicles is reduced.

The eyes of *Anguis* (Gugg, 1939) show the loss of two dorsal reversals
and much variation in number, but even one ring with only eight ossicles
has nasal and temporal minus and dorsal and ventral plus plates. The one
Anniella eye examined has only two reversals.

Xenosaurus newmanorum has the standard dorsal sequence and a total of
14 plates; if *X. grandis* indeed has a total of "about twenty" (Barrows and
Smith, 1947) this genus has a remarkable range of variation. The one eye of

Shinisaurus seen had 14 rectangular plates extending to the equator and having large corneal overlaps; the sequence is standard. In *Heloderma* the rectangular plates reach to the equator of the eye, the number is variable, and the overlaps are very poorly defined. A single eye of *Lanthanotus* is similar, but there are only 6 plates, two of which do not reach the corneal margin. *Varanus* has the standard dorsal sequence in a ring of 15 plates; the ring is rather flat, scarcely passing the inflexion of the sclera.

The Mosasauridae had thick plates in a rather flat ring that may, however, have extended to the orbital side of the inflexion of the sclera. No complete mosasaur rings appear to be known, but partial rings suggest a total of about 14 to 16 plates (Edinger, 1929). There were no gaps between the plates, and their edges of contact are bevelled, either the outer face on one edge and the inner on the other or both edges bevelled on the same face, outer or inner. It should, therefore, be possible to score the plates as plus, minus, or imbricating. In *Mosasaurus giganteus* some of the plates did not reach the corneal border of the ring. *Hainosaurus*, thought to have been a pelagic form, is believed to have lacked scleral ossicles. The proportions of the rings suggest that the relative size of the mosasaur cornea was similar to that of *Varanus*.

E. The Retina of a Diurnal Lizard

The general appearance of the retinae of several diurnal lizards, as seen by light microscopy, has been described by various workers, such as Detwiler (1923, *Eremias*) and Rochon-Duvigneaud (1943, *Lacerta, Chamaeleo*). Walls (1942, *Crotaphytus*) emphasized that diurnal lizards have a pure cone retina with single cones and double cones, while Vilter (1951, *Lacerta*) recognized that there are two types of single cones. Until recently our knowledge of the nervous structure of the retina rested solely on the work of Ramon y Cajal (1894, *Lacerta*). With the advent of electron microscopy it now appears that some of the results obtained by light microscopy may be misleading. Pedler and Tansley (1963) and Pedler and Tilly (1963) have made some studies of the fine structure of the retinas of geckos, and also of some material of *Lacerta*. We have, however, no general account of the fine structure of the retina of any primarily diurnal lizard; in fact the best known form is *Phelsuma*, a tertiarily diurnal descendant of secondarily nocturnal ancestors. I have therefore assembled a regrettably untidy account by extracting possibly relevant information from studies of chelonians, birds, and nocturnal lizards in addition to diurnal lizards.

The sensory retina consists of the pigment epithelium, the visual cell layer, and the nervous layers. It extends corneally from the entry of the optic nerve to the ora serrata (or ora terminalis) just on the orbital side of the inflexion of the sclera (Fig. 4). The conus papillaris arises from the head of the optic nerve, extends towards the centre of the lens, and tapers to a point that just fails to touch the lens. In *Anolis* and *Lacerta* the highly vascular conus is circular in cross section; it is heavily pigmented and contains neuroglial tissue. The blood supply to the conus enters via the optic nerve. The retina itself is completely avascular. The conus is believed to be related to the metabolic exchanges of the eye. The optic nerve consists wholly of bundles of efferent fibres invested by neuroglial tissue. Decussation at the optic chiasma is not complete, and a small proportion of the fibres passes to the ipsilateral centres of the brain (Armstrong, 1950, *Lacerta*).

The pigment epithelium consists of a single layer of cells. Between the pigment epithelium and the chorioid is Bruch's membrane (c. 0.7μ thick in *Chrysemys*) which consists of an elastic lamina sandwiched between the basement membranes of the chorioid capillaries and the pigment epithelial cells (Cohen, 1963b). The pigment cells have a basal zone, nuclear zone, apical zone, and zone of cell processes (Yamada, 1960, *Chrysemys*). The basal zone contains numerous minute tubular or vesicular invaginations, some of which reach the nuclear zone. There are long slender mitochondria ($3\mu \times 0.2\mu$) with longitudinal cristae in the nuclear zone. The perpendicularly oriented myeloid bodies in this region consist of flattened sacs that are continuous with the membranes of the endoplasmic reticulum. There is also an extensive network of smooth surfaced endoplasmic reticulum and scattered small clusters of ribosomes. At the middle level of the nuclei the cell membranes are joined by terminal bars forming Verhoeff's "membrane". In the apical zone the mitochondria and endoplasmic reticulum become less pronounced. There are small myeloid bodies and numerous pigment granules. The cell processes are 3μ–10μ long and about 0.7μ in diameter. They contain some endoplasmic reticulum, myeloid bodies, and dense pigment granules about $0.2\mu \times 1.0\mu$.

The nervous layers of the retina are well defined in diurnal lizards. The visual cell layer consists entirely of cones which are held together by a zone of terminal bars linking visual cells and neuroglial cells; this has long been known to light microscopists as the outer limiting "membrane" (Fig. 4). Detwiler (1923) reports small photomechanical changes in *Eremias*: the cones contract slightly in the light adapted retina and extend in the dark. The nuclei of the visual cells lie in the outer nuclear layer. In the outer plexiform layer the foot-pieces of the visual cells synapse with the bipolar and horizontal cells. The inner nuclear layer contains the nuclei of four cell types. Outermost are the horizontal cells that synapse with groups of visual cells. At the middle level are the nuclei of bipolar cells that synapse with visual cells on the one hand and with ganglion cells on the other. Here also are most of the nuclei of the neuroglial or Müller cells. Innermost in the inner nuclear layer are the nuclei of amacrine cells that synapse with the ganglion cells. The inner plexiform layer contains the synapses between the bipolar and amacrine cells and the ganglion cells. The ganglion cell bodies and their fibres passing to the optic nerve from the innermost layer bounded by the inner limiting membrane. The neuroglial or Müller cells pass radially through the whole thickness of the retina.

In *Lacerta* (Vilter, 1951) and *Anolis* there are three visual cell types: major single cones (type A_1), minor single cones (type A_2), and type B double cones (Fig. 12). I am at a loss to understand how so experienced an investigator as Polyak (1957) saw rods and cones but, apparently, no double cones in the retina of *Anolis*.

The single cones have six principal parts: the outer segment, the oil-droplet, the ellipsoid, the paraboloid lying in the region known as the myoid, the nucleus, and the footpiece. The outer segment is slender in relation to the diameter of the area on which the cell stands. In *Anolis* the oil-droplet of the major cone is bright yellow and about $4 \cdot 5\mu$ in diameter. It is believed to serve as an intraocular colour filter, absorbing the blue light which is most subject to scattering within the eye. Such scattered light would otherwise reduce the contrast of the image. The minor cone of *Anolis* has a colourless oil-droplet about 3μ in diameter. The ellipsoid always stains heavily; that of the major cell is stouter than that of the minor cell. The myoid, the region in which the slight photomechanical changes occur, contains the refringent body known as the paraboloid. Saxén (1955) has shown that in the frog

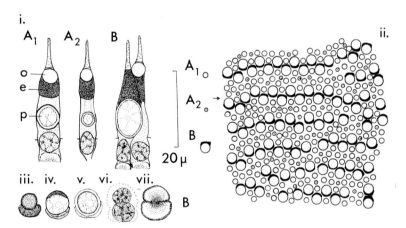

FIG. 12. Visual cells of *Anolis lineatopus*. i, Side views of cells; ii, tangential section of retina (semi-diagrammatic); iii to vii, tangential sections of a double cone, at the levels of, iii, the ellipsoids, iv and v, the myoid embracing the axial paraboloid, vi, the nuclei, and, vii, the footpieces. A_1, Major single cone; A_2, minor single cone; B, double cone, peripheral cell on the right in i; e, ellipsoid; o, oil-droplet; p, paraboloid.

Rana temporaria the paraboloid consists of glycogen. The nuclei, rounded in the major cones and oval in the minor cones, extend part way through the external limiting membrane. The cell continues vitreally into a fibre that terminates in an expanded pedicle that synapses with bipolar and horizontal cells.

The outer segment of the visual cell consists of a stack of lamellar sacs enclosed within a plasma membrane. It sits in a shallow depression in the inner segment to which it is attached by an eccentric narrow pedicle having the structure of a cilium without the central pair of filaments. Vitreal to the basal body of the ciliary pedicle is a centriole (Pedler and Tansley, 1963). Arising from the scleral margin of the inner segment of *Coleonyx* there are calycal processes embracing the outer segment (Dunn, 1966); these do not occur in *Lacerta*. The ellipsoid consists of closely packed mitochondria. The oil-droplet has no membrane of its own and lies free between the mitochondria in the peripheral part of the ellipsoid. Between the ellipsoid and the nucleus, in the myoid, is the Golgi system. The paraboloid of the major cone has cortical and medullary regions; it lacks a discrete membrane. The cortex consists of a tightly interwoven mass of tubules and vesicles in a granular matrix (Fig. 13, iii). The medulla consists of granular material. The fine structure of the minor cones has never been described, but Dunn (1966) found that the minor paraboloid of a gecko type C double cell consists only of tubules and vesicles without a discrete cortex. The outer surface membranes of the inner segments of the cones are thrown into a series of about 30–35 radially disposed folds per cell that form fins extending from the outer limiting membrane about two-thirds of the height of the inner segment. There are no fins on the surfaces of contact of the double cells.

The double cells consist of two unequal members, a bulky axial and a more slender peripheral cell. The membranes of the two cells are in close contact. The peripheral cell has a yellow oil-droplet like that of the A_1 cells, but has no paraboloid. The axial cell, in contrast, has no oil-droplet, but its ellipsoid surmounts a very large paraboloid. The peripheral ellipsoid fits around the axial ellipsoid and the peripheral myoid partly embraces the axial paraboloid in a crescent (Fig. 13, i). The axial cell, however, has a small lappet reflected back around the tip of the peripheral crescent (Fig. 13, ii). The axial nucleus is close to its paraboloid, but the peripheral nucleus lies a little deeper (Fig. 12). The double cells are evidently formed by an association of two cells. In *Anolis* there are occasional triple cells like those noted by Saxén (1953) in *Rana*. These triple cells consist of two peripheral cells flanking one axial element.

The two elements of a double cell are oriented vertically, one above the other. They are arranged in horizontal zig-zag rows with the peripheral cells approximately aligned and the axial cells alternately above and below them

(Fig. 12). Between the rows of double cells the two types of single cells are mixed together. Only rarely are two double cells of the same orientation in proximity, and this only where there is a break in the regularity of the mosaic (Fig. 12). The visual cell mosaic shows the greatest regularity on the nasal side of the retina; the regularity decreases towards the temporal side where it is disturbed by the foveae and is least on the dorsal and ventral sides where the double cells are mainly oriented transversely in relation to the long axis of the body. On the nasal side of the retina of *Anolis* the proportions are: major singles 57%, minor singles 14%, and doubles 29%.

All three visual cell types could be recognized in the temporal fovea of *Anolis*. They are all more slender and somewhat elongated, and both the major and minor singles lack a paraboloid. The visual cells in the central fovea are considerably elongated and so slender, about 1μ in diameter, that it was not possible to make out their structure.

The external limiting "membrane" is formed by terminal bars on the inner side of the plasma membranes of visual cells and Müller cells. They join the visual cells with Müller cells and the Müller cells with one another. The members of a double cell are not joined by terminal bars. All the separate visual cells are "insulated" from one another by Müller cells, but the members of a double cell are in contact from the level of the ellipsoid at least down to the level of the nuclei, that is on the vitreal side of the external limiting membrane. Scleral to the external limiting membrane, the Müller cells give off numerous fine processes between the fins of the visual cells. These processes contain vacuoles. A few processes may insinuate themselves between the double cells.

In the outer nuclear layer of *Lacerta viridis*, Ramon y Cajal (1894) distinguished three levels. The outer level contains the nuclei of "erect" cones that descend radially to their footpieces in the outer level of the outer plexiform layer, and the middle level contains the nuclei of "oblique" cones that descend obliquely to terminate in footpieces in the inner level of the outer plexiform layer. It is not clear whether these two cone types correspond to major and minor cones. The innermost of the outer nuclei belong to displaced bipolar cells. The displaced bipolar cells usually have an ascending process terminating in a Landolt's club, which may or may not reach

---

FIG. 13. *Lacerta viridis* (material from Dr. C. H. Pedler and Mrs. R. Tilly). The features of a standard tetrapod double cone are shown. Osmium tetroxide fixation. i: Transverse section of a double cone near the mid-level of the paraboloid; the peripheral cell (P) embraces the axial cell (A), the arrows lie on the peripheral side of the apposed cell membranes, and the axial cell contains a large paraboloid (pb); 15,000×. ii: Transverse section of a double cone from near the vitreal side of the paraboloid; the peripheral cell (P) embraces the axial cell (A), but a lappet (l) of the axial cell is reflected around the peripheral cell; the arrows lie on the peripheral side of the apposed cell membranes; 15,000×. iii: Transverse section of a double cone showing details of the paraboloid with its vesicular cortical region (c) and granular medulla (m): 45,000×

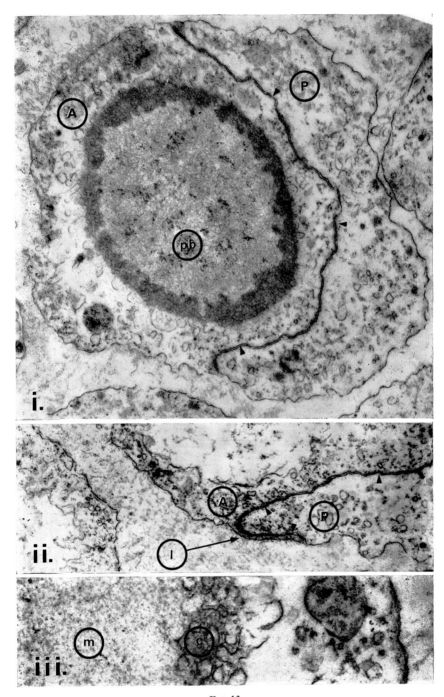

Fig. 13.

the external limiting membrane; some cells lack this process. The descending processes of the displaced bipolar cells send off a few short twigs with terminal boutons in the outer plexiform layer. The fine structure has not been described, but Cohen (1963a) believes that he has identified Landolt's clubs in pigeon retina as round processes between the Müller cells at the level of the outer limiting membrane.

The pedicles of the cones lie in the outer plexiform layer. The footpiece of the peripheral member of a double cell lies deeper than that of the axial cell and these two may synapse with different bipolar cells (Ramon y Cajal, 1894). The footpieces are complex and their relations with the other elements of the retina are incompletely analysed. All of the pedicles of lizard visual cells are of the complex polysynaptic type (Pedler, 1965; Underwood, 1968). The pedicles contain numerous synaptic vesicles and ribbons. There is some evidence that cone footpieces send out processes to contact adjacent cone footpieces. The double walled "cisternae" containing synaptic vesicles, described by Pedler and Tansley (1963, *Phelsuma*), may represent processes invaginated into the pedicle from which they arise (Evans, 1966, *Testudo*). A large number of, up to several hundred, bipolar cell processes may penetrate a pedicle; they enter from all directions, and assuredly many bipolar cells make contact with a single pedicle. A smaller number of horizontal cell processes also makes contact with the pedicle.

The horizontal cells occupy the outer level of the inner nuclear layer. Ramon y Cajal distinguished two types of horizontal cells: brush cells with dense horizontal branching over a limited area and star cells with long horizontal processes branching over a much larger area. The horizontal cell bodies are larger than those of the bipolar cells, and their cytoplasm contains a few mitochondria and Golgi bodies. As seen in electron micrographs these cells have large processes, up to 3μ in diameter, that spread in the inner level of the outer plexiform layer. They have a characteristic fibrillar cytoplasm with a few small mitochondria (Yamada and Ishikawa, 1965, *Clemmys*). Branches of the processes turn in a radial direction to synapse with visual cells.

Ramon y Cajal distinguished two major types of bipolar cells. The more numerous small bipolar cells are supposed to have ascending processes which send out a group of fibrils in the outer plexiform layer. Usually one fibril continues to the external limiting membrane to terminate in a Landolt's club. The more slender descending process follows an oblique course within the inner nuclear layer and then turns radially into the inner plexiform layer to give off a bundle of fibrils with terminal boutons. The large bipolar cells are supposed to lie in the outer level of the outer nuclear layer and to have arborizations arising directly from the cell body. They lack Landolt's clubs. Their descending processes are partly invested by Müller cells, but some of them are in direct contact with one another. Bundles of six to ten bipolar cell dendrites may have a common investment (Pedler and Tilly, 1963).

The amacrine cells occupy the inner level of the inner nuclear layer. They are large cells, larger than the bipolar cells. The nucleus is lobulated (Dowling and Boycott, 1965, species not indicated). Processes of the amacrine cells descend to the inner plexiform layer and synapse with processes of the bipolar cells. The processes of the amacrine cells contain clusters of vesicles in the immediate vicinity of the synaptic contacts. These processes are also believed to associate with processes of the ganglion cells to form post-synaptic dyads in contact with bipolar cells. The bipolar cells contain synaptic vesicles and synaptic ribbons at these dyad synapses. At some points amacrine cells appear to make presynaptic contacts with bipolar cells, even directly back onto the bipolar cell terminal that makes a dyad synapse (Dowling and Boycott, 1965).

The bodies of ganglion cells are partly invested by Müller cells, but there are some direct contacts with other ganglion cells (Pedler and Tilly, 1963). As seen by Ramon y Cajal (1894), some ganglion cells have diffuse processes in the inner plexiform layer and some form a plexus at a single or at several discrete levels. From the ganglion cells the nerve fibres pass to the optic nerve. The small fibres are in bundles invested by and partly infiltrated by the Müller cells, but the fibres are not separated by this investment. There are scattered large fibres that appear to be myelinated and are surrounded by two layers of radial fibre processes.

The Müller cells, or radial fibres, run through the thickness of the retina. The inner limiting membrane consists of two layers separated by about 80 mμ (Pedler and Tilly, 1963, *Phelsuma*). The inner layer is continuous with the fibrils of the vitreous humour, and the outer layer is formed by the flattened extremities of the processes of the Müller cells. The nuclei of the Müller cells lie mainly in the inner nuclear layer. The cytoplasm of the radial fibres is fibrillar. Their mitochondria lie mainly towards the outer limiting membrane.

The relative numbers of nuclei in the different layers of the retina give a rough indication of the nervous organization of the retina. Verriest *et al.* (1959) made counts, midway between the orbital pole and the periphery, of visual cell nuclei, displaced bipolar cell nuclei, inner layer nuclei, and ganglion cell nuclei. Dividing by the number of visual cell nuclei they give respectively displaced bipolar, inner cell, and ganglion cell quotients. It should be pointed out that such figures are crude because the number of nuclei counted in a section depends on their size and spacing and because the inner nuclear layer contains a variety of cell types. For five species of *Lacerta* they found quotients for displaced bipolars of from 0·1 to 0·5, for inner cells of 4·2–6·3, and for ganglion cells of 0·72–1·2.

The central fovea of *Anolis* lies slightly temporal to the orbital pole of the eye. The sides of the pit are rounded, with a radius of curvature of about 0·67 mm (adult male); the centre of the pit is parabolic. The transition between the two curves lies about 45μ from the axis. The thickness of the retina in the centre of the pit, measured from inner to outer limiting membrane, is about 35μ. In the centre of the fovea the distance from the outer limiting membranes to the basement of the pigment epithelium is about 120μ. The height of the visual cells could not be made out, but allowing for the thickness of the pigment epithelium is probably about 110μ. All nuclei are displaced from the centre of the fovea. The visual cells in the centre are about 1μ in diameter. The somewhat oval nuclei of the outer nuclear layer are stacked about 7 or 8 deep around the fovea. At the inner level of the outer plexiform layer, the footpieces of the visual cells form a well-defined single layer which is thrown into folds around the area of maximum retinal thickness. The inner nuclear layer builds up to a maximum of about 27 nuclei deep; the ganglion cell layer builds up to about 6 deep. This lengthening of the visual cells in the centre would appear to permit them to receive an image brought to a longer focus by refraction at the sides of the fovea (Pumphrey, 1948); in this lengthening of the visual cells the fovea of *Anolis* contrasts with that of birds, as shown in published figures (Rochon-Duvigneaud, 1943; Walls, 1942; Polyak, 1941).

The temporal fovea of *Anolis*, the only known non-avian form with a second fovea, lies about two-thirds of the way from the central fovea to the temporal ora terminalis. The fovea has round shoulders but is approximately conical in the centre, an unusual configuration. The slopes of the fovea subtend an angle of about 90° at the apex of the cone. At the centre of the fovea the distance between the two limiting membranes is approximately 85μ. The height of the visual cells in the centre of the fovea increases to about 32μ. In the centre of the fovea the major single cones are roughly 3μ in diameter, the minor cones about 2μ, and the double cones approximately $4·5\mu$. The nuclear layers continue across the centre of the fovea. The oval nuclei of the visual cells are stacked about 3 deep around the fovea. The layer of footpieces of the visual cells is well defined but not folded. The inner nuclear layer builds up to about 9 to 11 nuclei deep, and the ganglion cells to about 3 deep around the fovea (Fig. 4).

The ophthalmic artery links the cerebral branch of the internal carotid, within the braincase, with the superior orbital artery in the orbit. It emerges from the braincase with the optic nerve, gives off two branches passing through the sclera to the chorioid, a "hyaloid" vessel which enters the optic nerve and supplies the conus and a ciliary artery which passes through the sclera in company with the ciliary nerve. As mentioned in the section on embryology, Leplat (1922) is sure that the artery to the conus is not the hyaloid artery. The vein from the conus receives the vorticose veins draining the chorioid plexus and then joins the orbital sinus.

The ciliary artery accompanies the ciliary nerve temporo-ventrally and passes through the scleral cartilage proximal to the ora serrata and continues corneally inside the sclera through the connective tissue of the ciliary body. Just orbital to the root of the iris it divides; one branch crosses the transverse muscle and passes up on the nasal side of the iris to its dorsal side, the other branch extends around the temporal half of the iris (Fig. 5). Both vessels give off numerous centripetal capillaries which run to the pupillary margin. They then turn off and spread centrifugally, superficial to the centripetal vessels, to the periphery of the iris and to the ciliary body where they have numerous dichotomous branches. The capillaries run through the ciliary body close to the epithelium and drain into the chorioid plexus which is a dense network of narrow sinuses that are heavily pigmented; the plexus lies just outside the basement membrane of the pigment epithelium.

The ciliary ganglion of *Anolis* receives two roots, a shorter and stouter root from the oculomotor nerve and a longer and more slender root from the trigeminal nerve (Willard, 1915). From the ganglion emerge two ciliary nerves which pass dorsal to the optic nerve and accompany the ciliary artery through the sclera. They innervate the muscles of the ciliary body and iris. The two nerves separate at about the level at which the artery divides and pass around the eyeball at the level of the root of the iris.

F. The Retina of other Lizards and Amphisbaenians

The retina of all diurnal lizards examined, as well as that of the nocturnal *Heloderma* and fossorial *Anniella*, has only cones, both major single and double cells similar to those of *Anolis*. Minor single cones have been seen with certainty only in *Crotaphytus*, *Draco*, *Lacerta*, and *Anolis*; only for *Anolis* do we know the colour of their oil-droplets. Displaced bipolar cells are absent from *Crotaphytus*, *Phrynosoma*, *Agama*, *Chamaeleo*, and *Ameiva*, and they are very rare away from the retinal periphery in *Heloderma* (less than 1% of visual-cell nuclei). Displaced bipolar cells are found in *Lacerta*, *Psammodromus*, *Anguis*, *Gerrhonotus*, *Pseudopus*, *Anniella*, and *Varanus*; they range from about 50% of the number of visual-cell nuclei to about 10%. The inner nuclear quotient ranges from 10·5 (*Agama*) to 3·4 (*Anguis*), and the ganglion cell quotient ranges from more than one (*Agama* and *Phrynosoma*) down to 0·64 (*Pseudopus*).

The nocturnal lizard *Heloderma* and also the burrowing *Anniella* show loss of the yellow colour of the oil-droplets and of the fovea, but lack other obvious adaptive modifications. *Xantusia* has major single, minor single, and double cells with long and distinctly enlarged outer segments (Fig. 14). The colourless oil-droplets are so large as to suggest that their size is secondary and that they may be serving a light refracting function; otherwise the inner segments are not obviously modified. The double cells are loosely arranged in horizontal rows with many breaks, and are thus less regular than in *Anolis*. On the nasal side of the retina the proportions are (*X. vigilis*) major single cells 64%, minor single cells 11%, and double cells 25%. The displaced bipolar quotient is more than one, the inner nuclear quotient 5 to 6, and the ganglion cell quotient approximately one. The dark adapted retina of *Xantusia* does not show "visual purple" (Walls, 1942).

The pygopodid *Lialis* has major single, minor single, and double cells (Fig. 14). The outer segments are enlarged, but not proportionately as much as those of *Xantusia*. There are no oil-droplets, but the inner segments are otherwise little modified. The double cells are arranged in horizontal rows which zig-zag less than those of *Anolis*. Between the rows of double cells are rows of single cells. On the nasal side of the retina the proportions are major singles 54%, minor singles 8%, and doubles 38%. The displaced bipolar cell quotient is about 0·6, the inner nuclear quotient roughly 5, and the ganglion cell quotient about 1. *Delma* shows similar outer segments and also lacks oil-droplets (O'Day, 1939). *Aprasia* is similar and has a row of displaced bipolar cells; it is of particular interest that most of the visual cells lack paraboloids which were observed in only a few of the double cells (Fig. 14).

All of the geckos examined have major single and type B double cells as well as a second type of double cell, type C (Underwood, 1951a; Figs 14 and 15). The type C double cell consists of a major member which is like the major single elements and a minor member which appears to correspond to a minor single element (Underwood, 1968); the minor member may lack organelles present in the major member. The type B double cells are arranged in straight horizontal rows of considerable regularity. The major single and type C double cells occupy the rows between the type B doubles. The rows of type B doubles are aligned with one another vertically so that running up and down across the rows one passes over a series of doubles of the same orientation. In some geckos there is a small proportion of twin cells consisting of two single elements; these lie in the same rows as the single and type C double elements. The displaced bipolar cell quotient ranges from about 1 in *Hemidactylus* to 0·3 in *Gonatodes*, the inner nuclear quotient from 8 in *Coleonyx* to 3 in *Hemidactylus*, and the ganglion cell quotient from about 1·8 in *Sphaerodactylus parkeri* to 0·6 in *Gonatodes*.

The only eublepharine gecko examined is *Coleonyx* (Walls, 1942; Dunn, 1966; Fig. 14). It has very long cylindrical outer segments. There are no oil-droplets, but the inner segments are otherwise of the constitution and proportions found in diurnal lizard cones. Processes of the pigment epithelium

embrace the outer segments but do not intervene between the members of
the type C (D₂ of Dunn) double cells or of the triple cells. There is a single
incision in the lamellar sacs of the outer segments giving them a cardioid
outline in transverse section. The outer segments of the single cells are
about $3 \cdot 5\mu$ in diameter, and of the type B cells about 5μ in diameter. The
outer segment is attached by a well developed ciliary pedicle. There are
calycal processes around the bases of the outer segments. The mitochondria

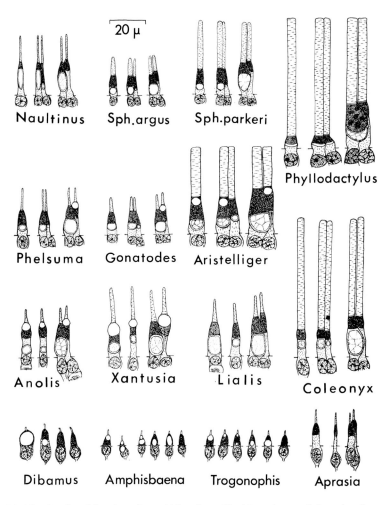

FIG. 14. Visual cells of lizards and amphisbaenians. *Naultinus elegans, Sphaerodactylus argus, Sphaerodactylus parkeri, Phyllodactylus xanti, Phelsuma cepediana, Gonatodes albogularis, Aristelliger praesignis, Coleonyx elegans, Anolis lineatopus, Xantusia vigilis, Lialis burtonii, Dibamus novaeguineae, Amphisbaena fuliginosa, Trogonophis wiegmanni*, and *Aprasia pulchella*.

of the ellipsoids are closely packed, with large ones in the centre and smaller ones peripherally.

Two types of paraboloids, granular and membranous, occur in *Coleonyx* (Dunn, 1966). Granular paraboloids have a central mass of granules surrounded by paired membranes, with additional granules between the pair of membranes. They are found in the single cells, in the twin cells, in the major members of the type C double and triple cells, and in the axial member of the type B double cells. The membranous paraboloids consist entirely of paired membranes enclosing granules, and are found in the minor members of the type C double cells and of the triple cells.

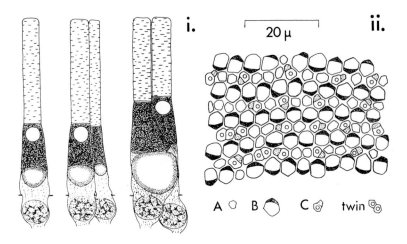

FIG. 15. Visual cells of the gecko *Aristelliger praesignis*. i, Side views of cells, the elements from left to right being single (type A) cell, type C double cell, and type B double cell; ii, tangential section of retina (semidiagrammatic). A, type A single cell; B, type B double cell; C, type C double cell.

All of the visual cells have radially disposed fins. The number of single cells ranges from 7·4% to 25·4% of the total number of cells. The type B double cells are both the most numerous and the most constant in proportion, with a range from 51·0% to 52·9%. The type C double cells consist of two apposed members, the minor being smaller in cross sectional area down to the level of the nuclei; they compose from 15·3% to 29·6% depending on the region of the retina. The twin cells consist of two major elements less closely apposed than in the double cells; they range from 1·7% to 6·2% of the total. Dunn (1966) also reported two types of triple cells, consisting of two major and one minor cell associated with one another like the members of the type C double cells. In the triplet$_1$ cells the arrangement of the three elements is linear; they constitute 1·1%–4·6% of the total. In the triplet$_2$ cells the grouping is triangular; they aggregate only 0·3%–1·7% of the total. Dunn finally reported finding a single quintuplet cell consisting of three major and two minor members. The dark adapted retina of *Coleonyx* shows a scotopic pigment that differs considerably from rhodopsin (Crescitelli, 1958).

The sphaerodactyline gecko *Gonatodes albogularis* has the outer segments of the visual cells a little larger than those in fully diurnal lizards. In the marginal areas of the retina the major single elements and the major members of the type C double cells may have small oil-droplets which do not fill the ends of the ellipsoids, but in by far the greater part of the retina they lack droplets (Fig. 14). Over nearly all of the retina the type B double cells have a normal sized, colourless oil-droplet. Oil-droplets and paraboloids are absent from the foveal visual cells. No visual pigment has been detected in the dark adapted retina. *Gonatodes annularis* is similar to *G. albogularis*, but *G. antillensis* has somewhat larger outer segments and lacks oil-droplets.

The *Sphaerodactylus* species examined lack all oil-droplets. In *S. argus* the outer segments are of about the same size as they are in *Gonatodes albogularis*, but in *S. parkeri* they are tall cylindrical elements. Some of the type C double cells of *S. parkeri* lack a paraboloid in the minor member. No scotopic pigment has been found in the dark adapted retina of *S. argus*, but there are probably two pigments in *S. parkeri* (Crescitelli, 1958).

The gekkonine *Aristelliger praesignis* has visual cells with large cylindrical outer segments. There are colourless oil-droplets in the single cells, in the peripheral and major members of the type B and type C double cells respectively, and in both members of the twin cells, but oil-droplets are lacking from the axial and minor members of the B and C cells respectively (Fig. 15). On the nasal side of the retina the proportions are: single cells 31%, type B doubles 50%, type C doubles 17%, and twin cells 2%. The structure of the other parts of the inner segments is not otherwise modified. *A. praesignis* of Jamaica has no fovea but *A. cochranae* of Navassa Island retains a shallow temporal fovea in combination with visual cells like those of *A. praesignis* (colour of oil-droplets not known). A scotopic pigment has been found in the dark adapted retina of *A. praesignis* (Crescitelli, 1958).

The visual cells of the diurnal species *Phelsuma cepediana* and *P. madagascariensis* have slender outer segments like those of other diurnal lizards (Fig.14; Tansley, 1961). The peripheral member of the type B double cell has an oil-droplet which is colourless in *P. madagascariensis*; its colour in *P. cepediana* is not known. The single and type C double cells lack oil-droplets. Some of the minor members of the type C doubles lack a paraboloid. In *Phelsuma* the ciliary pedicle of the outer segments is imperfectly developed. *Lygodactylus* is similar to *Phelsuma* (Pedler and Tansley, 1963; Pedler and Tilly, 1964).

The visual cells of *Hoplodactylus*, a nocturnal diplodactyline from New

Zealand, have large cylindrical outer segments, longer than those of *Aristelliger*; they all lack oil-droplets. Peripherally, and especially ventrally, in the retina the inner segments are of the usual proportions with round paraboloids as in *Aristelliger*. In the central parts of the retina, however, the paraboloids are hollowed on the scleral face, thus partly embracing the ellipsoid as in the advanced gekkonines. The diurnal *Naultinus* has slender, closely packed visual cells with fine outer segments like those of other diurnal lizards (Fig. 14). None of these cells however has an oil-droplet. The paraboloids of the major single and type B and type C double cells are elongated in conformity with the narrowness of the cells. The minor members of the type C double cells either have a small round paraboloid or lack this organelle. Examination of radial and tangential sections shows that a few minor single cells are not paired off with major singles to form type C doubles. A few major twin cells were also seen.

The other nocturnal gekkonines which have been studied have visual cells with very tall cylindrical outer segments (*Gehyra, Gekko, Hemidactylus, Phyllodactylus, Tarentola, Thecadactylus*). They lack all oil-droplets and have reduced crescentic paraboloids that partly embrace the vitreal ends of the ellipsoids (Fig. 14; Tansley, 1959; Pedler and Tilly, 1964). The ellipsoid of the axial member of the type B double cells stains more strongly with the acid fuchsin of Mallory's triple stain than does the peripheral ellipsoid; the ellipsoids of the major single and type C double cells resemble the latter. Twin cells are occasionally found. Pedler and Tilly (1964) show that in *Gekko* and *Hemidactylus* the central mitochondria of the axial ellipsoids are transformed into uniform electron dense bodies that do not section easily (Fig. 16). These bodies are of an apparently refringent material. In the same forms the footpieces contain double walled outlines formed by invaginations of the cell membrane to enclose processes of the radial fibres.

Apart from burrowing lizards that have already been discussed (*Anniella, Aprasia*), I have investigated well preserved material of *Dibamus* and the amphisbaenians *Trogonophis* and *Amphisbaena*. In all there appear to be only single cells of various types which resemble the published figures of embryonic visual cells in being small and rather variable (Fig. 14).

Trogonophis has the most fully developed visual cells, but they are less than 9μ high. The outer segments are small and conelike. There are vacuoles in most of the cells which, on the basis of their position, may be interpreted as oil-droplets and paraboloids. Some cells contain only oil-droplets which

---

Fig. 16. *Gekko gecko* (from Pedler and Tilly, 1964, *Vision Research*, by courtesy of Pergamon Press). Longitudinal section of an advanced gecko double rod fixed in osmium tetroxide. The refringent body of the axial ellipsoid is composed of transformed mitochondria (mr) and surrounded by unmodified mitochondria (mp). The paraboloid (pb) is hollowed to accommodate the axial ellipsoid. On the left side part of the peripheral cell (P) can be seen.

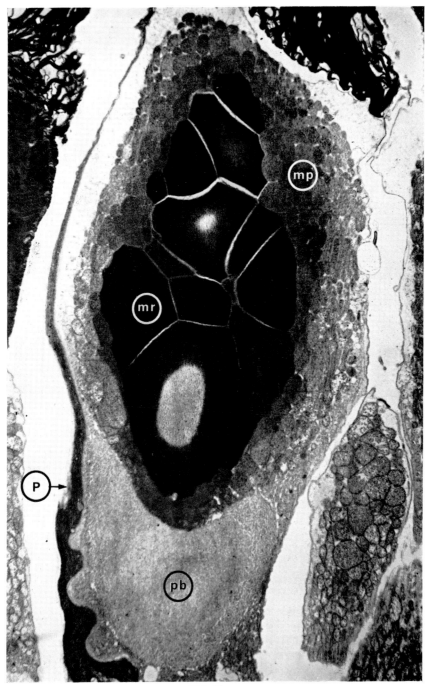

FIG. 16.

usually fill but do not distend the end of the ellipsoid, but a few have a paraboloid so large as to make a bulge between the ellipsoid and the nucleus. Some cells have both a small oil-droplet and a small paraboloid. A few cells have neither oil-droplet nor paraboloid. In tangential sections all the cells appear to stand alone without association to form doubles or twins. The retinal layers are well defined. In the outer plexiform layer there is a clear row of footpieces. Towards the centre of the retina, the inner nuclei out-number the outer nuclei by about four times and the ganglion cells are less numerous than the outer nuclei. The pigment epithelium is of a normal appearance with processes between the visual cells.

Amphisbaena has visual cells that are a little smaller, about 7–8μ high, and somewhat more irregular. Some of the visual cells have two large vacuoles, some have one very large vacuole, and some have none. The layers of the retina are still recognisable but less distinct than in *Trogonophis*. The pig-ment epithelium consists of columnar cells without any processes between the visual cells. There is no recognizable row of footpieces. The visual cells of *Dibamus* are about the same size as those of *Amphisbaena*, but far more irregular; some lack vacuoles, some have a vacuole near to the base of the cell, and some have enormous vacuoles which completely distort the form of the cell. None has a vacuole in the distal part of the cell in the position of an oil-droplet, and none has two vacuoles. The pigment epithelium is like that of *Amphisbaena*, with the pigmentation failing to reach the visual cells.

IV. Snakes

A. Orbit and Adnexae

In the more primitive and conservative snakes the orbits are separated by the bony walls of the braincase. The medial wall of the orbit is formed by the frontal and parietal bones which descend to meet the parasphenoid; the latter lies between the two trabeculae. The anterior wall of the orbit is formed by the prefrontal bone and the posterior by an expansion of the parietal and by the postorbital bone. The orbit is floored by the maxilla, pterygoid, and ectopterygoid which are usually very mobile.

The frontal and, to a lesser extent, the parietal, form a partial bony shelf of variable extent dorsal to the orbit. In some Boidae there is a separate supra-orbital bone, possibly homologous with the postfrontal of lizards. In some snakes with large eyes the braincase is raised and the frontals rest on a crest of the parasphenoid so that the eyes are separated by a bony interorbital septum. Finally, in other snakes, the bony septum is emarginated and a membrane extending between the frontals and the parasphenoid separates the orbits. In primitive snakes the optic nerve and the nerves to the eye-muscles emerge through the lateral walls of the braincase (between the frontal and parietal, through the frontal, or through the parietal). In more specialized snakes they pass through a larger aperture surrounded by the frontal, parietal, and parasphenoid.

There are six oculorotatory muscles. The four recti originate from bone or membrane around the optic foramen, and the two oblique muscles from the medial margin of the prefrontal bone. Bursalis, retractor bulbi, and depressor palpebralis inferior muscles are completely lacking. The levator bulbi muscle has shifted its insertions to become the retractor vomeris and retractor pterygoidei. Movement of the eye beneath the spectacle is rather limited.

The eye of all snakes is covered by a fixed transparent spectacle like that of some lizards. In most snakes the spectacle is surrounded and partly overlapped by the scales of the head. Some burrowing snakes lack a separate spectacle, and there is simply a transparent window in a smooth ocular shield covering the orbit and surrounding area. A conjunctival space is drained by the lachrymal duct through a single canaliculus. Snakes lack a nictitating membrane (Bellairs and Boyd, 1947).

Harder's gland is always large compared to that of lizards, extending from the anterior part of the orbit along its medial side ventral to (and sometimes around) the optic nerve and, usually, back into the temporal region. In *Mehelya* this postorbital extension of the gland is so large that the supralabial gland is locally reduced to accommodate it (Underwood, 1967a). The duct of Harder's gland passes forwards. There is usually no separate lachrymal gland.

In boid snakes the lachrymal duct arises by a broad canaliculus from the anteroventral corner of the conjunctival space. Most of the glandular tissue discharges into the canaliculus, but some patches discharge into the conjunctival space. In *Pareas* glandular tissue surrounds the upper part of the lachrymal duct and the anterior part of the conjunctival space and discharges into both. In the other primitive snakes the lachrymal canaliculus is narrow. Most of Harder's gland discharges directly into the lachrymal duct, but a few patches of glandular tissue discharge into the conjunctival space.

In more advanced snakes the canaliculus leaves the conjunctival space through a very narrow aperture, and its lower end projects into the lumen of the lachrymal duct. All of Harder's gland discharges directly into the lachrymal duct.

The ophthalmic and oculorotatory nerves pass anteriorly within the braincase, enclosed by the parietal bone, and typically emerge with the optic nerve; there are, however, separate foramina for the ophthalmic nerves in *Xenodermus*, *Fimbrios*, and *Achalinus*. The ophthalmic nerve passes dorsal to the optic nerve and ventral to the superior rectus and superior oblique muscles. It gives off a ciliary root and some fibres to the skin above the orbit.

The maxillary branch of the trigeminal passes ventral to the orbit, but sends a few fibres to it. The oculomotor nerve divides into two rami. The ramus superior gives off a ciliary root and then supplies the superior rectus. The ramus inferior goes to the inferior and anterior recti and inferior oblique muscles. The trochlear nerve to the superior oblique passes dorsal to the superior rectus muscle. The abducens nerve goes to the posterior rectus. The palatine branch of the facial nerve emerges from the Vidian canal and crosses the floor of the orbit.

The internal carotid artery divides to form the facial and cerebral arteries (Lüdicke, 1940). The cerebral artery enters the braincase via the Vidian canal. The facial artery passes ventral to the postorbital extension of Harder's gland to enter the orbit. It gives branches to Harder's gland and a few small branches to the skin and then divides. The smaller supraorbital artery passes dorsally and medially around the orbit. It sends branches to Harder's gland and the muscles of the eye and then becomes the ophthalmic artery which passes through the optic foramen into the braincase to anastomose with the cerebral circulation. The larger infraorbital branch passes ventral to the eye and accompanies the maxillary nerve forwards. There is no palatine artery.

The part of the orbital sinus within the orbit is not as large as in lizards, but the sinus extends outside the orbit ventral to Harder's gland (Bruner, 1907). It has several connections with the maxillary vein and receives a small vein from the nasal gland. The superior palpebral vein arises from the orbital sinus anteriorly and the inferior palpebral vein arises from the maxillary vein; the two veins join posterior to the eye and pass back to discharge into the orbital sinus. The secondary anterior cerebral vein arises from the posteromedial corner of the orbital sinus and enters the braincase. The posterior prolongation of the sinus beneath Harder's gland continues posteriorly into the lateral cephalic vein.

B. The Eyeball

The eyeball of snakes is approximately spherical or slightly elongated axially; this elongation is marked in *Typhlops*, *Leptotyphlops*, and *Rhinophis*. The cornea may be slightly more strongly curved than the rest of the eye, but there is no sharp change. The sclera is entirely fibrous, lacking scleral cartilage and ossicles. The cornea of *Natrix* subtends 125°, that of *Python* 135°; even diurnal snakes have a large cornea like that ordinarily found only in nocturnal animals (Rochon-Duvigneaud, 1943). The cornea is covered by a very thin epithelium. There is no Bowman's membrane, and Descemet's membrane is very thin. Orbital to the sclerocorneal junction the sclera is thick; it thins out towards the equator and thickens again orbitally. Schlemm's canal lies in the cornea near its junction with the sclera and opens into the ciliary veins (Fig. 17). The sclera and cornea are uniformly thin in forms with small eyes such as *Typhlops* and *Leptotyphlops*; there is no Schlemm's canal in these burrowing forms nor in *Boa* and *Eryx*. The pigmented chorioid is thinner than that of lizards and remains fused with the sclera. This thinness may be related to the development of the hyaloid circulation.

The ciliary zone is narrow, and the ciliary body is so reduced that Walls (1942) suggests that it may more appropriately be termed a "ciliary roll" (Fig. 17); *Typhlops*, *Leptotyphlops*, and *Rhinophis* lack even a ciliary roll (Fig. 10). The retina and pigment epithelium extend beyond the ora terminalis as a flat zone of simple columnar epithelium (the orbiculus ciliaris)

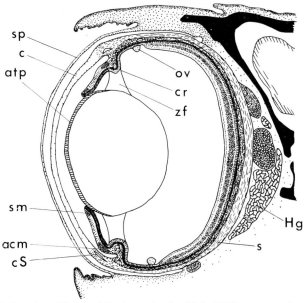

FIG. 17. Vertical section of the eye of *Natrix natrix*, after Walls (1942). acm, muscle of accommodation; atp, anterior pad of lens; c, cornea; cr, ciliary roll; cS, canal of Schlemm; Hg, Harder's gland; ov, orbicular vein; s, sclera; sm, sphincter muscle; sp, spectacle; zf, zonula fibres.

around which commonly runs a circular orbicular vein. This vein was not seen in *Typhlops*, *Leptotypholops*, *Boa*, *Charina*, *Epicrates*, *Eryx*, *Lichanura*, *Tropidophis*, or *Chersydrus*. The ciliary epithelium is thrown into an annular fold, which encloses connective tissue and blood vessels, at the root of the iris. The pectinate ligament is very small. The zonule fibres arise from the groove between the iris and the ciliary roll and from the posterior face of the ciliary roll.

The epithelium of the iris is not thickened at the pupillary margin; in *Typhlops* the outer epithelium is much thicker than the inner. The dilatator

c

fibres lie immediately on the outer face of the iridial epithelium and are believed to be of mesodermal origin. The epithelium of the iris is heavily pigmented; in *Typhlops* and *Leptotyphlops* the circumferential half of the inner epithelium is unpigmented. All the rest of the iris mesoderm contains striated muscle fibres which are concentrated at the root of the iris and around the margin of the pupil. The musculature of the root of the iris is much less developed in *Python* than in higher snakes. A transversalis muscle is always absent. The only musculature of the iris in *Typhlops*, and probably also in *Leptotyphlops*, is around the margin of the pupil. White and yellow pigment often lies superficial to the black pigment of the iris of snakes.

The lens is nearly spherical, lacks an annular pad, and has only a thin epithelium. In more specialized snakes there is generally an anterior pad, formed by thickening of the epithelium of the lens, so that the lens is even more nearly spherical (Fig. 17). The lens of snakes, unlike that reported for other reptiles, has sutures. Most of the fibres are too short to run from pole to pole, but terminate at each end on meridians running out from the pole. Each fibre meets an oppositely disposed fibre at each end along a meridionally disposed suture. The number of radial lamellae is high, from 201 to over 1100 (*Python molurus*). In general the lens is harder than that of other reptiles, but it is soft in some water snakes (*Natrix*). The lens is yellow in some of the more strongly diurnal snakes (*Coluber* and *Malpolon*).

Two mechanisms of accommodation have been described in snakes and, of the forms studied, only the python *Morelia* is reported to lack power of accommodation (Kahmann, 1932). All other snakes studied show forward displacement of the lens due to increased pressure in the posterior chamber. This pressure is generated by contraction of the musculature of the root of the iris forcing the lens corneally against the iris. In juvenile *Coronella* (Kahmann, 1932) the pupillary sphincter also squeezes the anterior face of the lens, thus increasing its curvature; this effect appears to be lost with age. In the amphibious *Natrix tessellata* the lens is not only displaced, but its anterior segment is also subject to considerable deformation, an effect also marked in *N. maura* and, to a lesser extent, in *N. natrix*.

There are two sets of zonule fibres. The anterior fibres arise from the front of the ciliary roll and pass dorsal to the anterior face of the lens. The other, and more variable, fibres arise from the posterior face of the ciliary roll.

The blood supply of eye and orbit has been well described by Lüdicke (1940). The ophthalmic artery divides to give rise to the nasal and temporal common ciliary arteries; these pass through the sclera to the chorioid where each gives off a hyaloid branch. The hyaloid branches unite to form the hyaloid artery ventral to the optic nerve. Each common ciliary divides to give a short ciliary artery that supplies the chorioid and a long ciliary artery that sends branches to the chorioid and extends to the root of the iris. These arteries enter the iris close to the horizontal meridian. Venous drainage is by two vessels in the vertical meridian. The course of the iris capillaries is mainly tangential, but they converge radially towards the two veins.

The hyaloid artery enters the posterior chamber of the eye ventral to the optic nerve. It supplies the conus, if present, and divides into nasal and temporal branches which run across the surface of the retina and give off small branches which form a network. The hyaloid vessels drain into the ringvein lying behind the ciliary roll and into the hyaloid vein passing posteriorly from the ventral side of the ringvein to the optic papilla. Mann (1929) states that, as in embryo mammals, the hyaloid vessels anastomose with and drain into the vessels of the chorioid plexus which forms outside the optic cup. In mammals, with the subsequent growth inwards of the optic cup to form the iris, the connections between hyaloid and chorioid circulations are severed and the hyaloid develops its own venous drainage. However, Mann found and figured small vessels passing from the ringvein through the orbicular epithelium into the chorioid circulation in adults of the African and Indian pythons and of the black and white cobra. She adds that there are no retinal veins, but this latter is certainly not true of most investigated snakes.

A few snakes are known to have a vascular conus arising from the optic nerve papilla (Jokl, 1923; Walls, 1942). It is reported to be bound by mesodermal tissue and not by neuroglia like the conus of lizards or birds. It is best developed and heavily pigmented in *Vipera berus*, small, non-vascular, and pigmented in *Eristocophis*, and well developed and unpigmented in *Lampropeltis*. Usually, as in *Malpolon*, there is a group of fibres that pass from the papilla to be lost in the vitreous humour. A number of snakes, such as *Epicrates* and *Coronella*, possess a conus in embryonic stages that is reduced or lost in the adult.

Lüdicke (1940) discovered a capillary network in the cornea. The vessels are, in *Coluber najadum*, mainly oriented vertically. This corneal network is supplied by small arteries to the scales surrounding the eye and is presumably, therefore, a conjunctival circulation. The venous drainage of the cornea is into the orbital sinus.

The optic nerve shows a "total resemblance to that of *Neoceratodus*" in which "the nerve fibres are blocked off by glial septa into fascicles, each with an axial core of (ependymal?) nuclei" (Walls, 1942, pp. 632 and 591). The optic nerve further differs from that of lizards in that there are numerous efferent fibres (Armstrong, 1951). These fibres are of unknown significance, but may provide vasomotor input to the hyaloid circulation.

C. The Retina

In snakes the pigmented processes of the pigment epithelium extend inwards and appear, by light microscopy, to embrace only the outer segments of the cones. There is thus no extension of the pigment in the forms which have only rods, such as *Typhlops*, or in forms in which the rod outer segments extend distal to the cones such as the Boidae and *Telescopus*. In forms in which the cones or transmuted cones reach the same level as the rods (*Vipera*) or extend distal to them (*Sibon*) or in which there are only cones (*Ahaetulla*), these cones are embraced by pigment processes; an exception is *Enhydris* in which the pigment does not embrace the upstanding cones. There are no known photomechanical changes in the pigment epithelium.

The visual cells of all known snakes lack oil-droplets and paraboloids. The parts of the visual cells are thus outer segment, ellipsoid, myoid (not contractile), nucleus, and foot-piece. In contrast to lizards many snakes have a duplex retina with both rods and cones together. There are no displaced bipolar cells in the retina of snakes.

The Typhlopidae and Leptotyphlopidae have only one type of visual cell with the ellipsoid close to the limiting membrane (Underwood, 1967a). These are here regarded as rods equivalent to the type D elements of other snakes. In *Typhlops jamaicensis* the closely packed visual cells are about 2μ wide and 16μ high with long, slightly tapering outer segments (Fig. 18). The nuclei are oval, closely packed, and stacked about 3 deep. The layers of the retina are well defined. The inner nuclear layer is 3 to 4 nuclei deep and more loosely packed than the layer of visual cells; the ganglion cells are 1 to 2 nuclei deep. The processes of the pigment epithelium are unpigmented. There is no vascular conus, but there are retinal vessels.

Leptotyphlops has visual cells which are a little less closely packed than those of *Typhlops*, and are of about the same width but only about 10μ high (Fig. 18). The outer segments are shorter and more cylindrical. The nuclei of the visual cells are similar, but stacked only 2 or 3 deep. The inner layer is 4 to 5 nuclei and the ganglion cell layer one nucleus deep. The pigment does not extend between the visual cells. There is no vascular conus, but there are retinal vessels.

The uropeltid *Rhinophis* (Baumeister, 1908) appears to have only rods. The nuclei are stacked two deep, the inner ones alternating with the outer ones. The inner nuclear layer is 4–5 nuclei deep and the ganglion cells are about two deep.

In the Henophidia and in some primitive Caenophidia there are single rods and single cones. The cones correspond to the type C elements of more complex snake retinas. The rods outnumber the cones; counts of tangential sections give ratios of 5:1 for *Tropidophis* and of 36:1 for *Pseudoboa*. The rods are taller than the cones, except perhaps in *Xenopeltis* and *Atractaspis*. The nuclei of the cones are usually more spherical than those of the rods and placed further sclerally, i.e., nearer to the limiting membrane; the rod nuclei are usually stacked in several rows. The outer nuclei are about twice as numerous as the inner nuclei (quotient 0·5, except in *Tropidophis*) and from 15 to 25 times the number of ganglion cells (quotients 0·07–0·04 except in *Tropidophis* and *Chersydrus*). Pigment from the epithelium does

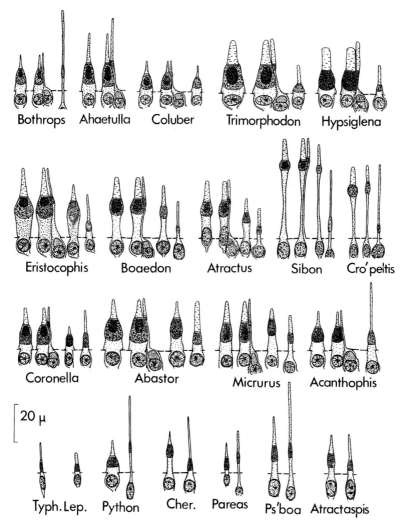

FIG. 18. Visual cells of snakes. *Bothrops atrox* (G. L. Walls preparation), *Ahaetulla nasuta* (G. L. Walls preparation), *Coluber constrictor* (G. L. Walls preparation), *Trimorphodon vandenburghi* (G. L. Walls preparation), *Hypsiglena ochrorhyncha* (G. L. Walls preparation), *Eristocophis mac-mahoni*, *Boaedon fuliginosus*, *Atractus trilineatus*, *Sibon nebulata*, *Crotaphopeltis hotamboeia*, *Coronella austriaca* (G. L. Walls preparation), *Abastor erythrogramma* (G. L. Walls preparation), *Micrurus fulvius* (G. L. Walls preparation), *Acanthophis antarcticus* (G. L. Walls preparation), *Typhlops jamaicensis*, *Leptotyphlops humilis*, *Python molurus* (G. L. Walls preparation), *Chersydrus granulatus*, *Pareas margaritophorus*, *Pseudoboa neuwiedii* and *Atractaspis dahomeyensis*.

not embrace the outer segments of the visual-cells. *Python* and *Boa* are known to show a visual purple in their dark adapted retinae (Walls, 1942).

Epicrates and the similar *Python* (Fig. 18) have very slender rods less than 1μ in diameter and about 40μ high with long slender myoids and outer segments about 30μ long. In radial sections the rods outnumber the cones by about 50:1. The stouter cones are 16μ tall, and their ellipsoids sit on the limiting membrane. *Tropidophis* is similar, but its visual cells are all stouter and the cones are less heavily outnumbered, so that the inner nuclear quotient is about 0·85 and the ganglion cell quotient about 0·11. In *Xenopeltis* (Bouin fixation) the rods and cones are of about the same height, and the rods have slender myoids (Underwood, 1967a).

Chersydrus has closely packed rods about 32μ high with slender outer segments about 24μ long and sessile ellipsoids (Fig. 18). The cones are about 22μ high and have ellipsoids about level with those of the rods. Ganglion cells are extremely sparse; the quotient is only 0·017 (see p. 40). In *Pareas* (Underwood, 1967a) the rods are about 22μ high with outer segments about 11μ long; their ellipsoids are a little distal to those of the cones which are about 16μ high. Counted in radial sections, the rods outnumber the cones by about 50:1. In *Atractaspis* the rods and cones are similar to those of *Pareas*, but the rods are not taller than the cones. In *Pseudoboa* both rod and cone ellipsoids are distal to the limiting membrane. The rods are about 48μ high with outer segments about 33μ long, and the cones are about 30μ high (Fig. 18).

The visual cell patterns of all other snakes can be related to the "viperine pattern", well shown by viperine snakes (Underwood, 1967a). *Vipera berus* is, furthermore, the only snake that has been studied in any detail by electron microscopy (observations of Underwood and Parry), although Yamada, *et al.* (1966) report briefly on *Elaphe climacophora* and I have made a few preliminary observations on *Heterodon platyrhinos* (Figs 19 and 20). The viperine pattern has four types of visual cells (Fig. 21). First are the small single rods, termed "type C'" by Walls (1942) to distinguish them from "type C" cones; as I find this rather confusing I have termed them "type D". Then there are small single cones (type C of Walls and the present writer), large single cones (type A) and large double cones (type B). The rods

---

Fig. 19. *Vipera berus* (specimen from Mr. D. J. Street). The features of a snake double cone are shown. Osmium tetroxide fixation. i: Transverse section of a double cone showing the peripheral ellipsoid (P) consisting of simple mitochondria apposed to the axial ellipsoid (A) containing refringent granules within the mitochondria; the arrows lie on the peripheral side of the apposed cell membranes; 20,000×. ii: Transverse section of a double cone between the ellipsoid and the external limiting membrane showing the slender peripheral cell (P) partly embedded in the axial cell (A); the small arrows lie on the axial side of the apposed membranes; the axial cell has a prominent Golgi system (G) and bears radial fins (f) between which are microvilli (v) from the Müller cells; 20,000×.

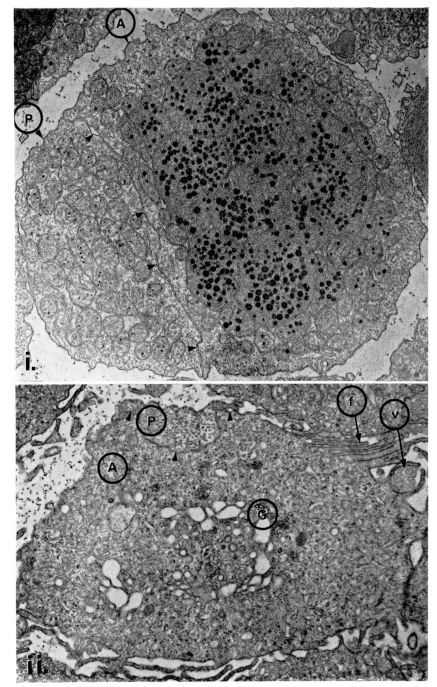

Fig. 19.

and the small single cones of the viperine pattern appear to correspond to the rods and cones of primitive snakes.

The outer segments contain the usual lamellar sacs or discs. The lamellar sacs of the rods of *Vipera* are a little less closely spaced than those of the cones. A peculiar feature seen in *Vipera*, but not in *Heterodon*, at the middle level of the outer segments, is tubules arising from the edges of the lamellar sacs and running lengthwise. Commonly between 8 and 16 are seen in one transverse section, but in one cell 46 were counted. The ciliary pedicle is well developed, but no ciliary rootlets were seen. All the visual cells of *Vipera* and *Heterodon* have calycal processes surrounding the bases of the outer segments. Between the ellipsoid and the nucleus is a well developed Golgi system that shows a tendency to circular disposition of the vacuoles and tubules. This region of the visual cells of *Vipera* has many inclusions; most prominent are large granular bodies up to 930 mμ in diameter like those described by Cohen (1963a) in pigeons and "multivesicular bodies" up to 800 mμ in diameter reminiscent of those found in the fat body of an insect by Locke and Collins (1966). The "myoids" of the visual cells bear fins which interdigitate with processes of the Müller cells. Scleral to these fins the visual cells of *Vipera* make numerous contacts with one another. Their cell membranes are separated by about 25 mμ. Contacts between all cell types were seen. At the free surfaces of the Müller cells ciliary structures are quite common; they lack the central pair of filaments.

The rods of *Vipera* (Fig. 21) are distinguished by their rather long, slightly tapering outer segments which are about 11μ by 2·5μ. Their ellipsoids have mitochondria up to about 1·1μ in diameter that contain very fine granules which are not more than 30 mμ in diameter. The small single cones have sharply tapering outer segments about 6μ long by 3μ wide at the base. The ellipsoid is similar to that of the rods but a little more bulky.

The large single and double cones are of a type unique to snakes. Tansley and Johnson (1956) reported that the cone ellipsoids of *Natrix* are refringent in the fresh retina. By light microscopy it can be seen that the ellipsoids of the type A cells and the type B axial cells have a differentiated medulla

FIG. 20. *Heterodon platyrhinos* (specimen from Dr. D. A. Rossman). The features of a snake double cone are shown. Osmium tetroxide fixation. i: Longitudinal section of a double cone through the peripheral cell showing the paranuclear body (pm) formed of a second aggregation of mitochondria within the cell and the nucleus (pn) indented to accommodate the paranuclear body; on each side is a Müller cell (M) between small (on the side of the peripheral cell) and broad arrows; at the level of the external limiting membrane (elm), a vestigial cilium (cm) can be seen in one of the Müller cells; 10,000×. ii: Longitudinal section of a double cone showing a Müller cell (M) separating the two members up to the level of the external limiting membrane (elm); the small arrows indicate the cell membranes of the peripheral cell (P) in which some paranuclear mitochondria (pm) are visible, and broad arrows indicate the cell membrane of the axial cell (A) in which a portion of the nucleus (an) can be seen; 20,000×.

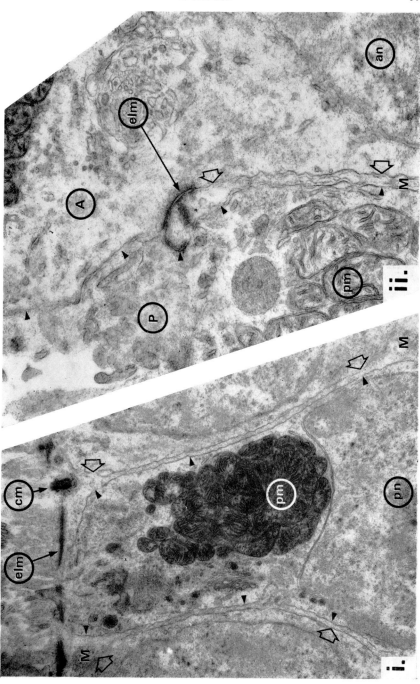

FIG. 20.

surrounded by a finely granular cortex. The large single cones of *Vipera* have a conical outer segment measuring about 7μ by $3 \cdot 5\mu$. The ellipsoid consists of a cortex of small mitochondria that tend to be oriented longitudinally around a medulla of large rounded mitochondria that contain numerous dense granules up to about 150 mμ across. These granules evidently constitute the refringent body seen by light microscopy. In *Elaphe* and *Heterodon* these refringent granules are mainly confined to the periphery of the mitochondria.

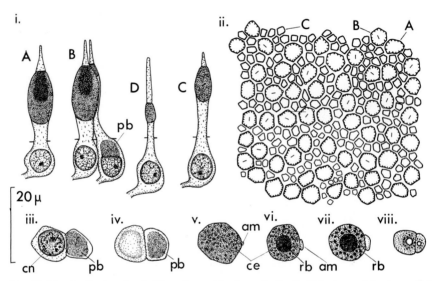

Fig. 21. Visual cells of snakes. i, *Vipera berus*, side views of cells; ii, *Helicops angulatus*, tangential section of retina (semidiagrammatic); iii to viii, *Helicops angulatus*, tangential sections of a double cone at the levels of, iii, the axial nucleus, iv, the axial myoid, v to vii, the axial ellipsoid, and, viii, the peripheral end of the ellipsoids. A, Large single cone; am, peripheral myoid; B, double cone; C, small single cone; ce, axial ellipsoid; cn, axial nucleus; D, rod; pb, paranuclear mitochondria; rb, refringent body.

The type B double cone has an axial member just like the type A cone with granules in the medullary mitochondria. The peripheral member has an outer segment about $1 \cdot 3\mu$ in diameter and electron micrographs show that it does not obviously taper. Calycal processes extend between the outer segments. There appears to be a tendency for both ciliary pedicles to lie on the same side of the pair of cells. The ellipsoid of the peripheral cell is much smaller than and closely applied to the axial ellipsoid. The two together appear somewhat pyriform in cross section. The mitochondria of the peripheral ellipsoid are like those of the rods. Vitreally the peripheral cell tapers to about $0 \cdot 5\mu$ in diameter and is partly sunk into the larger cell; thus it is sometimes difficult to recognise double cells in transverse section at this level by light microscopy. Between 1μ and 2μ scleral to the outer limiting membrane a Müller cell separates the two members so that, by light microscopy, the outer limiting membrane can be seen between them. They remain separated vitreal to this level. At this level the peripheral cell expands to accommodate the "paranuclear body", a feature, discovered by Walls, that is unique to the double cells of snakes. The paranuclear body is a second aggregation of mitochondria within the peripheral cell (Yamada et al., 1966) partly embracing the Golgi system of that cell. The nuclei of the peripheral cells of Vipera contrast with rounded nuclei of the other visual cells in being greatly lobed and invaginated (not seen by light microscopy). In Heterodon the nuclei are simply flattened on the mitochondrial side. The double cells are oriented in all directions, but the prevailing orientation is vertical.

Some visual cells of Vipera were counted and the following percentages obtained: rods 57%, small cones 5·5%, large single cones 29%, and double cones 8·5%. These figures may be somewhat biased in favour of the rarer cell types by selection of areas for micrography. The nuclei of the visual cells are stacked about two deep with the nuclei of the cones external and those of the rods internal. The pedicles are almost all of the complex type, suggesting that most of the rods are polysynaptic rods. Contacts between adjacent pedicles are rare. Rather commonly pedicles are penetrated by their own processes giving, in section, outlines of double membranes containing synaptic vesicles; sometimes two concentric double membranes are seen enclosing vesicles. All pedicles have synaptic ribbons with apical densities.

The horizontal cell nuclei form an incomplete layer in the inner nuclear layer. The nuclei of the bipolar cells form three or four rows. The amacrine cells form about two rows; contrary to the generalization of Dowling and Boycott (1965) for other vertebrate groups, the nuclei of the amacrine cells have smoothly rounded outlines.

The viperine pattern is seen with minor variations in Carphophis, Chionactis, Diadophis, Abastor, Farancia, Heterodon, Lycodonomorphus, Causus, Vipera, Micrurus, Liopholidophis, and Coronella. Counted in radial sections, there are 13 rods to every small single cone in Vipera, 8 to 1 in Abastor, and 0·4 to 1 in Coronella.

Crotaline snakes (Agkistrodon, Bothrops, and Crotalus) lack type C cones. The type A and B cones have long slender outer segments. The closely packed rods extend on long myoids slightly distal to the cones. The outer nuclei of Bothrops outnumber the inner, the quotient being 0·8. In Bothrops pigment barely extends into the processes of the epithelium. The dark adapted retina of Crotalus contains rhodopsin (Crescitelli, 1958). The Australian elapid

Acanthophis appears to agree with crotalines in the lack of type C cones; in addition to type A and B cells, it has rods "sitting" on the outer limiting membrane with long outer segments (Fig. 18).

In a number of nocturnal forms the myoids of the cones are elongated so that the cones lie distal to the rather numerous rods in a state of "permanent dark adaptation" (Walls, 1942, p. 166); the rod ellipsoids thus lie between the cone myoids. Walls termed this the "*Tarbophis* (= *Telescopus*) pattern". As this pattern has now been found in more forms and may show considerable variation, it is here termed the "two-tier pattern". It is seen in a moderate degree in *Bitis* (Walls, 1942, Fig. 189b) and *Enhydris* (Underwood, 1966, Fig. 1); the type A cones are the tallest, and the ellipsoids of the three types of cones lie distal to the rod ellipsoids with the outer segments of the cones reaching far distal to the outer segments of the rods. In *Bitis* there are 25 rods to every type C cone and in *Enhydris* 150 (Underwood, 1966). *Atractus*, *Boaedon*, and *Dasypeltis* are similar, but the outer segments of the cones are enlarged so that they are larger than the outer segments of the rods; *Telescopus* differs in that the outer segments of the cones are even larger, and the rods and cones are all of the same total height. *Atractus* has about 40 rods for every type C cone, and these cones are very rare or absent in the other three genera. What may be regarded as the extreme of "permanent dark adaptation" is shown by *Sibon*, *Dinodon*, *Crotaphopeltis*, and *Leptodeira* in which the ellipsoids of the transmuted cones are distal to the outer segments of the rods, and the outer segments of the transmuted cones are very large (Fig. 18). *Leptodeira* differs from *Sibon* and *Boaedon* in that it lacks type C cones. *Crotaphopeltis* differs in that it lacks type B double cells, although there are a few twin cells consisting of two type A members. The inner nuclear quotient ranges from about 1·2 in *Telescopus* to about 0·5 in *Sibon*; *Dasypeltis*, *Enhydris*, and *Leptodeira* are intermediate. Ganglion cell quotients are low, varying from 0·07 in *Sibon* to 0·2 in *Enhydris*. The processes of the epithelium are pigmented in *Dasypeltis* and *Sibon*, but not in *Enhydris* or *Telescopus*. The dark adapted retinas of *Dasypeltis* and *Telescopus* have a visual purple (Walls, 1942).

In a number of diurnal forms the rods are lost; as mentioned above they are already reduced in number in *Coronella*. There are then three types of sessile cones. The A and B cones have large ellipsoids and small tapering outer segments. The type C cones are much smaller than the type A and usually have a proportionately larger outer segment. This pattern is found in *Pseudaspis*, *Elaps*, *Coluber*, *Dromicus*, *Drymarchon*, *Helicops*, *Natrix*, and *Thamnophis*. The Australian elapids *Notechis* and *Denisonia* have small cones in addition to the large type A and B cones (O'Day, 1939). The sea-snake *Enhydrina* has a similar pattern with the small cells definitely cone-like in form.

In some more thoroughly diurnal forms the type C cones are also eliminated so that the retina contains only type A and type B cones. This is seen
in *Ahaetulla*, *Malpolon*, *Sepedon*, and, according to Yamada *et al.* (1966),
also in *Elaphe*.

There are, on the other hand, numerous nocturnal forms without type D
rods. One series of such forms is related to *Lampropeltis*. The cones of
Lampropeltis itself have outer segments which are slightly elongated, and
from this condition a series of steps leads through *Rhinocheilus*, *Cemophora*,
and *Arizona* to *Phyllorhynchus* in which the cylindrical outer segments of the
type A and B cells are about 20μ long and 5μ wide; these are by far the most
bulky outer segments known in any snakes. The type C cells are also enlarged but not to the same degree. *Lamprophis*, *Trimorphodon*, and *Hypsiglena* show a similar transformation, the first approximately matching
Cemophora and the latter *Phyllorhynchus*.

In all of these forms in which the type D rods are absent, the inner nuclei
outnumber the outer nuclei; the lowest quotient is $3 \cdot 3$ in *Helicops*. It ranges
from 5 to 6 in *Arizona*, *Phyllorhynchus*, *Sepedon*, *Trimorphodon*, and *Hypsiglena*, is $7 \cdot 7$ in *Coluber*, and reaches a maximum of 9 in *Ahaetulla*. The ganglion cell quotients are also high, ranging from $0 \cdot 4$ to $0 \cdot 5$ in *Helicops*, *Coluber*,
and *Sepedon* to as high as $0 \cdot 7$ to $1 \cdot 0$ in *Ahaetulla*, *Phyllorhynchus*, *Arizona*,
and *Hypsiglena*. The processes of the pigment epithelium embrace the outer
segments. *Hypsiglena* and *Phyllorhynchus* lack visual purple in the dark
adapted retina (Walls, 1942).

V. Rhynchocephalia

A. ORBIT AND ADNEXAE

The orbits of *Sphenodon* are large and there is a high interorbital septum
with the same membrane filled fenestrae as in *Ctenosaura*. The eye muscles
are very much as in lizards except for the retractor bulbi. The origin of that
muscle is similar, but it inserts by two slips, one near the entry of the optic
nerve and the other dorsolateral to the first (Säve-Södebergh, 1946).
Harder's gland has a similar relationship to the nictitating membrane, but
there is no lachrymal gland. The eyelids resemble those of lizards. There is a
tarsus in the lower lid and a cartilage in the nictitans. The tendon of the
nictitans passes around the eyeball, has a fibrous connection with the inner
part of the retractor bulbi muscle, and continues on its way to attach to the
dorsal side of the interorbital septum. The lachrymal canaliculi originate on
the margin of the lower lid and drain into the lachrymal duct as in lizards
(Bellairs and Boyd, 1947).

Blood is carried to the orbit by the temporal, palatine, and ophthalmic arteries and distributed in much the same way as in a lizard (O'Donoghue, 1919). The large orbital sinus is floored by a sheet of smooth muscle and receives a set of tributaries corresponding to those seen in lizards. The innervation is very similar to that of the lacertilian orbit.

B. The Eyeball

The eyeball of *Sphenodon* is large and the sulcus is pronounced. The sclera is partly fibrous and partly cartilaginous, the fibrous tissue being mainly external to the cartilage. The cartilaginous cup just overlaps the scleral ossicles. As in lizards the corneal epithelium is thin, but the substantia propria is thick. In an eye of 17 mm equatorial diameter the diameter of the cornea is 9·5 mm. Walls (1942) points out that in these proportions it agrees with *Iguana*. The corneal aperture is thus proportionately smaller than in nocturnal geckos. There are 16 (rarely 17) scleral ossicles (Fig. 22). The overlap pattern is indicated in Tables I and II. The expanded ossicles overlap corneally and have a distinct waist orbitally. The ring is rather flat.

The ciliary body resembles that of a lizard. There is little spongy tissue between the ciliary body and the sclera. It is unlikely that the ciliary body makes contact with the lens. There are no ciliary processes, and the zonule fibres arise from the whole width of the ciliary body. Walls (1942) describes the anterior zonule fibres as arising from the annular ridge formed by the ciliary-iris junction and passing radially inwards to fuse with both the capsule of the lens and the posterior face of the iris. The large canal of

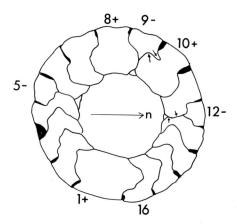

Fig. 22. Scleral ossicles of *Sphenodon punctatus*, after Gugg (1939). Plus (+) and minus (−) ossicles are indicated. n, Nasal direction.

Schlemm lies just internal to the sclera in the ciliary body and contains an annular nerve. The ciliary muscle fibres originate from the inner face of the sclera at the level of the root of the iris; they insert on about three-quarters of the width of the ciliary body as far as the ora terminalis.

The lens is fairly large and moderately flat, intermediate in its proportions between those of diurnal and nocturnal lizards. The pupil closes to a slit tilted slightly from the vertical. The iris thins gradually towards the margin of the pupil. Sphincter muscles are distributed over the whole of the iris, and the dilatator fibres lie behind them in contact with the epithelium of the iris. Both layers of the pars iridiaca retinae, especially the anterior, are heavily pigmented. The chorioid is similar to that of lizards of comparable size. It contains "peculiar spheroidal pigment cells with central nuclei suspended by delicate protoplasmic strands . . ." which "form a dense aggregation opposite the fovea" (Walls, 1942).

The optic nerve lacks septa between the fibre bundles. The retina is avascular, and the optic nerve entry is slightly concave and unpigmented. There is no trace of a conus. The well defined fovea lies at the orbital pole of the eye. The ora terminalis overlaps the scleral ossicles.

C. The Retina

Walls (1942) and Vilter (1951) disagree concerning the visual cells. On the basis of an examination of Walls' preparations it is clear that Vilter is correct in reporting both major and minor single cells (Walls does not comment on this). These single cells are like the cones of diurnal lizards, but the oil-droplet is colourless and the outer segment is considerably enlarged, being nearly as wide and as long as the inner segments. Walls calls these elements rods because he thought them to be low threshold receptors; Vilter calls them cones because they agree with chelonian and lacertilian cones in structure. Inspection of the dark adapted retina shows no evidence of visual purple (Walls, 1942). The double cells are very similar to the double cones of turtles and lizards except that, as in the single cells, the oil-droplet is colourless and the outer segments enlarged; the doubles appear to be vertically oriented.

Walls reported small droplet-free, cone-like elements in the retina, but Vilter regarded these as artifacts. Careful scrutiny of Walls' excellently fixed material leaves no doubt that these "dwarf cones" are perfectly discrete elements. They are rare and are largely confined to the peripheral parts of the retina but, once clearly recognized, can be distinguished under $100 \times$ magnification by their smaller size. Near the periphery of the fovea the paraboloids disappear from the visual cells, but elsewhere they retain their usual structure in an attenuated form.

Minor single cells extend almost to the centre of the fovea, and major single and double cells were followed in Walls' preparations to the centre of the fovea. The doubles, however, are few in number around the centre. The major single cells range from about 50μ high by 6μ or 7μ wide in peripheral areas to about 60μ high by 2·5μ wide in the centre of the fovea (Fig. 23). Outside the fovea the outer nuclear layer is just one nucleus deep with a scattered layer of displaced bipolar cells. The inner nuclear layer is 6 to 7 nuclei deep. There is a well-defined layer of foot-pieces in the outer plexiform layer.

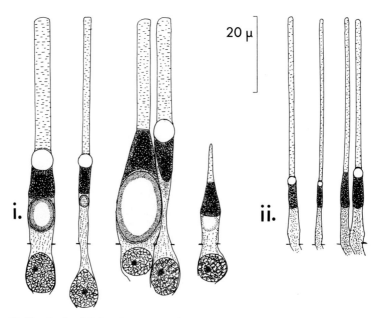

FIG. 23. Visual cells of *Sphenodon punctatus* (preparation of G. L. Walls). i, From near the nasal periphery; ii, in the central fovea. The elements from left to right are major single cell, minor single cell, double cell, and, in i only, dwarf cone.

VI. Testudines

A. ORBIT AND ADNEXAE

The orbit of turtles is walled by bone on three sides; its roof is formed by the postfrontal, frontal, and prefrontal, its anterior wall mainly by the prefrontal, and its floor largely by the palatine, with the participation of the maxilla and jugal. The interorbital septum continues anteriorly into the nasal septum and posteriorly into the lateral walls of the primary braincase.

The posterior border of the interorbital septum is perforated only by the optic foramen. The temporal muscles form the posterior wall of the orbit. In the Chelonioidea and Testudininae the interorbital septum is cartilaginous, rising from the trabecula communis at the level of the palatine bones to the frontals. In the Emydinae the interorbital septum is partly and in the Trionychoidea largely fibrous (Hoffmann, 1879). The orbits are reduced in the Chelidae.

The superior oblique muscle of *Chelonia* arises partly from the anterodorsal corner of the interorbital septum and partly from the frontal-prefrontal suture. The inferior oblique arises from the anteroventral corner of the interorbital septum. The anterior rectus muscle originates on the posterior and dorsal margins of the optic foramen, the superior rectus posterior to the optic nerve, and the inferior rectus anteroventral to the optic nerve. The posterior rectus originates by two bundles on the interorbital septum behind the optic nerve; the two bundles unite completely at their insertion. The retractor bulbi muscle originates by two bundles that arise partly from the posterior interorbital septum and partly from the presphenoid. The levator bulbi originates from the margin of the basisphenoid rostrum, the interorbital septum, and, by a separate bundle of fibres, from the vomer; it passes ventral to the eyeball to insert on the maxilla. The depressor palpebrae inferioris has a long origin on the lower border of the interorbital septum and passes ventral to the eyeball to insert on the lower lid.

The arterial blood supply resembles that of a lizard described above. The orbital sinus is also similar to that of lizards and has a strong sheet of smooth muscle in its floor. The principal tributaries are the frontal vein entering the anterior end and the palatine sinus entering the ventral side of the orbital sinus.

The variable lachrymal gland is very large in marine turtles in which it has been shown to excrete salt and is also large in brackish water forms. The histochemistry and fine structure have been described in *Chelonia* and *Caretta* (Abel and Ellis, 1966). Harder's gland is always present. The lachrymal duct is absent in all turtles; it was perhaps lost in association with aquatic habits.

The eyelids of chelonians, terrestrial as well as aquatic, are tilted so that the palpebral aperture rises posteriorly. The head of a floating turtle is generally brought to the surface of the water with the inclined palpebral aperture parallel with the water surface. The lower lid lacks a cartilaginous tarsus. The nictitans is withdrawn by a pyramidalis muscle which takes its origin on the orbital face of the eyeball and is innervated by the abducens nerve. A second tendon arises from the pyramidalis, passing posterior to the eyeball to insert on the lower lid which it serves as a levator. In *Carettochelys* the nictitating membrane is greatly reduced.

B. The Eyeball

The sclera contains a cup of cartilage similar in extent to that of lizards. In the marine *Dermochelys* the scleral cartilage is about a centimetre thick; in the freshwater *Trionyx* the fibrous tissue of the sclera is very thick. The sulcus is less pronounced than that of most lizards, and consequently there is less difference between the curvature of the cornea and the rest of the eyeball. The epidermal layer of the cornea is thick. There is no Bowman's layer, Descemet's layer is thin, and the endothelium is thick.

The scleral ring resembles that of lizards, but there are very rarely gaps between the ossicles (Fig. 24). The number of ossicles ranges from 6 to 13 and is commonly variable within a species. Sometimes an individual is asymmetrical. The ossicles are generally convex; in only a few forms do they extend corneally to enter the concavity of the sulcus. In some forms they are of regular shape and size, while in others they are irregular and of various sizes. There is commonly a plus ossicle approximately on the dorsal and one on the ventral side, and a minus ossicle on the nasal and on the temporal side.

The whole range of numbers of scleral ossicles occurs in the Testudinoidea. *Dermatemys* has 11 ossicles differing widely in size. *Chelydra* and *Staurotypus* have 13 and *Kinosternon* 11. In *Chelydra* they are varied, but in *Staurotypus* and *Kinosternon* they are fairly uniform; in the latter two the ossicles extend into the concavity of the sulcus. In *Platysternon* 9 subequal ossicles and a tenth very small one are found. Among the emydines *Emys* has 10, and *Batagur* and *Pseudemys* 11; the variation in size is not great. In the testudinines numbers range from 6 to 11, and the overlapping margins of the ossicles are far more irregular than in the Emydinae. *Geochelone elephantopus, G. gigantea, G. denticulata,* and *Kinixys* have 10 subequal ossicles; *Kinixys* has also an eleventh very small ossicle. In *Malacochersus* the number is reduced to 9. *Testudo horsfieldii* has 11, *T. hermanni* 8, and *T. graeca* 6 to 9. The Cheloniidae and Dermochelyidae are noteworthy for the denticulate periphery of the scleral ring and the irregularity of the overlapping borders. Ten ossicles are reported in *Chelonia,* 11 to 13 in *Caretta,* 12 in *Eretmochelys,* and 10 or 12 in *Dermochelys. Carettochelys* has 10 rather narrow, thin ossicles in a thick sclera. *Trionyx* has 10 and *Pelochelys* 9 ossicles which are rather narrow in the former and vary considerably in both. The pelomedusid *Pelusios* has 11 particularly wide ossicles which nearly reach the equator of the globe, but barely extend into the concavity of the sulcus. In the Chelidae, both *Chelodina* and *Emydura* have 13 ossicles, which are subequal in the latter.

König (1935) makes an instructive comparison between the corneal segments of the eyes of the amphibious terrapin *Emys,* the wholly terrestrial tortoise *Testudo*, and the wholly aquatic marine turtle *Caretta*. *Emys* has a relatively convex cornea (subtending an angle of approximately 70°) and a fairly thick lens which differs from that of a lizard in the thinness of the

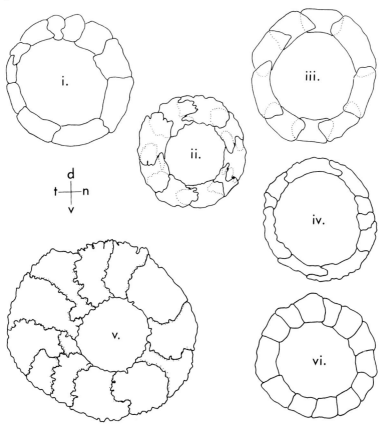

FIG. 24. Scleral ossicles of turtles. i, *Dermatemys mawii* (orientation not certain); ii, *Malacochersus tornieri*; iii, *Platysternon megacephalum*; iv, *Carettochelys insculpta*; v, *Eretmochelys imbricata*; vi, *Emydura novaeguineae*.

annular pad (Fig. 25). In *Testudo* the cornea is similar, but the lens is somewhat flatter. *Caretta* has a markedly less convex cornea (subtending only 38°) and a nearly flat ring of scleral ossicles extensively overlapped by the scleral cartilage; the lens is more convex than that of *Emys*.

The ciliary body differs conspicuously from that of a lizard in that the epithelium is thrown into a series of folds forming radially disposed ciliary processes (Fig. 26). Their tips touch the capsule of the lens except in *Caretta* in which there is a wide gap (König, 1935). The ciliary processes range from 34 in *Geochelone elephantopus*, through 35 to 40 in *Testudo graeca*, 55 to 60 in *Emys orbicularis*, and about 60 in *Caretta caretta*, to 66 in *Eretmochelys imbricata*. The regularity of the ciliary processes is interrupted on the ventral side by the remains of the embryonic fissure, and the processes are more closely spaced on the nasal than on the temporal side.

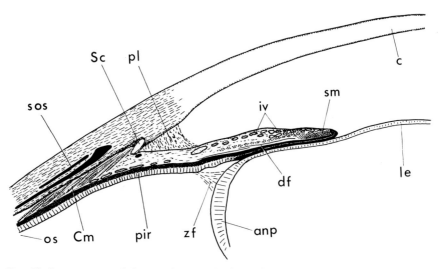

Fig. 25. Outer segment of the eye of *Emys orbicularis*, after König (1935). anp, annular pad; c, cornea; Cm, Crampton's muscle; df, dilatator fibres; iv, iris vessels; le, lens epithelium; os, ora serrata; pir, pars iridiaca retinae; pl, pectinate ligament; Sc, canal of Schlemm; sm, sphincter muscle; sos, scleral ossicles; zf, zonula fibres.

As in lizards a transversalis muscle passes through the chorioid fissure. Radial muscle fibres in the ciliary folds between the epithelium and blood vessels extend to the inner face of the sclera at the level of the sulcus. External to the radial fibres, at the level of the inner ends of the processes, are circular muscle fibres. The powerful transversalis muscle runs from the nasal side of the sclera partly to the ventral side of the lens and partly to the connective tissue of the ciliary body. The zonula fibres arise in the grooves between the ciliary processes and run inwards to join the capsule of the lens. The fibres of the transversalis muscle join the zonula fibres so that the muscle does not insert directly onto the lens. The canal of Schlemm lies just within the sclera at the sclerocorneal junction; it is a circular vessel with thin endothelium. A few small radial vessels communicate with the capillaries of the ciliary body. In *Caretta* some blood vessels, with numerous branches to the capillaries of the ciliary processes, run in the sclera at about the level of Schlemm's canal.

The iris is similar to that of a lizard. The circular muscle fibres are particularly strongly developed, especially around the pupillary margin. Some oblique fibres run from one circular bundle to another. In *Testudo* the circular musculature is noticeably less powerful than in *Emys* and more fibres run obliquely. There are radial fibres close to the iris epithelium which do not reach the margin of the pupil. These fibres are also relatively few in *Testudo*. Both layers of iris epithelium are heavily pigmented, but the pigment of the inner epithelium ceases at the level of the tips of the ciliary processes.

The course of *Testudo*'s ciliary artery is similar to that of a lizard. It enters the posteroventral quadrant of the eyeball and divides to encircle the pupil

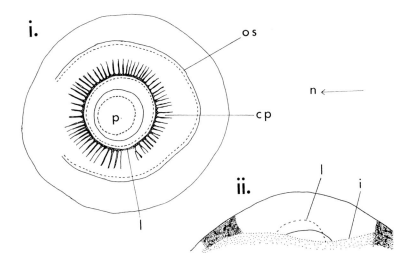

Fig. 26. Accommodation in *Emys orbicularis*, after König (1935). Dotted outlines indicate positions in accommodation. i, Inner view of outer segment; ii, dorsal view of outer segment. cp, Ciliary processes; i, iris; l, lens; n, nasal direction; os, ora serrata; p, pupil.

at about the level of the root of the iris. The ring vessels give off a fine network of closely spaced irregular vessels over the whole area of the iris. From this network radial vessels run through the ciliary body, one through each ciliary process. The vessels divide orbital to the ciliary folds and anastomose before passing back into the chorioid circulation. The two nerves that accompany the ciliary artery part and pass around the eye at the level of the canal of Schlemm, thus forming a ring. They meet on the ventral side of the eye and give off a branch which passes orbitally. This branch divides, encircles the iris at the level of the ring artery, and gives off fibres to the iris.

Out of water the cornea of *Emys* is the principal refracting surface, hence its strong curvature. Under water, however, little refraction occurs at the corneal surface. The powerful sphincter muscle of the iris is believed to compensate for this reduction in refraction by squeezing the anterior face of the lens and thus greatly increasing its curvature (Fig. 26). The eye is thus very strongly accommodated under water. The terrestrial *Testudo* has no need of such great powers of accommodation, the lens is flatter, and the iris sphincter is less powerful. In the marine *Caretta*, which never comes ashore except to lay eggs, the curvature of the cornea is reduced and the lens is more strongly curved.

C. THE RETINA

The retina of chelonians is non-vascular; the optic nerve entry is unpigmented, and there is no trace of conus. There is commonly an area centralis, but only in *Trionyx* is a fovea definitely known to occur. The outer nuclear layer includes displaced bipolar cells which compose 50% of the nuclei in this layer in *Emys*, *Malaclemys*, and *Pseudemys* and 40% in *Testudo* (Verriest et al., 1959). Horizontal fibres are prominent in the outer plexiform layer, especially in *Chelydra*. There are many nuclei in the inner plexiform layer, again especially in *Chelydra*. The inner nuclear quotient ranges from 3·0 in *Emys* to 3·7 in *Pseudemys*, and the ganglion cell quotient from 0·72 in *Testudo* to 0·37 in *Pseudemys* (Verriest et al., 1959).

There are single and double cones with oil-droplets which are virtually identical in structure with those of lizards. It has been claimed that the oil-droplets are of many colours, but Walls (1942) found only red, orange, yellow, and colourless droplets. In addition to the major single cones there are, in *Chelydra*, some minor single cones as in lizards (Fig. 27); I have not seen these in *Emys* or *Chrysemys*. Although it has been stated that turtles have only cones in the retina, Walls (1942) found rods in the forms which he examined. These rods have outer segments which are considerably wider but not much longer than those of cones. There is no oil-droplet, but there is a paraboloid.

Counted in radial sections, the rods make up about 40% of the single cells in *Chelydra serpentina*, 25% in *Emydoidea blandingii*, and 2·5% in *Chrysemys picta*. Verriest et al. (1959) found no rods in *Emys orbicularis*, but do report them in *Malaclemys terrapin*, *Pseudemys ornata*, and *Testudo graeca*. They also report some double cells with a paraboloid in both members in *Testudo*. From the study of radial sections it is evident that the double cells are vertically oriented and tend to be arranged in horizontal rows. It is not known how the differently coloured oil-droplets are distributed among the various types of visual cells. Köttgen and Abelsdorff (1895), in a careful study with the techniques then available, found no visual purple in *Emys orbicularis*; it should be noted, however, that this is the only species which has been recently reported to lack rods. Some form known to have a high proportion of rods must be examined before we can assume that turtles lack rhodopsin or a similar visual pigment.

Yamada (1960) has made some observations on the fine structure of the chelonian retina. The structure of the cones is much like that of lizards. There is a connecting cilium between the inner and outer segments. The paraboloid is similar. There are fins that interdigitate with the processes of the radial fibres. The pigment epithelium has already been described.

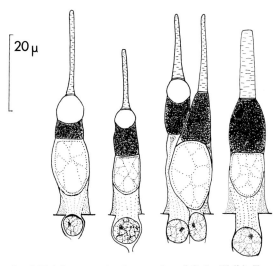

Fig. 27. Visual cells of *Chelydra serpentina* (preparation of G. L. Walls). From left to right, the elements are major single cone, minor single cone, double cone, and rod.

VII. Crocodilia

A. Orbit and Adnexae

The orbits of recent crocodilians, apparently like those of the fossil Eusuchia and earlier Mesosuchia, open on the dorsal side of the head. In the primitive Protosuchia and the aberrant Sebecosuchia the skull is rather deep and the orbits are decidely lateral. In the marine Thalattosuchia the orbits are lateral and turned somewhat forwards.

The orbits are separated by a cartilaginous interorbital septum extending between the frontal and palatine bones. The ossified rostrum of the basisphenoid extends into the posterior end of the interorbital septum. The palatine partly floors the medial side of the orbit, and the ectopterygoid crosses its floor posteriorly. There is no bony anterior or posterior wall, but laterally the jugal walls the orbit. Externally the orbit is bordered by the jugal, lachrymal, prefrontal, frontal, and postorbital bones.

The superior oblique muscle arises from the inner edge of the process of the frontal bone which descends to meet the palatine (Rathke, 1866). The inferior oblique muscle originates immediately ventral to the superior oblique.

The anterior rectus muscle arises from the interorbital septum just ventral to the optic nerve. The superior rectus arises further posteriorly, from about the middle of the lateral wing of the basisphenoid. The inferior rectus arises from the base of the basisphenoid rostrum. The posterior rectus arises dorsal to the superior rectus from the anterolateral wing of the basisphenoid. The rather weak retractor bulbi muscle consists of two bundles of fibres which originate posterior to the optic nerve, one above the other, from the wing of the basisphenoid; they insert on the sclera near the corneal segment of the eye. The striated depressor palpebralis inferior muscle arises by two heads, one from the anterior corner of the pterygoid and the other from the side of the basisphenoid rostrum; the fibres spread out laterally and dorsally into an aponeurosis in the lower lid. The maxillary branch of the trigeminal nerve passes between the two heads of the depressor. The striated levator palpebralis superior muscle has a tendinous origin from the bony margin of the orbit, and its fibres spread anteriorly and laterally to the upper lid. There are also smooth muscle fibres in the lids.

Crocodilians differ from other reptiles in that closure of the eye is said to be effected mainly by movement of the upper lid which contains a bony tarsus. The lower lid, on the other hand, has no tarsus. The nictitating membrane contains a cartilage and has two folds on its outer surface. The tendon of the nictitans passes round behind the eyeball dorsal to the optic nerve and into the pyramidalis muscle. This muscle arises on the antero-medial face of the inner segment of the eyeball and passes posteriorly, embracing the retractor bulbi muscle, to meet the tendon; it is innervated by the abducens nerve. The large Harder's gland discharges on the inner face of the nictitans. The lachrymal gland lies on the medial side of the orbit. Three to eight canaliculi on the anteromedial margin of the lower lid join to form the lachrymal duct which passes anteriorly through the foramen in the lachrymal bone. The marine *Crocodylus porosus* also has patches of glandular tissue on the conjunctiva of the lower lid, and its lachrymal duct arises by a single aperture on the lower lid.

The optic, abducens, and oculomotor nerves emerge from the braincase together between the basisphenoid and orbitosphenoid bones. The oculo-motor nerve sends a branch to the external rectus and, shortly after entering the orbit, bears the ciliary ganglion which receives a branch from the nasal ramus of the ophthalmic nerve. The oculomotor continues and supplies the posterior rectus, inferior rectus, and inferior oblique muscles. Three nerves arise from the ciliary ganglion: one enters the eyeball close to the optic nerve and two pass laterally to enter the eye near the sclerocorneal junction. The ophthalmic division of the trigeminal nerve gives off a frontal and a nasal ramus. The nasal ramus sends a branch to the skin of the upper and lower lids, passes forwards, and, beneath the superior oblique muscle, gives off several more twigs to the skin of the lids. The maxillary branch of the trigeminal nerve also sends fibres to the lids and branches to the con- junctiva and Harder's gland.

The internal carotid artery divides into facial and cerebral branches. The cerebral artery passes through a canal into the pituitary fossa where it gives off the orbital artery. The latter passes between the inferior and posterior rectus muscles and, between them and the optic nerve, forms a rete mirabile. The orbital artery continues as the ophthalmic artery which anastomoses with the cerebral circulation and with the temporal artery to the muscles of the eye and to the nictitating membrane, an artery to the striated muscle of the lower lid, and an artery to the temporal muscles.

No account has been found of the venous drainage of the orbit.

B. The Eyeball

The large eyeball of crocodilians is nearly spherical and lacks a sulcus. The cornea subtends an angle of 128°, and the binocular field of view is estimated at 25°. The sclera contains a cup of cartilage which reaches to the level of the ciliary body; corneal to the ciliary body the fibrous sclera is thickened. The cornea and its epithelium are thin. There is no Bowman's membrane, Descemet's membrane is thin, but the endothelium is thick. There are no scleral ossicles in Recent crocodilians, but they are known in some fossil forms. The thalattosuchian *Geosaurus* had about 14 interdigitating plates with denticulate inner and outer margins, and ossicles are also known in *Metriorhynchus*. The mesosuchian *Pelagosaurus* had about 16 plates. The much branched canal of Schlemm lies in the fibrous tissue of the sclera and drains into veins in the sclera.

The ciliary body has about 110 processes which extend from the ora serrata to the equator of the lens. Ventrally the position of the embryonic fissure is indicated by some irregularity in the ciliary processes, but there is no transversalis muscle. The ciliary muscle consists largely of separate fibres which run meridionally from the fibrous sclera on the orbital side of Schlemm's canal to the chorioid where they just overlap the ora serrata. White granules overlie the black pigment and give the fairly thin iris a golden appearance. The pupil is vertical. A thin layer of fibres runs across the iris parallel to the pupillary margins; these fibres curve around the ends of the pupil and cross one another there. Dilator fibres appear to be absent. The lens is large and thick, and the annular pad is greatly reduced. The lens has more than 900 radial lamellae of great regularity, but the sutures are poorly defined and of limited extent. The zonule fibres are very fine. Experiments indicate that accommodation is slow and of limited extent (Beer, 1898).

The ciliary artery divides on the temporal side of the iris: one branch runs dorsally posterior to the pupil and then turns anteroventrally and the other runs anteriorly and then dorsally anterior to the pupil. From these vessels small, radial, centripetal vessels form loops at the pupillary margin. The drainage is also by radial vessels. The corneal vessels, as in snakes, form a predominantly vertically oriented network. The network is not flat but three-dimensional (Lüdicke, 1940), implying that the vessels penetrate the substance of the cornea. At many points the vessels are double, presumably paired arterioles and venules. There are also capillaries in the optic nerve.

C. The Retina

The tapetum lucidum of the retina lies on the dorsal side of the eye. The chorioid behind it is thick and vascular but is thinner elsewhere. Those pigment cells lying outside the area of the tapetum have long pigmented processes extending between the outer segments of the visual cells. Those in the centre of the tapetum are heavily charged with guanin crystals which extend into the processes; only the tips of these processes have melanin granules. The processes of cells lying dorsal and ventral to the centre of the tapetum contain melanin, but only the cell bodies contain guanin.

Near the centre of the retina, above the optic papilla, there is a horizontally elongated area centralis; this implies that there is a finer mosaic of visual cells with concomitant higher resolution in this region. The optic papilla has some pigment, but there is no conus. The retina is avascular.

Crocodilian visual cells lack oil-droplets. As in turtles there are single and double cones and single rods, but in crocodilians the rods are the most numerous (Fig. 28). The rods are about 50μ high, with large cylindrical outer segments about 30μ long and $5-6\mu$ wide. Outside the area of the tapetum the cones are about 25μ high and have small tapering outer segments. The outer segments of the cones become larger and more bulky near the centre of the tapetum until, in its centre, they are quite rod-like in form although their outer segments are still somewhat smaller than those of the rods. Photomechanical changes are reported by Laurens and Detwiler (1921) in the retina of *Alligator*: in light the myoids of the rods expand and in darkness they contract, the total movement being about 4μ. The cones show smaller changes, about 2μ, but they extend in darkness and contract in light. The pigment processes migrate less than do the cones, extending about $1\cdot6\mu$ in light and contracting in the dark. The dark adapted crocodilian retina contains rhodopsin (Crescitelli, 1958).

The nuclei of the visual cells are stacked about one and a half rows deep, the inner nuclei 4 to 5 rows deep, and the ganglion cells form a single irregular layer (Walls, 1942).

Kalberer and Pedler (1963) have studied the fine structure of the retina of

Alligator. Irregularities of the lamellar sacs of the outer segments are common, and some outer segments are partly empty. The ciliary structure of the pedicles of the outer segments is so poorly developed that Kalberer and Pedler saw only one. Occasional inner segments contain whorls of what appear to be outer segment lamellae. The mitochondria of the ellipsoids are generally arranged lengthwise. More than three-quarters of the cells, including many rods, possess paraboloids consisting of rather loosely

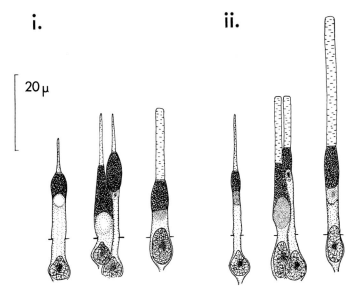

FIG. 28. Visual cells of *Alligator mississippiensis* (preparation of G. L. Walls). i, Near the ventral periphery; ii, near the centre of the tapetum. From left to right, the elements are single cone, double cone, and rod.

arranged granular material without a differentiated cortex. Between the paraboloid and the nucleus is the Golgi system. Groups of several visual cells with their inner segmental membranes in contact are quite common; there may be as many as eleven cells in such a group. These groups, however, are quite distinct from the class B double cells. Near the retinal centre Kalberer and Pedler found a ratio of ten rods to one cone. The inner nuclear quotient was 2·9 in a central area and 1·7 in a peripheral area, and the ganglion cell quotient 0·42 centrally and 0·14 peripherally. Radial fibres are numerous, especially peripherally, and their nuclei comprise from one-tenth to one-sixth of the total inner nuclei. The outer plexiform layer contains numerous large, typically cone-type, pedicles synapsing with a great number of dendrites; I have termed these polysynaptic pedicles (Fig. 29). Far less numerous

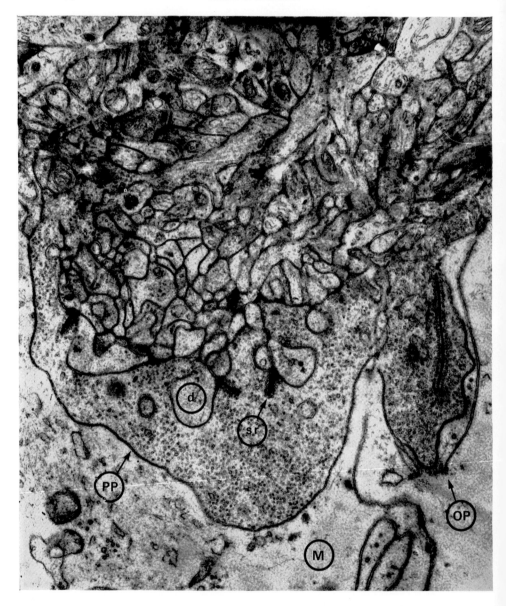

FIG. 29. *Alligator mississippiensis* (from Kalberer and Pedler, 1963, *Vision Research*, by courtesy of Pergamon Press). Transverse section through adjacent polysynaptic pedicle (PP) and oligosynaptic pedicle (OP) contrasting the two types. The polysynaptic pedicle can be seen to receive many dendrites (d) from the neurons with which it synapses; some of the synapses are associated with synaptic ribbons (sr). In the oligosynaptic pedicle only one large synaptic ribbon can be seen. The pedicles are invested by Müller cells. Osmium tetroxide fixation; 17,500×.

are small, typically rod-type pedicles synapsing with only a few dendrites; these were termed oligosynaptic pedicles (Fig. 29).

VIII. Scleral Ossicles of Extinct Forms

We rarely know more of the optic anatomy than the size and orientation of the orbits in wholly extinct reptiles. There are however scattered records of scleral ossicles; this subject has been reviewed in detail by Edinger (1929), and more recently summarised by Romer (1956). The information given below is drawn from these sources. There are several difficulties attending the study of the scleral ossicles of fossil forms. As the plates do not articulate with the rest of the skull, the ring can very easily fall out and be lost, and in most forms the ring readily falls apart so that the individual ossicles become scattered. Furthermore they are usually rather delicate and easily damaged.

The occurrence of scleral ossicles and the numbers reported are noted in Table III. Mosasaurs and the fossil groups of crocodilians have already been mentioned above with their Recent relatives. The 13 plates of *Trachodon* figured by Edinger are well enough preserved that they can be scored as 1,7 plus and, depending on orientation, 5,10 or (less likely) 3,11 minus. Some well preserved specimens of *Pterodactylus* have a scleral ring with no trace of sutures, so that it seems likely that there was one solid ring of bone. The plates of the plesiosaur *Pliosaurus* have a denticulate outer margin reminiscent of the scleral ring of marine turtles.

IX. General Discussion

A. SCLERAL OSSICLES

Scleral ossicles are present in many bony fish, but only the Crossopterygii, with 20 to 28 rectangular plates, have more than four of them. In some extinct amphibians there are from 20 to 32 scleral ossicles. The absence of scleral ossicles from Recent Amphibia is evidently secondary. Thus the scleral ossicles have a long history prior to the emergence of amniotes, and cannot be derived from the circumorbital bones of fish as suggested by Walls (1942).

It is worthwhile to consider what the palaeontologist may infer from scleral ossicles in those rare cases in which they are well preserved. If the ring of ossicles is flat or only slightly convex in a terrestrial form, it indicates that there was a sharp change of curvature between the corneal and orbital segments of the eye and a well developed sulcus. This rather strongly indicates good powers of accommodation and probable diurnal habits. The inner and outer diameters of the ring give an indication of the relative size of the cornea. An inner diameter of one-third or less of the outer indicates diurnal habits. A large inner diameter must be due to a proportionately larger cornea and

gives a fair indication of adaptation to dim illumination. If the scleral ring
has the form of a slice of a sphere this indicates reduction of the sulcus and

TABLE III

Occurrence and Numbers of Scleral Ossicles in some Extinct Groups[1]

	Ossicles
Seymouriamorpha	
Seymouria	c. 20
Gephyrostegus	c. 30
Captorhinomorpha	
Labidosaurus	present
Bolosaurus	c. 20
Pelycosauria	
Haptodus	present
Dimetrodon	present
Therapsida	
Titanophoneus	c. 18
Galechirus	present
Dicynodontia	present
Theriodontia	rare
Ictidosauria	not known to occur
Eosuchia	
Prolacerta	c. 14
Askeptosaurus	c. 12
Thalattosaurus	14, overlapping
Saurischia	
Brachiosaurus	present
Plateosaurus	c. 16
Diplodocus	present, no sutures visible
Ornithischia	
Monoclonius, Prosaurolophus,	
Protoceratops, Psittacosaurus,	
Saurolophus	present
Trachodon	13
Pterosauria	
Ctenochasma, Pterodactylus (part)	present
Pteranodon	12
Rhamphorhynchus	14 or 15
Pterodactylus (part)	13
Plesiosauria	
Pliosaurus	present
Plesiosaurus, Cimoliosaurus	13
Peloneustes, Trinacromerum	14
Ichthyosauria	
Ophthalmosaurus	14
Ichthyosaurus	13–17

[1] The numbers are taken largely from Edinger (1929) and Romer (1956).

diminished powers of accommodation. If the size of such a ring suggests that the eye is large in relation to the orbit, this also indicates nocturnal habits with continuing importance of vision. The retention of scleral ossicles that are small in relation to the size of the orbit would suggest burrowing habits or (as in *Heloderma*) nocturnal habits with reduced importance of vision.

The rare cases in which an exact count of the scleral ossicles of a fossil form can be made are most likely to be useful in forms related to Recent reptilian groups. Mammals and crocodilians are of special interest, for they are both groups in which Recent members have lost their scleral ossicles in association with nocturnal habits, but in which scleral ossicles are present in some fossil antecedents. We may reasonably assume that the ancestral lines leading to Recent mammals and Recent crocodilians retained diurnal habits, or had at least not gone far in the conversion to nocturnality, as long as the fossil record shows them to retain scleral ossicles.

B. Orbit

The palaeontologist is more often able to make out features of the orbit than of the scleral ossicles. A large orbit and high interorbital septum with the orbital boundaries well defined by the prefrontal and postorbital bones indicates a large eye. A large eye does indicate that vision is important in the life of the animal, but of itself does not afford a basis for distinguishing between diurnal and nocturnal habits. Reduction of the height of the interorbital septum (as compared with related forms) indicates a reduction in the size of the eyes which may be associated with a reduced importance of vision under conditions of dim illumination. In burrowing lizards and snakes the orbital glands occupy a large part of the orbit so that the orbit becomes large in relation to the size of the eye, but loses its well-rounded shape. The external margins of the orbit formed by the prefrontal, lateral border of the frontal, and postorbital show marked reduction and rounding off in burrowing forms so that the orbit becomes much less clearly defined.

C. Nictitating Membrane

Although Walls (1942) appears to disagree, it seems quite probable that the nictitating membrane is homologous with the lower lid of Recent Amphibia. The amphibian lower lid has a tendon which arises from its margin and passes posteriorly around both the eyeball and the retractor bulbi muscle to attach to the medial wall of the orbit. The tendon has a fibrous association with the retractor bulbi muscle. The eye is closed by movement of the lower lid; when the eye is open the lid is thrown into folds at the ventral margin of the orbit. The lachrymal duct arises, on the lateral face of the lower lid, by two canaliculi which pass anteriorly and unite. The relations of the nictitating membrane are similar: a tendon passes posteriorly from its free margin around the retractor bulbi muscles to attach, in *Sphenodon* and lizards, to the medial wall of the orbit, and the lachrymal duct arises, usually by two canaliculi, lateral to the nictitating membrane.

In chelonians, *Sphenodon*, and crocodilians there are two divisions of the retractor bulbi muscle; it is clearly the lateral one that becomes the bursalis muscle in lizards. In chelonians and crocodilians the origin of the tendon of the nictitans is transferred from the orbital wall to the pyramidalis muscle on the surface of the eye. Possibly the pyramidalis is derived from fibres of the lateral retractor bulbi muscle that already had an association with both the eyeball and the tendon.

D. Accommodation

In fishes and Recent amphibians accommodation is effected by movement of the whole lens. The transversalis muscle of amniotes appears to represent the ventral protractor lentis muscle of Amphibia. In water the cornea is not an effective refracting surface as the refractive index of the corneal tissue is similar to that of water; in air the cornea becomes the principal refracting surface. The refractive effect of the cornea is increased by the development of the scleral sulcus with increase of the corneal curvature. A shortening of the optic axis in relation to the equatorial diameter of the eye accompanies the reduced focal length of the optical system. The ring of scleral ossicles maintains the concavity of the sulcus, bringing the ciliary body into proximity with the lens. Radial muscle fibres in the ciliary body presumably originated in the amniotes. The thickening of the lens capsule around the equator to form an annular pad brings it into contact with the ciliary body. The development of ciliary processes presumably facilitates contraction of the ciliary body and thus squeezing of the lens. The widespread occurrence of ciliary processes in chelonians, crocodilians, mammals, and birds suggests that they were developed early in amniote history. The absence of ciliary processes in *Sphenodon* and lizards is evidently secondary, as is the mechanism of accommodation in snakes.

Many reptiles are adapted to vision in both air and water. This poses special problems, for during immersion in water the whole of the refraction has to be effected by the lens. Crocodilians have very limited powers of accommodation and do not appear to have adapted their vision to the amphibious habit. Both turtles and snakes, with very different primary mechanisms of accommodation, have the same supplementary mechanism. The lizard *Amblyrhynchus*, and perhaps also *Dracaena*, should be examined in this respect. *Amblyrhynchus* is able to feed underwater on seaweed, and presumably vision plays some part in this. Sea-snakes are said to increase their depth of vision in air by contraction of the pupil to pinhole size, thus obviating the need for a supplementary accommodation mechanism.

Only a few reptiles, such as the marine turtles in which the corneal curvature has been reduced due, apparently, to its unimportance under water, are so fully aquatic that their eyes are not adapted for aerial vision.

E. Nocturnal Adaptations

Nocturnal forms generally show an increase in the aperture of the pupil, in the relative area of the cornea, and in the aperture of the lens. These changes all tend to reduce visual acuity and thus to reduce the usefulness of the accommodation mechanism. The increase in the size of the cornea leads to a reduction of the scleral sulcus and thus to a reduction in the functional significance of the scleral ossicles in maintaining the sulcus. In the partially nocturnal Pygopodidae and some of the geckos we find very marked variations in the scleral ossicles. In the Recent and nocturnal Crocodilia the scleral ossicles and most of the power of accommodation are absent.

In mammals contact between the lens and ciliary body is absent as are the scleral ossicles.

A few reptiles adapt to dim illumination by reducing the primary importance of the eye. The lizard *Heloderma* is the clearest example, and *Lanthanotus* may be similar. In *Heloderma* the eye shows some reduction in size and is simplified; it appears that chemoreception is of primary importance (Bogert and del Campo, 1956). The turtle *Chelus* probably belongs in this category, since it has small orbits and small eyes, and lives on the bottom lying in wait for prey which is perceived by other cues. Also comparable are the snakes *Acrochordus* and *Chersydrus* which have very small eyes and live in coastal waters that are presumably very muddy.

F. Burrowing Adaptations

Burrowing habits subject the eye to mechanical stresses, expose the eye to much dirt (unless there is already a spectacle), and take the animal into a world of darkness in which vision cannot have primary importance. In most burrowing squamates, with the notable exception of *Anniella*, the eye is covered by a transparent spectacle; this prevents dirt from entering the conjunctival space and presents a smooth external surface. Mechanical stress and reduced importance of vision both tend to result in reduction in the size of the eye. Although the size of the eye diminishes, the orbital glands continue to be important for the irrigation of Jacobson's organ and thus

D

come to occupy a proportionately larger part of the orbit. Both the diminished importance of vision and the diminished size of the eye tend to reduce the importance of accommodation—a small eye has a greater depth of focus and less resolution. The muscles of accommodation are, therefore, lost in burrowing forms. With diminution of the size of the eye there is usually reduction of the scleral cartilage and ossicles. At an early stage in the reduction of the eye the fovea disappears and the vascular conus is reduced.

G. The Retina

Fish, amphibians, birds, and mammals have a duplex retina, and therefore it seems likely that the duplex condition in chelonians, crocodilians, and snakes is a primitive amniote feature. The idea that this pattern represents a common heritage is further supported by the occurrence of rhodopsin as the rod pigment in most of these groups. Recent Amphibia have single and double cones and red and green rods; they are the only animals with two anatomically distinct types of rods, and the green rod is probably a feature peculiar to them. Chelonians and crocodilians have single and double cones and one type of single rod; this pattern, also found in *Ornithorhynchus*, marsupials, and birds, is probably that basic to amniotes.

Walls (1942) postulated transmutation (termed a "Walls transformation"; Underwood, 1968) of cones into "rods" in geckos and *Sphenodon* and partial transmutation in the Pygopodidae and *Xantusia*. He documented in some detail a case of transmutation from cones to rods in snakes, and transmutation in geckos is now supported in detail by the existence of intermediate conditions. Since these transmuted elements are clearly not rods in the usual sense as is indicated by the ratio of outer to inner nuclei and by the lack of any scotopic pigment resembling rhodopsin (Crescitelli, 1958; Walls, 1942), I have termed them "polysynaptic rods" (Underwood, 1968).

The conditions in a number of snakes help in the interpretation of these transmuted elements. In snakes with a boid-pattern retina, with a high proportion of single rods, there are many outer nuclei in comparison with the number of inner nuclei, indicating a high level of summation. These rods are presumably the usual oligosynaptic elements. However, snakes with a high proportion of cones, or with cones only, have relatively numerous inner nuclei compared with outer nuclei. In the series of forms leading from a pure cone condition to the pure secondary rod condition of *Phyllorhynchus* and *Hypsiglena*, there is little change in the ratio of inner to outer nuclei. This suggests that there are no important changes in the neural connections of the visual cells during transmutation. The "rods" of *Hypsiglena* and *Phyllorhynchus* are structurally the same as single and double cones apart from the size and shape of their outer segments, and I suggest that their neural connections are similar. These "rods" are therefore interpreted as visual cells that mediate cone-type vision at reduced levels of illumination, or "polysynaptic rods" (Underwood, 1968).

The concept of a meaningful distinction between oligosynaptic rods and polysynaptic rods (or low threshold cones) is supported by consideration of the snakes with a two-tier retina. All have a high proportion of slender, closely packed (evidently oligosynaptic) rods with the outer nuclei stacked in several rows as in a boid retina. Despite this high proportion of rods, they have adapted to nocturnality by extending the cones in a state of "permanent dark adaptation" and enlarging their outer segments. That adaptation to nocturnality has involved transmutation of cones in the presence of a large number of oligosynaptic rods seems clearly to argue that cones mediate a different kind of vision regardless of threshold, and thus that these snakes have converted from "rod plus high-threshold cone vision" to "rod plus low-threshold cone vision".

The crocodilian retina is of especial interest. The transmutation of the cones in the tapetal area indicates that there has been a Walls transformation. The existence of rods with polysynaptic pedicles in company with (polysynaptic) cones strongly suggests that cells with rod-like outer segments have acquired cone-type footpieces, a mosaic transformation of cellular anatomy termed a "Pedler transformation" (Underwood, 1968). In geckos, as in snakes, there is no marked change in the ratio of inner to outer nuclei in association with transmutation. This is the basis for the suggestion that we recognize oligosynaptic ("ordinary") rods, polysynaptic rods (or scotopic cones), and "ordinary" (polysynaptic) cones (Underwood, 1968). The dwarf cones of *Sphenodon* are perhaps vestigial oligosynaptic rods reduced to functional insignificance.

Walls (1942) stressed that one of the major questions concerning the retina is the significance of the double cells. They have not been much studied, presumably because they are not known in placental mammals. It has been suggested that they may serve as detectors of polarized light (Underwood, 1968). The structure of the double cones of turtles and lizards seems compatible with this view. The large refringent organelle, the paraboloid, would subject incident light to preferential refraction and internal reflection in the plane of polarization. One of the two outer segments is aligned with the axial cell and the other lies to one side. Comparison of the two signals should permit detection of the polarization of the incident light. The advanced Gekkoninae, in which the paraboloid is reduced, have a refringent body in the ellipsoid of the axial cell so that the same interpretation could apply. This interpretation does not suggest a significance for the increased proportion of double cells in the Gekkota, for the straight horizontal rows of double cells, or for the second type of double cell found only in geckos.

The double cells of snakes also have a refringent body in the axial ellipsoid so that they too could be polarized light analysers. According to this hypothesis double cones would not have appeared in snakes until the refringent type A cones had been developed.

The retinas of many reptiles are noteworthy for the number and variety of cell types. These cells have a number of prominent and precisely arranged organelles, and there are various mosaic arrangements which reach a maximum of precision in geckos. The radial orientation of the cells in a single layer makes them peculiarly accessible to precise investigation. Once the types of cells in a given retina have been clearly characterised, then variation in their structure, relative numbers, and orientation is readily recognised by routine techniques. The studies of Saxén (1954 and 1956) on the development of the visual cells of frogs give us much information which probably applies to reptiles as well. It is an additional point of interest that at intermediate stages in evolutionary transformation the central parts of the retina are more advanced and the peripheral parts more conservative; it is as though evolutionary changes start with that region of the retina that is the first to differentiate in ontogeny (or is the one used for the most critical visual analysis).

X. Systematic Discussion

A. Testudines

The absence of the lachrymal duct is certainly secondary and associated with aquatic habits. The tilt of the palpebral aperture argues strongly that Recent terrestrial chelonians are of aquatic origin. Unfortunately it is unlikely that primarily terrestrial turtles would be recognized as such in the fossil record, but the presence of a lachrymal foramen would give a strong indication that the conversion to aquatic habits had not been completed. One special feature of chelonian eyes, namely the simultaneous appearance of accommodation by contraction of the ciliary muscles and of contraction of the iris sphincter, is clearly an adaptation to vision both in air and in water.

The pattern of visual cells in chelonians appears to be that of primitive amniotes. The duplicity of the retina is probably an inheritance from amphibian ancestors, but the most nocturnal turtles have more cones than rods in the retina. Nocturnal turtles apparently lack anatomical modifications of the cones comparable to those of the nocturnal lizards and snakes.

B. Lepidosauria

1. *General*

The disappearance of the ciliary processes is evidently a lepidosaurian feature, but of obscure significance. The behaviour of lizards suggests that they accommodate rapidly, but so do birds which retain the ciliary processes.

2. *Rhynchocephalia*

The eye of *Sphenodon* has relatively few primitive features (Walls, 1942); the simple condition of the retractor bulbi musculature is presumably one. Walls' estimate that the eye of *Sphenodon* is, in essence, a lacertilian eye with some modifications for nocturnal habits seems to be fully justified.

The droplet-free dwarf cones appear to correspond with the rods of turtles. Their rarity and their cone-like form suggests that they are not functionally rods and, indeed, that they are not functionally significant. This implies a strong commitment to cone-type vision. The subsequent enlargement of the outer segments of the cones is evidently associated with secondarily nocturnal habits. Considering the remarkably low operating body temperature of modern *Sphenodon*, we may well wonder at the circumstances under which its ancestors became so completely committed to cone-type vision, presumably with concomitant diurnal habits. It suggests that their ancestors experienced low air temperatures, either at high elevations or high latitudes.

3. *Lacertilia and Amphisbaenia*

Lizards are clearly a primarily diurnal group fully committed to cone-type vision with the elimination of the droplet-free elements that still persist in *Sphenodon*. The structure of the eye of primarily diurnal lizards varies moderately; this is hardly surprising in a group that was already radiating in the Jurassic. We see two noteworthy adaptations to arboreal habits, the extreme ocular mobility and limited visual field in the chameleons and the development of a second fovea in anoles. The number and pattern of scleral ossicles has systematic value. In particular this evidence may help the systematic analysis of the iguanian stock.

Study of the eyes indicates rather clearly that most burrowing lizards and amphisbaenians are descended from diurnal forms. This holds for the Scincidae, Teiidae, Anguidae, Anniellidae, Feyliniidae, and Dibamidae. These forms, as far as they have been studied, show various stages of reduction in the development of a diurnal eye; there are no alterations of the course of development that might be adaptively related to the new habit. Careful experiment shows that the greatly reduced eyes of *Amphisbaena* are still sufficiently sensitive to light to be of possible functional significance (Gans and Bonin, 1963; Steven, 1963), whereas the snake *Typhlops jamaicensis* shows obvious and acute embarrassment when illuminated. The Pygopodidae contrast with the above forms in showing conversion to burrowing habits from a condition of visual adaptation to dim illumination. *Aprasia* shows simplification of the eye rather than simple arrest of its development. In the course of ontogeny some features (e.g., scleral cartilage) are eliminated whereas others (e.g., visual cells) continue to develop and differentiate fully.

It would be interesting to study the more extensively modified form *Ophidiocephalus*, but this is unfortunately still known from the type specimen only.

The nocturnal lizards of the families Pygopodidae, Gekkonidae, and Xantusiidae are remarkable for the variety of degrees of modification which survive and provide abundant examples of the Walls transformation. With continued dependence on cone-type vision in feeding at reduced levels of illumination, there was presumably selective pressure bearing on both ends of the "acuity-sensitivity seesaw". These lizards clearly offer attractive material for study of visual performance. That these nocturnal lizards are, like *Sphenodon*, of diurnal ancestry is fairly certain. They do not operate at the remarkably low body temperature of *Sphenodon*, but many do operate at lower body temperatures than most diurnal lizards. Whilst the Pygopodidae are surely, and the Xantusiidae probably, related to the Gekkonidae, study of their visual cells strongly suggests that they have separately converted cones to polysynaptic rods, and indeed that within the Gekkonidae there may have been several such conversions. Probably they shared not a common commitment to nocturnality, but a common habit that offered the opportunity to convert from diurnal to nocturnal habits. It is possible that the ancestors of *Sphenodon* and of Recent lizards were diurnal and dependent on cone-type vision under conditions of low temperature. They may have found themselves in a situation of rising temperatures; while *Sphenodon* and the ancestors of the presently nocturnal lizards may have avoided these higher temperatures by becoming nocturnal, the ancestors of the presently diurnal lizards adapted to operation at higher body temperatures. The fossil record suggests that most of the present diversification of lizards had taken place by the Cretaceous. Thus the extinction of many reptile stocks in the Cretaceous probably occurred after the hypothetical changes suggested above.

The structure of the eyes has already been used in the classification of geckos (Underwood, 1951b). All geckos share a unique type of double cell, the type C. The Eublepharinae clearly diverged early, for they retain eyelids and a nictitating membrane; all, however, appear to be fully nocturnal. The Diplodactylinae presumably diverged from an early spectacled gecko stock before the origin of the Gekkoninae. They have apparently all made a full conversion to nocturnality, except *Naultinus* the retina of which indicates that it is tertiarily diurnal. From Kluge's (1967) studies it appears that the Gekkoninae include the central stock of spectacled geckos. *Aristelliger* has a diagrammatically perfect primitive nocturnal gecko retina. In *Phelsuma* and *Lygodactylus*, the loss of some oil-droplets is evidence of further conversion to nocturnal habits, followed by tertiary reversion to diurnal habits. The visual cell pattern of *Gonatodes*, taken in conjunction with the other anatomical evidence of Kluge, suggests that the Sphaerodactylinae originated from just such a stock as is represented by *Lygodactylus*. The most advanced Gekkoninae combine the three lobed, vertical pupil with highly modified visual cells. None of these advanced Gekkoninae appears to have reverted to diurnal habits.

Kluge (1967) argued that a high number of scleral ossicles, in excess of 14, is primitive for geckos and I had found this convincing. Elevated numbers are found throughout the Eublepharinae and Diplodactylinae, the two groups that retain the most features judged primitive on comparative anatomical grounds. The more advanced Gekkoninae and Sphaerodactylinae have stable, and never more than slightly elevated, numbers. However, in the light of the evidence of overlap patterns I feel bound to reconsider this view. Numerous geckos with 14 ossicles show an overlap pattern that is similar to that of *Sphenodon* and *Varanus* and identical with that of such diverse lizards as iguanids, skinks, and xenosaurs. Since there are other ways of arranging 14 ossicles in a well developed ring, it is surely more likely that *Sphenodon* and these diverse lizard groups share a common inheritance than that there is some functional or developmental reason why they should converge upon the same detailed pattern. The very variety of patterns in some geckos would seem further to argue against the operation of selection pressures tending to stabilize patterns. The reduction of ossicles in the dorsal and ventral parts of the ring has evidently occurred in several gecko stocks. The combination of a ring of uniform width with an irregular overlap pattern, and with a high number of reversals may help to define a group of advanced Gekkoninae, probably including *Gekko* and *Uroplatus*.

The diurnal Ascalabota—Iguanidae, Agamidae, and Chamaeleonidae— are here regarded as a stock that has adapted to elevated body temperatures and in which vision is of primary importance in feeding, territorial, and courting behaviour. In the Autarchoglossa (sensu Camp, 1923), however, although the eye may still be elaborately developed, the system of chemo-reception involving the tongue and the organ of Jacobson is also elaborated and affords many of the leading cues in behaviour. This difference is underlined by the reduction of the eye of the nocturnal and burrowing forms. The Amphisbaenia, it may be noted, are autarchoglossan in character.

4. *Serpentes*

The great differences between the eyes of snakes and those of other reptiles have impressed all who have made comparative studies. Indeed if the eyes and optic tectum (Senn, 1966) be removed from a snake, the rest of the animal is sufficiently like a lizard that most students place them as suborders of one order. However, if we examine the eye, there is nothing about it to suggest that its owner is a reptile, let alone one related to lizards. Walls (1942) brought the subject into prominence by drawing inferences concerning the early history of snakes. Further study has in general supported his view that the ancestors of snakes were adapted to burrowing and further suggested that they converted from nocturnal to burrowing habits. The differences between the eyes of snakes and lizards are interpreted as the results of initial modification associated with nocturnal habits, followed by simplification associated with burrowing habits. The pygopods in some measure parallel these changes. After snakes or their ancestors returned to the surface, an augmentation of visual function and a re-elaboration of the eye resulted in a pattern of structure and development differing from that of lizards in a number of respects.

There is little variation in the structure of the non-sensory parts of the eye in snakes. The condition of the lachrymal duct has some systematic value and so may the presence or absence of an orbicular vein. With almost no accurate prior information to guide him and with the chaotic ideas of snake classification then current to mislead him, Walls made a remarkable survey of the retinas of snakes. The variety in their structure was so great that he concluded (p. 640) that "the snakes alone have rung as many changes upon their visual-cell patterns as have all the other vertebrates put together". I have attempted an assessment of the systematic significance of this wealth of new data (Underwood, 1967a, b). Although some snakes have a simplex retina, the distribution of duplicity in vertebrates strongly indicates that it is primitive for snakes. The fact that the one snake examined by spectrophoto-metric techniques has rhodopsin like that of amphibians, crocodilians, birds, and mammals supports the view that it is a primitive amniote duplicity. Since the ancestors of *Sphenodon* were probably at least functionally simplex and since the ancestors of all Recent lizards were structurally as well as functionally simplex, this has implications for the ancestry of snakes.

The relationship between lizards and snakes is not in doubt. The pattern of the visual cells of *Sphenodon* suggests that there were ancestral Lepido-sauria with a duplex retina like that of turtles. Presumably this duplicity was inherited by the ancestral Squamata. The stock ancestral to Recent lizards developed functional and structural simplicity; the rhynchocephalian stock ancestral to *Sphenodon* developed functional simplicity whilst retaining structural traces of duplicity. Ancestral snakes on the other hand become nocturnal and then fossorial or secretive whilst retaining a functionally and structurally duplex retina with cones and oligosynaptic rods. This inter-pretation suggests that the division of the Squamata into snakes and lizards is ancient and antedates the origins of any of the groups of Recent lizards.

In the early evolution of snakes the chemoreceptor system was elaborated and the eye simplified. The refringent organelle disappeared from the cones and with this the double cones were lost, giving rise to the boid type of retina. With their return to the surface snakes remained nocturnal, but made more use of their eyes. Three processes in the re-elaboration of the eye were perhaps associated: the development of the unique ophidian mechanism of accommodation, the acquisition of refringent organelles by some of the cones, and the formation of double cones. I believe that these were crucial changes for the radiation of the snakes above the Henophidian level, for most Caenophidia show this advanced pattern of eye structure. A few Caenophidia, however, are known to have a boid type of retina. These are *Pareas*, *Atractaspis* (which is certainly not a viperid), *Calamelaps* (probably related to *Atractaspis*), and *Pseudoboa* (which I had placed in the Lycodontinae).

I had initially assumed (Underwood, 1967a) that the development of refringent cones and double cones gave rise to the viperine type of retina with squat cones as in *Vipera* itself. I now find grounds for supposing that the two-tier pattern with tall cones appeared first. Counts of the nuclear layers strongly suggest that the boid type of retina contains oligosynaptic rods, for the outer nuclei greatly outnumber the inner nuclei. Those higher snakes with double cones that also have many more outer than inner nuclei are forms with two-tier retinas such as *Sibon*, *Dinodon*, *Crotaphopeltis* and *Leptodeira*; these too, therefore, presumably have a high proportion of oligosynaptic rods. One of these genera, *Crotaphopeltis*, has type A twin cells, but does not appear to have type B double cells; it may be that this represents a primitive absence rather than a secondary loss. *Vipera* has few, if any, oligosynaptic rods.

I therefore advance the following hypothesis that may at least have heuristic value. With the reinstatement of vision as an important sense, there was an increase in the proportion of cones in the presence of a high density of rods containing rhodopsin or a similar scotopic pigment. As the numbers of cones increased, they extended scleral to the rods, giving rise to a two-tier retina. The inner tier consisted of oligosynaptic rods interrupted only by the "stalks" of the tall cones. The neural connections of these rods gave maximum sensitivity with low acuity. The outer tier consisted of cones uninterrupted by rods, and their neural connections gave high acuity with relatively low sensitivity. However, the sensitivity was slightly increased in some forms by enlargement of the outer segments. This condition is found in the Dipsadinae, Boiginae, and some of the Lycodontinae. Following the achievement of visual acuity and a greatly increased role of vision in the life of the animal, a "Pedler transformation" took place, and some rods acquired polysynaptic pedicles, no doubt at some cost in sensitivity. As this transformation progressed, more and more of the visual cells contributed to the acuity of the image, and there were no longer functional reasons for segregation of the rods and cones in two tiers; thus the viperine pattern arose. The Pedler transformation resulted in conversion of a duplex heterosynaptic retina into a duplex polysynaptic retina. Judging by the thickness of their nuclear layers this latter pattern is found in some Lycodontinae, in Viperinae, in some Elapidae, and in one colubrid (*Coronella*). With an increasing commitment to diurnal habits, a diminishing proportion of the outer segments of the small non-refringent visual cells differentiated as rods, until some stocks arrived at a pure-cone retina and lost the biochemical system for the synthesis of scotopic pigments. This pattern occurs in some Lycodontinae, some Elapidae, most Natricidae, and most Colubridae. Finally, some Natricidae and Colubridae made a tertiary conversion to nocturnal habits, and their visual cells underwent a "Walls transformation" from cones to polysynaptic secondary rods. Some stocks, especially the Crotalinae and Homalopsinae, require further investigation in the light of this interpretation.

C. CROCODILIA

It may be significant that the only archosaurs to survive the Cretaceous are nocturnal. Since the modern family Crocodylidae is known from the Cretaceous, and since no fossil member of the modern suborder, the Eusuchia, is known to have scleral ossicles, we may suppose that they were already nocturnal before the other Archosauria become extinct.

Acknowledgements

My own studies of the retina have been immeasurably aided by the generosity of people in many parts of the world who sent me material. These include: Mr J. Alexander (*Enhydris, Eristocophis*), Dr A. d'A. Bellairs (*Aprasia, Delma, Lialis, Pygopus, Trogonophis*). Dr W. C. Brown (*Dibamus*), Dr R. Bustard (*Delma, Lialis*), Dr E. Mc.Callan (*Amphisbaena*), Dr T. Devaraj (*Acrochordus, Enhydrina*), Dr M. G. Emsley (*Micrurus*), Mr M. Eudey (*Anniella*), Miss A. G. C. Grandison (*Pseudorhabdion*), Dr M. Hecht (*Epicrates*), Dr A. Greenhall (*Leptodeira, Polychrus*), Dr J. Hendrickson (*Draco, Xenopeltis*), Mr B. Hughes (*Atractaspis, Calamelaps*), Mr J. Jefferies (*Boaedon*), Mr B. deJong (*Gonatodes*), Dr J. Kenny (*Helicops, Pseudoboa*), Dr L. Klauber (*Coleonyx, Gehyra, Phyllodactylus*), Dr A. Kluge (*Coleonyx, Xantusia*), Mr R. J. Knowles (*Vipera*), Dr K. Koopman (*Anolis*), Mr B. Lewis (*Cyclura, Epicrates, Tropidophis*), Dr S. Minton (*Carphophis, Conophis, Diadophis, Tantilla*), Dr K. Norris (*Leptotyphlops*), Dr J. Price (*Pseudoboa, Thecadactylus*), Mr G. R. Proctor (*Aristelliger*), Dr W. B. Quay (*Helicops, Leptodeira, Lioheterodon*), Dr V. C. Quesnel (*Gonatodes, Sibon*), Mr J. D. Romer (*Calliophis, Gekko, Pareas, Ptyas*), Dr D. Rossman (*Heterodon,*

Toluca), Mr C. Shore (*Boaedon, Crotaphopeltis*), Mr P. Soderberg (*Chersydrus, Erpeton, Homalopsis, Dendrelaphis*), Dr N. G. Stephenson (*Hoplodactylus, Naultinus*), Mr D. J. Street (*Vipera*), Dr A. M. Taub (*Dinodon*), Mr M. W. F. Tweedie (*Xenopeltis*), Mr J. Vinson (*Phelsuma*), and Mr J. Visser (*Elaps, Lamprophis, Lycodonomorphus, Pseudaspis*). I have received many courtesies from Dr E. E. Williams at the Museum of Comparative Zoology. At the British Museum Mr D. Cooper prepared sections of many retinas for me, Miss D. Parry took me on my first excursion into electron microscopy, and Miss A. G. C. Grandison has greatly facilitated my work in the Reptile Section. Latterly I have profited from discussions with Dr C. M. Pedler and Mrs R. Tilly of the Institute of Ophthalmology. My first steps into the study of the retina were greatly encouraged by the enthusiastic interest of the late Dr Gordon Walls. Later through the courtesy of Dr H. Barlow, Dean of the School of Optometry, Berkeley, California, I had the special privilege of examining the microscopical preparations of Dr Walls. Finally, the editors subjected my manuscript to a most thorough scrutiny.

References

The three most important references are Franz (1934), Walls (1942), and Rochon-Duvigneaud (1943).

The relatively few works published prior to 1940 that are cited here are mainly those that are not cited by Walls. An attempt has been made to cover the literature since 1940.

Abel, J. H. and Ellis, R. A. (1966). Histochemical and electron microscopic observations on the salt secreting lachrymal glands of marine turtles. *Am. J. Anat.* 118, 337–358.

Armstrong, J. A. (1950). An experimental study of the visual pathways in a reptile (*Lacerta vivipara*). *J. Anat.* 84, 146–167.

Armstrong, J. A. (1951). An experimental study of the visual pathways in a snake (*Natrix natrix*). *J. Anat.* 85, 275–288.

Barrows, S. and Smith, H. M. (1947). The skeleton of the lizard *Xenosaurus grandis* (Gray). *Kans. Univ. Sci. Bull.* 31, 227–281.

Baumeister, L. (1908). Beiträge zur Anatomie und Physiologie der Rhinophiden. *Zool. Jb., Abt. Anat.* 26, 423–526.

Beer, T. (1898). Die Accommodation des Auges bei den Amphibien. *Pflügers Arch. ges. Physiol.* 73, 501–534.

Bellairs, A. d'A. (1949a). Observations on the cranial anatomy of *Anniella*, and a comparison with that of other burrowing lizards. *Proc. zool. Soc. Lond.* 119, 887–904.

Bellairs, A. d'A. (1949b). The anterior braincase and interorbital septum of Sauropsida, with a consideration of the origin of snakes. *J. Linn. Soc. (Zool.)* 41, 482–512.

Bellairs, A. d'A. and Boyd, J. D. (1947). The lachrymal apparatus in lizards and snakes. I. The brille, the orbital glands, lachrymal canaliculi and origin of the lachrymal duct. *Proc. zool. Soc. Lond.* 117, 81–108.

Bogert, C. M. and del Campo, R. M. (1956). The gila monster and its allies. The relationships, habits and behavior of the lizards of the family Helodermatidae. *Bull. Am. Mus. nat. Hist.* 109, 1–238.

Bonin, J. J. (1965). The eye of *Agamodon anguliceps* Peters (Reptilia, Amphisbaenia). *Copeia* 1965, 324–331.

Bruner, H. L. (1907). On the cephalic veins and sinuses of reptiles, with description of a mechanism for raising the venous blood-pressure in the head. *Am. J. Anat.* 7, 1–118.

Camp, C. L. (1923). Classification of the lizards. *Bull. Am. Mus. nat. Hist.* 48, 289–481.

Cohen, A. I. (1963a). The fine structure of the visual receptors of the pigeon. *Expl Eye Res.* 2, 88–97.

Cohen, A. I. (1963b). Vertebrate retinal cells and their organization. *Biol. Rev.* 38, 427–459.

Crescitelli, F. (1958). The natural history of visual pigments. *Ann. N.Y. Acad. Sci.* 74, 230–255.

Detwiler, S. L. (1923). Studies on the retina. Photomechanical responses in the retina of *Eremias argus. J. exp. Zool.* 37, 89–99.

Dowling, J. E. and Boycott, B. B. (1965). Neural connections of the retina: Fine structure of the inner plexiform layer. *Cold Spring Harb. Symp. quant. Biol.* 30, 393–402.

Dunn, R. F. (1966). Studies on the retina of the gecko *Coleonyx variegatus.* I. The visual cell classification. II. The rectilinear visual cell mosaic. III. Photoreceptor cross-sectional area relationships. *J. Ultrastruct. Res.* 16, 651–692.

Edinger, T. (1929). Über knöcherne Scleralringe. *Zool. Jb., Abt. Anat.* 51, 163–226.

Eigenmann, C. H. (1909). Cave vertebrates of America. A study in degenerative evolution. *Publs Carnegie Instn* 104, 1–241.

Etheridge, R. (1964). The skeletal morphology and systematic relationships of sceloporine lizards. *Copeia* 1964, 610–631.

Evans, E. M. (1966). On the ultrastructure of the synaptic region of visual receptors in certain vertebrates. *Z. Zellforsch. mikrosk. Anat.* 71, 499–516.

Franz, V. (1934). Vergleichende Anatomie des Wirbeltierauges. *In* "Handbuch der Vergleichenden Anatomie der Wirbeltiere" (L. Bolk, E. Göppert, E. Kallius and W. Lubosch, eds.) 2(2), 989–1292. Urban und Schwarzenberg, Berlin and Wien.

Gans, C. and Bonin, J. J. (1963). Acoustic activity recorder for burrowing animals. *Science, N.Y.* 140, 398.

Gugg, W. (1939). Der Skleralring der plagiotremen Reptilien. *Zool. Jb., Abt. Anat.* 65, 339–416.

Hanke, V. (1912). Die rudimentären Sehorgane einiger Amphibien und Reptilien. *Arch. vergl. Ophthal.* 6, 323–342.

Hoffmann, C. K. (1879–1890). Reptilien. *In* "Klassen und Ordnungen des Thier-Reich's" (H. G. Bronn, ed.) 6(3) 3 vols. 1–2086. C. F. Winter'sche Verlagshandlung, Leipzig.

Jokl, A. (1923). Über den Verschluss der fötalen Augenbecherspalte, die Entwicklung der Sehnerveninsertion und die Bildung ektodermaler und mesodermaler Zapfen im embryonalen Reptilienauge. *Z. Anat. EntwGesch.* 68, 523–618.

Kahmann, H. (1932). Sinnesphysiologische Studien an Reptilien. II. Über die Akkommodation im Schlangenauge mit Bemerkungen über die Akkommodation der Echsen und über den Akkommodations-Apparat. *Zool. Jb., Abt. Physiol.* 52, 295–337.

Kalberer, M. and Pedler, C. H. (1963). The visual cells of the alligator: An electron microscopic study. *Vision Res.* 3, 323–329.

Kluge, A. G. (1962). Comparative osteology of the eublepharid lizard genus *Coleonyx* Gray. *J. Morph.* 110, 299–332.

Kluge, A. G. (1967). Higher taxonomic categories of gekkonid lizards and their evolution. *Bull. Am. Mus. nat. Hist.* 135, 1–59.

König, D. (1935). Der vordere Augenabschnitt der Schildkröten und die Funktion seiner Muskulatur. *Jena Z. Naturw.* 69, 223–284.

Köttgen, E. and Abelsdorff, G. (1895). Die Arten des Sehpurpurs in der Wirbelthierreihe. *Sber. preuss. Akad. Wiss.* **38**, 921–926.

Lakjcr, T. (1926). "Studien über die Trigeminus-versorgte Kaumuskulatur der Sauropsiden." C. A. Reitsel, Copenhagen.

Läsker, G. (1934). Der vordere Augenabschnitt bei *Lacerta serpa* und Geckonen und die Funktion seiner Muskeln. *Jena Z. Naturw.* **69**, 15–82.

Laurens, H. and Detwiler, S. R. (1921). Studies on the retina. The structure of the retina of *Alligator mississippiensis* and its photomechanical changes. *J. exp. Zool.* **32**, 207–234.

Leplat, G. (1921). Sur le devéloppement de la musculature interne de l'oeil des reptiles. *Bull. Acad. r. Belg. Cl. Sci.* **7**(5), 748–752.

Leplat, G. (1922). Recherches sur le devéloppement du cone papillaire de l'oeil des reptiles. *C.r. Ass. Anat.* **17**, 195–200.

Locke, M. and Collins, J. V. (1966). Sequestration of protein by the fat body of an insect. *Nature, Lond.* **210**, 552–553.

Lüdicke, M. (1940). Über die Kapillargebiete des Blutgefäss-Systems im Kopf der Schlangen (*Tropidonotus natrix* L. und *Zamenis dahli* Fitz.). *Z. Morph. Ökol. Tiere* **36**, 401–445.

Mann, I. (1929). Some observations on the vascularization of the vertebrate eye. *Trans. ophthal. Soc. U. K.* **49**, 353–392.

McDowell, S. B. and Bogert, C. M. (1954). The systematic position of *Lanthanotus* and the affinities of the anguinomorphan lizards. *Bull. Am. Mus. nat. Hist.* **105**, 1–142.

O'Day, K. J. (1939). The visual cells of Australian reptiles and mammals. *Trans. ophthal. Soc. Aust.* **1**, 12–20.

O'Donoghue, C. H. (1919). The blood vascular system of the tuatara *Sphenodon punctatus*. *Phil. Trans. R. Soc.* B **210**, 175–252.

Oelrich, T. M. (1956). The anatomy of the head of *Ctenosaura pectinata* (Iguanidae). *Misc. Publs Mus. Zool. Univ. Mich.* **94**, 1–122.

Olney, J. W. (1968). Centripetal sequence of appearance of receptor-bipolar synaptic structures in developing mouse retina. *Nature, Lond.* **218**, 281–282.

Pedler, C. H. (1965). Duplicity theory and microstructure of the retina. Rods and cones: a fresh approach. *In* "Ciba Foundation Symposium on Physiology and Experimental Psychology of Colour Vision" (C. E. Wolstenholme and J. Knight, eds.), 52–88. J. and A. Churchill, London.

Pedler, C. H. and Tansley, K. (1963). The fine structure of the cones of a diurnal gecko (*Phelsuma inunguis*). *Expl Eye Res.* **2**, 39–47.

Pedler, C. H. and Tilly, R. (1963). The radial fibres of the reptilian retina. *J. Anat.* **97**, 626–627.

Pedler, C. H. and Tilly, R. (1964). The nature of the gecko visual cell: A light and electron microscopic study. *Vision Res.* **4**, 499–510.

Polyak, S. (1941). "The Retina." Univ. Chicago Press, Chicago.

Polyak, S. (1957). "The Vertebrate Visual System." Univ. Chicago Press, Chicago.

Pumphrey, R. J. (1948). The theory of the fovea. *J. exp. Biol.* **25**, 299–312.

Ramón y Cajal, S. (1894). "Die Retina der Wirbelthiere." Bergmann, Wiesbaden.

Rathke, M. H. (1866). "Untersuchungen über die Entwickelung und den Körperbau der Krokodile." (W. von Wittich, ed.) F. Vieweg und Sohn, Braunschweig.

Rochon-Duvigneaud, A. (1943). "Les Yeux et la Vision des Vertébrés." Masson et Cie, Paris.

Romer, A. S. (1956). "Osteology of the Reptiles." Univ. Chicago Press, Chicago.

Säve-Södebergh, G. (1946). On the fossa hypophyseos and the attachment of the retractor bulbi group in *Sphenodon*, *Varanus* and *Lacerta*. *Ark. Zool.* **38A**(11), 1–24.

Saxén, L. (1953). An atypical form of the double visual cell in the frog (*Rana temporaria* L.). *Acta anat.* **19**, 190–196.

Saxén, L. (1954). The development of the visual cells. Embryological and physiological investigations on Amphibia. *Suomal. Tiedeakat. Toim.* Ser. 4A, **23**, 1–93.

Saxén, L. (1955). The glycogen inclusion of the visual cells and its hypothetical role in the photomechanical responses. Histochemical investigation during frog ontogenesis. *Acta anat.* **25**, 319–330.

Saxén, L. (1956). The initial formation and subsequent development of the double visual cells in Amphibia. *J. Embryol. exp. Morph.* **4**, 57–65.

Schwartz-Karsten, H. (1933). Über Entwicklung und Bau der Brille bei Ophidiern und Lacertiliern und die Anatomie ihrer Tränenwege. *Morph. Jb.* **72**, 499–540.

Senn, D. G. (1966). Über das optische System im Gehirn squamater Reptilien. Eine vergleichend-morphologische Untersuchung, unter besonderer Berücksichtigung einiger Wühlschlangen. *Acta anat.*, Supplement **52**, 1–87.

Stephenson, N. G. (1960). The comparative osteology of Australian geckos and its bearing on their morphological status. *J. Linn. Soc. (Zool.)* **44**, 278–299.

Stephenson, N. G. and Stephenson, E. M. (1956). The osteology of the New Zealand geckos and its bearing on their morphological status. *Trans. R. Soc. N.Z.* **84**, 341–358.

Steven, D. M. (1963). The dermal light sense. *Biol. Rev.* **38**, 204–240.

Svanidze, I. K. (1959). Development of the optic nerve and retina in the rock lizard. *Dokl. Akad. Nauk SSSR* **126**, 441–442.

Tansley, K. (1959). The retina of two nocturnal geckos, *Hemidactylus turcicus* and *Tarentola mauritanica*. *Pflügers Arch. ges. Physiol.* **268**, 213–220.

Tansley, K. (1961). The retina of a diurnal gecko *Phelsuma madagascariensis longinsulae*. *Pflügers Arch. ges. Physiol.* **272**, 262–269.

Tansley, K. and Johnson, B. K. (1956). The cones of the grass-snake's eye. *Nature, Lond.* **178**, 1285–1286.

Underwood, G. (1951a). Reptilian retinas. *Nature, Lond.* **167**, 183–185.

Underwood, G. (1951b). On the classification and evolution of geckos. *Proc. zool. Soc. Lond.* **124**, 469–492.

Underwood, G. (1957). On lizards of the family Pygopodidae: A contribution to the morphology and phylogeny of the Squamata. *J. Morph.* **100**, 207–268.

Underwood, G. (1966). On the visual-cell pattern of a homalopsine snake. *J. Anat.* **100**, 571–575.

Underwood, G. (1967a). "A Contribution to the Classification of Snakes." Brit. Mus. (Nat. Hist.), London.

Underwood, G. (1967b). Symposium on colubrid snake systematics: A comprehensive approach to the classification of higher snakes. *Herpetologica* **23**, 161–168.

Underwood, G. (1968). Some suggestions concerning vertebrate visual cells. *Vision Res.* **8**, 483–488.

Verriest, G., de Rouck, A. and Rabaey, M. (1959). Étude comparative de l'histologie rétinienne et de l'électrorétinogramme chez les batraciens et chez les reptiles. *Biol. Jaarb.* **27**, 102–191.

Vilter, U. (1951). Valeur morphologique des photorécepteurs rétiniens chez la hatterie (*Sphenodon punctatus*). *C.r. Séanc. Soc. Biol.* **145**, 20–23.

Walls, G. L. (1938). The microtechnique of the eye with some suggestions as to material. *Stain Technol.* **13**, 69–72.

Walls, G. L. (1942). The vertebrate eye and its adaptive radiation. *Bull. Cranbrook Inst. Sci.* (19), 1–785.

Willard, W. A. (1915). The cranial nerves of *Anolis carolinensis*. *Bull. Mus. comp. Zool. Harvard* **59**, 17–116.

Williams, E. E. and Hecht, M. K. (1955). "Sunglasses" in two anoline lizards from Cuba. *Science, N.Y.* **122**, 691–692.

Winckels, A. (1914). Das Auge von *Voeltzkowia mira*. Ph.D. Thesis, Universität Bonn.

Yamada, E. (1960). The fine structure of the pigment epithelium in the turtle eye. *Anat. Rec.* **136**, 305.

Yamada, E. and Ishikawa, T. (1965). The fine structure of the horizontal cells in some vertebrate retinae. *Cold Spring Harb. Symp. quant. Biol.* **30**, 383–392.

Yamada, E., Ishikawa, T. and Hataé, T. (1966). Some observation on the retinal fine structure of the snake *Elaphe climacophora*. *Sixth Int. Cong. Electron Microsc.*, *Kyoto* **2**, 495–496.

CHAPTER 2

The Nose and Jacobson's Organ

THOMAS S. PARSONS

Department of Zoology, University of Toronto, Toronto, Ontario, Canada

I. Introduction

The variation in nasal anatomy between the living orders of reptiles is great enough that little can be said about the class in general. However, before treating each order separately I have included a brief section outlining the major regions and structures of the nose, considering their homologies within the reptiles and also within the tetrapods generally. Following this the gross anatomy of the nose in each order is described. Then the histology, the embryology, and finally the nasal glands are considered. Although some dissections were made, this study is primarily a review of the quite extensive literature. Since this stresses gross anatomy, treats embryology relatively briefly, and passes very lightly over histology, so does this chapter.

The bibliography omits some older papers and those which only mention the nose in passing; exceptions are made in cases in which no other papers mention the group or form being considered, and certain classic papers are cited despite their age. I have tried to make the bibliography reasonably comprehensive, and the older papers which are not cited can be tracked down in the bibliographies of the works here cited.

The scope of this review must naturally be limited, and there are many related topics which bear on the questions being considered but cannot be dealt with here. The skeletal structures of the nasal area have thus been omitted, and the olfactory nerves and lobes considered but briefly. On the other hand I have dealt with the nasal glands as fully as I could; the lack of detail reflects the meagerness of the literature on this topic.

A major problem is terminology. The more important of the earlier papers, those of Seydel (1896), Nick (1912), and Fuchs (1915), contain different combinations of German and Latin terms, a usage followed by Parsons (1959a). Most names have here been anglicized unless this made them become exceedingly awkward, in which case they are retained unchanged. Such a mixture is not ideal, but is preferable to coining yet more terms. The major synonyms are cited, but some others, particularly older German ones, are omitted as the original papers are of little more than historic interest.

The nasal apparatus consists of a modified tube and the nomenclature of some of its specializations needs to be settled. Thus outpocketings or invaginations of the wall refer to foldings or other modifications of the epithelium that cause it to project into the tubular lumen. Inpocketings or evaginations are pockets, cavities, or depressions of the wall which will widen the hollow space.

II. Major Regions and Structures of the Reptilian Nose

A. Vestibulum nasi

The vestibulum nasi of all living reptiles is an essentially tubular portion of the nasal cavity extending from the external naris to the cavum nasi proprium. The vestibulum is almost always clearly separable from the cavum by the far greater diameter of the latter. There is, in addition, commonly (*Sphenodon*, many turtles and squamates) a ridge in the lateral nasal wall marking the boundary. In crocodilians the structure is somewhat different; here the vertical portion of the nasal cavity is considered to be the vestibulum. Although it is typically rather short and simple, the vestibulum may, especially in certain lizards, be quite long and complex, and no generalizations can safely be made concerning its structure.

The reptilian vestibulum can thus be defined with reasonable precision on the basis of gross structure. Unfortunately this is not the case in all other tetrapods, especially mammals; in the latter the shape of the nasal cavity is quite different and the vestibulum is commonly defined as that part of it which is lined by stratified squamous epithelium like that of the skin in contrast to the rest of the nasal cavity which is lined by columnar epithelium. Such a histological definition appears to be impractical when treating reptiles. Not only is the histology of reptilian noses poorly known, but Eckart (1922) has shown that there is considerable variation in the extent of stratified epithelium within the nasal cavities of members of the family Agamidae and similar variation may well occur in other groups.

A third and embryological definition of the vestibulum is frequently cited but rarely, if ever, used. It characterizes the vestibulum as that part of the nasal cavity formed from relatively unmodified ectoderm invaginated at some stage in development to form a tubular connection between the external naris and the cavum nasi proprium from the embryonic nasal placode. The nasal embryology of few reptiles is known in enough detail to insist that the invagination indeed results in the vestibulum, and the placode does not have sharp margins but rather merges with the surrounding ectoderm.

The variety of definitions emphasizes the difficulty of making homologies between the vestibula of different reptiles and, indeed, of tetrapods generally. Theoretically the embryological definition would be the most suitable, yet it has been shown to be unworkable. The morphological and histological definitions are not equivalent and cannot both reflect homologies. The former is used primarily for convenience, but the vestibulum thus defined appears to be quite comparable in all orders of reptiles. The external nasal gland of all orders of reptiles commonly arises from the posterior portion of the vestibulum as defined by gross structure. Exact comparisons with members of other classes are more difficult and, perhaps, not yet profitable.

B. Ductus nasopharyngeus

The nasopharyngeal duct is here used to refer to any tubular connection between the cavum nasi proprium and the internal naris or choana. The usage is not intended to suggest anything concerning its origin or the nature of the palate. As here defined, this duct varies greatly in length depending on the development of a secondary palate (*sensu lato*) and the consequent posterior displacement of the choanae. It is always a simple tube with a minimum of special associated structures. *Sphenodon* lacks a nasopharyngeal duct; the duct is short in most lizards, better developed in snakes, quite long in turtles, and reaches its maximum development in crocodilians. The duct is lined by various sorts of epithelia which are not sensory.

An enormous literature deals with the embryology and nature of the nasopharyngeal duct. Beyond the standard embryological descriptions, there are series of papers by Fuchs (1907, 1908, and 1915) and by the students of Fleischmann (see Thäter, 1910), mainly polemic in content with magnification of minor differences of terminology. Their arguments are briefly reviewed by Parsons (1959a).

Fuchs distinguished two types of nasopharyngeal ducts and used different terms for each. The term nasopharyngeal duct was restricted to that part of the oral cavity which is separated off by the formation of an extensive secondary palate; such a duct is found only in crocodilians and mammals. The analogous duct of other reptiles, believed to be formed entirely from tissue of nasal, that is placodal, origin, he termed Choanengang or choanal duct. This distinction does not seem as sharp as Fuchs thought it. Certainly the difference between lizards and crocodilians is clear cut, but the turtles appear partially to bridge the gap. Fuchs' statement (1907, 1915) that the nasopharyngeal duct of turtles is formed entirely from placodal tissue remains to be proven; I do not believe that it is. Fuchs also did not believe that turtles have a true secondary palate, but claimed that it was an extended primary palate, another distinction that seems rather questionable. While Fuchs is certainly correct in stressing the difference between crocodilians and other reptiles, the term nasopharyngeal duct is here used in a more general sense, recognizing however that such ducts are not always homologous.

C. Cavum nasi proprium

The portion of the nasal cavity lying between the vestibulum and the nasopharyngeal duct is termed the cavum nasi proprium. It forms a relatively large, and complex chamber, the shape of which varies greatly among reptiles, even among those of a single order. Sensory epithelium partially, and to a very variable extent, lines the caval walls; such epithelium occurs neither in the vestibulum nor the nasopharyngeal duct. Different sections of this chamber are frequently recognized and defined on the basis of the conchae which are, therefore, considered below.

D. Conchae

The name concha is used in several ways and has been differently defined, even to the point of mutual exclusion. Most workers have defined the term concha in a general sense to mean any projection of the lateral wall of the nasal cavity into this cavity; in reptiles, such projections occur only in the cavum nasi proprium. However, certain authors have proposed more restricted definitions. Gegenbaur (1873) and Solger (1876) restricted the term to simple lamellar projections (=Muscheln), while projections enclosing cavities and hence more or less U-shaped in section were referred to as pseudoconchae or concha-like projections (a variety of German names are used). According to their definition, the structure normally called the concha in squamates is really a pseudoconcha. However, de Beer (1937) restricted the term concha to projections which *do* contain a space, the latter being occupied in most cases by the external nasal gland; his definition is, thus, the reverse of that used by Gegenbaur and Solger.

The homologies of the various conchae (*sensu lato*) among the different groups of tetrapods are quite uncertain. Amphibians are usually considered to lack conchae, although de Beer (1937) claimed that urodeles possess one. Turtles have no definitive conchae, although there are certain structures which are often, but with little reason, said to represent them. All other tetrapods have at least one concha. Table I shows what appear to be the most probable homologies.

The scheme adopted suggests that there was a single primitive concha and that this remains the most prominent and almost always the first to develop embryologically. Most groups have independently developed additional conchae. The homologies here suggested bear no relation to the more restricted concepts of conchae mentioned previously: the squamate concha is generally (though not invariably) a concha *sensu* de Beer, while the concha posterior of *Sphenodon* is a concha *sensu* Gegenbaur.

TABLE I

Homologies of Conchae

Sphenodon	Squamata	Crocodilia	Aves	Mammalia
			Concha anterior	
Anterior concha				
Posterior concha	Concha	Preconcha + Concha	Concha media	Maxilloturbinal
				Nasoturbinal
		Postconcha	Concha posterior	
				Ethmoturbinal

Although these homologies are probably the most widely accepted, there is some disagreement. Peter (1906) postulated that the crocodilian post-concha and avian concha posterior are homologous with the mammalian nasoturbinal, and some other workers have agreed with this. While such a homology is possible, there is no compelling evidence in its favor and it seems phylogenetically improbable. Hoppe (1934) believed the squamate concha and rhynchocephalian concha posterior to be the homologs of the crocodilian postconcha; this appears improbable. Finally de Beer (1937), relying in part on his restricted definition of concha, homologized the squamate concha with the crista semicircularis rather than with the maxilloturbinal of mammals.

These problems have been considered elsewhere (see Peter, 1906; Matthes, 1934; Parsons, 1959a), and further discussion is not necessary here. The presently available evidence is insufficient to permit more than guess-work; more definitive summaries must await further studies of the anatomy and embryology of the nasal cavities and capsules.

E. JACOBSON'S ORGAN

The literature concerning Jacobson's organ is very extensive. Although there has been general agreement on its homologies in the Rhynchocephalia, Squamata, and Mammalia, there has been no consensus concerning the situation in other tetrapod groups. Detailed reviews are available (Parsons, 1959a; major older reviews include those by von Mihalkovics, 1898; Zuckerkandl, 1910b, and Matthes, 1934), and only a brief outline is needed here.

In *Sphenodon*, squamates, and mammals Jacobson's organ arises at an early embryonic stage as a medial outpocketing of the nasal pit in the area which will be just medial to the anterior end of the choanae. In *Sphenodon* it retains this position, while the Jacobson's organ of squamates becomes associated with the mouth as the growth and anterior fusion of the choanae breaks its connection with the nasal cavity. Its further development in mammals varies. In crocodilians and birds, the first stage in its development resembles that described above, but it quickly disappears and is totally lacking in late embryos and adults.

The situation in amphibians and turtles is quite different. Seydel (1895 and 1896) recognized a homolog of Jacobson's organ in both groups and suggested that Jacobson's organ may be distinguished from the remaining sensory portions of the nasal epithelium on the basis of three characters: 1. It develops more or less ventrally and medially (the normal olfactory epithelium tends to lie dorsally within the nasal cavity). 2. It is innervated by nerves running to the accessory rather than the main portion of the olfactory bulb. 3. It lacks Bowman's glands which are found in the olfactory epithelium of virtually all tetrapods. Seydel used these criteria to homologize a variable number of patches and bands of sensory epithelium in the ventral half of the cavum nasi proprium of turtles with the Jacobson's organ of other reptiles. Amphibians are quite variable and outside the scope of this discussion.

III. Adult Anatomy of the Nasal Organs

A. Testudines

1. *General*

Although the nasal cavity has been studied in quite a few different turtles, most of the descriptions are both old and incomplete. The following genera have been described: *Chelydra* (Nick, 1912), *Kinosternon* (Hoffmann, 1879–1890; Parsons and Stephens, 1968), *Sternotherus* (Parsons and Stephens, 1968), *Clemmys* (McCotter, 1917; I assume that his "*Chrysemys punctata*" = *Clemmys guttata*), *Chrysemys* (Seydel, 1896), *Emys* (Solger, 1876; Seydel, 1896), *Pseudemys* (Nemours, 1930; Parsons, 1959a), *Geochelone* (Hoffmann, 1879–1890), *Testudo* (Seydel, 1896; Matthes, 1934), *Caretta* (Gegenbaur, 1873), *Chelonia* (Solger, 1876; Nick, 1912; Parsons, 1959a), *Eretmochelys* (Hoffmann, 1879–1890; Fuchs, 1915), *Dermochelys* (Hoffmann, 1879–1890; Nick, 1912), *Trionyx* (Hoffmann, 1879–1890; Seydel, 1896), and *Pelomedusa* (van der Merwe, 1940). Major reviews include those of Matthes (1934) and Parsons (1959a). A few other papers describe only certain regions or features and are cited below. For this study I have dissected single specimens of *Emydoidea blandingii*, *Chelonia mydas*, and *Chelus fimbriatus*. I have also checked certain points on sectioned heads of some turtles and have a description of the nose of *Trionyx* in preparation.

2. *Vestibulum*

In all the turtles so far studied, the vestibulum (=anterior nasal canal, Einführungsgang, Vorhof) appears to be a relatively simple tubular structure which leads almost directly posterior from the external naris to the cavum nasi proprium; in some cases, *e.g. Chelydra*, it may run posteroventrally (Figs 1–7). Although the vestibulum is typically short, it may be elongated

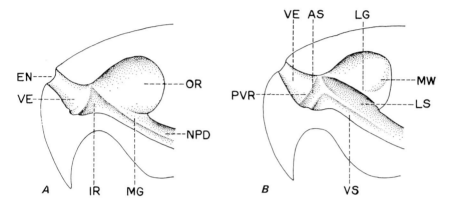

FIG. 1. Nasal cavities of *Chelydra serpentina* (after Nick, 1912). A. Lateral view of the medial wall of the nasal cavity. B. Medial view of the lateral wall of the nasal cavity.
AS, Anterior sulcus; EN, External naris; IR, Intermediate region; LG, Lateral Grenzfalte; LS, Lateral sulcus; MG, Medial Grenzfalte; MW, Muschelwulst; NPD, Nasopharyngeal duct; OR, Olfactory region; PVR, Postvestibular ridge; VE, Vestibulum; VS, Ventral sulcus.

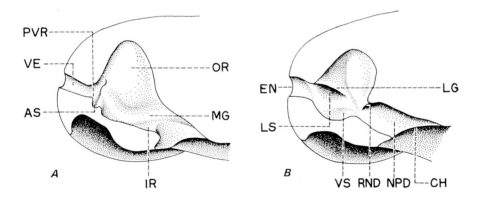

FIG. 2. Nasal cavities of *Emydoidea blandingii*. A. Lateral view of the medial wall of the nasal cavity. B. Medial view of the lateral wall of the nasal cavity.
AS, Anterior sulcus; CH, Choana; EN, External naris; IR, Intermediate region; LG, Lateral Grenzfalte; LS, Lateral sulcus; MG, Medial Grenzfalte; NPD, Nasopharyngeal duct; OR, Olfactory region; PVR, Postvestibular ridge; RND, Recess of the nasopharyngeal duct; VE, Vestibulum; VS, Ventral sulcus.

in forms such as *Chelus* (Fig. 7), trionychids, and *Carettochelys* that possess elongated snouts. The latter genus and most trionychids have, along the medial wall of the vestibulum, a distinct ridge which may be seen within the external naris. In cross section the vestibulum is typically circular, often becoming vertically elliptical posteriorly.

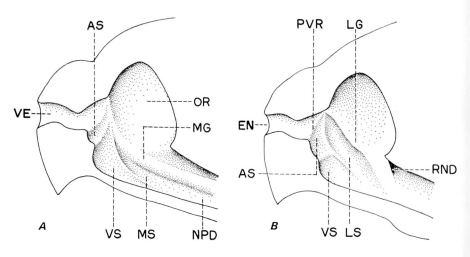

FIG. 3. Nasal cavities of *Emys orbicularis* (after Seydel, 1896). A. Lateral view of the medial wall of the nasal cavity. B. Medial view of the lateral wall of the nasal cavity.
AS, Anterior sulcus; EN, External naris; LG, Lateral Grenzfalte; LS, Lateral sulcus; MG, Medial Grenzfalte; MS, Medial sulcus; NPD, Nasopharyngeal duct; OR, Olfactory region; PVR, Post-vestibular ridge; RND, Recess of the nasopharyngeal duct; VE, Vestibulum; VS, Ventral sulcus.

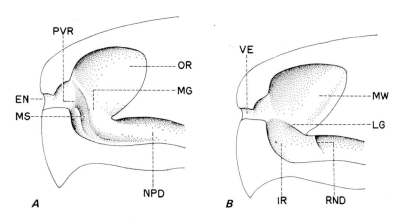

FIG. 4. Nasal cavities of *Testudo graeca* (mainly after Seydel, 1896). A. Lateral view of the medial wall of the nasal cavity. B. Medial view of the lateral wall of the nasal cavity.
EN, External naris; IR, Intermediate region; LG, Lateral Grenzfalte; MG, Medial Grenzfalte; MS, Medial sulcus; MW, Muschelwulst; NPD, Nasopharyngeal duct; OR, Olfactory region; PVR, Postvestibular ridge; RND, Recess of the nasopharyngeal duct; VE, Vestibulum.

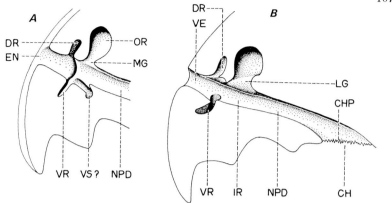

FIG. 5. Nasal cavities of *Chelonia mydas*. A. Lateral view of the medial wall of the nasal cavity. B. Medial view of the lateral wall of the nasal cavity.
CH, Choana; CHP, Choanal papilla; DR, Dorsal recess; EN, External naris; IR, Intermediate region; LG, Lateral Grenzfalte; MG, Medial Grenzfalte; NPD, Nasopharyngeal duct; OR, Olfactory region; VE, Vestibulum; VR, Ventral recess; VS, Ventral sulcus.

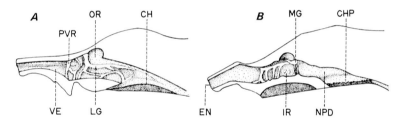

FIG. 6. Nasal cavities of *Trionyx ferox*. A. Lateral view of the medial wall of the nasal cavity. B. Medial view of the lateral wall of the nasal cavity.
CH, Choana; CHP, Choanal papillae; EN, External naris; IR, Intermediate region; LG, Lateral Grenzfalte; MG, Medial Grenzfalte; NPD, Nasopharyngeal duct; OR, Olfactory region; PVR, Postvestibular ridge; VE, Vestibulum.

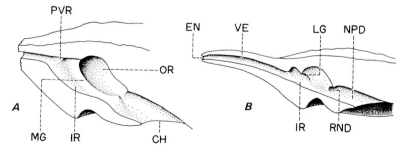

FIG. 7. Nasal cavities of *Chelus fimbriatus*. A. Lateral view of the medial wall of the nasal cavity. B. Medial view of the lateral wall of the nasal cavity.
CH, Choana; EN, External naris; IR, Intermediate region; LG, Lateral Grenzfalte; MG, Medial Grenzfalte; NPD, Nasopharyngeal duct; OR, Olfactory region; PVR, Postvestibular ridge; RND, Recess of the nasopharyngeal duct; VE, Vestibulum.

The duct of the external nasal gland, if present, commonly enters the dorsolateral wall of the vestibulum near the posterior end of the latter. In *Pelomedusa* this duct may empty into the anterior end of the cavum nasi proprium; unfortunately van der Merwe's (1940) figure is not clear on this point, but he describes the duct as entering the cavum rather than the vestibulum. In sectioned material of *Podocnemis expansa*, the duct appears to enter almost exactly at the boundary between the two regions, and I cannot definitely tell with which it is more associated. The duct of the external nasal gland enters the anterodorsal part of the cavum in kinosternids (Parsons and Stephens, 1968).

In some cases there are modifications serving to close off the external nares when the turtle is submerged, for example the highly vascularized (erectile) tissue around the vestibulum of *Caretta* (Walker, 1959). This tissue forces the walls of the vestibulum together and seals off the entrance when the animal is at rest under water; the nares are apparently kept open when the animal is active. Similar erectile tissue has been described around much of the nasal cavities of *Chelonia*, *Dermochelys*, and *Eretmochelys* (Nick, 1912; Fuchs, 1915). No such modifications have been reported for other turtles.

3. *Cavum nasi proprium*

The cavum nasi proprium (=eigentliche Nasenhöhle, Haupthöhle, principal nasal chamber) is most conveniently described separately for two groups, one containing *Chelydra*, kinosternids, *Testudo*, emydines, *Trionyx*, and *Chelus*, while the sea turtles form the second. *Pelomedusa* is poorly known, but seems to be more or less comparable to members of the first assemblage.

In members of both groups, the cavum nasi proprium can be divided into two main parts, an olfactory region (=innere Riechgrube, pars olfactoria, recessus superior posterior) and an intermediate region (=cella media plus various recesses, pars respiratoria). The former is a dorsal or posterodorsal pouch opening broadly into the intermediate region, while the latter lies between the vestibulum and the nasopharyngeal duct. Most of the olfactory region is lined by olfactory epithelium with Bowman's glands. The intermediate region is partly lined by non-sensory or respiratory epithelium. It also contains varying amounts of sensory epithelium that lacks Bowman's glands and is believed to be the homolog of the Jacobson's organ of other reptiles.

In the emydines and similar forms (Figs 1–4 and 6–9), the olfactory region is almost always relatively large, forming the dorsal half of the cavum nasi proprium. Two ridges, the medial Grenzfalte (=mediale Grenzleiste) and lateral Grenzfalte (=concha, laterale Grenzleiste), separate it from the intermediate region. The medial Grenzfalte often extends posteriorly along the wall of the nasopharyngeal duct. Typically the olfactory region is approximately as high as it is long; its width is roughly half either of the other two dimensions. The medial side of the olfactory region is generally flat, but it may be slightly protruding (as in *Emydoidea*) or hollowed (as in *Emys* and other forms). The lateral wall is similar, but shows a greater tendency to protrusion.

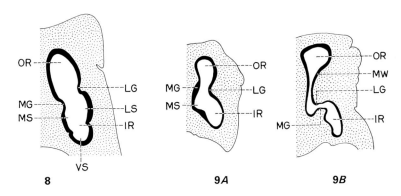

FIG. 8. Transverse section through the cavum nasi proprium of *Emys orbicularis* (after Seydel, 1896).

FIG. 9. Transverse sections through the cavum nasi proprium of *Testudo graeca* (after Seydel, 1896). A. Through the anterior part of the cavum. B. Through the posterior part of the cavum.

IR, Intermediate region; LG, Lateral Grenzfalte; LS, Lateral sulcus; MG, Medial Grenzfalte; MS, Medial sulcus; MW, Muschelwulst; OR, Olfactory region.

Protrusion is most marked in *Testudo* in which the lateral Grenzfalte forms the ventral margin of a prominent projection into the cavum. This swelling, and also the lateral Grenzfalte, has sometimes been considered to be a concha, but it bears little resemblance to the conchae of other forms and is apparently found in only a few turtles; the rather vague term Muschelwulst is thus retained. Although Seydel (1896) reports the presence of a low Muschelwulst in emydines, these often lack conspicuous inpocketing of the nasal wall except for the lateral Grenzfalte. A well developed Muschelwulst is apparently known only in *Testudo*, but smaller ones occur in *Kinosternon* and, possibly, *Chelydra* and *Emydoidea*. The entire olfactory region, with the exception of the dorsal surfaces of the medial and lateral Grenzfalten and the extreme posteroventral portion, is lined by sensory (olfactory) epithelium in all species, sections of which have been studied.

The intermediate region, that portion of the cavum nasi proprium ventral to the two Grenzfalten, is more complex, having several low ridges along its walls with shallow sulci between them. Often these ridges are not obvious upon gross dissection; their form should only be described from the study of sectioned material. Most species have a rather low postvestibular ridge (=Grenzwall) encircling the anterior end of the intermediate region, but it appears to be lacking in kinosternids (Parsons and Stephens, 1968). *Chelydra, Chrysemys, Emys,* and *Emydoidea* show a similar ridge a short distance posterior to this; this second ridge is absent in *Testudo* and either absent or recognizable only in sectioned material in *Chelus*. The area between these two ridges forms the anterior sulcus (=anterior ventromedial sulcus, pars anterior of Jacobson's organ). It may be either U-shaped, with the dorsal side incomplete, or circular, but the ventral portion is always the longest anteroposteriorly.

One or more low ridges run anteroposteriorly within the more posterior part of the intermediate region. *Testudo* has only one such ridge; it lies ventromedially on the wall of the cavum and thus forms the ventral boundary of a medial sulcus (=Jacobson's organ, part of pars dorsalis of Jacobson's organ) which is bounded dorsally by the medial Grenzfalte. It is the only sulcus present in *Testudo*. In *Chelydra*, on the other hand, there is a ventrolateral, but no ventromedial, longitudinal ridge; thus *Chelydra* has a lateral sulcus (=part of pars dorsalis of Jacobson's organ) and a broader ventromedial sulcus. In *Emys* both the ventrolateral and ventromedial ridges are present and, with the two Grenzfalten, separate three sulci, lateral, ventral (=pars ventralis of Jacobson's organ), and medial. *Clemmys* (?; *Chrysemys punctata* of McCotter, 1917) has three ridges and hence four longitudinal sulci, the extra sulcus being ventromedial. *Kinosternon* and *Sternotherus* resemble *Chelydra* in having a ventrolateral and lacking a ventromedial ridge; however, they also possess a transverse ridge which separates the ventromedial sulcus into two parts (the middle and posterior ventromedial sulci of Parsons and Stephens, 1968). Details of the ridges and sulci are not available for the other forms.

In those forms which have been studied histologically, the sulci are lined by sensory epithelium which lacks Bowman's glands. The remainder of the intermediate region (the ventral surfaces of the Grenzfalten, the various ridges, and, in *Testudo*, the ventral and lateral walls) bears non-sensory or respiratory epithelium.

The duct of the medial nasal gland enters the intermediate region. In *Testudo* its opening lies on the ventral surface of the medial Grenzfalte just dorsal to the anterior end of the medial sulcus, while in *Emys* it is near the dorsomedial corner of the anterior sulcus. The duct of this gland is further discussed in the sections on Jacobson's organ and on the glands.

Trionyx was studied by Hoffmann and also by Seydel (1896) who states that its nasal cavities generally resemble those of emydines, but that its olfactory region is relatively smaller. Work now in progress confirms Seydel's observations and shows the presence of numerous ridges in the intermediate region (Fig. 6); further description must await the preparation and study of more sectioned material.

Apparently the pattern in *Pelomedusa* is basically the same as in emydines; ridges and sulci are present in the intermediate region. However the cursory description by van der Merwe (1940) mentions and figures a dorsal recess, apparently at the anterior end of the intermediate region, into which the duct of the external nasal gland empties, and also a medial recess in the same area. Examination of sections of *Podocnemis expansa* suggests that the dorsal recess is merely the base of the duct. The medial recess may be the dorso-medial end of the anterior sulcus.

The second, and quite different, arrangement of the cavum nasi proprium is seen in sea turtles, both *Dermochelys* and cheloniids (Figs 5 and 10). The olfactory region is basically similar to that in other species, but is smaller

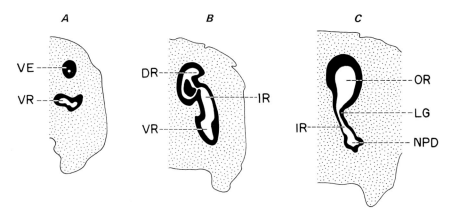

FIG. 10. Transverse sections through the nasal cavity of *Eretmochelys imbricata* (after Fuchs, 1915). A. Through the anterior end of the nasal cavity. B. Through the anterior part of the cavum nasi proprium. C. Through the posterior part of the cavum nasi proprium.
DR, Dorsal recess; IR, Intermediate region; LG, Lateral Grenzfalte; NPD, Nasopharyngeal duct; OR, Olfactory region; VE, Vestibulum; VR, Ventral recess.

and does not extend as far anteriorly. It forms a pocket the shape of two-thirds of a sphere with the base open to the posterior part of the intermediate region. Medial and lateral Grenzfalten, similar to those of other turtles, mark the boundary between the regions, but the medial one is not very prominent. However, since the olfactory region extends farther medially than the adjacent portion of the intermediate region, the boundary is marked by quite a sharp angle. There is no Muschelwulst. As in other turtles, the olfactory region is lined by sensory epithelium.

The intermediate region in sea turtles consists of a central tube (=cella media + pars posterior of the recessus inferior) with prominent pouches extending dorsally and ventrally from its anterior end. This tube, with the vestibulum and nasopharyngeal duct, forms a straight open channel from the external naris to the choana. There is no postvestibular ridge, but the far greater diameter of the cavum clearly distinguishes it from the vestibulum. There is in *Chelonia*, but apparently not in *Dermochelys*, a rather distinct groove in the floor of the intermediate region running posteriorly and very slightly laterally from the ventral recess; possibly this groove represents the ventral sulcus of other turtles.

The ventral recess (=pars anterior of recessus inferior, recessus inferior, untere Ausbuchtung) of cheloniids is a moderately large pocket, wide mediolaterally but narrow anteroposteriorly, projecting ventrally from the anterior part of the intermediate region. Its ventral end curves anteriorly, especially near its lateral side, and is the anterior-most portion of the cavum nasi proprium. A small but distinct ridge marks the opening of the ventral recess laterally, but medially a quite prominent groove connects the dorsal and ventral recesses. In *Dermochelys* the entire nasal cavity is shorter than in cheloniids and hence is set at a steeper angle; this reduces the space available for the ventral recess to a small ventromedial pit off the anterior part of the intermediate region.

The dorsal recess (=obere Ausbuchtung, recessus superior anterior, recessus superior and medialis) is a somewhat larger pocket, and is also far wider mediolaterally than anteroposteriorly. Its medial portion is large and has been considered to form a separate medial recess (Nick, 1912). As in the case of the ventral recess, the lateral margin of the opening to the dorsal recess of cheloniids is marked by a small ridge; medially the two recesses are connected by a groove. Gegenbaur (1873) considered the transverse bar of tissue between the dorsal recess and the olfactory region to represent the concha.

Sensory epithelium without Bowman's glands lines the recesses and, in cheloniids, the medial groove between the recesses and the ventral sulcus. The remainder of the intermediate region is lined by non-sensory respiratory epithelium.

In adult, but not late embryonic, *Dermochelys* the erectile tissue, which surrounds the nasal cavities in all sea turtles, increases greatly in volume and markedly constricts the entire nasal cavity (Nick, 1912). The vestibulum, main portion of the intermediate region, and nasopharyngeal duct become very narrow, and the medial half of the dorsal recess and the olfactory region are thus virtually isolated from the rest of the nasal cavity. The ventral recess and the lateral portion of the dorsal recess are closed. An essentially similar situation occurs in *Chelonia*, but the closure is here effected by filling with secretion rather than by constriction via erectile tissue (Nick, 1912).

The head of *Chelonia* dissected by me had some material within the nasal cavities, yet these were hardly full, and it was impossible to tell whether the filling accumulated before or after death.

4. *Nasopharyngeal duct*

The nasopharyngeal duct (= Ausführungsgang, part of Choanengang, hinterer Nasengang, posterior nasal canal) forms a relatively simple tube leading from the cavum nasi proprium to the choana (= internal naris). Its length is quite variable, depending mainly on the extent of the secondary palate (*sensu lato*; Fuchs, 1907, 1908, and 1915, pointed out that this is not the equivalent of the mammalian secondary palate and, in his later papers, termed the palate of turtles an extended primary palate). The nasopharyngeal duct is longest in cheloniids, but seems always to be present even in those forms, such as *Dermochelys* and *Chelus*, in which there is no bony secondary palate. Although Hoffmann (1879–1890) figures a cross section of the nose of *Kinosternon* sp. (his *Cinosternum rubrum*) in which the cavum nasi proprium appears to open directly into the oral cavity, a well developed nasopharyngeal duct is present in that genus (Parsons and Stephens, 1968). Fuchs (1907) discusses the extent of the bony palate in a large variety of turtles but performed few dissections, so his descriptions do not necessarily show the length of the nasopharyngeal ducts.

In cross section the nasopharyngeal duct appears roughly oval with the long axis vertical. The medial Grenzfalte of the cavum nasi proprium generally extends posteriorly into the nasopharyngeal duct as a rather low ridge along the anterior half or more of the medial wall. This continuation of the Grenzfalte is most marked in *Chelydra*, *Testudo*, and emydines, but also occurs in sea turtles; it is not seen in *Chelus*. Dorsolaterally there is, in *Chelydra*, *Kinosternon*, *Sternotherus*, *Testudo*, emydines, *Pelomedusa*, and *Chelus*, a recess of the nasopharyngeal duct (= sinus maxillaris of von Mihalkovics, 1898, and Nemours, 1930; it bears no real resemblance to the maxillary sinus of mammals). This recess projects anteriorly between the anterior end of the nasopharyngeal duct and the posteroventral part of the olfactory region. It is lacking in sea turtles. *Trionyx* possesses a recess in the same general area, but its structure does not resemble closely that seen in other forms.

The nasopharyngeal ducts open into the oral cavity through a pair of variably elongated oval choanae. In most turtles there are ridges, flaps, or papillae along the lateral choanal margins. I have described these in cheloniids (Parsons, 1958), emydines (Parsons, 1960), and turtles generally (Parsons, 1968). *Dermatemys* has a lateral flap bearing three to five irregular papillae. Among the chelydrids, chelydrines have a lateral flap with a single, rather blunt papilla at its anterior end, *Claudius* only a flap or ridge, and *Staurotypus* and kinosternines a lateral flap with an irregular bulge which might be considered a papilla. There is more variation among the testudinids: *Platysternon* possesses a lateral ridge or small flap, sometimes with a single papilla; emydines may have no special structures, a ridge, a flap, or a flap with a single papilla near its anterior end; and testudinines possess a rather deeply set lateral ridge or flap. Most cheloniids have a single papilla near the anterolateral corner of the choana, but *Chelonia* has a series of them along the lateral margin. There are no special structures in *Dermochelys*. *Carettochelys* has a large lateral flap with an irregular margin but no clear papillae. In the trionychids there is a well developed lateral flap; in *Trionyx* it bears numerous small papillae, in *Pelochelys* two or three larger papillae, and in the other genera one or two papillae or bulges. Pelomedusids have only a small antero-lateral ridge and chelids lack any special structures. Examples of these structures are shown in Fig. 11.

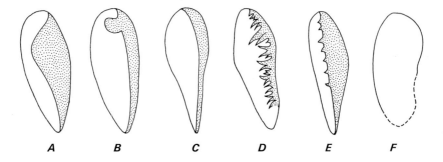

FIG. 11. Left choanae of various turtles in palatal view. The choanal flaps and papillae are stippled. A. *Kinosternon hirtipes*. B. *Geoemyda funerea*. C. *Pseudemys scripta*. D. *Chelonia mydas*. E. *Trionyx spinifer*. F. *Chelus fimbriatus*.

5. *Jacobson's organ*

Turtles clearly do not possess a typical Jacobson's organ and are often said to lack one completely. However, as noted in the general section, Seydel (1896) postulated that all the sensory epithelium of the intermediate region was the Jacobson's organ, basing this mainly on the position of this epithelium in *Testudo*, of Bowman's glands, the innervation by nerves leading to the accessory olfactory bulb (the medial branch of the olfactory nerve).

Seydel's evidence concerning the glands has never been disputed. Zuckerkandl (1910a), Fuchs (1915), McCotter (1917), and Parsons (1959a) have all agreed with Seydel concerning the innervation, but some workers, most recently Loew (1956), have denied that the innervation of the dorsal and ventral portions of the nose of turtles is as discrete as Seydel believed. My own observations, and hence my conclusions, are in complete agreement with Seydel's (Parsons, 1959a, 1967). Although Seydel's first point, the primitive ventromedial position of Jacobson's organ, has been commonly accepted, Loveridge and Williams (1957) do not consider the testudinines to be primitive; thus the organ is probably ventral rather than ventromedial in primitive turtles.

Various authors have accepted the homologies here postulated, but have disagreed on the use of the term Jacobson's organ. Some have called all homologous structures Jacobson's organ; thus the term would be applied to several isolated patches of sensory epithelium, forming part of the lining of the cavum nasi proprium and differently arranged in amphibians, turtles, and other reptiles, a very awkward usage. Other workers, with whom I agree, restrict the term to those cases in which the organ develops as a distinct medial outpocketing of the embryonic nasal pit and do not use it when describing turtles.

At least three other theories have been proposed. von Mihalkovics (1898) and von Navratil (1926) postulate that the duct of the medial nasal gland is homologous with Jacobson's organ. Although both these authors report that the duct is lined with sensory epithelium and innervated by a branch of the olfactory nerve, this has been denied by Zuckerkandl (1910a) and Parsons (1959a), and the theory is hence invalidated.

The second alternative is that of Peter (1906) and others who agree that the sensory areas of the intermediate region do not look like the Jacobson's organ of other forms and do not develop in the same way; they deny the presence of any Jacobson's organ in turtles.

Finally, Loew (1956) denies that all the sensory epithelium of the intermediate region is supplied by the medial branch of the olfactory nerve and thus considers only the medial sulcus to be the Jacobson's organ. His statement that the Jacobson's organ develops in the same manner as in other reptiles is in conflict with embryological findings (Parsons, 1959a).

Most other workers have refused to commit themselves on the presence or absence of a Jacobson's organ in turtles, but these problems remain of some importance in considering the phylogeny of reptiles. If, as I believe, the sensory epithelium of the intermediate region is the homolog of Jacobson's organ, then turtles possess a pattern of nasal anatomy radically different from that seen in all other amniotes; this would seem to imply a very early origin for the order Testudines, although secondary simplification is also possible. The problem has been discussed in greater detail in earlier papers (Parsons, 1959b, 1967).

Testudines show no trace of a lachrymal duct.

E

B. RHYNCHOCEPHALIA

1. *General*

Adult specimens of *Sphenodon* have rarely been available for dissection, and much of our knowledge of their gross nasal anatomy comes from immature specimens and very late embryonic stages. The most detailed study is that by Hoppe (1934); other original sources are Osawa (1898), Broom (1906), Fuchs (1908), Pratt (1948), and Bellairs and Boyd (1950). Göppert (1903) studied the palate. Major secondary references include those of Matthes (1934), Malan (1946), and Parsons (1959a). The following description and accompanying figures (Figs 12 and 13) are based entirely on these papers.

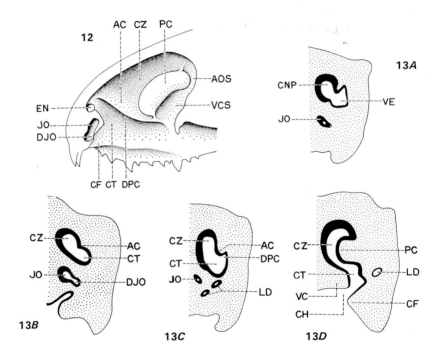

FIG. 12. Medial view of the lateral wall of the nasal cavity of *Sphenodon punctatus* (after Hoppe, 1934).

FIG. 13. Transverse sections through the nasal cavity of *Sphenodon punctatus* (after Broom, 1906, and Fuchs, 1908). A. Through the vestibulum. B. Through Jacobson's organ. C. Through the anterior concha. D. Through the posterior concha.

AC, Anterior concha; AOS, Antorbital space; CF, Choanal fold; CH, Choana; CNP, Cavum nasi proprium; CT, Choanal tube; CZ, Conchal zone; DJO, Duct of Jacobson's organ; DPC, Dorsal pocket of the choanal tube; EN, External naris; JO, Jacobson's organ; LD, Lachrymal duct; PC, Posterior concha; VC, Vomerine cushion; VCS, Ventral conchal space; VE, Vestibulum.

2. *Vestibulum*

The vestibulum (= anterior chamber, anterior nasal tube, Vorhof) is very short and runs almost directly medially from the external naris. Laterally it is roughly cylindrical, but medially it expands slightly so that the entire structure is somewhat mushroom-shaped. The cavum nasi proprium extends posteriorly from the medial half of the vestibulum; there is no clear boundary on the lateral wall, but medially a small postvestibular ridge is present. The ducts of two glands enter the vestibulum near its posterior end, that of the external nasal gland dorsally and that of the medial nasal gland ventrally.

3. *Cavum nasi proprium*

The cavum nasi proprium of *Sphenodon* is a relatively complex chamber containing two conchae; both are supported by simple lamellar projections of the nasal capsule and hence are not considered true conchae by de Beer (1937). The anterior concha (= part of concha, vordere Muschel) extends posteroventrally across the lateral wall of the cavum from a point just posterodorsal to the vestibulum. Its posterior end, which lies ventral to the center of the cavum, curves dorsally to meet the anterior end of the posterior concha (= concha, part of concha, hintere Muschel). The latter then extends posteriorly and dorsally nearly to the posterior end of the cavum. The anterior concha projects ventromedially into the cavum, while the posterior concha projects medially or dorsomedially with the free edge curling ventrally. The presence of two conchae was first noted by Hoppe (1934); most authors have reported but one, presumably either the posterior or the two together considered as one.

The various parts of the cavum nasi proprium are usually defined in terms of their relationships to the conchae. That portion ventral to the conchae is commonly termed the choanal tube (= Choanengang); this is not the same as a ductus choanalis, a term which refers to the nasopharyngeal duct, a structure not present in *Sphenodon*. The choanal tube extends dorsolaterally beneath the two conchae. Hoppe (1934) calls the extension under the anterior concha the dorsal pocket of the choanal tube (= dorsale Tasche des Choanenganges), and that under the posterior concha the ventral conchal space (= ventraler Muschelraum). The main portion of the choanal tube plus its dorsal pocket forms a rather widely open connection between the vestibulum and the choana; the ventral conchal space lies dorsal to the posterior end of the choana and not in the main respiratory channel.

Most of the cavum nasi proprium dorsal to the choanal tube is termed the conchal zone (= Muschelzone). The small part posterior to the posterior concha is generally recognized as a separate area, the antorbital space (= Antorbitalraum), but it is very small in *Sphenodon* and not really distinct from the conchal zone. The latter can be subdivided into a more or less vertical region lying medial to the posterior concha (= Stammteil) and a recess dorsolateral to the posterior concha (= Sakter, dorso-lateraler Muschelraum). There is no distinct boundary between these two regions.

The dorsal surface of the cavum nasi proprium, the lateral wall dorsal to the conchae, the dorsal surfaces of the conchae, and the dorsal half of the medial wall all bear sensory epithelium while the remaining areas, mainly the choanal tube and ventral portion of the antorbital space, are lined by respiratory (non-sensory) epithelium (Hoppe, 1934). Osawa (1898) stated that the entire medial wall and antorbital space bear sensory epithelium but his description otherwise agrees with that by Hoppe.

Sphenodon lacks a nasopharyngeal duct and the cavum nasi proprium opens directly into the oral cavity through the choana (= inner choana). Since there is no palatal fusion posterior to the premaxillae, the choanae are very long openings below the middle three-quarters (roughly) of the cavum. They are quite wide, but inconspicuous in palatal view. Anteriorly they appear to enter the oral cavity from the sides of the head, an appearance caused by the prominent choanal folds (= Choanenfalten, Gaumenfortsätze) which extend medially into the oral cavity along the ventral margins of the choanae. Between these folds and dorsal to them the base of the internasal wall forms a large, laterally projecting plate, the vomerine cushion (= Vomerpolster). Thus the ventral portion of the choanal tube extends ventrolaterally between the conchae and the vomerine cushion, and then ventromedially between the choanal fold and the vomerine cushion to enter the oral cavity.

4. *Jacobson's organ*

The Jacobson's organ (= vomeronasal organ) of *Sphenodon* is a moderately long tubular structure lying in the nasal septum beside the anteroventral portion of the choanal tube. It is longitudinally oriented and its posterior end lies slightly more dorsal than its anterior end. The mushroom body characteristic of the Squamata is lacking. Only the dorsal half of Jacobson's organ is lined with sensory epithelium.

In *Sphenodon* Jacobson's organ retains its presumably primitive association with the nasal cavity. It opens into the anteroventral corner of the choanal tube and is connected with both the oral and nasal cavities. The earlier workers (Osawa, 1898; Broom, 1906; Fuchs, 1908) stated that a very short duct leaves the lateral side of Jacobson's organ near its center and enters the medial surface of the choanal tube opposite and slightly anterior to the entry of the lachrymal duct. Hoppe (1934) described the anterior end of Jacobson's organ as curving laterally to enter the anterolateral wall of the choanal tube through a common opening with the lachrymal duct and ascribed the earlier reports to a reliance on transverse sections. However, Malan (1946), Pratt (1948), Bellairs and Boyd (1950) all support the earlier descriptions. In late embryos, some sectioned in the frontal plane, the duct of Jacobson's organ appears to leave from near the anterior end of the organ and to enter the choanal tube anteromedially, opposite and anterior to the opening of the lachrymal duct (Parsons, 1959a). Further study, probably including careful dissections of large specimens, appears desirable.

C. SQUAMATA

1. *General*

The Squamata are much the largest and most diversified order of Recent reptiles and, as might be expected, their nasal anatomy has been accorded most attention. However, many of the descriptions are very short and incomplete; a large number of the papers cited are descriptions of late stages in the development of the skull, and the nasal cavities are treated only in passing. Although many of the more important of these papers on skulls are included, the following list of previously described genera is not complete, though it includes most of the useful, original descriptions of squamate noses.

List of Previously Described Genera

Sauria

IGUANIDAE: *Anolis* (Nemours, 1930; Malan, 1946; Pratt, 1948; Stebbins, 1948; Bellairs and Boyd, 1950; Armstrong *et al.*, 1953; Stimie, 1966); *Callisaurus* (Stebbins, 1948); *Crotaphytus* (Stebbins, 1948); *Ctenosaura* (Stebbins, 1948; Oelrich, 1956); *Cyclura* (Matthes, 1934); *Dipsosaurus* (Stebbins, 1948); *Iguana* (Solger, 1876; Malan, 1946; Pratt, 1948; Stebbins, 1948); *Leiosaurus* (Born, 1879); *Liolaemus* (Born, 1879); *Phrynosoma* (Malan, 1946; Stebbins, 1948); *Sauromalus* (Stebbins, 1948); *Sceloporus* (Born, 1879; Malan, 1946; Stebbins, 1948); *Tropidurus* (Solger, 1876); *Uma* (Stebbins, 1943; Stebbins, 1948); *Uta* (Malan, 1946; Stebbins, 1948).

AGAMIDAE: *Agama* (Malan, 1946; Pratt, 1948; Bellairs and Boyd, 1950; Barry, 1953; Eyal-Giladi, 1964); *Amphibolurus* (Born, 1879; Pratt, 1948); *Calotes* (Göppert, 1903; Eckart, 1922; Pratt, 1948); *Ceratophora* (Eckart, 1922); *Cophotis* (Eckart, 1922); *Draco* (Born, 1879); *Otocryptis* (Eckart, 1922); *Physignathus* (Pratt, 1948); *Uromastix* (Gegenbaur, 1873).

CHAMAELEONIDAE: *Chamaeleo* (Solger, 1876; Born, 1879; Zuckerkandl, 1910a; Haas, 1937; Malan, 1946; Haas, 1947; Pratt, 1948; Bellairs and Boyd, 1950); *Microsaura* (Malan, 1946; Engelbrecht, 1951); *Rhampholeon* (Frank, 1951).

GEKKONIDAE: *Coleonyx* (Pratt, 1948; Stebbins, 1948); *Gehyra* (Born, 1879); *Gekko* (Seydel, 1899; Beecker, 1903; Göppert, 1903); *Hemidactylus* (Pratt, 1948; Bellairs and Boyd, 1950); *Hoplodactylus* (Pratt,

1948); *Lepidodactylus* (Born, 1879); *Lygodactylus* (Pratt, 1948); *Oedura* (Webb, 1951); *Pachydactylus* (Malan, 1946); *Palmatogecko* (Webb, 1951); *Phyllodactylus* (Stebbins, 1948); *Stenodactylus* (Pratt, 1948); *Tarentola* (Born, 1879; Hafferl, 1921).

PYGOPODIDAE: *Aprasia* (Underwood, 1957); *Lialis* (Pratt, 1948; Bellairs and Boyd, 1950).

XANTUSIIDAE: *Xantusia* (Malan, 1946; Stebbins, 1948; Bellairs and Boyd, 1950).

TEIIDAE: *Ameiva* (Solger, 1876; Pratt, 1948); *Cnemidophorus* (Göppert, 1903; Malan, 1946; Stebbins, 1948); *Teius* (Malan, 1946); *Tupinambis* (Pratt, 1948; Bellairs and Boyd, 1950).

SCINCIDAE: *Ablepharus* (Born, 1879; Malan, 1946); *Acontias* (Malan, 1946); *Chalcides* (Born, 1879; Pratt, 1948); *Dasia* (Born, 1879); *Emoia* (Born, 1879); *Eumeces* (Stebbins, 1948); *Lygosoma* (Born, 1879); *Mabuya* (Göppert, 1903; Malan, 1946; Pratt, 1948; Bellairs and Boyd, 1950); *Nessia* (Pratt, 1948); *Scelotes* (Malan, 1946); *Scincus* (Born, 1879); *Sphenomorphus* (Born, 1879); *Tiliqua* (Pratt, 1948).

LACERTIDAE: *Lacerta* (Leydig, 1872a; Gegenbaur, 1873; Born, 1879; von Mihalkovics, 1898; Beecker, 1903; Göppert, 1903; Fuchs, 1908; Krause, 1922; von Navratil, 1926; Pratt, 1948; Bellairs and Boyd, 1950).

CORDYLIDAE: *Cordylus* (Malan, 1946); *Gerrhosaurus* (Malan, 1946; Pratt, 1948); *Platysaurus* (Malan, 1946).

ANGUIDAE: *Anguis* (Leydig, 1872a; Seydel, 1899; Broman, 1920; von Navratil, 1926; Pratt, 1948; Bellairs and Boyd, 1950; Negus, 1958); *Gerrhonotus* (Stebbins, 1948); *Ophisaurus* (Solger, 1876; Malan, 1946; Pratt, 1948).

ANNIELLIDAE: *Anniella* (Malan, 1946; Stebbins, 1948; Bellairs, 1949b; Toerien, 1950).

VARANIDAE: *Varanus* (Born, 1879; Malan, 1946; Pratt, 1948; Bellairs, 1949a; Bellairs and Boyd, 1950; Shrivastava, 1963).

Amphisbaenia

AMPHISBAENIDAE: *Amphisbaena* (Fischer, 1900; Göppert, 1903; Pratt, 1948; Bellairs and Boyd, 1950); *Monopeltis* (Malan, 1946); *Rhineura* (Bellairs and Boyd, 1950).

TROGONOPHIDAE: *Trogonophis* (Fischer, 1900; Pratt, 1948; Bellairs and Boyd, 1950).

Serpentes

TYPHLOPIDAE: *Anomalepis* (Haas, 1968); *Liotyphlops* (Haas, 1964); *Typhlops* (Zuckerkandl, 1910a; Bellairs and Boyd, 1950).

LEPTOTYPHLOPIDAE: *Leptotyphlops* (Haas, 1959).

UROPELTIDAE: *Rhinophis* (Baumeister, 1908).

ANILIIDAE: *Xenopeltis* (Bellairs, 1949a).

BOIDAE: *Constrictor* (Gegenbaur, 1873); *Eryx* (Bellairs and Boyd, 1950); *Python* (Solger, 1876; Dieulafé, 1904–1905; Matthes, 1934).

COLUBRIDAE: *Acrochordus* (Kathariner, 1900); *Cerberus* (Kathariner, 1900); *Coronella* (Leydig, 1872b); *Dasypeltis* (Pringle, 1954); *Drymarchon* (Parsons, 1959a); *Elaphe* (Nemours, 1930); *Enhydris* (Kathariner, 1900); *Homalopsis* (Kathariner, 1900); *Lamprophis* (Pringle, 1954); *Natrix* (Leydig, 1872b; Solger, 1876; Born, 1883; von Mihalkovics, 1898; Kathariner, 1900; Beecker, 1903; Göppert, 1903; Thäter, 1910; Broman, 1920; von Navratil, 1926); *Storeria* (Parsons, 1959a); *Thamnophis* (Macallum, 1883).

ELAPIDAE: *Hemachatus* (Pringle, 1954).

HYDROPHIIDAE: *Hydrophis* (Kathariner, 1900); *Laticauda* (Kathariner, 1900); *Pelamis* (Kathariner, 1900).

VIPERIDAE: *Causus* (Pringle, 1954; Sülter, 1962); *Crotalus* (Solger, 1876; Parsons, 1959a); *Vipera* (Solger, 1876; Peyer, 1912; Bellairs, 1942; Bellairs and Boyd, 1950).

A large number and variety of lizards and amphisbaenians were studied by Malan (1946), Pratt (1948), Stebbins (1948), and Bellairs and Boyd (1950); these are the basic references for any work on lacertilian nasal anatomy. The snakes have not been as well studied, but the papers of Bellairs (1942 and 1949a), Bellairs and Boyd (1950), and Parsons (1959a) are the most convenient starting points for further work.

As usual there are problems of terminology, both taxonomic and anatomical. When possible I have translated the name used by the original describer into the currently accepted version, although the old name is frequently cited as well. Even if the correct modern name was assigned, there remains the possibility that the specimen was misidentified in the first place. Hence conclusions based primarily or entirely on the older papers may be accepted only with reservations. I have tried to give most of the anatomical synonyms, but others could certainly be added. In the descriptions, the terms larger and smaller are relative, and refer to a standard head size.

For this study I dissected a single specimen of *Epicrates striatus* and two each of *Iguana iguana* and *Heterodon platyrhinos*.

2. *Vestibulum*

The vestibulum (= anterior chamber, anterior and respiratory chambers, anterior nasal tube, anterior nasal tube and anterior chamber, atrium, äussere Nasenhöhle, Nasenvorhof, Nasenvorhöhle, vestibulum and Mittelraum, Vorhöhle) is variable and often complex in squamates. It is always a more or less tubular connection between the external naris (= apertura narium externa, äussere Nasenloch, äussere Nasenöffnung) and the cavum nasi proprium, but varies greatly in length and course. The vestibulum is shown in Figs 14 through 22.

In most squamates the external naris is lateral rather than terminal on the snout and hence enters the lateral side of the vestibulum. However, in certain aquatic snakes, such as *Acrochordus* and *Cerberus*, the external naris is dorsal and the vestibulum runs ventrally to reach the cavum nasi proprium (Fig. 22); in some amphisbaenians such as *Monopeltis* (Malan, 1946), *Leposternon*, *Rhineura*, and *Tomuropeltis* (Gans, *pers. comm.*), the external naris is ventral, and the vestibulum thus extends dorsally. The nares of some species of *Typhlops* are directed ventrally; those of *Lanthanotus* are directed dorsally. In many squamates the vestibulum runs anteriorly from

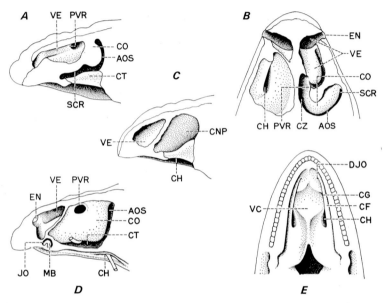

Fig. 14. Nasal cavities of *Iguana iguana*. A. Superficial lateral dissection. B. Deeper lateral dissection. C. Medial view of the lateral wall of the nasal cavity. D. Dorsal view of the nasal cavities; the concha is removed on the left side. E. Ventral view of the palate.
AOS, Antorbital space; CF, Choanal fold; CG, Choanal groove; CH, Choana; CNP, Cavum nasi proprium; CO, Concha; CT, Choanal tube; CZ, Conchal zone; DJO, Duct of Jacobson's organ; EN, External naris; JO, Jacobson's organ; MB, Mushroom body; PVR, Postvestibular ridge; SCR, Subconchal recess; VC, Vomerine cushion; VE, Vestibulum.

the external naris before turning posteriorly towards the cavum; such a course probably helps to prevent sand and other debris from becoming lodged within the nose (see below).

All snakes, as far as is known, have a very short and simple vestibulum, except for that of *Laticauda*, which contains folds. It may, as in *Python*, run directly medially or, more commonly as in *Heterodon* and *Crotalus*, anteromedially to enter the cavum. In aquatic forms with dorsally placed external nares, it runs ventrally. The vestibulum is frequently separated from the

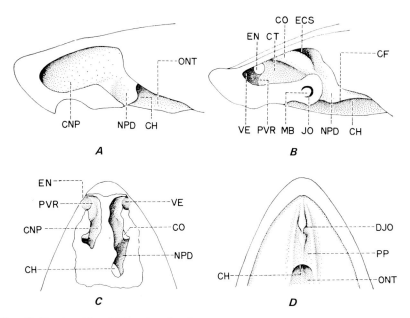

FIG. 15. Nasal cavities of *Heterodon platyrhinos*. A. Lateral view of the medial wall of the nasal cavity. B. Medial view of the lateral wall of the nasal cavity. C. Dorsal view of the nasal cavities; the dissection on the right side is deeper. D. Ventral view of the palate.
CF, Choanal fold; CH, Choana; CNP, Cavum nasi proprium; CO Concha; CT, Choanal tube; DJO, Duct of Jacobson's organ; ECS, Extraconchal space; EN, External naris; JO, Jacobson's organ; MB, Mushroom body; NPD, Nasopharyngeal duct; ONT, Orbitonasal trough; PP, Primary palate; PVR, Postvestibular ridge; VE, Vestibulum.

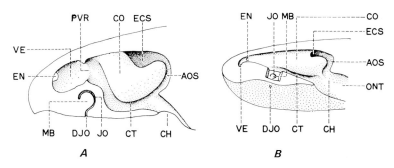

FIG. 16. Medial views of the lateral walls of the nasal cavities of squamates. A. *Lacerta viridis* (after Leydig, 1872a). B. *Python sebae* (after Matthes, 1934).
AOS, Antorbital space; CH, Choana; CO, Concha; CT, Choanal tube; DJO, Duct of Jacobson's organ; ECS, Extraconchal space; EN, External naris; JO, Jacobson's organ; MB, Mushroom body; ONT, Orbitonasal trough; PVR, Postvestibular ridge; VE, Vestibulum.

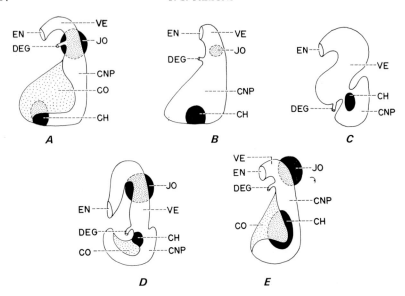

FIG. 17. Diagrams of the nasal cavities of squamates in dorsal view (after Pratt, 1948). A. *Hoplodactylus pacificus*. B. *Anolis roquet*. C. *Chamaeleo "calcaratus"*. D. *Varanus bengalensis*. E. *Amphisbaena alba*.
CH, Choana; CNP, Cavum nasi proprium; CO, Concha; DEG, Duct of the external nasal gland; EN, External naris; JO, Jacobson's organ; VE, Vestibulum.

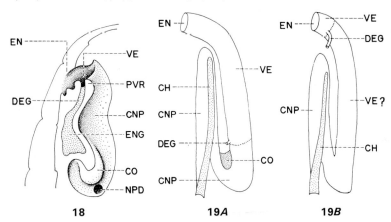

FIG. 18. Dorsal view of the nasal cavity of *Natrix maura* (after Kathariner, 1900).

FIG. 19. Diagrams of the nasal cavities of agamids in dorsal view (after Eckart, 1922). The dotted line marks the boundary between the stratified squamous (vestibular) epithelium and the columnar (caval) epithelium. A. *Calotes versicolor*. B. *Otocryptis wiegmannii*.

CH, Choana; CNP, Cavum nasi proprium; CO, Concha; DEG, Duct of the external nasal gland; EN, External naris; ENG, External nasal gland; NPD, Nasopharyngeal duct; PVR, Postvestibular ridge; VE, Vestibulum.

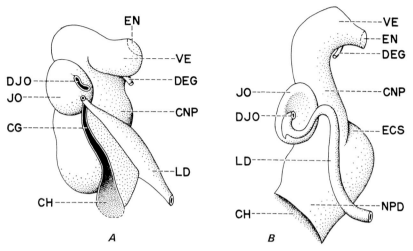

FIG. 20. Ventral views of the nasal cavities of squamates (after Bellairs and Boyd, 1950). A. *Anguis fragilis*. B. *Eryx conicus*.
CG, Choanal groove; CH, Choana; CNP, Cavum nasi proprium; DEG, Duct of the external nasal gland; DJO, Duct of Jacobson's organ; ECS, Extraconchal space; EN, External naris; JO, Jacobson's organ; LD, Lachrymal duct; NPD, Nasopharyngeal duct; VE, Vestibulum.

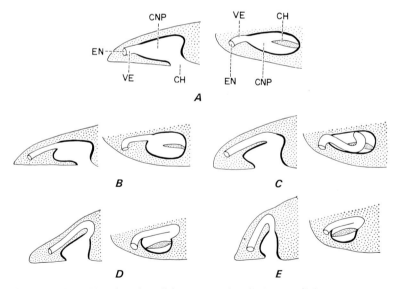

FIG. 21. Nasal cavities of lizards to show different types of vestibula (after Stebbins, 1948). Diagrammatic lateral views (to the left) and dorsal views (to the right) showing a possible sequence of types, not a phylogenetic series, leading to the "*Uma*-type" of iguanids. A. *Gerrhonotus*. B. *Coleonyx*. C. *Dipsosaurus*. D. *Callisaurus*. E. *Phrynosoma*.
CH, Choana; CNP, Cavum nasi proprium; EN, External naris; VE, Vestibulum.

cavum by a postvestibular ridge (= pseudoconcha, separating fold, Vorhofs-muschel). Kathariner (1900) found this ridge to encircle completely the inner end of the vestibulum in several aquatic snakes such as *Natrix maura* (his *Tropidonotus viperinus*), but in other forms (*e.g.*, *Crotalus*) it appears to be present only on the posterolateral portion of the border. In *Heterodon* I could see no ridge, and the vestibulum and cavum are not grossly separable. The vestibulum is lined by stratified squamous epithelium and receives the duct of the external nasal gland. The point of entrance of this duct varies; commonly it enters the posterolateral margin of the vestibulum, but in *Rhinophis* it enters anteromedially (Baumeister, 1908) and in *Xenopeltis* ventrally (Bellairs, 1949a).

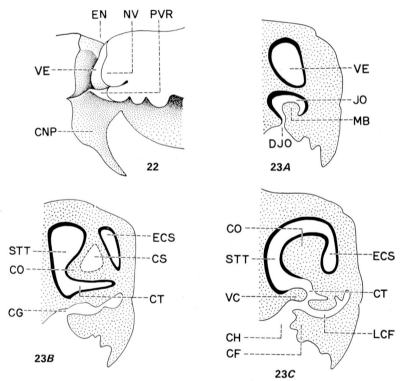

FIG. 22. Medial view of the lateral wall of the anterior part of the nasal cavity of *Cerberus rhynchops* (after Kathariner, 1900), showing the ventral fold in the cavum nasi proprium.

FIG. 23. Transverse sections through the nasal cavity of *Lacerta agilis* (after Beecker, 1903). A. Through the vestibulum and Jacobson's organ. B. Through the concha. C. Through the choana.

CF, Choanal fold; CG, Choanal groove; CH, Choana; CNP, Cavum nasi proprium; CO, Concha; CS, Conchal space; CT, Choanal tube; DJO, Duct of Jacobson's organ; ECS, Extraconchal space; EN, External naris; JO, Jacobson's organ; LCF, Lateral choanal fissure; MB, Mushroom body; NV, Nasal valve; PVR, Postvestibular ridge; STT, Stammteil; VC, Vomerine cushion; VE, Vestibulum.

In most lizards the postvestibular ridges are well developed, frequently encircling the opening from the vestibulum into the cavum. As in snakes the vestibulum is lined by stratified squamous epithelium and receives the duct of the external nasal gland. In most cases the duct enters the postero-lateral portion of the vestibulum. In amphisbaenians it enters ventrally, ventrolaterally in *Amphisbaena* and *Trogonophis* (Fischer, 1900) and ventro-medially in *Monopeltis* (Kritzinger, 1946). The major variation is in the length and degree of development of the vestibulum.

The simplest pattern, and quite probably the most primitive, is that seen in most leptoglossans plus a variety of other forms including *Lialis* (Pygopo-didae), *Gerrhonotus* (Anguidae), and *Amphisbaena* (Amphisbaenidae). The vestibulum is a relatively short and small chamber which extends medially or anteromedially from the external naris and then turns posteriorly (Fig. 16A). Its posterior end joins the anterior end of the cavum nasi proprium. The vestibulum is thus J- or L-shaped in dorsal view. Some workers have used different names for the parts of the vestibulum, terming the first, more or less transverse portion the anterior chamber, anterior nasal tube, or vesti-bulum, and the second, longitudinal portion the respiratory chamber, anterior chamber, or Mittelraum.

There are numerous relatively minor variations on this pattern. Many scincids have exceptionally short vestibula. In the gekkonids *Coleonyx* and *Phyllodactylus*, the vestibulum is slightly longer, but is still shorter than the cavum nasi proprium and not otherwise modified. Usually the vestibulum is circular or oval in transverse section, but in *Cnemidophorus* its dorsal end extends laterally so that it appears T-shaped in section. Another variant is the presence of a small ventral diverticulum or blind sac of the vestibulum. In anguids Malan (1946, p. 119) described it as "a large blind sac leading from the posterior wall of the external nares and lying beneath the anterior part of the true nasal cavity and lateral to the organ of Jacobson" (see Fig. 20A). Stebbins (1948) did not find such a diverticulum in *Gerrhonotus* or *Anniella* although Toerien (1950) described and figured a small one in the latter genus. Bellairs and Boyd (1950) figured, but did not mention, an apparently similar structure in *Rhineura*.

In four families of lizards the vestibulum is greatly enlarged. *Varanus* (Varanidae) possesses an extremely elongate vestibulum which runs a con-siderable distance anteromedially from the external naris before turning posteriorly to enter the cavum nasi proprium (Fig. 17D); it is thus U-shaped in dorsal view. Although the vestibulum is at least twice the length of the cavum, the pattern is otherwise quite similar to that in the groups previously described. Malan (1946) and Shrivastava (1963) described a ventral diverti-culum of the vestibulum, but Bellairs (1949a) did not mention or figure it.

In the Chamaeleonidae the vestibulum is elongate and, in most cases, very large in diameter, while the cavum nasi proprium is reduced (Fig. 17C). There is some variation between the different genera and among the species of *Chamaeleo* (Haas, 1937; Malan, 1946; Pratt, 1948; Engelbrecht, 1951; Frank, 1951), but all possess a greatly enlarged vestibulum, the posterior end of which lies dorsolateral to the cavum. The connection between these chambers is thus through the ventromedial surface of the vestibulum and dorsolateral surface of the cavum.

The complex vestibulum of the Iguanidae has been studied in detail by Stebbins (1943 and 1948) who, in his later paper, described three patterns found in this family (Figs 14 and 21). The *"Dipsosaurus*-type" of nasal structure occurs in *Crotaphytus*, *Ctenosaura*, *Dipsosaurus*, *Iguana*, and *Sauromalus*, and apparently also in *Cyclura*, *Leiosaurus*, and *Liolaemus* if earlier descriptions are correct. The vestibulum is elongate and extends posteriorly dorsolateral to the anterior half or more of the cavum nasi proprium. Near the posterior end of the vestibulum there is a relatively narrow opening directed medially or ventromedially into the cavum. In some forms, such as *Dipsosaurus*, the vestibulum is S-shaped, going dorsomedially from the external naris, then posterolaterally, and finally dorsomedially to reach the cavum. In other forms, such as *Iguana*, the vestibulum extends medially from the external naris and then turns posteriorly; it is L-shaped in dorsal view. *Iguana* also has a prominent ridge along the ventromedial surface of the vestibulum.

The *"Uma*-type" pattern occurs in *Callisaurus*, *Holbrookia*, *Phrynosoma*, *Sceloporus*, *Uma*, and *Uta*. In these genera the vestibulum extends postero-dorsally and slightly medially from the external naris as a long, relatively straight tube. It then curves anteroventrally and slightly laterally to enter the posterodorsal corner of the cavum nasi proprium. The latter lies ventro-lateral to the long first portion of the vestibulum. In *Phrynosoma* the snout is extremely short and the vestibulum extends almost directly dorsally at first and then turns ventrally to reach the cavum.

The *"Anolis*-type" pattern is known only in *Anolis*. In this genus the entire nasal apparatus is reduced and the vestibulum is relatively short, extending medially from the external naris and then posteriorly to enter the anterior end of the cavum nasi proprium. Although *Anolis* thus possesses a vestibulum essentially like that of *Lacerta* and many other lizards, it seems probable that it is not primitive but rather represents a reduction and simplification of the *"Dipsosaurus*-type" which is found in most iguanids.

In the Agamidae the problem of defining the vestibulum becomes acute, and the homologies of its various parts cannot at present be determined. Only the papers of Eckart (1922) and Pratt (1948) give enough detail on the critical points, and they are followed here. The gross morphology appears quite similar in all agamids. The vestibulum extends medially from the external naris and then turns posteriorly as a long duct-like structure which, near its posterior end, opens ventrolaterally into the posterodorsal part of the cavum nasi proprium. The general pattern thus resembles that seen in iguanids, being intermediate between the "*Dipsosaurus*-type" and the "*Uma*-type".

Consideration of the point of entrance of the duct of the external nasal gland and of the boundary between stratified squamous and columnar sensory epithelia unfortunately complicates the issue (Fig. 19). In *Calotes* (Eckart, 1922; his figures illustrating these points are mislabelled, and apparently Pratt, 1948, did not realize this) and *Agama*, *Amphibolurus*, and *Physignathus* (Pratt) the duct of the external nasal gland enters the nasal cavity near the posterior end of the vestibulum (as defined by gross structure) and the boundary between the different epithelial types appears to be in the same area; these genera thus resemble the iguanids. However, in *Cophotis* (Eckart) the epithelial boundary occurs at approximately the mid-point of the tubular "vestibulum" and the duct of the gland enters its anterior third. In *Ceratophora* and *Otocryptis* (Eckart) both the epithelial boundary and the entrance of the duct are very close to the anterior end of the "vestibulum". The constancy of the gross pattern would suggest that this is the stable feature and should be followed in defining homologies; the correlation between the positions of the epithelial boundary and point of entrance of the glandular duct suggests the reverse.

The vestibulum seems to keep foreign substances such as sand grains or water from entering into the nasal cavity. The elongation and complication of the iguanid vestibulum is closely related to this function (Stebbins, 1943 and 1948). That portion of the vestibulum just inside the external naris frequently extends somewhat dorsally; thus sand particles entering the nose will tend to be restricted to the very beginning of the vestibulum by gravity and may easily be blown out at exhalation. This system would appear to be most efficient in *Phrynosoma* which spends much of its time half buried in the sand. The vestibular epithelium is apparently capable of hyperplasia in *Anguis* (Pratt, 1948); soil particles become trapped in the cellular debris and secretions of the external nasal gland, and the whole mass may be expelled by a sudden exhalation.

Nearly all squamates have a layer of cavernous erectile tissue surrounding the vestibulum and in many forms this may act as a valve to close the external naris. Leydig (1872a) first described this erectile tissue and stated that, in *Lacerta*, it contained some elastic fibers but no muscles. Almost all later workers have reported the presence of smooth muscle fibers radially arranged around the vestibulum. Despite passing mention in many descriptions of the nose, detailed accounts of the cavernous tissue and its action are not common (Bruner, 1907; Kathariner, 1900; Stebbins, 1948). Bruner described the veins of the head and considered the effects of changes in the venous blood pressure. He noted that the swelling of the cavernous tissue can completely close the external naris in *Phrynosoma* but not in *Lacerta*. In both *Lacerta* and *Natrix* the vestibulum is surrounded by a venous plexus, but the drainage from this plexus is quite different in the two forms.

The variation in this erectile tissue has been described in a series of lizards (Stebbins, 1948). However, too few forms are known in enough detail to say more than that the amounts and positions of thickened areas of the tissue vary greatly. In some forms a greatly thickened area adjacent to the external naris can presumably act as a nasal valve closing the naris. This occurs in *Gerrhonotus*, *Anniella*, and *Uma* and similar iguanids, but not in *Coleonyx*, *Phyllodactylus*, *Xantusia*, and other iguanids. The nasal valve is commonly at the posterior margin of the external naris. A valve similar to that in lizards has been reported in various aquatic snakes, but the position of this valve is quite variable (Kathariner, 1900). It lies posteriorly in *Cerberus* (Fig. 22) and *Natrix*, ventrally in *Enhydris* and *Pelamis*, and anteriorly in *Laticauda*. There are apparently no detailed descriptions of the valve in any terrestrial snakes, but its presence, at least in sand inhabiting forms, would seem quite probable.

A longitudinal, subnasal smooth muscle has been described in snakes (Lapage, 1928). It is probably associated with the opening and closing of the vestibulum, but its action is unknown although it has been implied that it is a dilator of the vestibulum. Malan (1946) studied similar smooth muscles in a series of lizards and found them to run between various points on the nasal capsule around the margin of the vestibulum; she thus believed the muscle to be a constrictor of the external naris. Dilator fibers within the cavernous tissue oppose the action of the more superficial constrictor muscles and force blood out of the sinuses of the cavernous tissue.

3. *Cavum nasi proprium*

The cavum nasi proprium (= eigentliche Nasenhöhle, Nasenhaupthöhle, olfactory chamber, posterior nasal chamber, primary nasal chamber, principal cavity, true nasal cavity) of squamates is basically rather simple. Typically there is a single concha (= cornet, Muschel, muschelförmige Wulst, Muschelwulst, pseudoconcha, turbinal) projecting into the cavum from the lateral wall of a simple cavity; in some forms this concha is lost. The subdivisions of the cavum are defined on the basis of their relationships to the concha. Since the concha varies greatly in size, shape, and place of attachment, these subdivisions cannot be recognized in all forms and are probably not strictly comparable in all cases. Figures 14 to 21 and 23 to 27 show the cava of various squamates.

Most of the parts of the cavum can be seen in a relatively simple form such as *Lacerta* (Figs 16A and 23). As in *Sphenodon* the cavum is divided into three main zones. The region anterior and ventral to the concha is the choanal tube (= Choanengang, ductus respiratorius, lower nasal chamber) which leads from the vestibulum to the nasopharyngeal duct (if present) or the choana. In some forms in which the concha is attached far dorsally, or in which the free margin of the concha is curled ventrally or ventrolaterally, there is a subconchal recess (= Aulax, lateral recess of the nasal sac, recessus intraconchale) off the choanal tube lying ventral or ventrolateral to the concha; *Lacerta* lacks this recess. The part of the cavum posterodorsal to the choanal tube is divided into the conchal zone (= Muschelzone, olfactory chamber) beside the concha and the antorbital space (= Antorbitalraum) posterior to it. The conchal zone is further divided into a more or less vertical Stammteil (= ductus olfactorius) lying medial to the concha and an extraconchal space (= cavum extraconchale, dorsal conchal zone, lateral recess, Sakter, seitlicher Nebenraum, sinus maxillaris, upper nasal chamber) lying dorsal and dorsolateral to the concha.

The vestibulum is most complicated in the Varanidae, Chamaeleonidae, Iguanidae, and Agamidae, and these forms also have the most complex cavum nasi proprium. All the others, as far as is known, resemble *Lacerta*. Two types of epithelium line the cavum. Non-sensory respiratory epithelium lies ventrally and lines mainly the choanal tube, while sensory olfactory epithelium lies dorsally and lines mainly the conchal zone. The exact position of the boundary between these epithelial types is known in but few forms and thus detailed comparisons are still impossible.

In lacertids (Figs 16A and 23) the concha is well developed, but the cavum remains a rather widely open cavity. The concha is attached ventrolaterally and projects freely into the cavum for but a short distance posterior to its attachment; hence the extraconchal space is large and the subconchal recess absent. In transverse section the concha appears narrow at its attachment to the caval wall; distally it widens and becomes nearly circular. A large conchal space (= cavum conchale) contains the external nasal gland.

The cavum of gekkonids (Figs 17A and 16) is relatively wide and low. In some forms the vestibulum is elongate and partially overlies the cavum, opening into it from the dorsomedial side, but in most of the genera studied the general pattern is similar to that in *Lacerta* except for the shape of the concha. In gekkonids it is a very thin plate, attaching to the ventrolateral caval wall and extending dorsomedially. Its free margin curls ventrally and ventrolaterally. Thus both the extraconchal space and the subconchal recess are well formed. The various descriptions differ slightly, but the concha appears, in most cases at least, to be supported almost entirely by a simple lamella of cartilage although there is a small conchal space anteriorly near its base.

The nasal anatomy of pygopodids is poorly known. The cavum nasi proprium of *Lialis* "is not strongly developed, though elongated and of normal sensory function" (Pratt, 1948, p. 182) and diagrams show a fairly large concha. Figures of *Aprasia* (Underwood, 1957) also show a well developed concha.

Xantusia (Xantusiidae) appears to resemble *Lacerta* in the structure of the cavum although its concha seems somewhat larger. Malan (1946) commented on its resemblance to gekkonids, and Stebbins (1948) stressed the similarities to scincids.

The cavum nasi proprium of teiids is reported to resemble that of *Lacerta* (Malan, 1946; Pratt, 1948). However, Malan figured the concha of *Teius* as attaching to the dorsolateral rather than the ventrolateral wall of the cavum. The concha and conchal space, the latter containing the external nasal gland, are well developed and large. The concha of *Cnemidophorus* is very large, nearly filling the cavum (Stebbins, 1948). It is attached in the normal fashion to the ventrolateral caval wall. However, this attachment continues posteriorly around the concha and "is continuous with a membranous lamella that connects the ventromedial surface of the concha with the basal portion of the nasal septum" (Stebbins, 1948, p. 199; Fig. 27). Thus, the choanal tube forms a fairly simple duct-like connection between the vestibulum and the choana. It is completely separated, except at its anterior end, from the conchal zone and antorbital space. These two regions form a large blind sac lying above the concha which bulges dorsally into them. No other lizard has been described with the concha attached to the septum and with the dorsal parts of the cavum isolated as a blind sac.

The Scincidae are a large and apparently composite family and have been much studied. In all cases the cavum nasi proprium appears quite similar to that of *Lacerta*. The concha is large and normally contains a well developed conchal space, although the concha is, in some forms, supported for part of its length only by a simple lamella of cartilage as in gekkonids (Malan, 1946). In forms possessing a very short vestibulum, this may enter the cavum anterolaterally rather than anteriorly. In *Eumeces* (Stebbins, 1948) the entire cavum is somewhat flattened dorsoventrally and the cartilage within the concha has lateral thickenings. Such a flattening has not been reported in other forms.

Cordylids resemble scincids and *Lacerta* in their nasal anatomy but few details or figures of these forms are available (Malan, 1946; Pratt, 1948). Malan noted that the conchal space is small in some cordylids.

In anguids (Fig. 20A) the concha is apparently slightly larger, but usually flatter, than in *Lacerta*. The conchal space is greatly reduced and much of the concha is supported by a simple lamella of cartilage. Correlated with the reduction in the development of the conchal space is a reduction in the size of the external nasal gland. The concha is attached to the lateral or dorso-lateral wall of the cavum nasi proprium and extends medially or ventro-medially. Its free margin is rolled ventrally or ventrolaterally so that the subconchal recess is well formed. Malan (1946) and Pratt (1948) interpreted this recess as a diverticulum of the nasal cavity pushing into the conchal space through the very incomplete floor of that space. The subconchal recess is lined by sensory epithelium in *Ophisaurus* (Malan, 1946), but by respiratory epithelium in *Anguis* (Pratt, 1948). Because of the dorsally placed attach-ment of the concha, there is no extraconchal space.

Anniella (Anniellidae) was described by Stebbins (1948) as being very similar to the anguid *Gerrhonotus*, with the concha attached to the dorso-lateral caval wall and a greatly reduced conchal space; most of the relatively large external nasal gland lies lateral to the nasal capsule. Malan (1946) was interested largely in the cartilaginous nasal capsule and was probably referring primarily to that when commenting that the two families are quite different, as the nasal cavity of *Anniella* does resemble that of anguids.

Although *Varanus* (Varanidae) has a greatly elongated vestibulum, the cavum nasi proprium is quite well developed (Fig. 17D). It is relatively small and short. The vestibulum enters the anterior end of the cavum, and the choana lies ventral to its center. The concha is moderately large, has a conchal space containing the external nasal gland, and is attached dorso-laterally. There is no extraconchal space, but the subconchal recess is very large, the exact size and shape showing specific variation. The lateral wall of the concha may send a medial projection into this recess. Much of the sub-conchal recess, which is continuous with the choanal tube posteroventrally and with the large antorbital space posteriorly, lies outside of the cartila-ginous nasal capsule; such an extracapsular extension is, as far as I am aware, unique among squamates. The two pairs of lachrymal ducts of *Varanus* (see the section on the nasopharyngeal duct below) are also peculiar; one duct enters each choanal tube quite far dorsally, just ventral to the anterior part of the concha.

In chamaeleonids (Fig. 17C) the structure of the cavum nasi proprium varies considerably in details, but in all it is the most greatly reduced of any reptiles and has very little if any sensory epithelium. The vestibulum usually enters the cavum either dorsally or dorsolaterally, and the cavum is a simple cavity leading to the choana. A concha is lacking, although Haas (1937) has postulated that the postvestibular ridge is its homolog, and hence the various regions of the cavum cannot be recognized. The air can generally pass in a straight line from the vestibulum to the oral cavity.

Iguanids (Figs 14, 17B, 21 and 24) are variable. Forms of the "*Dipsosaurus*-type" (Stebbins, 1948; see the section on the vestibulum above), such as *Iguana*, have the most complex cavum nasi proprium. A very large concha is attached to the dorsolateral caval wall and nearly fills the cavum, and a well developed conchal space contains the external nasal gland. The opening from the vestibulum lies dorsolaterally, at the top of the concha and directly dorsal to the more lateral opening to the choana. The extraconchal space is lacking, but the subconchal recess is very large, extending far dorsally lateral to the posterior half of the concha and communicating throughout its height

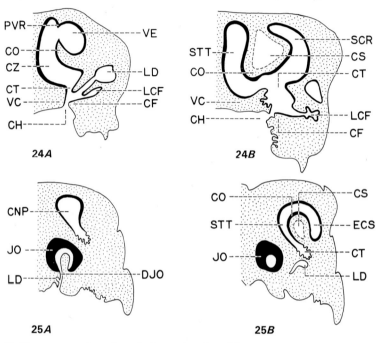

FIG. 24. Transverse sections through the nasal cavity of *Iguana iguana* (after Malan, 1946). A. Through the anterior part of the cavum nasi proprium. B. Through the posterior part of the cavum nasi proprium.

FIG. 25. Transverse sections through the nasal cavity of *Thamnophis sirtalis* (after Macallum, 1883). A. Through Jacobson's organ. B. Through the concha.

CF, Choanal fold; CH, Choana; CNP, Cavum nasi proprium; CO, Concha; CS, Conchal space; CT, Choanal tube; CZ, Conchal zone; DJO, Duct of Jacobson's organ; ECS, Extraconchal space; JO, Jacobson's organ; LCF, Lateral choanal fissure; LD, Lachrymal duct; PVR, Postvestibular ridge; SCR, Subconchal recess; STT, Stammteil; VC, Vomerine cushion; VE, Vestibulum.

with the high but very short antobital space. The cavum projects well anterior to its connection with the vestibulum, lying ventromedial to the latter. In some forms with this type of nasal structure, especially those in which the vestibulum is more S-shaped, the concha is not as large as in *Iguana*, but its general structure is similar.

Iguanids of the "*Uma*-type" and the "*Anolis*-type" lack a concha. A slight bulge in the roof of the cavum nasi proprium of *Uma* (Stebbins, 1948) may well represent the concha, but it is very small and poorly developed. In this genus, and similar forms, the cavum is a small oval cavity connecting the vestibulum to the choana. Sensory epithelium is reduced, and no subdivisions of the cavum can be recognized. The vestibulum connects with the posterodorsal (dorsal in *Phrynosoma*) portion of the cavum, and the choana is ventral. *Anolis* possesses a very simple cavum. The vestibulum opens into its anterior part, while the oral connection is well posterior. The cavum is rather depressed and lacks a concha.

Agamids (Fig. 19) also possess a much reduced and simplified cavum nasi proprium (the cavum defined on gross features; see discussion above in the section on the vestibulum). The vestibulum enters the cavum dorsolaterally at or near the posterior end of the latter and the large choana extends for most or all of the length of the caval floor. A very small, dorsally attached concha lies just anterior to the connection with the vestibulum of some forms; in other forms there is no concha. The cavum thus resembles that of iguanids of the "*Uma*-type", although in agamids the vestibular connection is even farther posterior.

In amphisbaenians (Fig. 17E) the cavum nasi proprium is quite large but very simple. The concha is relatively small and broadly attached to the lateral wall of the cavum; in transverse section the latter is C-shaped. Thus the extraconchal space is small or even absent, and there is no subconchal recess. In forms in which the external naris is ventrally placed on the snout, the vestibulum enters the anterior end of the cavum from the ventral side. There is no distinct antorbital space.

There seems to be comparatively little variation in the cavum nasi proprium of snakes (Figs 15, 16B, 18, 20B and 25). However, comparatively few forms have been studied and the group is not as well known as are the lizards. In most snakes, *e.g.*, *Lamprophis*, *Natrix*, *Thamnophis*, and *Causus*, the cavum is essentially similar to that of *Lacerta*. There is a moderately developed concha attaching along the ventrolateral or lateral caval wall and surrounding a conchal space. The latter contains part of the external nasal gland. The posterior end of the concha projects posteriorly into the cavum towards the rather small antorbital space. There is a large extraconchal space which is continuous with the antorbital space posteriorly. The subconchal recess is lacking. The distribution of sensory olfactory epithelium and non-sensory respiratory epithelium is similar to that of lizards.

Several relatively minor variants on this pattern occur. In some forms the nasal cavities are relatively short and in these the concha tends to run from anterodorsal to posteroventral, but the general relationships remain the same. *Heterodon* displays a relatively slight slope of the concha, and in *Crotalus* it becomes considerably closer to a vertical position. Different species of the latter genus have been figured by Solger (1876), Dullemeijer (1959), and Parsons (1959a); all three papers disagree on the details of the shape of the concha. In *Constrictor* the concha apparently does not have a freely projecting posterior end but is attached to the lateral caval wall throughout its length. The concha of *Typhlops* is relatively reduced but otherwise normal (Zuckerkandl, 1910a; Haas, 1964 and 1968). Another, and more striking, variation has been reported in *Python*, *Xenopeltis*, and *Hemachatus*. In these three genera there is a prominent extension of the extraconchal space which extends anterolaterally (*Xenopeltis*) or anteriorly (*Python* and *Hemachatus*) from its anterolateral portion. The terms used for this large blind sac, the lateral recess or seitlicher Nebenraum, are also used for the extraconchal space in general. In *Python* and *Hemachatus*, but not in *Xenopeltis*, the concha bulges laterally into this blind sac which is, thus, C-shaped in transverse section.

A variety of aquatic snakes show varying degrees of reduction of the olfactory apparatus (Kathariner, 1900). *Natrix maura* (his *Tropidonotus viperinus*) is essentially the same as the more terrestrial members of that genus except that the posterior part of the concha is supported by a simple lamella of cartilage, and the conchal space is thus much restricted (Fig. 18). The free margin of the concha has been figured by Kathariner as turning dorsally. If this is actually the condition and not an artifact of the sectioning, it is a unique feature; in other squamates the free conchal margin either extends straight out from the caval wall or turns ventrally. *Cerberus* (Fig. 22) is more highly modified. The very small concha forms a ridge along the dorsolateral caval wall. Olfactory epithelium is present dorsally and dorsomedially. A special feature in this form is a transversely oriented flap extending dorsally and laterally from the ventral and medial walls of the cavum almost at its anterior end; the flap could probably act as a valve closing off the entrance to the cavum (Fig. 22). The other genera such as *Acrochordus*, *Pelamis*, and *Laticauda* are even more highly modified. There is no concha and the cavum is a simple tubular structure. In *Acrochordus* it is a narrow tube surrounded by venous sinuses. The sensory, olfactory epithelium is greatly restricted, lying mainly in a rather small groove along the caval roof; in *Laticauda* olfactory epithelium also occurs on part of the medial and lateral walls and in *Acrochordus* on part of the lateral caval wall.

The connection between the cavum nasi proprium and the oral cavity varies greatly in squamates; some resemble *Sphenodon* and have no trace of a nasopharyngeal duct, some have that duct well developed, and some are rather intermediate, lacking a true nasopharyngeal duct but having various modifications which produce a functional and, sometimes, a structural duct. It is hence most convenient to discuss all of these structures below, even though many of them properly belong to the cavum.

4. Nasopharyngeal duct

The palate of squamates was very intensively studied in Germany around 1900. The most important papers are those by Busch (1898), Seydel (1899), Beecker (1903), Göppert (1903), Hofmann (1905), Fuchs (1908), Thäter (1910), Fuchs (1915), and Haller (1921); their work is reviewed by Barge (1937). Lakjer (1927) treated the skeletal structures of the palate. More recently Malan (1946) and Bellairs and Boyd (1950) have studied this region with special emphasis on the relationships of the lachrymal duct. Much of this literature is concerned with the embryology of the palate and comparisons between the various types of secondary palates found in different groups of amniotes and disputes that are peripheral to this chapter and hence are touched upon only briefly. Unfortunately few works considered both the nasal cavities and the palate, and the relationships between the choana and the deeper portions of the nose often remain unclear.

Most lizards lack a true nasopharyngeal duct (= choanal tube, part of choanal tube, part of Choanengang, conduit choanal); their cavum nasi proprium leads directly to the choana (= Choanenspalte, internal naris, outer choana). The structure is essentially the same as in *Sphenodon* and can be seen best in transverse sections (Figs 23C, 24B, and 26). The choanal tube

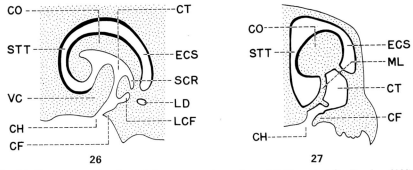

FIG. 26. Transverse section through the cavum nasi proprium of *Gekko gecko* (after Beecker, 1903).

FIG. 27. Transverse section through the cavum nasi proprium of *Cnemidophorus tessellatus* (after Stebbins, 1948).

CF, Choanal fold; CH, Choana; CO, Concha; CT, Choanal tube; ECS, Extra-conchal space; LCF, Lateral choanal fissure; LD, Lachrymal duct; ML, Membranous lamella between concha and nasal septum; SCR, Subconchal recess; STT, Stammteil; VC, Vomerine cushion.

has a more or less horizontal dorsal portion lying ventral to the concha. From near the lateral end of this dorsal portion the choanal tube extends ventromedially to the choana. The opening between the two portions of the choanal tube is commonly termed the inner choana and the more ventral portion of the choanal tube is often called the nasopharyngeal duct (= absteigender Schenkel des Choanenganges). The ventral end of the internasal wall expands laterally, thus forming a median plate that lies dorsomedial to the ventral portion of the choanal tube and forms the medial border of the choana; this plate is the vomerine cushion (= Gaumenmittelfeld, Mittel-platte, Vomerfeld, vomerine pad, Vomerpolster). Lateral and slightly ventral to it lies the choanal fold (=Choanenfalte, Gaumenblatt, Gaumenfalte, Gaumenfortsatz, mediale Seitenfalte, palatine fold; some authors do not consider all these terms to be synonymous, but there is no agreement about the various distinctions which have been suggested). This fold lies ventro-lateral to the ventral portion of the choanal tube and forms the lateral margin of the choana. There is often a groove of very variable size extending laterally or dorsolaterally from the ventrolateral wall of the ventral portion of the choanal tube; this is the lateral choanal fissure (= choanal groove, fissura palatina lateralis, Winkeltasche) into which the lachrymal duct may open. Posterior to the choana there is a median orbitonasal trough (= nasal groove, Nasalmulde, Orbitalgewölbe, Orbitalmulde) lying between and dorsal to the posterior ends of the choanal folds of the two sides.

All squamates differ from *Sphenodon* in that there is some fusion between the vomerine cushion and choanal fold so that the choana is shortened in all of the former. This fusion starts near the anterior end of the original choana, leaving a very small anterior portion of the choana as the duct of Jacobson's organ; there is no direct connection between this duct and the nasal cavity in adult squamates. The extent of the fusion varies considerably, but in most lizards it is not great and the adult choana lies ventral to much of the conchal zone of the cavum nasi proprium. In other cases the fusion extends farther posteriorly, and in such cases there may be a nasopharyngeal duct formed dorsal to the fused choanal fold and vomerine cushion and posterior to the cavum. The surface formed by this fusion, though frequently called a secondary palate, is not comparable to the mammalian secondary palate, but is really a continuation of the primary palate with, at least in most cases, the adult choana being a part of the embryonic choana and not a new and more posterior opening (cf. Fuchs, 1908). The palate of some scincids has been considered a true secondary palate (Fuchs, 1908), but the scincid condition has also been compared to that of other squamates although the adult choana may be posterior to the embryonic one (Haller, 1921).

In many squamates the fusion between the vomerine cushion and choanal fold of each side occurs mainly along the dorsal part of the contact. Thus ventrally, on the palatal surface, there may be a distinct choanal groove (= part of choanal groove, Choanenrinne, part of fissura palatina lateralis, Nasengaumenspalte, part of Winkeltasche) marking the line of fusion (Figs 14 and 20A). Posteriorly this groove is continuous with the choana and, in its deeper parts, with the lateral choanal fissure. Its anterior end is marked by the opening of the duct of Jacobson's organ. Such a complete choanal groove occurs in the Iguanidae (although the anterior end may be a canal rather than a groove in some forms), Agamidae, Chamaeleonidae, Gekkonidae, and Pygopodidae. An apparently complete groove is found in the Scincidae, Lacertidae, and Cordylidae; however, in these families it is probable that the anterior end of the groove is actually part of the lachrymal duct (see Bellairs and Boyd, 1950, for further discussion). In the Anguidae and Anniellidae the choanal groove is very nearly complete, but stops just posterior to the duct of Jacobson's organ. The situation in the Amphisbaenia apparently varies and there is some disagreement between different workers; Bellairs and Boyd (1950) reported an essentially complete groove in *Trogonophis* but incomplete ones in *Rhineura* and *Amphisbaena*. The groove is incomplete, failing to reach the duct of Jacobson's organ, in the Xantusiidae and Teiidae. Finally in the Varanidae and snakes the fusion between the vomerine cushion and choanal fold is more extensive ventrally, and there is almost no choanal groove left.

As already noted, the anteroposterior extent of the fusion, and hence the position of the adult choana, varies. Although in most lizards the fused area is short and the choana long, there are numerous cases in which more extensive fusion occurs. Also in some forms the orbitonasal trough is deep and narrow so that it forms what has been called an open nasopharyngeal duct. Such a structure may function as a duct with the tongue forming its floor when the mouth is closed (Göppert, 1903). The choanal folds, which normally continue posteriorly to the choanae, may approach each other and so increase the separation between the orbitonasal trough and the rest of the oral cavity; this is the case in chamaeleonids. The region can vary even within a family. For example, although most iguanids have a long choana underlying most of the cavum nasi proprium, the choana is short and well posterior in *Anolis*. The choana is restricted to a very small opening under the extreme posterior end of the cavum in the burrowing anniellids and amphisbaenians.

The greatest variation in the choanal area occurs in the infraorder Leptoglossa. Teiids have normal long choanae and lacertids and cordylids are quite similar to them, although they may have slightly more fusion and shorter choanae. In *Xantusia* (Xantusiidae) the choanal structure is like that of lacertids except that the posterior portions of the choanal folds are greatly enlarged so that they overlap in the midline; the orbitonasal trough is thus virtually isolated from the rest of the mouth and functions as a single median nasopharyngeal duct. Among the scincids all stages from the lacertid condition of the choanae to well formed nasopharyngeal ducts are seen; even within a single genus the variation can be very large. The genera studied by Busch (1898), Göppert (1903), and Malan (1946) can be divided into seven groups: 1. with the choanal folds essentially as in lacertids (*Chalcides* and *Eumeces*); 2. with the folds as in lacertids but meeting in the midline to restrict further the choanae (*Mabuya* and *Scelotes*); 3. with the choanal folds meeting in the midline to form a functional median nasopharyngeal duct (*Ablepharus* and *Mabuya*); 4. with the choanal folds overlapping in the midline to form a functional median nasopharyngeal duct (*Ablepharus* and *Tiliqua*); 5. with the choanal folds fusing to form a true median nasopharyngeal duct (*Mabuya*); 6. with the choanal folds and elongated vomerine cushion touching to form functional paired nasopharyngeal ducts (*Acontias*); and 7. with the choanal folds and elongated vomerine cushion fusing to form true paired nasopharyngeal ducts (*Typhlosaurus*).

In all snakes the vomerine cushion and choanal folds are well fused, so that the choanal grooves are obliterated and short paired nasopharyngeal ducts are formed. The choanae open posteriorly into the anterior end of the rather deep orbitonasal trough (Figs 15, 16B and 20B). Most snakes have a very short snout, and thus the choanae are well forward on the palate despite the presence of nasopharyngeal ducts.

Malan (1946) and Bellairs and Boyd (1950) have described the relationships of the lachrymal duct (= nasolacrimal duct, Tränennasengang) to the choanal groove. Although their interpretations differ in places, their observations are in agreement. The following summary is based primarily on the work of Bellairs and Boyd. In most lizards the lachrymal duct runs forward beside the choanal groove and ends at the duct of Jacobson's organ. Generally, as in iguanids, agamids, chamaeleonids, gekkonids, scincids, lacertids, anguids, and anniellids, the duct has one or more, often long, openings into the groove. In the Gekkonidae the openings are near the anterior end of the groove only. The choanal groove is much reduced in the Teiidae, but the lachrymal duct does open into the lateral choanal fissure. In pygopodids and xantusiids there are no such openings. *Varanus* (Varanidae) has two lachrymal ducts on each side. The shorter, mentioned in the section on the cavum nasi proprium, enters the choanal tube; the longer has a small opening to the ventral part of the choanal tube near the posterior end of the choana and then continues to the duct of Jacobson's organ. Malan (1946) and Shrivastava (1963), but not Bellairs (1949a) or Bellairs and Boyd (1950), reported a connection between the two lachrymal ducts of the same side. *Lanthanotus* (Lanthanotidae) and *Sibynophis* (Colubridae) resemble *Varanus* in possessing two lachrymal foramina on each side (McDowell and Bogert, 1954). The Amphisbaenia vary. In *Trogonophis* there is an anterior connection between the groove and the duct; this is absent in *Rhineura* or *Amphisbaena*. In all snakes the lachrymal duct runs directly to the duct of Jacobson's organ without any connection to the nasal cavity.

5. *Jacobson's organ*

Jacobson's organ (= Nebengeruchsorgan, vomeronasal organ) is more highly developed in squamates than in other animals. The organ was first reported in squamates by Rathke (1839) who considered it to be a nasal gland. The homology of the Jacobson's organs of mammals and squamates has been universally accepted since the papers of Leydig (1872a, b). Almost all of the cited papers on the squamate nasal region include descriptions of this organ; the older literature has been reviewed by Zuckerkandl (1910b). Figures 14 through 17, 20, 23, 25, 28 and 29 show the Jacobson's organ of various forms.

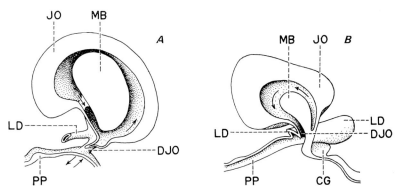

FIG. 28. Reconstructions of the Jacobson's organ of lizards. A. Posterior view of the Jacobson's organ of *Varanus bengalensis* (after Bellairs, 1949a). B. Anterior view of the Jacobson's organ of *Anguis fragilis* (after Bellairs and Boyd, 1950).
CG, Choanal groove; DJO, Duct of Jacobson's organ; JO, Jacobson's organ; LD, Lachrymal duct; MB, Mushroom body; PP, Primary palate.

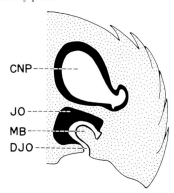

FIG. 29. Transverse section through the Jacobson's organ of *Anguis fragilis* (after Broman, 1920). CNP, Cavum nasi proprium; DJO, Duct of Jacobson's organ; JO, Jacobson's organ; MB, Mushroom body.

Although Jacobson's organ starts its embryological development as an outpocketing of the nasal cavity (see the section on embryology below), it is, in all adult squamates, separated from the nose by the extension of the primary palate or so-called secondary palate. A small portion of the primitive (embryonic) choana is retained anterior to the fused area and becomes the duct of Jacobson's organ (= Stenson's duct). The organ itself is a nearly spherical structure, with the ventral side invaginated into the sphere and nearly filling its center, so that only a very narrow lumen is left. This invagination is the mushroom body (= concha of Jacobson's organ, fungiform eminence, Kolben des Organon Jacobsoni, pilzenförmige Wulst). The very narrow duct leads dorsally from the palate and enters the lumen of the organ by a somewhat curved path, starting medially and spiralling posterodorsally and then laterally and anteriorly to the lateral side of the lumen of Jacobson's organ (Fig. 28). The dorsal wall and sides of Jacobson's organ are formed by thick sensory epithelium; thin, non-sensory, ciliated epithelium covers the mushroom body and lines the duct.

Most of the variation in the Jacobson's organ of squamates is in the degree of development. The organ is largest in snakes, even in aquatic ones with generally reduced olfactory structures, and varanids, and smallest in certain lizards, especially arboreal forms in which the entire olfactory system is poorly developed. In some iguanids, most notably *Anolis*, Jacobson's organ is much reduced and possibly nonfunctional (Pratt, 1948; Stimie, 1966). Eckart (1922) reported reduction of this organ in agamids; in *Calotes* only a very small mushroom body was found and none at all in *Ceratophora*, *Cophotis*, and *Otocryptis*. Chamaeleonids show the most extreme degree of reduction of Jacobson's organ, and it may well lack any sensory function in this family. The organ is a small simple pit without any mushroom body in *Microsaura* and some species of *Chamaeleo* and is completely lacking, at least in adults, in *Rampholeon* and other species of *Chamaeleo* (Zuckerkandl, 1910a; Brock, 1941; Malan, 1946; Haas, 1947; Pratt, 1948; Engelbrecht, 1951; and Frank, 1951).

The variation in the size of Jacobson's organ is reflected in its innervation. As in all tetrapods, Jacobson's organ is innervated by a special part of the olfactory nerve, usually called the medial trunk of the olfactory nerve or the vomeronasal nerve, which arises from the accessory olfactory bulb. In all cases there is a very good correlation between the degrees of development of Jacobson's organ and of the accessory olfactory bulb. Although it has been suggested that the nervus terminalis is associated with Jacobson's organ, the function of the nerve is uncertain, and there does not appear to be any correlation between its size or even presence and the development of Jacobson's organ. The relationship between Jacobson's organ and the accessory olfactory bulb (Zuckerkandl, 1910a) and the accessory bulb (Crosby and Humphrey, 1939a, b) have been described in a series of species; a review of the nerves of Jacobson's organ is found in the work of Parsons (1959a).

In almost all squamates the anterior end of the lachrymal duct enters the medial side of the duct of Jacobson's organ (cf. Bellairs and Boyd, 1950, for most of this section). The relationships of the duct to the choanal groove have been considered above in the section on the nasopharyngeal duct. In gekkonids, pygopodids, iguanids, agamids, teiids, and varanids, in the amphisbaenians *Amphisbaena* and *Rhineura*, and in snakes, the lachrymal duct enters the duct of Jacobson's organ without complications (see Fig. 28A). The lachrymal duct of *Xantusia* (Xantusiidae) enters the lumen of Jacobson's organ rather than its duct, the opening lying just dorsomedial to the origin of the duct of Jacobson's organ. In lacertids and scincids the anterior opening of the lachrymal duct is at the medial side of the opening of the duct of Jacobson's organ into the oral cavity and thus enters both the latter duct and the mouth. The amphisbaenian *Trogonophis* is somewhat similar but the opening of its lachrymal duct is longer and opens into both the duct of Jacobson's organ and the choanal groove. In anguids and anniellids the lachrymal duct opens to the oral cavity at the anterior end of the choanal groove just posteromedial to the duct of Jacobson's organ. Finally, in chamaeleonids the lachrymal duct enters the oral cavity at the anterior end of the choanal groove, in the region in which Jacobson's organ should be. Unfortunately there seem to be no detailed descriptions of the anterior end of the lachrymal duct in any chameleons that possess Jacobson's organs as adults.

There has been comparatively little work done on the functional aspects of the anatomy of Jacobson's organ. Since it is partly lined by olfactory epithelium and is innervated by the olfactory nerve, it is universally considered to be an olfactory receptor. However, the means by which the particles being sensed enter the organ is not clear. One view is that fluid from the mouth is sucked into the organ (Broman, 1920). Pressure from the tongue or material within the mouth, if applied ventral to the mushroom body, could force that body dorsally, thus restricting the lumen; relaxation and a return to the original position would draw fluid into Jacobson's organ. An alternative view notes that the tongue of many squamates is very thin and flexible and thus unsuited for applying pressure to the palate (Pratt, 1948). The particles are supposed to enter the stream of lachrymal fluid in the choanal groove and then be carried to the duct of Jacobson's organ and into that organ by ciliary action. The possibility exists, at least in some forms such as varanids, that the tips of the tongue may be inserted into the ducts of Jacobson's organs. Pratt further suggested that the rather complex spiral pattern of the organ's duct permits a ciliary current to enter, traverse, and leave Jacobson's organ via its single duct. The problem has been reviewed, and difficulties noted in both theories (Bellairs and Boyd, 1950). Not all squamates use the same method of drawing particles into Jacobson's organ. The hypothesis of ciliary transport suggested by experiments on *Lacerta* (Pratt,

1948) seems well supported and is probably used by many or even most lizards. However, the choanal groove does not reach the duct of Jacobson's organ in snakes and some lizards. The direct insertion of the tips of the tongue into the duct of Jacobson's organ, and the subsequent transport of the particles thus brought into the duct by the cilia of that duct, appears possible in snakes and varanids; however, in most lizards the duct is too narrow to admit the tips of the tongue. Experiments are needed on a greater variety of forms before any reliable conclusions may be reached.

D. CROCODILIA

1. General

The nasal cavities of crocodilians are more complex than those of any other living reptiles. However, the variation within the order is exceedingly small and one description will suffice for all of them. Most of the literature is based on late embryos or juvenile specimens. The earliest major work is that of Rathke (1866); Bertau (1935) presented the most detailed consideration of the group although his work was mainly embryological. Four genera have been studied: *Alligator* (Rathke, 1866; Gegenbaur, 1873; Reese, 1901; Nemours, 1930; Bertau, 1935; Parsons, 1959a), *Caiman* (Rathke, 1866), *Melanosuchus* (Bertau, 1935), and *Crocodylus* (Rathke, 1866; Solger, 1876; Hoffmann, 1879–1890; Meek, 1893 and 1911; Shiino, 1914; Bertau, 1935). Dieulafé (1904–1905) studied a form identified only as "un crocodile", presumably *Crocodylus*. The nasal anatomy of *Gavialis* has, to my knowledge, never been described, but was figured by Brühl (1886). The major reviews of crocodilian nasal anatomy are those by Matthes (1934) and von Wettstein (1954). For this study I dissected one specimen of *Caiman crocodilus* (= *C. sclerops*).

Many of the descriptions have been based on relatively small specimens, but even cursory examination demonstrates extreme allometric changes with growth.

2. Vestibulum

The vestibulum (= part of vestibule, part of Vorhof, Vorhöhle) is a short tubular structure leading ventrally from the external naris (= apertura externa nasi, äussere Nasenloch, äussere Nasenöffnung), which is located near the anterior end of the long snout on a small dorsal projection; in *Crocodylus* the external nares of opposite sides are closer together than in *Alligator* or *Caiman*, but the difference is not great. The ventral part of the vestibulum is slightly wider than the dorsal part and curves posteriorly to enter the cavum nasi proprium. The postvestibular ridge is lacking, and the angle in the nasal cavity is taken as the boundary between the vestibulum and the cavum. The vestibulum (Figs 30, 31 and 32) is lined by stratified squamous epithelium which gradually merges with the columnar epithelium of the cavum. The duct of the external nasal gland enters the posteromedial side of the vestibulum.

The mechanism for opening and closing the external naris (Fig. 33) has been studied in detail by Bellairs and Shute (1953) and earlier by Bruner (1897) and Bertau (1935). There is some cavernous erectile tissue containing

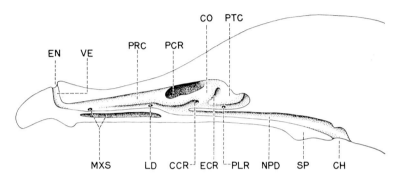

FIG. 30. Medial view of the lateral wall of the nasal cavity of *Alligator mississippiensis* (after Gegenbaur, 1873; Bertau, 1935; and Parsons, 1959a).
CCR, Caviconchal recess; CH, Choana; CO, Concha; ECR, Extraconchal recess; EN, External naris; LD, Lachrymal duct; MXS, Maxillary sinus; NPD, Nasopharyngeal duct; PCR, Preconchal recess; PLR, Posterolateral recess; PRC, Preconcha; PTC, Postconcha; SP, Secondary palate; VE, Vestibulum.

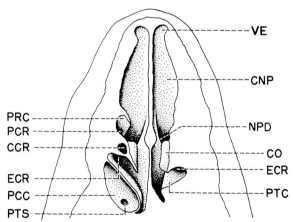

FIG. 31. Dorsal view of the nasal cavities of *Caiman crocodilus*. The dissection is deeper on the left side.
CCR, Caviconchal recess; CNP, Cavum nasi proprium; CO, Concha; ECR, Extraconchal recess; NPD, Nasopharyngeal duct; PCC, Postconchal cavity; PCR, Preconchal recess; PRC, Preconcha; PTC, Postconcha; PTS, Postturbinal sinus; VE, Vestibulum.

smooth muscle fibers at the anterior margin of the external naris, but this tissue, which is similar to that seen in other reptiles, is not the major factor in narial control. A relatively large smooth muscle, the dilator muscle of the naris (= Öffnungsmuskel), runs from the posterior wall of the external naris to the premaxilla at the posterior margin of the bony external nasal aperture.

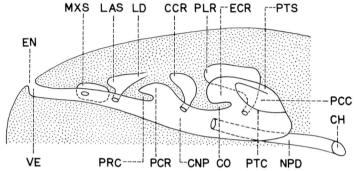

FIG. 32. Diagram of the crocodilian nasal cavity in dorsal view to show the various recesses and sinuses (after Bertau, 1935, and Parsons, 1959a).
CCR, Caviconchal recess; CH, Choana; CNP, Cavum nasi proprium; CO, Concha; ECR, Extra-conchal recess; EN, External naris; LAS, Lachrymal sinus; LD, Lachrymal duct; MXS, Maxillary sinus; NPD, Nasopharyngeal duct; PCC, Postconchal cavity; PCR, Preconchal recess; PLR, Posterolateral recess; PRC, Preconcha; PTC, Postconcha; PTS, Postturbinal sinus; VE, Vestibulum.

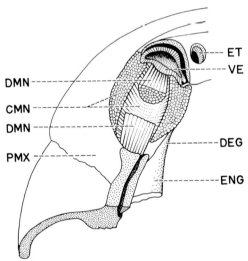

FIG. 33. Diagrammatic dorsal view of the narial muscles of *Alligator mississippiensis* (after Bellairs and Shute, 1953).
CMN, Constrictor muscle of the naris; DEG, Duct of the external nasal gland; DMN, Dilator muscle of the naris; ENG, External nasal gland; ET, Erectile tissue; PMX, Premaxilla; VE, Vestibulum.

Its contraction draws the posterior wall of the naris posteriorly, thus opening the external naris. This muscle is opposed by the constrictor muscle of the naris (= Verschlussmuskel), a circular smooth muscle which surrounds the dilator. Its contraction forces the dilator to elongate, thus closing the external naris. Both of these muscles, which form most of the small narial projection on the snout, develop in place from mesenchyme and are innervated by the cranial sympathetic nerve.

3. Cavum nasi proprium

The cavum nasi proprium (= Haupthöhle) of crocodilians is quite unlike that of any other Recent reptiles (Figs 30, 31, 32 and 34). There are, in the adult, three conchal formations on the lateral caval wall.

> 1. Anteriorly the preconcha (= anterior turbinal, atrioturbinal, inferior turbinal, vordere äussere Riechmuschel, vordere Muschel) forms a dorsolateral projection into the cavum. It is quite wide and low and is

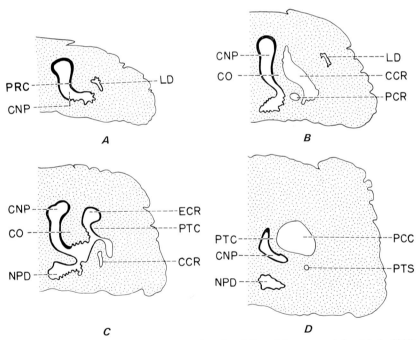

FIG. 34. Transverse sections through the nasal cavity of *Crocodylus porosus* (after Meek, 1911). A. Through the preconcha. B. Through the anterior part of the concha. C. Through the posterior part of the concha. D. Through the postconcha.
CCR, Caviconchal recess; CNP, Cavum nasi proprium; CO, Concha; ECR, Extraconchal recess; LD, Lachrymal duct; NPD, Nasopharyngeal duct; PCC, Postconchal cavity; PCR, Preconchal recess; PRC, Preconcha; PTC, Postconcha; PTS, Postturbinal sinus.

F

supported by an inpocketing of the cartilaginous nasal capsule. In *Alligator* the preconcha extends along the anterior half of the lateral caval wall.

2. The posteroventral corner of the preconcha is continuous with the concha (= cornet, Hauptmuschel, innere Riechmuschel, middle turbinal, upper turbinal). The latter forms a prominent projection of the lateral caval wall which extends posteriorly from the preconcha and then turns posterodorsally. A horizontal groove along the medial surface of the anterior half of the concha in *Alligator* has been described only by Bertau (1935). The more posterior portion of the concha projects posteriorly into the cavum. Although the concha does contain a small conchal cavity medially, its dorsolateral attachment to the nasal capsule is much restricted and supported only by a simple lamella of cartilage; it is, thus, a true concha (*sensu* Gegenbaur, 1873). In *Alligator* the opening to the nasopharyngeal duct lies ventral to the anterior end of the concha.

3. The postconcha (= ethmoturbinal, faux cornet, hintere äussere Riechmuschel, hintere Muschel, posterior turbinal, pseudoconcha) forms a relatively low but prominent swelling of the posterolateral caval wall. It is nearly the full height of the cavum posteriorly, but anteriorly it becomes restricted to the ventral half of the caval wall and lies ventro-lateral to the posterior end of the concha. The postconcha is supported by a hollow, more or less hemispherical, inpocketing of the cartila-ginous nasal capsule.

The description given in the preceding paragraph is based primarily on *Alligator*; *Caiman* and *Melanosuchus* are essentially the same. Although *Crocodylus* is very similar to these three genera, there are a few differences. Its concha is simpler and forms a prominent bulge which extends from anteroventral to posterodorsal without curving. The connection with the preconcha is smaller and the two are almost completely separate in the adult. In *Crocodylus* the opening to the nasopharyngeal duct lies more posteriorly, ventral to the center rather than the anterior end of the concha. The general proportions of the parts of the cavum nasi proprium also differ. In *Alligator* the anterior end of the concha lies approximately one half to two-thirds of the way posteriorly; in *Crocodylus* it is two-thirds to three-quarters of the way from the anterior to the posterior end. The published figures show considerable variation in both genera, and ontogenetic size changes have not been studied (most workers have examined relatively small specimens). In larger specimens the anterior section is elongated, and the part posterior to the preconcha is relatively shorter than in smaller ones.

Some authors have attempted to divide the cavum nasi proprium into the three regions that are recognized in *Sphenodon* and squamates. (1) The choanal tube (= Choanengang) is defined as the part of the cavum anterior to the entrance of the nasopharyngeal duct and ventral to the preconcha; (2) the conchal zone (= Muschelzone) is defined as the part dorsal to the choanal tube; and (3) the antorbital space (= Antorbitalraum) is defined as the posterior part of the cavum. The indistinct anterior boundary of the antorbital space has been delimited in two ways, either by the posterior end of the concha or by the opening from the cavum into the nasopharyngeal duct. The choanal tube may be functionally significant as the passageway for the respiratory current of air. Yet the differences in shape between the cava of crocodilians and of squamates suggests that the proposed homologies are dubious. Thus most workers do not apply these terms to crocodilians. Nor can the anterior half of the cavum be considered a part of the vestibulum (Bertau, 1935).

Crocodilians have a series of seven recesses and sinuses off the cavum nasi proprium. The first four of them lie within the cartilaginous nasal capsule, and the remaining three are extracapsular. Wegner (1958) has considered the sinuses within the bony skulls of many forms, including some relatively large specimens with skulls more than 70 mm long. The following descriptions are based largely on Bertau's (1935) reconstructions of late embryos with supplementary information from other papers. *Alligator* and the exceedingly similar *Caiman* and *Melanosuchus* are considered first and then compared to *Crocodylus*.

The preconchal recess (= anterior nasal pouch, interturbinal sinus) is a rather small pocket lying in the dorsolateral wall of the cavum between the preconcha and the concha. It is widely open to the cavum and extends a short distance anteriorly from its opening, lying lateral to the posterodorsal part of the preconcha. The preconchal recess is one of the smallest of the recesses and sinuses of the crocodilian nose.

The extraconchal recess (= side cavity) lies between the concha and the postconcha and is a rather narrow cavity extending the full height of the cavum nasi proprium. It is obliquely placed, with its dorsal end posterior to the ventral end and its lateral margin anterior to the medial; it thus lies lateral to the posterior part of the concha. The opening of the extraconchal recess into the main part of the cavum is slit-like, but farther laterally it becomes more widely open.

The last two intracapsular sinuses lie within the cartilage supporting the postconcha. The wall of the postconcha is very thin and the entire structure is hollow, containing a large postconchal cavity (= Höhle in der Post-concha, posterior nasal pouch, Sinus der Pseudoconcha). The cavity is connected to the other parts of the nasal cavity only through the narrow duct-like postturbinal sinus. The latter runs posteriorly from the ventrolateral corner of the extraconchal recess and lies within a canal in the cartilage, ventrolateral to the postconchal space. The posterior end of the postturbinal sinus turns dorsally to enter the ventrolateral margin of the posterior end of the postconchal cavity.

The caviconchal recess (= mid-turbinal sinus, ventro-lateral diverticulum) is an extracapsular sinus that opens into the cavum nasi proprium ventral to the anterior half of the concha. It extends anterolaterally from this opening as a moderately large sinus and then turns posterodorsally and gradually narrows at its posterodorsal end. Most of the caviconchal recess thus forms a rather digitiform cavity lying parallel and just anterior to the extraconchal recess. The caviconchal recess lies along the base of the posterior half of the concha.

The posterolateral recess (= hintere laterale Nebenhöhle) is a medium-sized sinus lying ventral to the extraconchal recess, postturbinal sinus, and postconchal cavity. Its narrow connection with the cavum is through the ventrolateral caval wall, ventral to the center of the postconcha.

The last of the extracapsular sinuses, the maxillary sinus, was absent in Bertau's (1935) material and presumably first appears only in older specimens. The large sinus lies within the maxilla ventral to the anterior half of the cavum nasi proprium. Gegenbaur (1873), who figured the sinus, neither mentioned nor illustrated any connection with the nasal cavity. Hoffmann (1879–1890; *Crocodylus*) figured it as opening into the anteroventral part of the lateral caval wall, and Nemours (1930; young *Alligator*) found a similar opening. However, Nemours also reported that the maxillary sinus opened farther posteriorly, in the region of the start of the nasopharyngeal duct, of a larger *Alligator*; Bertau (1935) suggested that either the maxillary sinus had merged with the caviconchal recess or, more probably, that the thin wall between these two sinuses had been overlooked by Nemours. The opening to the maxillary sinus is, thus, probably well anterior in the lateral caval wall, ventral to the anterior end of the preconcha and anterior to the opening of the lachrymal duct. The crocodilian maxillary sinus is almost certainly an independent development and not homologous to the maxillary sinus of mammals (most fossil reptiles, including pelycosaurs, lack maxillary sinuses; A. S. Romer, *pers. comm.*).

The recesses and sinuses of *Crocodylus* are generally similar to those of *Alligator*, though the former genus lacks the posterolateral recess. Although they are otherwise similar, the caviconchal and extraconchal recesses of *Crocodylus* are more vertically oriented than those of *Alligator*, and the extraconchal recess of the former is relatively larger. *Crocodylus* also differs in having not only the postturbinal sinus, but possesses another duct-like connection to the postconchal cavity. This second tube runs anteriorly from the ventrolateral corner of the anterior end of the postconchal cavity, passes dorsomedial to the postturbinal sinus's entrance into the extraconchal recess and ventral to the extraconchal recess, and enters the posteroventral end of the caviconchal recess.

The lachrymal duct (= ductus nasolacrimalis, Tränenkanal, Tränennasengang) enters the cavum nasi proprium through its ventrolateral wall, ventral to the posterior part of the preconcha. The duct is greatly enlarged lateral to the nasal cavity and forms a lachrymal sinus (= sinus nasolacrimalis) which frequently includes a blind sac (the saccus lacrymalis of Bertau, 1935) extending a short distance anterior to the entrance of the lachrymal duct into the cavum. The sac is very irregular in size and shape and was completely absent in one late embryo of *Melanosuchus* (Bertau, 1935).

As in other reptiles, the cavum is lined by sensory olfactory epithelium posterodorsally and non-sensory respiratory epithelium anteroventrally. The lining of the dorsal parts of the preconchal and extraconchal recesses is of olfactory epithelium, but their ventral parts and all of the other recesses and sinuses have only respiratory epithelium. Within the cavum itself respiratory epithelium is found anterior and ventral to the conchae, while the remainder of the cavum is lined by olfactory epithelium.

4. *Nasopharyngeal duct*

The nasopharyngeal duct (= conduit respiratoire, Gaumenrohr, hinterer Nasengang, Nasenrachengang, posterior nares, ventral passage) of crocodilians is a very long narrow tube leading to the choana (= posterior naris, sekundäre Choane, tertiäre Choane) from the middle or posterior part of the cavum nasi proprium, ventral to the concha. Its development has been studied by Voeltzkow (1899), Fuchs (1908), and most recently Müller (1965). Although they differ concerning details of the embryology, all agree that, in crocodilians with development parallel to that in mammals, there is a true secondary palate. All but the anterior end of the nasopharyngeal duct is thus considered to be a part of the primary oral cavity and is separated from the remainder of that cavity by the secondary palate.

The nasopharyngeal duct extends posteriorly nearly to the back of the skull so that the choana is well posterior to the orbit. Its length is approximately the same as that of the cavum nasi proprium. Although for much of their embryonic development the posterior parts of the two nasopharyngeal ducts form a single median tube, in postembryonic stages there is a complete septum and the nasopharyngeal ducts and choanae of the two sides are separate. There are no recesses or other specializations of the duct which, despite its length, is a very simple tubular structure in those forms studied.

5. *Jacobson's organ*

Adult crocodilians lack a Jacobson's organ. Although there has been much dispute concerning this organ in embryos, there is almost unanimous agreement about the adult condition. Crocodilians also lack an accessory olfactory bulb (Zuckerkandl, 1910a; Crosby and Humphrey, 1939b; Parsons, 1959a) which supports the theory that Jacobson's organ is either lacking or at least nonfunctional.

The arguments concerning rudiments of Jacobson's organ in embryos have been reviewed many times, by Peter (1906), Zuckerkandl (1910b), Matthes (1934), Bertau (1935), and Parsons (1959a), and need not be repeated here. Several small and apparently unrelated pockets have been reported in many different areas and stages and thought to represent this organ; these range in location from the duct of the external nasal gland (von Mihalkovics, 1898) to the dorsal side of the nasopharyngeal duct (Reese, 1901, and others). However, few recent workers have accepted any of these identifications. Instead they have postulated that crocodilians have only the slightest indication of a Jacobson's organ in early embryonic stages, a conclusion based on a figure of Voeltzkow's (1899) which will be discussed below in the section on embryology, and that this quickly disappears leaving no trace of that organ in later embryos or adults.

E. EXTINCT GROUPS

Since no soft parts are available for study, and since the nasal capsules were presumably cartilaginous and hence not preserved (Romer, 1956), the nasal anatomy of the various extinct groups of reptiles is almost totally unknown. All that can generally be seen is the position of the external nares and choanae.

In certain aquatic or partially aquatic forms the external nares were placed quite far posteriorly on the often elongated snout. Sometimes, as in *Mesosaurus* and ichthyosaurs, they lay laterally and at the base of the snout; in other cases they were, as in certain eosuchians such as *Champsosaurus*, set well dorsally. Phytosaurs and some sauropods, such as *Diplodocus* and *Brachiosaurus*, presented rather extreme cases in which the external nares opened on a mound which formed the most dorsal part of the skull and lay posterior to the choanae.

The nasal cavities were greatly modified in ornithopod dinosaurs of the subfamily Lambeosaurinae (Fig. 35). In these forms the bones of the snout were greatly elongated, forming a prominent crest on the dorsal surface of the skull. The nasal passages lay largely within these crests where they might, as in *Procheneosaurus*, *Corythosaurus*, and *Lambeosaurus*, form large chambers or, as in *Parasaurolophus*, long U-shaped tubes. The chambers or tubes of the two sides usually appear to have been connected, but we do not know whether the nasal cavities were actually interconnected or whether there was a soft septum between them. The function of these crests has been the subject of much speculation. The most recent analysis is that of Ostrom

(1961), who believed that the increased size and complexity of the nasal passages probably served to increase the area lined by sensory epithelium and hence was olfactory in function.

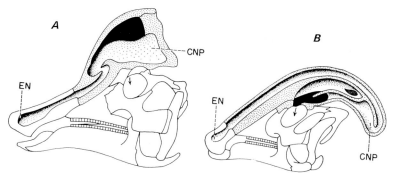

FIG. 35. Nasal passages in the bony skulls of lambeosaurine dinosaurs (after Ostrom, 1961). The arrows indicate the dorsal opening of the "choanal canal" leading from the nasal cavities to the palate. A. *Corythosaurus excavatus.* B. *Parasaurolophus cyrtocristatus.*
CNP, Cavum nasi proprium; EN, External naris.

The nasal cavities of some of the more advanced therapsids presumably approached the mammalian condition. A secondary palate was well developed. Casts of the nasal cavities of two genera (*Diademodon* and *Nythosaurus*) show grooves believed to represent a series of ethmoturbinals (Watson, 1913; Brink, 1957).

IV. Histology of the Nasal Organs

A. GENERAL

Most of our knowledge of the histology of the nasal organs comes from relatively brief descriptions or passing mention in the papers cited in the section on gross anatomy, with the single outstanding exception of the work of Gabe and Saint Girons (1964) on *Sphenodon*. There has been almost no work done on the electron microscopy of reptilian nasal tissues. Hopkins (1926) reported that the olfactory receptor cells of the turtle *Chrysemys* resemble very closely those of frogs; Bloom (1954), Reese (1965), and others have studied the latter with the electron microscope and possibly their work may be taken as giving an indication of the structures to be expected in reptiles, but it is hoped that electron microscopic work on the latter will soon be forthcoming. The following descriptions are based entirely on the cited literature, although original photographs of nasal tissues of *Clemmys* are included.

B. VESTIBULUM

In all the described cases the epithelial lining of the reptilian nasal vestibulum is stratified squamous epithelium continuous with and very similar to the skin (Fig. 36); such a lining by skin is sometimes used as the definitive characteristic of a vestibulum. The epithelium varies considerably in thickness between different species, but appears to be of a relatively even thickness within any given species. It is possibly thinnest in some squamates, but too few forms have been described to permit safe generalizations. Basally, there is frequently a single layer of columnar or cuboidal cells with large nuclei (Osawa, 1898; Kathariner, 1900; Eckart, 1922; Parsons, 1959a). I suspect that such a basal layer is always present, but other workers have not mentioned it specifically. Superficially, the cells are squamous and become progressively more cornified towards the lumen of the vestibulum. The epithelium is dry and, in most cases, lacks all but the large external and medial nasal glands. However, Osawa (1898) has reported typical goblet cells in the middle of this epithelium in *Sphenodon*, and Fischer (1900) found crypts which resemble mucous glands ("die ich fast als Schleimdrüsen ansprechen möchte", p. 448) in amphisbaenians. Although in most cases this epithelium has a relatively smooth surface, there may, in some squamates, be low folds with crypts between them.

The epithelium is underlain by connective tissue which usually contains many venous sinuses and forms functional erectile tissue that may, especially in squamates, act as a nasal valve. The variation in the thickness and development of such erectile tissue is great and is briefly discussed in the section on adult anatomy. Only a few workers have mentioned the presence or absence of a layer of pigment cells within this connective tissue: *Sphenodon* has few pigment cells in some areas and none in others (Osawa, 1898), hydrophiids have many pigment cells (Kathariner, 1900), and a well developed pigment layer occurs in the agamids *Ceratophora* and *Otocryptis* although there is almost no pigment there in *Calotes* and *Cophotis* (Eckart, 1922). Leydig (1872a) has reported the absence of pigment within the epithelium of *Lacerta*, but did not mention its presence or absence in the underlying connective tissue.

Although most of the vestibulum, as defined by gross morphology, is lined by stratified squamous epithelium, the parts closest to the cavum nasi proprium may show a transition to the epithelial types of that region. In at least some turtles respiratory epithelium lines the posteriormost part of the vestibulum. Late embryos of *Chrysemys* show a transition between the two epithelial types (Parsons, 1959a), but Seydel (1896) reported a sharp boundary between them in *Testudo*. Osawa (1898), but not Hoppe (1934), reported respiratory epithelium in the posterior vestibular region of *Sphenodon*; I suspect that this difference reflects differences in the concept of the vestibulum, and that the entire vestibulum, as here defined, is lined by stratified squamous epithelium. In crocodilians Bertau (1935) stated that the typical vestibular epithelium merges with respiratory epithelium in the

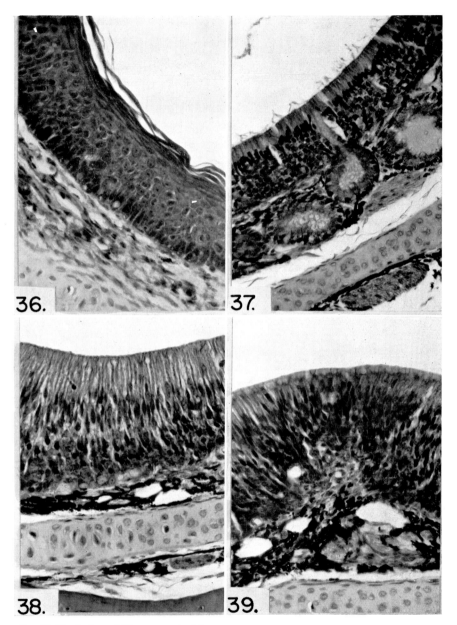

Fɪɢ. 36. Vestibulum of *Clemmys caspica leprosa.*

Fɪɢ. 37. Olfactory epithelium and Bowman's glands of *Clemmys caspica leprosa.*

Fɪɢ. 38. Vomeronasal epithelium from the lateral sulcus of *Clemmys caspica leprosa.*

Fɪɢ. 39. Respiratory epithelium from the intermediate region of *Clemmys caspica leprosa.*

All four figures are transverse sections, 10μ thick, stained with haematoxylin and eosin, and magnified approximately 120 times.

ventral portion of the vestibulum. In almost all squamates the entire vesti-bulum is lined by stratified squamous epithelium, the exceptions being certain agamids (Eckart, 1922; see discussion in the section on adult anatomy). In these forms true olfactory epithelium is said to be present in what is, grossly, part of the vestibulum. Any respiratory or olfactory epithelium which may be present in the vestibulum resembles that of the cavum nasi proprium described below.

C. Cavum nasi proprium

In all reptiles there are two types of epithelium lining the cavum nasi proprium. Sensory olfactory epithelium is typically located posterodorsally within the cavum and non-sensory respiratory epithelium anteroventrally; the distribution of these types has been considered in the section on adult anatomy. In agamids sensory epithelium may extend into what is, in its gross structure, part of the vestibulum (Eckart, 1922). There is, in turtles, a third type of caval epithelium, the so-called vomeronasal epithelium, the sonsory epithelium of the intermediate region. This type is believed to be the homolog of the Jacobson's organ of other reptiles (see below).

The most detailed description of the histology of the cavum is that by Gabe and Saint Girons (1964), while Allison (1953) has presented a useful review, based largely on mammals but also including some on reptiles.

The olfactory epithelium is high columnar and frequently pseudo-stratified (Fig. 37). It is 75μ high in *Lacerta* (Krause, 1922), and it appears to be approximately 120μ high in Gabe and Saint Girons' (1964) photograph of *Sphenodon*. Although Hoffmann (1879–1890) gave the height of the olfactory epithelium of *Emys* as $600–800\mu$, his figures for other turtles indicate a height of about 150μ and suggest the possibility of an error. Only in *Hydrophis* (Kathariner, 1900), do Bowman's glands fail to develop from the olfactory epithelium and to extend into the underlying connective tissue. The epithelium lacks other glands, and cilia occur only as the special olfactory hairs on the sensory cells. The three types of cells of the olfactory epithelium are sensory (= olfactory or receptor) cells, sustentacular (= supporting) cells, and basal cells.

The sensory cells are bipolar neurons, whose cell bodies normally lie within the basal half of the epithelium. The small cell bodies are spindle-shaped and have fine basophilic Nissl bodies in the scanty cytoplasm (Allison, 1953). Hoffmann (1879–1890) stated that, in *Emys*, the cell bodies are roughly 15 by 12μ, but some of his measurements are highly questionable, and thus these cannot be accepted without further studies. The spherical nuclei are richer in chromatin than those of the sustentacular cells (Gabe and Saint Girons, 1964). Basally, each sensory cell gives rise to a single unmyelinated axon which passes through the basement membrane and runs to the olfactory bulb; together these axons constitute the olfactory nerve. The thinness of the axons makes their histological demonstration difficult. The second process of the cell body, the peripheral process or olfactory rod, is long and thin, extending to the surface of the epithelium where it has a slight terminal swelling. From this swelling project the olfactory hairs.

The nature of the olfactory hairs, recently shown to be cilia (Cordier, 1964; but see below in the discussion of Jacobson's organ), is not well known, although, since they presumably are the actual olfactory receptors, they have been noted by many workers. Each sensory cell of mammals and reptiles bears from 8 to 12 of these hairs which appear to be extensions of the cell membrane and are very short (Allison, 1953); in lower vertebrates they are frequently much longer. Such short olfactory hairs were figured as long ago as 1894 by Retzius in *Natrix*. However, most earlier workers (Leydig, 1872a; Hoffmann, 1879–1890; Macallum, 1883; Hopkins, 1926; and Kolmer, 1927) have stated that the hairs are long, and more recently Cordier (1964) has also mentioned long ones in reptiles. Hopkins described two types of olfactory hairs, long motionless ones up to 75μ long and short motile ones up to 30μ long, in *Chrysemys*. The long hairs extend to the surface of the 40μ thick layer of mucus covering the epithelium, and their ends are in contact with the air. The olfactory hairs are damaged and shortened by many reagents including ethanol and distilled water (Hopkins, 1926); probably this extreme sensitivity, which prevents many techniques such as those used by Gabe and Saint Girons (1964) from demonstrating them, is responsible for the discrepancies in the various descriptions of their size.

Some variation occurs in the sensory cells of *Gekko* (Kolmer, 1927). Some cells, mainly in the peripheral parts of the olfactory area, are larger, with bigger nuclei than the normal sensory cells and a larger peripheral swelling. These cells each bear a single flagellum (= olfactory hair?). Kolmer also figured, but did not otherwise mention, a sensory cell from *Emys* in which there is a large crystaloid inclusion. There are, to my knowledge, no other reports of variations in the sensory cells of reptiles.

The sustentacular cells are columnar and typically heptagonal or octagonal in cross section with the peripheral processes of the sensory cells lying at the corners of the sustentacular cells. The latter have oval nuclei which tend to lie slightly peripheral to the cell bodies of the sensory cells. The sustentacular cells also have finely granular cytoplasm (Hoffmann, 1879–1890), found to be acidophilic and to contain PAS positive granules by Gabe and Saint Girons (1964). Presumably these granules are the olfactory pigment which Allison (1953) described as yellow or light brown. The nature of this pigment, which is also present in some of the cells of Bowman's glands, is unknown, but it appears to be important for olfaction (Allison, 1953). The basal ends of the sustentacular cells are compressed by the cell bodies of the sensory cells and by the basal cells and, according to Hoffmann (1879–1890) and Allison (1953), are often forked or branched; Macallum (1883) denied that they are forked.

The basal cells are small, lie along the basement membrane, and are probably found in most, if not all, forms (Hoffmann, 1879–1890; Eckart, 1922; Allison, 1953; Gabe and Saint Girons, 1964), although many workers have not mentioned them.

There is, thus, a tendency for a layering of the nuclei within the olfactory epithelium, with those of the sustentacular cells most peripheral, those of the sensory cells in the middle, and those of the basal cells most basal. This layering is quite distinct in the agamid *Cophotis* (Eckart, 1922), but in other forms it is only a tendency, and no clear layers can be distinguished.

The respiratory epithelium is also columnar, frequently pseudostratified, and contains ciliated, goblet, and basal cells (Fig. 38). It is lower than the olfactory epithelium, being 25μ high in *Lacerta* (Krause, 1922), approximately 50μ high in *Emys* (Hoffmann, 1879–1890), and, judging by the figures of Gabe and Saint Girons (1964), 60 to 70μ high in *Sphenodon*. The name respiratory is almost always used for the lining of the non-olfactory portions of the nose. It does not imply any function in gas exchange.

The basal cells, although probably of widespread occurrence, have been described but rarely. They appear to resemble those of the olfactory epithelium. They are conical or pyriform and have clear vesicular nuclei and homogeneous cytoplasm (Gabe and Saint Girons, 1964). The ciliated cells, which form much of the epithelium, have round or oval central nuclei with rather diffuse chromatin and nearly homogeneous cytoplasm. Some authors have reported similar ciliated cells in the olfactory epithelium, but more recent workers have denied their presence there.

Typical goblet cells, with basal nuclei and much of the cytoplasm filled with secretion, are very numerous in the respiratory epithelium of all reptiles. Gabe and Saint Girons (1964) found the secretory products in them to be strongly PAS positive and suggested an acid mucopolysaccharide secretion.

In many forms, some areas of the respiratory epithelium are composed almost entirely of goblet cells, thus forming, in effect, small multicellular glands. These have been described as small tubular mucous glands and crypts in *Testudo* (Seydel, 1896). Although few such glandular areas have been found in *Emys* (Seydel, 1896), there are, especially in the posterior part of the cavum nasi proprium, numerous shallow crypts lined mainly by goblet cells in late embryos of *Chrysemys* (Parsons, 1959a). Goblet cells are especially numerous in *Sphenodon*, and this form also has short tubular glands composed entirely of typical goblet cells with a PAS positive secretion ventral to the concha (= posterior concha?) (Gabe and Saint Girons, 1964). In crocodilians Bertau (1935) found many unicellular glands, presumably goblet cells, in folds of the epithelium near the anterior end of the cavum but few glands in the linings of the recesses and sinuses. Folding of the epithelium with shallow, generally longitudinal crypts between the folds is very common in squamates. Such crypts, which are generally most numerous posteriorly and are lined mainly or even entirely by goblet cells, have been described in *Lacerta* (Krause, 1922), *Thamnophis* (Macallum, 1883; Parsons, 1959a), and various aquatic snakes (Kathariner, 1900). The subconchal recess of *Anguis* is lined entirely by mucus secreting, presumably typical goblet, cells (Pratt, 1948), although the same area of the closely related *Ophisaurus* is lined with olfactory epithelium (Malan, 1946). Only in *Chamaeleo* are these glands few and poorly developed (Haas, 1937).

In forms with reduced olfactory areas the respiratory epithelium extends around much or all of the cavum nasi proprium. It is, thus, very extensive in some aquatic snakes (Kathariner, 1900) and lines the entire cavum of *Chamaeleo* (Haas, 1937) and *Uma* (Stebbins, 1943); in the latter genus, Stebbins mentions Bowman's glands but is apparently referring to goblet cells as the former do not occur in respiratory epithelium.

There are two reports of different types of respiratory epithelium. In *Dermochelys* Nick (1912) found stratified squamous epithelium, like that of the nasopharyngeal duct, lining part of the intermediate region of the cavum, while in *Varanus* Bellairs (1949a) described the epithelium of much of the subconchal recess as intermediate between olfactory and respiratory epithelium. Since he stated that this epithelium did not give rise to any nerve fibers, it must be considered respiratory rather than olfactory. The study of more forms might well result in the recognition of more variation in the histology of the non-sensory regions of the cavum nasi proprium.

The epithelium of the cavum is, in *Sphenodon*, underlain by a basement membrane which is very thin under the respiratory epithelium but well developed under the olfactory epithelium (Gabe and Saint Girons, 1964). Beneath the membrane there is a layer of connective tissue containing many nerves and blood vessels, both especially numerous in the olfactory regions (Krause, 1922, for *Lacerta*). Kathariner (1900) reported that the blood vessels are particularly well developed in *Acrochordus*. The subepithelial connective tissue of *Dermochelys* is typical cavernous tissue (Nick, 1912). The Bowman's glands project into the connective tissue under the olfactory regions, and there are many collaginous but few elastic fibers (Gabe and Saint Girons, 1964).

Pigment cells often occur in the subepithelial connective tissue. The pigment has, like that within the sustentacular cells of the olfactory epithelium, been referred to as olfactory pigment, and Negus (1958), who observed many black pigment cells in the connective tissue of *Anguis*, used the term for both; the relationship, if any, between them appears to be unknown. Pigment cells have been reported in *Lacerta* (Leydig, 1872a) and *Thamnophis* (Macallum, 1883) in which they are most numerous around the nerves, blood vessels, and Bowman's glands, and beneath the respiratory but not the olfactory epithelium of *Pelamis* (Kathariner, 1900). Probably such pigmentation, which is generally associated with the connective tissue system, is common, but I know of no other reports of it.

D. Nasopharyngeal Duct

There are descriptions of the histology of the nasopharyngeal duct for four turtles (Figs 39 and 40), and they are all slightly different. Seydel (1896) found respiratory epithelium lining the nasopharyngeal duct of *Testudo*, and Nick (1912) described low columnar epithelium merging with the epithelium of the cavum in *Chelydra*. Late embryos of *Chrysemys* appear to have one or two layers of cuboidal or low columnar cells lining the nasopharyngeal duct (Parsons, 1959a). Finally, in *Dermochelys*, Hoffmann (1879–1890) and Nick (1912) reported stratified squamous epithelium; in embryos there is a single layer of columnar cells superficially, but this layer disappears after hatching. As already noted, this stratified epithelium of the nasopharyngeal duct also lines part of the cavum nasi proprium in *Dermochelys*.

In all the squamates so far described respiratory epithelium similar to that of the cavum nasi proprium continues to the choana where it meets the stratified squamous epithelium of the palate. Such respiratory epithelium is found even in the imperfectly formed nasopharyngeal duct of *Xantusia* (Stebbins, 1948). The only crocodilian that has been described is *Alligator*; Reese (1901) reported one or two layers of cuboidal or low columnar cells in a late embryo. He could see no cilia in the nasopharyngeal duct.

E. Jacobson's Organ

Although the histology of Jacobson's organ of squamates has been considered by many workers, few have studied that organ in turtles or *Sphenodon*. There are marked differences between the orders of reptiles in the gross structure of Jacobson's organ, but whether these are reflected in histological differences is virtually unknown. Crocodilians lack Jacobson's organ, except in early embryonic stages, and hence need not be considered here.

The sensory epithelium of the intermediate region of turtles (= Jacobson's organ) resembles the olfactory epithelium in the form and arrangement of its cells (Seydel, 1896). The one notable difference is the total absence of Bowman's glands in the intermediate region (Fig. 41). In *Testudo*, but not in *Emys*, Seydel found the basal region of the epithelium to have prominent evaginations; these extend nearly to the middle of the epithelium and contain the nerve fibers leaving the sensory cells of Jacobson's organ. In late embryos of *Chrysemys* there are no such evaginations, although the epithelial base is somewhat irregular (Parsons, 1959a). There are no studies of the cytology of Jacobson's organ in turtles, and details of the structure of its epithelium are unknown. Although von Mihalkovics (1898) and von Navratil (1926), both of whom also noted the sensory epithelium lacking Bowman's glands in the intermediate region of the cavum nasi proprium, reported that sensory epithelium representing Jacobson's organ lines the duct of the medial nasal gland in turtles, this has been denied by all other workers and I can see no sensory epithelium there.

The histology of the Jacobson's organ of *Sphenodon* has been described only by Osawa (1898), who admitted that his material was poorly preserved, and Pratt (1948), who was interested primarily in the gross structure. Both stated that the organ is lined by high, sensory epithelium dorsally and low, ciliated epithelium ventrally, and that the subepithelial connective tissue contains many blood vessels. In the latter character *Sphenodon* resembles mammals more than it does other reptiles (Broman, 1920). There are no glands associated with Jacobson's organ except, possibly, the orbital glands; the lachrymal duct enters the nasal cavity very close to Jacobson's organ.

Despite the numerous studies of the Jacobson's organ of squamates, there are, to my knowledge, no recent detailed descriptions of its histology. Dorsally, and on the sides, the organ is lined by high sensory epithelium, and ventrally there is lower non-sensory epithelium covering the mushroom body. The duct of Jacobson's organ is lined by stratified squamous epithelium, except for *Anguis* in which the anterolateral wall is ciliated (Pratt, 1948).

The sensory epithelium is very high and well developed, its height being 400–500μ in *Natrix* (von Mihalkovics, 1898, and Krause, 1922), and 95μ in *Anguis* (Negus, 1958). In snakes the basal nine-tenths of the epithelium appears as tightly packed polygonal columns interspersed with small amounts of connective tissue containing a network of capillaries. Such columns are not clearly formed in lizards, but the capillary network is present, and the basic structure appears to be similar (Beard, 1889, and von Mihalkovics, 1898). The columns, whose formation has been discussed by Beard (1889) and Parsons (1959a), develop only in the later embryonic stages after the epithelium has nearly attained its adult height. Connective tissue and capillaries extend into the epithelium dividing it into the columns. Beard reported that capillaries are not present at the earliest stages in the development of the columns of lizards, but they do seem to be there at all stages in *Thamnophis* (Parsons, 1959a). The columns not only become longer in the later stages, but also narrower and more numerous; this presumably requires the splitting of existing columns, but there are no descriptions of this occurring or reports of partially divided columns.

The sensory epithelium probably contains the same three cell types as does the olfactory epithelium of the cavum nasi proprium. Basal cells are mentioned only by Allison (1953); although his description is said to apply to both mammals and reptiles, it is based mainly on the former, and basal cells are possibly absent in reptiles. The sustentacular and sensory cells were first adequately described by Retzius (1894). The former are very high columnar cells, extending the entire height of the epithelium, which, in *Natrix*, have long spindle-shaped nuclei which lie in essentially a single row near the peripheral border of the epithelium (Kolmer, 1928). In *Anguis*, the sustentacular cells are rare or even absent (Pratt, 1948), but "there is a transition from sustentacular to goblet cells" (p. 174) at the boundary between the sensory and non-sensory regions. All workers agree that Bowman's glands are lacking in Jacobson's organ.

The sensory cells are bipolar neurons like the olfactory cells of the cavum and make up most of the sensory epithelium (Wright, 1883, and many later workers). Retzius (1894), who studied *Natrix* stained by the Golgi method, confirmed the bipolar nature of the cells and found no ganglionic cells in the epithelium despite previous reports of their presence. Since the nerve of Jacobson's organ is part of the olfactory nerve, ganglionic cells would not be expected and, indeed, their presence would be very difficult to explain (Parsons, 1959a). The many small and densely packed cell bodies of the sensory cells form the columns of the epithelium, and nerve fibers leave from the ends of the columns; the fibers are very rare in the intercolumnar connective tissue (Wright, 1883). In *Natrix* the nuclei of the sensory cells are 6 or 7μ by 5μ (Wright, 1883) and up to 50μ deep between the base of the epithelium and its periphery (Kolmer, 1928). Leydig (1872a) described rigid but easily destroyed hairs at the peripheral ends of the sensory cells, and Retzius (1894) figured short olfactory hairs exactly like those of the olfactory cells of the cavum. Allison (1953), however, denied the presence of olfactory hairs in Jacobson's organ, and stated that, although previous workers had thought their absence might be caused by their extreme sensitivity and rapid loss after death, he had evidence that such is not the case. Allison's evidence is based on mammalian material as is much of his general description, but Cordier (1964) reported similar findings in reptiles. Recently the Jacobson's organ of *Anguis* has been shown, electron microscopically, to lack cilia but to have numerous long microvilli which resemble poorly fixed cilia under the light microscope (Bannister, 1968).

Much of the older literature on Jacobson's organ concerns the nature of the epithelial columns. Leydig (1872b), who originally described them, considered the columns to be composed of ganglionic cells, a view supported by Wright (1883) and Beard (1889) and opposed by Born (1883), who believed the columns to represent glands. Although the work of Retzius (1894) should have ended the dispute, von Mihalkovics (1898) still argued

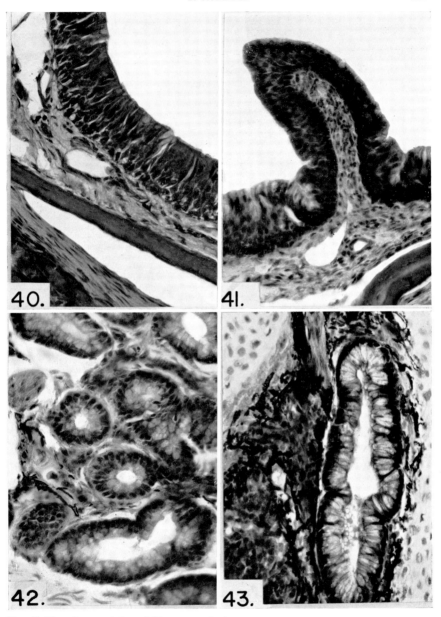

FIG. 40. Nasopharyngeal duct of *Clemmys caspica leprosa*.
FIG. 41. Choanal flap of *Clemmys caspica leprosa*. Dorsal is to the right.
FIG. 42. External nasal gland of *Clemmys caspica leprosa*.
FIG. 43. Medial nasal gland of *Clemmys caspica leprosa*.
All four figures are transverse sections, 10μ thick, stained with haematoxylin and eosin, and magnified approximately 120 times.

the ganglionic nature of the columns, and discussion of this disagreement continued at least until 1910 (Zuckerkandl, 1910b). The only reference to ganglionic cells (or at least presumably ganglionic cells) of which I am aware after that date is Pratt's (1948, p. 174) mention of "a zone of what are generally accepted as granular neurones" basal to the sensory and sustentacular cells of *Anguis*.

The mushroom body is covered by low columnar ciliated epithelium, 15μ high in *Thamnophis* and *Anguis* (Wright, 1883; Negus, 1958). There are no reports of basal cells within this epithelium; goblet cells, so abundant in the respiratory epithelium of the cavum nasi proprium, are apparently absent. Although, as noted above, Pratt (1948) mentioned them in his description of *Anguis*, no other workers have noted their presence, and Krause (1922) specifically reported their absence in *Lacerta*. Thus, as in other reptiles and unlike the situation in mammals, the Jacobson's organ of squamates has no glands, but it is closely associated with the lachrymal duct (as described in the section on adult anatomy).

The epithelium of Jacobson's organ is underlain by connective tissue containing nerves, blood vessels, and pigment cells. The blood vessels do not form a plexus of sinuses around the organ as they do in mammals and, to a lesser extent, in *Sphenodon* (Broman, 1920, and Negus, 1958). Pigment cells are very common in the connective tissue; according to Leydig (1872a) they are, in *Lacerta*, concentrated around the nerves and more numerous here than in the subepithelial tissue of the cavum.

The only mention of the histology of a vestigial Jacobson's organ in a squamate is that of *Chamaeleo* (Haas, 1947). It is lined by a compound columnar epithelium, the cells of which have elliptic nuclei, and a basal layer containing more tightly packed nuclei which are described only as not being elliptical. Other details are lacking, so that this form remains, histologically, almost unknown. The reduced Jacobson's organ in *Anolis* resembles histologically that organ in *Lacerta* (Armstrong *et al.*, 1953).

V. Embryology of the Nasal Organs

A. EARLY EMBRYOLOGY

The early embryology of reptilian noses has been studied by many workers. Turtles were considered by Seydel (1896) and crocodilians by Voeltzkow (1899), but most of the classic papers, those by Rathke (1839), Born (1879 and 1883), Beard (1889), and Peter (1900), describe squamates, especially *Lacerta* and *Natrix*. *Sphenodon* has been little studied. This early work was carefully reviewed by Peter (1906). Although there are numerous more recent works, such as those by Beecker (1903) and Hoppe (1934), most of them are concerned primarily with the later stages; such emphasis on later stages is especially marked in studies of the palate, although Fuchs (1907, 1908, and 1915), Thäter (1910), and Dohrer (1912) made passing mention of earlier stages. Parsons (1959a) presented an extensive review of the earlier work.

The early stages in the nasal embryology are very similar in all groups of reptiles. This similarity can be seen in sectioned material, such as is shown in Figs 44, 45 and 46, and even better in intact embryos. The latter are here represented only by *Eretmochelys* (Fig. 47), but several forms are figured in the literature: turtles by Voeltzkow (1903), Dohrer (1912), and Deraniyagala (1939), *Sphenodon* by Schauinsland (1903), squamates by Rathke (1839) and Born (1879 and 1883), and *Crocodylus* by Voeltzkow (1899).

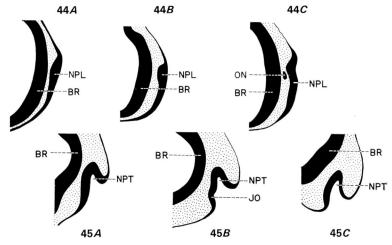

FIG. 44. Transverse sections through the nasal placodes of reptiles (after Parsons, 1959a). A. *Chrysemys picta*. B. *Thamnophis* sp. C. *Alligator mississippiensis*.

FIG. 45. Transverse sections through the nasal pits (early stages) of reptiles (after Parsons, 1959a). A. *Chrysemys picta*. B. *Oxybelis* sp. C. *Alligator mississippiensis*.

BR, Brain; JO, Jacobson's organ; NPL, Nasal placode; NPT, Nasal pit; ON, Olfactory nerve.

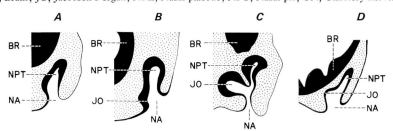

FIG. 46. Transverse sections through the nasal pits (later stages) of reptiles. A. *Chrysemys picta* (after Parsons, 1959a). B. *Sphenodon punctatus* (after Parsons, 1959a). C. *Thamnophis* sp. (after Parsons, 1959a). D. *Crocodylus niloticus* (after Voeltzkow, 1899).

BR, Brain; JO, Jacobson's organ; NA, Naris; NPT, Nasal pit.

The first stage in the nasal development is the formation of the nasal placode (= Riechfeld, Riechplakode, Riechplatte), a thickening of the epithelium on the ventrolateral surface of the snout (Fig. 44). The placode, which is roughly circular with the ventral margin slightly flattened, is not sharply distinct from the surrounding epidermal epithelium, but gradually merges with it. During this, and the immediately succeeding stages, the epidermis is

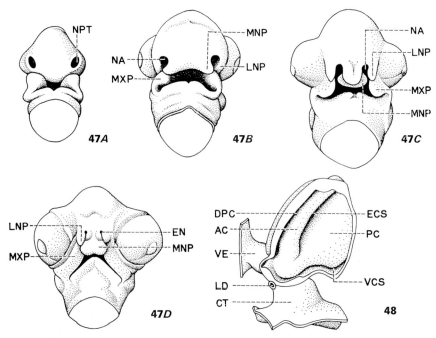

Fig. 47. Anterior views of the head of *Eretmochelys imbricata* embryos showing the development and fusion of the lateral and medial nasal processes (after Voeltzkow, 1903). A through D are successive stages.

Fig. 48. Medial view of the lateral wall of the nasal cavity of 4·5 mm headlength embryo of *Sphenodon punctatus* (after Hoppe, 1934).

AC, Anterior concha; CT, Choanal tube; DPC, Dorsal pocket of the choanal tube; ECS, Extra-conchal space; EN, External naris; LD, Lachrymal duct; LNP, Lateral nasal process; MNP, Medial nasal process; MXP, Maxillary process; NA, Naris; NPT, Nasal pit; PC, Posterior concha; VCS, Ventral conchal space; VE, Vestibulum.

formed by simple cuboidal epithelium with the nuclei located near the centers of the cells; the higher placodal epithelium is columnar and, probably, pseudostratified. The nuclei are mostly basal in position, but there are very numerous peripherally placed mitotic figures in squamates and turtles; in crocodilians the nuclei of the placodal cells are frequently central or even peripheral in position.

The placode soon becomes indented to form a nasal pit (= Nasenfurche,

Nasengrube, Nasenmundrinne, Riechgrübchen, Riechgrube). Early stages in the development of this pit are shown in Figs 45 and 47A. The margins of the nasal pit are slightly raised and an inpocketing occurs at its center or the region just dorsal to its center. This inpocketing is caused by the rapid division of the placodal cells (Peter, 1900). The olfactory nerve begins its development at approximately the time when the nasal pit appears. Fibers grow out from the cells of the nasal epithelium and extend towards the brain. These fibers are accompanied by cells which may give rise to the Schwann cells of the olfactory nerve (see Parsons, 1959a). In squamates, but apparently not in other reptiles, even early nasal pit stages show a small groove in the medial wall of the nasal pit which marks the first appearance of Jacobson's organ. There is no change in the histology at this stage although some variation in the thickness of the nasal epithelium can be seen; it is typically thickest dorsally and anteriorly.

As the nasal pit develops it becomes deeper and, relatively at least, narrower. At first it extends dorsomedially, but it soon becomes dorsally and then dorsolaterally oriented (Fig. 46). The pit also elongates antero-posteriorly; the anterior end remains on the ventrolateral surface of the snout in a nearly terminal position and the posterior end extends into the roof of the mouth. There is thus a single, anteriorly widest naris (= Einführungs-spalte, Nasenspalte) on each side (Fig. 47). In most reptiles the nasal pit extends a short distance anterior to the anterior end of the naris; this anterior extension is termed the apikale Blindsack in the German literature. The histological picture remains essentially the same as in the earlier stages and the nasal epithelium is still thickest anteriorly and dorsally. There is no distinct boundary between the nasal and epidermal epithelia.

Jacobson's organ becomes well formed at this stage (Fig. 46B). In squamates the small groove seen in the previous stage has become a large, nearly spherical pit off the ventromedial wall of the nasal pit with thick epithelium like that of the nasal pit and a large lumen. Jacobson's organ is, at this stage, frequently as large as the rest of the nasal pit and is apparently well developed in all squamates since it is large even in *Chamaeleo* (Haas, 1947). The Jacobson's organ of *Sphenodon* appears as a small groove in the ventromedial nasal wall, slightly later than but much like that of squamates. In crocodilians there is apparently a very transitory groove representing Jacobson's organ that is found only at this stage. Its greatest development is in *Crocodylus* (Voeltzkow, 1899; his figure is here reproduced as Fig. 46D); in *Alligator* I saw only a smaller and less conspicuous inpocketing of the same region (Parsons, 1959a). Turtles are said, by almost all workers, to lack any such inpocketing. However, Loew (1956) has reported the presence of a typical (i.e., more or less squamate-like) Jacobson's organ in *Emys*. His figures show a small groove or pit, roughly comparable to that of *Crocodylus*

(Fig. 46D). While the nasal pit does curve slightly (Fig. 46A), there does not appear to be any distinct groove (Seydel, 1896; Fuchs, 1907; Parsons, 1959a; see also the discussion of Jacobson's organ in adult turtles).

In the Squamata the concha first appears in the later stages of the development of the nasal pit. It is basically the same as in the adult, an invagination of the lateral or ventrolateral nasal wall into the pit. Although the concha is small, the lumen of the pit extends laterally dorsal to it, thus forming a small extraconchal space, in *Lacerta* and *Thamnophis* (Peter, 1906, and Parsons, 1959a). At the same stage there may develop a small evagination (= choanal diverticulum) of the ventrolateral nasal wall, opposite Jacobson's organ, into which the anterior end of the lachrymal duct will later empty (Born, 1879 and 1883, and Bellairs and Boyd, 1950); however, this duct is not formed until later stages. The few described embryos of *Sphenodon* lack a concha at this stage, but this could as easily reflect the inadequacy of the material as the absence of a concha. Those turtles of which there are embryological studies lack prominent Muschelwülste, so that when that structure first appears is unknown. In crocodilians the conchae are not present at this stage, but, in *Crocodylus*, Voeltzkow (1899) and Shiino (1914) have described a small dorsolateral invagination into the nasal pit. This invagination must rapidly disappear, as it was not noted in a series of embryos of *Alligator* (Parsons, 1959a). The presence of this invagination makes the nasal pit Y-shaped in transverse section, and Shiino considered the medial arm of the Y to represent Jacobson's organ. However, this arm lies well dorsal to the groove here considered to be Jacobson's organ, and does not seem to be related to it; yet none of the described specimens show both structures, and hence Shiino's theory cannot be disproved.

The final event in the early nasal embryology is the separation of the external naris from the choana. Medially the nasal pit is bounded by the medial nasal process (= innerer Nasenfortsatz, medialer Nasenfortsatz) and laterally by the lateral nasal process (= äusserer Nasenfortsatz, lateraler Nasenfortsatz). The latter, together with the maxillary process (= Oberkieferfortsatz), extends ventrally so that the naris comes to lie ventrally rather than ventrolaterally (Fig. 47). The ventral ends of the medial and lateral processes meet and fuse ventral to the center of the nasal pit. Apparently the fusion occurs more rapidly in squamates than in turtles since the stage with tightly appressed nasal processes is rarely encountered in squamates. The ventral surface of the fused processes is the primary palate. Only a small opening remains at the anterior end of the naris on the external surface of the snout; this is the external naris and quickly becomes closed by a plug of more or less isodiametric cells, the Füllgewebe (see Weber, 1950, for details). Posteriorly the much longer, slit-like choana opens into the anterior part of the oral cavity.

B. LATER EMBRYOLOGY

1. *General*

The earlier stages in the nasal embryology, during which the basic structures of the nose are formed, are relatively similar in all reptiles; in the later stages, the members of each order gradually attain their characteristic adult specializations. Thus each order must be treated separately but, since the adult structure has been treated in some detail, the individual treatments can be relatively short.

There is a huge but generally disappointing literature on the later nasal embryology of reptiles (see Peter, 1906, and Parsons, 1959a). Many papers contain some mention of later embryos; however, few of these accounts are detailed. Thus, although many other works were used and are cited below, most of the following descriptions are based on a comparatively small number of papers: Seydel (1896) and Parsons (1959a) on turtles, Hoppe (1934) on *Sphenodon*, Born (1879 and 1883) and Parsons (1959a) on squamates, and Meek (1911) and Bertau (1935) on crocodilians.

2. *Testudines*

The only turtles whose later nasal embryology has been studied in any detail are *Chrysemys* and *Emys* (Seydel, 1896; Fuchs, 1907 and 1915; Thäter, 1910; Kunkel, 1912; Loew, 1956; Parsons, 1959a); other forms are known only from casual mention of one or two specimens. In both *Chrysemys* and *Emys* the cavum nasi proprium gradually attains its adult configuration. The two Grenzfalten are first indicated by a thinning of the epithelium covering them and only later become ridges projecting into the cavum. The development of the sulci is more complex. At first the entire ventral part of the cavum, especially laterally, has thinner epithelial walls than the dorsal part. They become progressively thicker, first ventromedially, then ventrally, and finally ventrolaterally. The sulci first appear as quite narrow grooves which gradually widen out to form the broad, shallow sulci of the adult. As they widen, the epithelium lining them becomes thicker while that lining the intervening ridges and the Grenzfalten becomes thinner. Neither *Chrysemys* nor *Emys* has a well formed Muschelwulst, but some indication of one may be present in very late embryos. All the descriptions are in general agreement except for that of Loew (1956) who figured, in all stages, a moderately prominent groove, interpreted as the Jacobson's organ and apparently corresponding to the medial sulcus. Other workers only found the medial sulcus at later stages and then less prominently.

The external and medial nasal glands develop as solid, rod-like outgrowths of the vestibulum which later branch and develop lumina. Besides these, there is, in *Chrysemys*, a small dorsal recess of the vestibulum which projects dorsally from the extreme posterior end of the vestibulum in certain late embryonic stages (Parsons, 1959a). This recess is absent in the latest embryos of *Chrysemys* and has not been reported in any other forms. The external naris is plugged, for most of the later embryonic stages, by its hypertrophied epithelial lining.

The development of the nasopharyngeal duct has been much studied and fought over (Fuchs, 1907, 1908, 1911, and 1915; Thäter, 1910; Dohrer, 1912), and the literature is filled with polemics. Fuchs believed that the progressive posterior restriction of the choana is accomplished by fusion at the anterior part of the primitive choana until only its extreme posterior end remains open. Thäter denied that there is fusion and claimed that the posterior displacement of the choana is caused by differential growth. Differential growth certainly occurs (Fuchs mentions it), but it also seems most probable that there is fusion so that the primary palate is extended posteriorly during the later embryonic stages.

3. *Rhynchocephalia*

Only a few embryos of *Sphenodon* have been studied and its nasal embryology is very incompletely known. The vestibulum develops as in other reptiles. Both medial and external nasal glands grow out from it and, for most of the later embryonic stages, the vestibulum is plugged by a solid mass of cells. The choana remains, throughout the later embryonic and adult stages, in essentially its original condition, that is as a long opening ventral to most of the cavum nasi proprium.

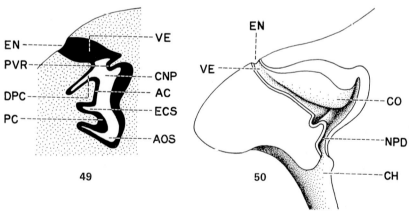

Fig. 49. Frontal section through the nasal cavity of an embryo of *Sphenodon punctatus* (after Parsons, 1959a).

Fig. 50. Medial view of the lateral wall of the nasal cavity of a 5 mm headlength embryo of *Crocodylus porosus* (after Meek, 1911).

AC, Anterior concha; AOS, Antorbital space; CH, Choana; CNP, Cavum nasi proprium; CO, Concha; DPC, Dorsal pocket of the choanal tube; ECS, Extraconchal space; EN, External naris; NPD, Nasopharyngeal duct; PC, Posterior concha; PVR, Postvestibular ridge; VE, Vestibulum.

There are, however, changes in the cavum nasi proprium. Figure 48 shows the youngest of the embryos studied by Hoppe (1934) in which the nasal processes have fused, and Fig. 49 shows a slightly older but similar specimen. Even at the stages figured, almost all of the adult structures are present, but their relationships are not the same as in the adult. The main difference is in the arrangement of the anterior and posterior conchae; in these embryos they lie parallel and very close to each other. Their anteroventral ends are joined and their posterodorsal ends separate. Thus the region corresponding to the extraconchal space of squamates (the dorso-laterale Muschelraum of Hoppe) forms a slit-like recess between the conchae, and the dorsal pocket of the choanal tube is a long, nearly vertical slit lying anterior to the anterior concha. As the embryo grows, the cavum elongates and the dorsal ends of the conchae gradually become separated by a greater distance until the adult condition is reached. With this spreading of the conchae like the two leaves of a hinge, the extraconchal space becomes merely the dorsal part of the conchal zone and the dorsal pocket of the choanal tube comes to lie ventral to the anterior concha.

Jacobson's organ and the lachrymal duct quickly attain their adult configurations and change but little in the stages studied by Hoppe (1934). His descriptions of embryos differ from those given by all other workers in exactly the same fashion as his descriptions of adults differ from those of others. This discrepancy has been discussed in the section on adult anatomy.

4. Squamata

Although numerous workers have studied embryos of different squamates, there is very little to be said concerning the later stages in their nasal embryology. Almost all the embryological work has been done on only four genera, *Lacerta*, *Anguis*, *Natrix*, and *Thamnophis*. All of these possess rather similar and quite simple nasal cavities; almost nothing is known concerning the development of the complex vestibulum of other families of lizards, of the dorsally attached concha in some lizards, or of other such specializations. The great variability in adult anatomy must be reflected in considerable embryological variation, but the details of the latter have, to my knowledge, never been described. For example, only a passing mention documents the nasal embryology of *Varanus* (Sṅrivastava, 1963).

The development of the vestibulum in the well known forms is simple. Throughout the later embryonic stages the external naris is plugged by a mass of isodiametric cells (Weber, 1950). The vestibular epithelium is simple, rather low columnar, with the nuclei basally located in the cells. The external nasal gland develops as a solid outgrowth of the vestibular wall, usually dorsally, as in other reptiles. Squamates typically lack a medial nasal gland, but a small ventral outgrowth of the posterior part of the vestibulum of *Varanus* has been described by Shrivastava (1963), and is believed to represent this gland. Judging by Shrivastava's figures, the complex course of the adult varanid vestibulum develops only in the later embryonic stages; in earlier embryos, as in embryos and adults of *Lacerta* and snakes, the vestibulum is a simple passage from the external naris to the cavum nasi proprium.

Formation of the concha permits recognition of all the major parts of the cavum nasi proprium. In the well studied squamates the concha first appears in the early embryonic stages. The later changes are, except in the region of the choana, not important. The histological differentiation of the epithelial lining proceeds gradually, with the epithelium of the sensory areas becoming very thick while only simple columnar epithelium lines the non-sensory regions.

In all squamates there is further restriction of the primitive choana (Pratt, 1948; Bellairs and Boyd, 1950; and Parsons, 1959a). There has been some dispute over how this occurs. Fuchs (1908 and 1911) and most other workers believe that both fusion and differential growth occur, but Thäter (1910) postulated differential growth only. The arguments are exactly the same as the ones just discussed concerning turtles. The lachrymal duct grows forward from the orbit and enters the anterior end of the primitive choana laterally, thus producing a structure closely comparable to that of the adult *Sphenodon*. With the further fusion and extension of the primary palate, a small part of the anterior end of the primitive choana is left open as the duct of Jacobson's organ. The presence or absence of a choanal groove, the length of the adult choana, and the presence or absence of a nasopharyngeal duct all depend on the extent of the fusion which occurs and have been considered in the section on the adult anatomy.

Jacobson's organ is well formed in the early embryonic stages as a more or less spherical pocket at the medial side of the choana. With the further extension of the primary palate its duct becomes separated from the choana. The mushroom body develops as an outpocketing of the floor of the organ and the epithelium covering it becomes thinner as that lining the rest of the organ becomes thicker. Only in quite late stages, when the epithelium has nearly attained its adult thickness, does the columnar structure of the sensory epithelium, discussed above in the section on histology, develop. The Jacobson's organ, which is normally developed in early embryos of *Chamaeleo*, grows but little in later stages, and the mushroom body never develops (Haas, 1947); presumably a similar course is followed in other lizards in which Jacobson's organ is reduced.

5. *Crocodilia*

In crocodilians the vestibulum remains very small and simple, and gives rise to the external nasal gland in the same manner as in other reptiles.

There is no Jacobson's organ in later embryonic stages; some workers have disagreed on this point, as has been noted in the section on adult anatomy, but their views have not been generally accepted. The development of the nasopharyngeal duct and secondary palate has been studied by several workers including Voeltzkow (1899), Fuchs (1908), and Müller (1965 and 1967). Although there are complications when the process is considered in detail, basically there is further fusion to extend the primary palate as in turtles and snakes, and the roof of the mouth posterior to the primitive choanae becomes inpocketed to form a groove. A secondary palate converts this groove into the nasopharyngeal ducts. In late embryos the posterior part of the duct is a median structure, but postembryonically the septum reaches to the choanae and separates the right and left nasopharyngeal ducts.

The development of the cavum nasi proprium with its three conchae and several sinuses and recesses is more complex. Successive stages are shown in Figs 50 through 52; although they show different genera, they represent the changes which could be observed in any one genus. The lachrymal duct grows forward from the orbit and, throughout most of the later embryonic period, enters the cavum in the same fashion as it does in the adult.

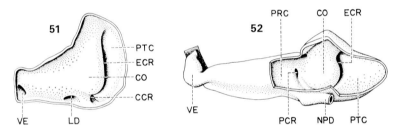

Fig. 51. Medial view of the lateral wall of the cavum nasi proprium of an 11 mm headlength embryo of *Melanosuchus niger* (after Bertau, 1935).

Fig. 52. Medial view of the nasal cavity of a 19·5 mm headlength embryo of *Alligator mississippiensis* with part of the medial wall removed (after Bertau, 1935).

CCR, Caviconchal recess; CO, Concha; ECR, Extraconchal recess; LD, Lachrymal duct; NPD, Nasopharyngeal duct; PCR, Preconchal recess; PRC, Preconcha; PTC, Postconcha; VE, Vestibulum.

The first conchal structure to appear is called the concha. It forms a prominent projection into the cavum from most of the length of the lateral caval wall (Fig. 50). In later stages, the cavum extends farther posteriorly and the postconcha appears as a posterolateral projection into it (Fig. 51); actually the cavum grows around the postconcha rather than the latter swelling out into a large cavity. Finally the original concha becomes largely subdivided by a vertical slit-like depression; the longer but lower anterior part is the preconcha and the shorter but more prominent posterior part the concha of the adult (Fig. 52). The changes in the shapes of the conchae during the final embryonic stages are not very great. The concha becomes relatively thinner, appearing as a long ridge in the adult rather than a nearly hemispherical swelling as in the embryo.

The extraconchal recess can be recognized as soon as the postconcha is distinct and the preconchal recess is the slit separating the preconcha from the concha. The caviconchal recess also develops at a fairly early stage, before the differentiation of the preconchal recess. The other recesses and sinuses do not develop until very late embryonic or even postembryonic stages, the maxillary sinus being the last to appear (Bertau, 1935). All of them begin as small outpocketings from the cavum nasi proprium and gradually enlarge until the adult condition is attained. The postconchal cavity is, embryologically, merely the greatly enlarged end of the post-turbinal sinus, and the latter, in turn, is an outgrowth of the extraconchal recess. Bertau (1935) has considered the later stages in the development of the crocodilian nose in considerable detail and presented many excellent reconstructions of the various stages; for further details the reader is referred to his paper.

VI. Nasal Glands

A. BOWMAN'S GLANDS

Almost all reptiles have Bowman's glands (= glandulae olfactoriae) throughout the olfactory epithelium of the cavum nasi proprium (Fig. 37). Although generally very numerous, these glands may be few in number in aquatic snakes such as *Acrochordus* in which they occur in only a part of the olfactory epithelium (Kathariner, 1900). The greatest variation is found in the Hydrophiidae; many occur in *Laticauda*, few in *Pelamis*, and none in *Hydrophis*, the last being the only known reptile with olfactory epithelium and without Bowman's glands (Kathariner, 1900). The glands appear to be completely lacking in all non-sensory portions of the nasal cavity and in Jacobson's organ.

The shape of the Bowman's glands varies. General descriptions (Kolmer, 1927; Allison, 1953) refer to them as generally simple and tubulo-alveolar. In turtles only the alveolar form occurs (Hoffmann, 1879–1890; Seydel, 1896; von Mihalkovics, 1898; Parsons, 1959a). In *Sphenodon* the glands are generally tubular (Osawa, 1898, and Gabe and Saint Girons, 1964), although some alveolar glands have also been reported by Osawa. Although many workers have mentioned their presence in various squamates, few have noted the shape of the Bowman's glands; there are two reports of tubular structure (*Thamnophis*, Macallum, 1883; and *Pelamis*, Kathariner, 1900) and two of alveolar structure (*Lacerta*, Krause, 1922; and late embryos of *Thamnophis*, Parsons, 1959a). Hoffmann (1879–1890) stated that the Bowman's glands of *Crocodylus* resemble those of mammals, which suggests a tubular structure. Only Macallum (1883) and Osawa (1898) have reported any branched Bowman's glands in reptiles. The body of the gland always lies within the subepithelial connective tissue, and a very narrow duct pierces the olfactory epithelium. Although Leydig (1872a) thought that some of these ducts might join the external nasal gland, all the more recent workers have denied this.

Although there are various discrepancies in the descriptions of the histology of the Bowman's glands, most workers agree that they are formed of simple epithelium, with the columnar or pyramidal cells of the main part of the gland and the lower cuboidal cells of the duct having elongate basal nuclei (Osawa, 1898; Krause, 1922; Allison, 1953; Gabe and Saint Girons, 1964). The descriptions by Hoffmann (1879–1890) and Macallum (1883) differ in reporting central nuclei and spherical rather than columnar cells respectively. The columnar cells are 32–35μ high and 12–14μ in diameter in sea turtles (Hoffmann, 1879–1890) and 30μ high in *Sphenodon* (Gabe and Saint Girons, 1964). Although Osawa (1898) described typical goblet cells in the Bowman's glands of *Sphenodon*, Gabe and Saint Girons (1964) found none in that genus, and no other authors have reported their presence there. Allison (1953) and Negus (1958) noted yellowish olfactory pigment granules within the cells of Bowman's glands, but in neither case is it clear if such pigment occurs in all forms or only in mammals, with which their works are primarily concerned. Hoffmann (1879–1890) also reported an apparently similar pigment in *Eretmochelys* and *Dermochelys*, but only in a mass of small spherical cells with large central nuclei which he described as filling the lumen of the gland; such cells have not been reported by any other workers, and Hoffmann's description cannot, therefore, be accepted without further evidence.

Bowman's glands develop from the olfactory epithelium only in the latest embryonic stages (Parsons, 1959a). At that time they are simple alveolar glands with simple, essentially cuboidal epithelium which becomes very low and nearly squamous in the ducts.

There is no general agreement on the nature of the secretion of Bowman's glands. Although Osawa (1898) described the cytoplasm of the cells as finely reticulated distally and granular only basally, Krause (1922) and Gabe and Saint Girons (1964) reported small secretory granules distally. Krause described them only as acidophilic, but Gabe and Saint Girons found the granules to be strongly PAS positive and suggested that the secretion is either a neutral mucopolysaccharide or a glycoprotein in a broad sense. Oledzka-Slotwinska (1961) reported similar findings in *Lacerta*, but stated that in *Natrix* and *Vipera* the secretion is an acid mucopolysaccharide. Negus (1958) had been unable to demonstrate mucus in *Anguis*, and Allison (1953) considered the secretion of Bowman's glands to be neither typically serous nor mucous. Since the secretion bathes the olfactory hairs and is restricted to the olfactory region, it may well be of importance in olfaction.

B. EXTERNAL NASAL GLAND

The external nasal gland (= äussere Nasendrüse, dorsal nasal gland, lateral nasal gland, lateral nasal gland of Müller, laterale Nasendrüse, nasal gland, Nasendrüse, obere Nasendrüse, seitliche Nasendrüse, superior nasal gland) is usually the largest of the nasal glands in reptiles. It lies outside of the cartilaginous nasal capsule, dorsal or lateral to the nasal cavity. The duct of the gland enters the vestibulum, typically posterodorsally and near the anterior end of the cavum nasi proprium. Hoffmann (1879–1890), van der Merwe (1940), Pratt (1948), and Parsons and Stephens (1968) have described cases in which the duct enters the anterior part of the cavum, and others have noted its entrance at the boundary between the vestibulum and the cavum; probably there is variation in this point, but the differences in descriptions could also be due to varying definitions of the vestibulum. The gland is commonly, though far from invariably, a fairly compact mass lying within connective tissue. Although Reese (1925) mentioned a distinct capsule, Oelrich (1956) has denied that a true capsule exists. The connective tissue surrounding the gland is rich in capillaries (Reese, 1925, and Philpott and Templeton, 1964).

Most workers who have described the external nasal gland termed it a branched tubular mucous gland (Fig. 42). However, Röse (1893), Reese (1925), Pratt (1948), Stebbins (1948), and Bellairs (1949a) all have referred to acini or alveoli; possibly in some forms the gland is best described as tubulo-acinar since Leydig (1873) mentioned that the ends of the tubules are somewhat swollen. Taub (1966) considered the gland to be serous rather than mucous. Recently there has been much work done on the salt secreting ability of this gland. Although most such work has been performed on birds, salt secretion has also been studied in certain lizards (e.g., by Philpott and Templeton, 1964, in *Dipsosaurus*). It should be noted here that the salt secreting gland of marine turtles, although often called the nasal gland (Benson *et al.*, 1964, etc.), is not a nasal gland but one of the orbital glands, probably the lachrymal (Franz, 1934; Abel and Ellis, 1966). The natrial gland of hydrophiid snakes may be oral rather than nasal (Dunson and Taub, 1967; Taub and Dunson, 1967; Dunson, 1968). I know of no references to salt secretion by a true nasal gland in any reptiles other than lizards.

In all reptiles the external nasal gland appears to be innervated by the ramus lateralis nasi of the ethmoidal nerve, a branch of the ophthalmic division of the trigeminal (terminology that of Willard, 1915). Other names that apparently refer to the same nerve are nervus externus narium (Gaupp, 1888), lateral branch of the ramus ethmoidalis (Malan, 1946), lateral ramus of the ethmoidal nerve (Bellairs, 1949a; Frank, 1951; Bellairs and Shute, 1953), and lateral ethmoid nerve (Oelrich, 1956). Most of these studies were of squamates, but turtles (Gaupp, 1888) and crocodilians (Gaupp, 1888; Bellairs and Shute, 1953) have also been described. The nerve fibers actually innervating the gland must be autonomic and hence not part of the tri- geminal nerve strictly speaking. Gaupp (1888) and Bellairs (1949a) both mentioned communications between the ethmoidal nerve and the palatine branch of the facial nerve (through the ethmoidal ganglion of Willard, 1915), and presumably the autonomic fibers join the ethmoidal nerve there. This connection is absent in crocodilians (Bellairs and Shute, 1953), and sympa- thetic fibers join the nerve more proximally.

As far as is known, the embryology of the external nasal gland is very similar in all reptiles (Röse, 1893; Hoppe, 1934; Bertau, 1935; Pratt, 1948; Parsons, 1959a). Although normally the first of the nasal glands to develop, it is not present until quite late embryonic stages. The gland first appears as a solid rod-like projection from the dorsal, or lateral, wall of the vestibulum close to the latter's boundary with the cavum nasi proprium. It grows posteriorly and branches repeatedly until the adult configuration is attained. In all embryonic stages the lumina of the duct and tubules are very small and often completely absent; they become much wider at about the time of hatching. Röse (1893) reported a regression in the size of this gland in the latest embryonic stages of Crocodylus, but Bertau (1935) found no evidence of this in Crocodylus or other crocodilians. Certainly the normal pattern appears to be for the gland to reach its adult proportions in the latest embryonic stages and then to enlarge more slowly, maintaining approxi- mately the same relative size in all later stages.

The external nasal gland of Testudo is very large with its posterior part lying lateral to the lateral Grenzfalte between the cartilaginous nasal capsule and the bony skull and with its anterior part lying dorsal to the anterior portion of the cavum nasi proprium, again external to the nasal capsule (Seydel, 1896). The rather short duct pierces the nasal capsule and enters the dorsolateral vestibular wall immediately anterior to the postvestibular ridge. Chelydra apparently resembles Testudo closely (Nick, 1912). In Emys, the gland resembles that of Testudo except that it is smaller, the more posterior lateral portion being absent, and its duct enters the vestibulum more dorsally (Seydel, 1896; cf. von Mihalkovics, 1898, who described the duct as lateral). Chrysemys resembles Emys (Parsons, 1959a). Kinosternon has a well developed gland whose duct enters the anterior part of the cavum nasi proprium (Parsons and Stephens, 1968). In both cheloniids and Dermochelys, there is no external nasal gland (Hoffmann, 1879–1890; Nick, 1912; Fuchs, 1915). According to van der Merwe (1940), the duct of this gland enters a dorsal recess of the nose in Pelomedusa; this recess appears to me to be an expanded terminal portion of the duct. Otherwise the gland resembles that of *Emys*. The only other descriptions of this gland in turtles are those by Hoffmann (1879–1890), and unfortunately his descriptions of glands are frequently in disagreement with those of other workers. He reported it to be very large and dorsally located in *Kinosternon*, smaller but more elongated and laterally placed in *Geochelone*, and long and entirely laterally located in *Trionyx*.

The external nasal gland of *Sphenodon* is a rather compact structure lying lateral to the cavum nasi proprium (Hoppe, 1934; Malan, 1946; Pratt, 1948). In general it resembles that of squamates, except that *Sphenodon* lacks a conchal space to accommodate the gland. Pratt considered the gland to be only weakly developed.

There are brief descriptions of the external nasal glands of many lizards. The commonest pattern is that of a fairly large gland lying lateral to the cavum nasi proprium and outside of the cartilaginous nasal capsule with much of its tissue filling the conchal space; its duct runs anteriorly to enter the posterior part of the vestibulum. Such a structure has been reported in *Ctenosaura*, *Dipsosaurus*, *Iguana*, *Sauromalus*, *Lialis*, *Xantusia*, teiids, scincids, *Lacerta*, cordylids, *Gerrhonotus*, and *Varanus* (Malan, 1946; Pratt, 1948; Stebbins, 1948; and others). Gekkonids, *Anniella*, and amphisbaenids are basically similar except that the conchal space is reduced or lacking so that most of the gland lies lateral to the nasal capsule (Fischer, 1900; Malan, 1946; Pratt, 1948; Stebbins, 1948; and others). The gland is somewhat reduced in *Anolis*, *Anguis*, and *Ophisaurus* (Malan, 1946, and Pratt, 1948), but they are otherwise similar to the forms mentioned in the previous sentence. In chamaeleonids, the rather small gland lies posterolateral to the posterolateral corner of the nasal capsule (Haas, 1937; Malan, 1946; Pratt, 1948; Engelbrecht, 1951). The external nasal gland of *Uma*, and other similar iguanids, retains its primitive position lateral to the nasal capsule, but, with the elongation of the vestibulum, its duct runs medially or posteriorly from the posterior part of the gland to the posterior end of the vestibulum. Agamids are more variable. *Agama* and *Calotes* resemble *Uma*, but in *Cophotis* the duct enters the middle of the vestibulum (as defined by gross structure), and in *Ceratophora* and *Otocryptis* the anterior end of the vestibulum (Eckart, 1922; Pratt, 1948; Barry, 1953); thus, in the last three genera, the gland lies posterior to the vestibular end of its duct. In agamids, the gland varies in size but is never very large.

The external nasal gland of snakes has long been known. It was first described by Müller (1829) who, according to Leydig (1873), thought that its duct joined the lachrymal duct and thus entered the mouth; Leydig corrected this error and gave the first adequate description of the gland. Despite this early work, numerous subsequent papers, and the survey by Smith and Bellairs (1947), even the gross structure of this gland is known in only a few forms. Typically, the gland resembles that of most lizards, lying lateral to the nasal capsule and extending posteriorly into the conchal space. However, its size is very variable, and in many forms the gland does not reach posteriorly as far as the concha. Judging by the figures and descriptions of Smith and Bellairs (1947), Baumeister (1908), Reese (1925), and Darevsky (1956), the gland is large in *Macropisthodon*, *Malpolon*, some *Natrix*, *Pareas*, *Psammophis*, *Rhinophis*, *Thamnophis*, and *Xenopeltis*; medium-sized in *Agkistrodon*, some *Ahaetulla*, *Cerberus*, *Coluber*, *Dasypeltis*, and some *Natrix*; and small in some *Ahaetulla*, *Anilius*, *Eryx*, *Naja*, *Ptyas*, *Uropeltis*, and *Vipera*. Leydig (1873) was unable to find this gland at all in *Vipera*, but subsequent workers (Bellairs, 1942; Smith and Bellairs, 1947; Dullemeijer, 1956) have reported it to be a small, more or less spherical body lying immediately posterior to the vestibulum. The only snake apparently lacking the external nasal gland is *Pelamis* (Kathariner, 1900); however it is present in other hydrophiids and the other groups of marine snakes (Kathariner, 1900, and Smith and Bellairs, 1947).

In most squamates the gland has a single duct, but there are two in *Uma* (Stebbins, 1943), more than one in *Iguana* (Pratt, 1948), and one or more ducts in snakes (Smith and Bellairs, 1947; no details given). Little is known concerning the position of the duct within the body of the external nasal gland; in teiids (Malan, 1946; Stebbins, 1948) it is central and in *Gerrhonotus* it is ventrolaterally placed (Stebbins, 1948). Although the duct normally enters the dorsolateral wall of the vestibulum, it is ventral or ventrolateral in amphisbaenians (Fischer, 1900, and Pratt, 1948) and anteromedial in *Rhinophis* (Baumeister, 1908).

In all crocodilians the external nasal gland is an oval body lying dorsolateral to the anterior portion of the cavum nasi proprium (Röse, 1893; Reese, 1925; Bertau, 1935). Its posterior end is at the level of the preconcha. From the gland, a long duct extends anteriorly to the posterior wall of the vestibulum. Röse (1893) reported the presence of two ducts, one entering the vestibulum posterolaterally and the other posteromedially, but other workers, such as Bellairs and Shute (1953), have described only a single duct. The duct of the gland is longer in *Crocodylus* than in *Alligator* or *Melanosuchus* so that, despite the longer snout in the first genus, the gland lies in the same position in all crocodilians (Bertau, 1935). Although the external nasal gland of crocodilians was first reported by Stannius (1848), both Hoffmann (1879–1890) and Dieulafé (1904–1905) were unable to find it and stated that crocodilians lack nasal glands.

The histology of the external nasal gland has been studied by few workers and almost exclusively in squamates, although Reese (1925) also observed crocodilian material. The glandular tubules have large lumina and are lined by high columnar cells with light colored, highly vacuolated cytoplasm and

G

strongly acidophilic granules within the vacuoles (Krause, 1922) or with clear or finely granulated cytoplasm (Reese, 1925). The nuclei are basal, apparently often pycnotic (Krause, 1922) or large and frequently flattened (Reese, 1925). Krause, but not Reese, also mentioned smaller cells with large, light colored, central nuclei and without any secretion lying between the secretory cells. The secretory cells have also been described as very low columnar or cuboidal, with basal nuclei and clear cytoplasm distally (Kathariner, 1900) or as resembling the mucous cells of mammals (Stebbins, 1943). This gland is formed of simple columnar epithelium in *Dipsosaurus* (Philpott and Templeton, 1964). It contains mucous cells and other, more numerous cells typical of those found in other salt-secreting glands. The latter possess many mitochondria and have a very large plasmalemmal surface area due to infoldings of the cell margins and extensive lateral interdigitations between adjacent cells (electron microscopic as well as light microscopic observations).

The duct of the external nasal gland apparently varies considerably in its histological structure. It usually possesses a large lumen (Reese, 1925; Dullemeijer, 1956) and may have an intraglandular enlargement, the latter being present in *Gerrhonotus* and *Cnemidophorus* but not in *Uma* (Stebbins, 1948). The width of the duct and the height of its epithelium varies (Stebbins, 1948) as, apparently, does the method of branching. Oelrich (1956) described each tubule as entering one main duct, but Leydig (1872a) reported that the main duct was trifurcated. The epithelium of the main duct has been referred to as columnar (Kathariner, 1900; Stebbins, 1943), pseudostratified columnar (Stebbins, 1948; in *Cnemidophorus* but not *Gerrhonotus*), respiratory, i.e., ciliated columnar plus goblet cells (Reese, 1925; Pratt, 1948), and stratified cuboid (Stebbins, 1948; in *Gerrhonotus*); the differences are probably specific ones in most cases. Krause (1922), who furnished the most detailed description, found columnar epithelium composed of cells with central nuclei, vacuolated cytoplasm basally, and cytoplasm containing acidophilic granules peripherally. These cells form a simple epithelium in the smaller ducts of *Lacerta*, but in the main duct they are surrounded by a basal layer of cuboidal cells.

C. MEDIAL NASAL GLAND

Many turtles possess a second large nasal gland, the medial nasal gland (= glandula nasalis interna, Jacobsonsche Drüse, Septaldrüse, septale Nasendrüse, untere Nasendrüse). It is a branched tubular gland, lying between the nasal cavity and the nasal septum, and with a duct entering the ventromedial part of the anterior end of the cavum nasi proprium (Fig. 43). The gland is innervated by the nervus septi narium, a branch of the ophthalmic division of the trigeminal, in *Trionyx* (Gaupp, 1888). The embryology of this gland has been studied only in *Chrysemys* in which it first appears shortly after the formation of the external nasal gland as a solid rod of cells projecting posteriorly, apparently from the extreme posterior end of the medial vestibular wall (Parsons, 1959a). Since, in adults, the gland enters the cavum rather than the vestibulum, it is possible that it actually arises from the extreme anterior end of the cavum, although this does not appear to be the case in embryos. Its further development by elongation, branching, and the opening of lumina resembles that of the external nasal gland.

The duct of the medial nasal gland of *Testudo* has a narrow lumen and opens into the anterodorsal corner of the medial sulcus (Seydel, 1896). The duct extends posteriorly and is partly covered by the paraseptal process of the septal cartilage. Numerous, very small acini and tubules surround and enter the duct. The gland itself is large and lies medial and ventromedial to the middle third of the cavum nasi proprium. Seydel considered it to be a mucous gland. In *Emys*, the gland is quite similar but much smaller; its duct enters the dorsomedial end of the anterior sulcus (Seydel, 1896).

Less is known about this gland in other turtles. In *Chelydra* (Nick, 1912), it is a small gland, apparently resembling that of *Emys*; its long duct is lined by stratified epithelium and enters the medial side of the anterior sulcus. Hoffmann's (1879–1890) figures show this gland as very large in *Trionyx*. In *Pelomedusa*, a short duct enters the cavum from this gland with the latter described only as lying between the nasal cavity and septum (van der Merwe, 1940). Finally, in sea turtles, both cheloniids and *Dermochelys*, the gland is completely lacking (Nick, 1912; Fuchs, 1915). Hoffmann (1879–1890) also reported its absence in *Dermochelys* but thought it was large in the cheloniid *Eretmochelys*, apparently mistaking some of the cavernous tissue surrounding the nose for a medial nasal gland.

The duct of the medial nasal gland has been considered the Jacobson's organ of turtles by von Mihalkovics (1898) and von Navratil (1926) both of whom studied *Emys*. Their descriptions of the gland itself and the gross structure of the duct, which they term the Jacobsonschen Gang, agree with that given by Seydel (1896). The duct is said to be oval in section and, near its entrance into the cavum, to have a lumen that measures 120μ by 40μ and to be lined by 40μ high columnar epithelium. Posteriorly the duct widens to 400 or 500μ by 250μ and is lined by 90 or 100μ high olfactory epithelium. The latter is said to have three or four rows of nuclei and to be surrounded by pigment cells (von Mihalkovics, 1898). Further, von Mihalkovics stated that a large branch of the medial division of the olfactory nerve runs to the gland and then along its duct. His observations were supported by those of von Navratil, but, as noted in the section on the Jacobson's organ of turtles, all other workers have disagreed, and several have specifically denied that the duct of the medial nasal gland is lined by sensory epithelium and that it is innervated by part of the olfactory nerve. Despite their rejection of von Mihalkovics' theory, some workers, such as Plate (1924), have continued to call this gland the Jacobsonsche Drüse, because they consider the gland homologous to one sometimes called that in amphibians, and because it does enter the region of the nasal cavity believed to represent the Jacobson's organ of turtles.

Sphenodon has a somewhat similar, and probably homologous, medial nasal gland (= untere Vorhofsdrüse, ventral nasal gland). It is a single, unbranched, glandular tube extending posteriorly and slightly ventro-laterally along the base of the nasal septum from the ventral wall of the vestibulum (Hoppe, 1934; Parsons, 1959a; Malan, 1946, and Pratt, 1948, mention the gland but give no details). Hoppe noted that it first appears in the embryo at about the same stage as does the external nasal gland. The duct enters the anteroventral wall of the vestibulum near the medial margin of the latter; this is very close to the point where the medial nasal gland enters the nasal cavity of turtles, but in *Sphenodon* the gland enters the vestibulum and in turtles the cavum nasi proprium. Such a difference is not a strong argument against the homology of the gland in these forms since there is no evidence that the vestibulo-caval boundary is exactly the same in both.

D. OTHER GLANDS

The respiratory epithelium of the cavum nasi proprium of all reptiles contains numerous goblet cells. These may become concentrated in certain areas to produce what are functionally multicellular glands as has been described above in the section on the histology of the cavum.

Shrivastava (1963) considered the ventral diverticulum of the vestibulum in *Varanus* to be glandular and von Mihalkovics (1898) figured tubules lying just dorsal to the nasopharyngeal duct of *Emys*. Since there are no descriptions of these structures, they can only be mentioned here.

The only remaining gland is that termed the internasal gland (= Inter-nasaldrüse, mediale Nasendrüse) of *Rhinophis* (Baumeister, 1908). This gland does not resemble the medial nasal gland of turtles and *Sphenodon*; it is not known from any other squamates; it has been described only by Baumeister. Thus I prefer to treat it separately as a gland distinct from all others (as did Baumeister who suggested the name internasal gland as an alternative to medial nasal gland, although he used the latter in his descriptions). It forms a large pouch-like structure in the medial and ventromedial wall of the vestibulum or anterior end of the cavum nasi proprium, just posterior to the plane of the external nares, and has numerous smaller pouches opening into it. The gland has up to four layers of large polygonal cells with large, centrally located nuclei and light colored, nongranular, homogeneous cytoplasm; these cells Baumeister considered to be glandular. Basal to them, there is a single layer of columnar cells which is continuous with the nasal epithelium. Although the columnar structure suggests that the gland may be caval rather than vestibular, Baumeister believed that this is not the case and stated that it was probably an integumentary derivative.

VII. Discussion

It would seem appropriate to conclude this description of reptilian nasal anatomy with a discussion of the evolution of the nose in the various groups and a consideration of what this tells us concerning the evolution of reptiles generally. Unfortunately this is very difficult, and the conclusions must be taken as tentative and probably unreliable. I have already attempted such discussions (Parsons, 1959b, 1967) and can add little here. The major problems remain the same: we unfortunately do not know enough about primitive reptiles in general and about the most reptile-like amphibians and the most primitive reptiles (see Olson, 1965, for a discussion of the possible relationships of some of the Cotylosauria *sensu* Romer, 1956) in particular, and we know essentially nothing about the nasal cavities of any of the extinct species.

Among the living forms, the Testudines certainly seem the most distinctive. In all other reptiles, and indeed in all other amniotes, the Jacobson's organ appears in very early embryonic stages as an inpocketing of the ventromedial nasal wall; in turtles the ventral part of the nasal cavity appears to be the homolog of Jacobson's organ. In almost all other amniotes there are one or more projections of the lateral nasal wall, conchae in a broad sense; in turtles, although the lateral Grenzfalte or the Muschelwulst may be homologous structures, there are no well formed conchae. When conchae are missing in other amniotes, such as in various iguanid lizards, they have surely been lost secondarily, but there is no evidence that turtles ever had them. Turtles not only differ from other amniotes in these characters, but they also resemble closely the salamanders; the main differences appear to be caused by the shape of the head, flattened in urodeles and high in turtles.

These observations suggest that, in their nasal anatomy, turtles are very primitive and that they probably diverged from the main line of reptilian evolution before any of the other surviving groups. Unfortunately, there is evidence from the structure of the ear and of the circulatory system suggesting that the line culminating in mammals is the most divergent and the first to separate off from the basal stock (see Parrington, 1958, and Parsons, 1959b, for discussion and references). None of the lines of evidence is completely convincing and the only safe conclusion that can be reached is that the Testudines are a very distinct, and presumably old, order; this has never been doubted.

At lower taxonomic levels, too, nasal anatomy adds little to our knowledge of reptilian phylogeny. All of the currently recognized orders are clearly distinct and generally families show considerable uniformity of pattern. There are exceptions, such as the Iguanidae, but the differences are not such that the generally accepted relationships are called into question. It is possibly noteworthy that, in its nasal anatomy, *Dermochelys* resembles the cheloniids more closely than any other forms; this supports the idea that the two are closely related and that *Dermochelys* is not, as has sometimes been suggested (*e.g.*, by Deraniyagala, 1939), the sole representative of a distinct suborder. Malan (1946) believed that her findings on the nasal anatomy of lizards confirmed earlier work on their classification, but she considered mainly characters of the nasal capsule, and Stebbins' (1948) work demonstrated that ecological factors must also be considered in any attempt to relate lacertilian nasal anatomy and phylogeny.

It is impossible to reconstruct the nasal anatomy of a primitive reptile or to give the typical features for the class as a whole. The simplest assumption is that a pattern resembling that of most turtles (forms like *Emys*; not sea turtles) is primitive. This allows most specializations to be additions of various modifications and requires the loss of very few structures. However, it is entirely possible, and may even be probable, that some of the apparently primitive characters of turtles, such as the absence of conchae or the simple tubular shape of the vestibulum, represent secondary simplifications from a more complex ancestral structure. At the present even speculation appears unprofitable.

The descriptions given in this work should make it clear that much remains to be learned concerning the nasal structure of living reptiles. Although the gross anatomy of a large number of forms has been studied, there are still many which have never been described in detail; for example turtles of the groups Dermatemydidae, Platysterninae, and Carettochelyidae (classification that of Romer, 1956) have never been studied, and other families are only poorly known. There are also many groups of squamates that have been studied inadequately or not at all. The histology is poorly known. Most of the numerous references contain only brief asides on histology, and almost no cytological descriptions exist. Even these few show that there is great histological and cytological variation. Very few forms have been studied embryologically. Although little major variation has been noted in the nasal development of those forms which have been described, this could reflect our ignorance as easily as a general constancy of embryological pattern.

Acknowledgements

I wish to thank several people for their assistance in the preparation of this paper: Dr. M. C. Parsons for criticizing the manuscript and preparing the drawings, Drs. C. S. Churcher and C. Gans as well as several editorial reviewers for criticizing the manuscript, Dr. E. E. Williams for providing some of the specimens for dissection, and Miss B. M. Hall for assistance in the preparation of the manuscript. The work was carried out with the support of Grant A-1724 from the National Research Council of Canada.

References

Abel, J. H. and Ellis, R. A. (1966). Histochemical and electron microscopic observations on the salt secreting lacrymal glands of marine turtles. *Am. J. Anat.* 118, 337–357.

Allison, A. C. (1953). The morphology of the olfactory system in the vertebrates. *Biol. Rev.* 28, 195–244.

Armstrong, J. A., Gamble, H. J. and Goldby, F. (1953). Observations on the olfactory apparatus and the telencephalon of *Anolis*, a microsmatic lizard. *J. Anat.* 87, 288–307.

Bannister, L. H. (1968). Fine structure of the sensory endings in the vomero-nasal organ of the slow-worm *Anguis fragilis. Nature, Lond.* 217, 275–276.

Barge, J. A. J. (1937). Mundhöhlendach und Gaumen. *In* "Handbuch der vergleichenden Anatomie der Wirbeltiere", (L. Bolk, E. Göppert, E. Kallius and W. Lubosch, eds), Vol. 3, pp. 29–48. Urban und Schwarzenberg, Berlin and Wien.

Barry, T. H. (1953). Contributions to the cranial morphology of *Agama hispida* (Linn.). *Annale Univ. Stellenbosch* (A)29, 55–77.

Baumeister, L. (1908). Beiträge zur Anatomie und Physiologie der Rhinophiden. Integument, Drüsen der Mundhöhle, Augen und Skeletsystem. *Zool. Jb., Abt. Anat.* 26, 423–526.

Beard, J. (1889). Morphological studies. Nr. 4. The nose and Jacobson's organ. *Zool. Jb., Abt. Anat.* 3, 753–783.

Beecker, A. (1903). Vergleichende Stilistik der Nasenregion bei den Sauriern, Vögeln und Säugethieren. *Morph. Jb.* 31, 565–619.

Bellairs, A. d'A. (1942). Observations on Jacobson's organ and its innervation in *Vipera berus. J. Anat.* 76, 167–177.

Bellairs, A. d'A. (1949a). Observations on the snout of *Varanus*, and a comparison with that of other lizards and snakes. *J. Anat.* 83, 116–146.

Bellairs, A. d'A. (1949b). Observations on the cranial anatomy of *Anniella*, and a comparison with that of other burrowing lizards. *Proc. zool. Soc. Lond.* 119, 887–904.

Bellairs, A. d'A. and Boyd, J. D. (1950). The lachrymal apparatus in lizards and snakes.— II. The anterior part of the lachrymal duct and its relationship with the palate and with the nasal and vomeronasal organs. *Proc. zool. Soc. Lond.* 120, 269–310.

Bellairs, A. d'A. and Shute, C. C. D. (1953). Observations on the narial musculature of Crocodilia and its innervation from the sympathetic system. *J. Anat.* 87, 367–378.

Benson, G. K., Phillips, J. G. and Holmes, W. N. (1964). Observations on the histological structure of the nasal glands of the turtle. *J. Anat.* 98, 290.

Bertau, M. (1935). Zur Entwicklungsgeschichte des Geruchsorgans der Krokodile. *Z. Anat. EntwGesch.* 104, 168–202.

Bloom, G. (1954). Studies on the olfactory epithelium of the frog and the toad with the aid of light and electron microscopy. *Z. Zellforsch. mikrosk. Anat.* **41**, 89–100.

Born, G. (1879). Die Nasenhöhlen und der Thränennasengang der amnioten Wirbelthiere. I. *Morph. Jb.* **5**, 62–140.

Born, G. (1883). Die Nasenhöhlen und der Thränennasengang der amnioten Wirbelthiere. III. *Morph. Jb.* **8**, 188–232.

Brink, A. S. (1957). Speculations on some advanced mammalian characteristics in the higher mammal-like reptiles. *Palaeont. afr.* **4**, 77–96.

Brock, G. T. (1941). The skull of the chameleon, *Lophosaura ventralis* (Gray); some developmental stages. *Proc. zool. Soc. Lond.* B110, 219–241.

Broman, I. (1920). Das Organon vomero-nasale Jacobsoni—Ein Wassergeruchsorgan! *Arb. anat. Inst., Wiesbaden (Anat. Hefte, Abt. I)* **58**, 137–191.

Broom, R. (1906). On the organ of Jacobson in *Sphenodon*. *J. Linn. Soc., Zool.* **29**, 414–420.

Brühl, C. B. (1886). "Zootomie aller Thierklassen für Lernende, nach Autopsien skizzirt", pp. 137–140. Alfred Hölder, Wien.

Bruner, H. L. (1897). New nasal muscles in the Reptilia. *Anat. Anz.* **13**, 217–218.

Bruner, H. L. (1907). On the cephalic veins and sinuses of reptiles, with description of a mechanism for raising the venous blood-pressure in the head. *Am. J. Anat.* **7**, 1–117.

Busch, C. H. (1898). Beitrag zur Kenntniss der Gaumenbildung bei den Reptilien. *Zool. Jb., Abt. Anat.* **11**, 441–500.

Cordier, R. (1964). Sensory cells. *In* "The Cell" (J. Brachet and A. E.Mirsky, eds), Vol. 6, pp. 313–386. Academic Press, New York.

Crosby, E. C. and Humphrey, T. (1939a). A comparison of the olfactory and the accessory olfactory bulbs in certain representative vertebrates. *Pap. Mich. Acad. Sci.* **24**(2), 95–104.

Crosby, E. C. and Humphrey, T. (1939b). Studies of the vertebrate telencephalon. I. The nuclear configuration of the olfactory and accessory olfactory formations and of the nucleus olfactorius anterior of certain reptiles, birds, and mammals. *J. comp. Neurol.* **71**, 121–213.

Darevsky, I. S. (1956). On the structure and function of the nasal gland of *Malpolon monspessulanus* Herm. (Reptilia, Serpentes). *Zool. Zh.* **35**, 312–314 [in Russian].

deBeer, G. R. (1937). "The Development of the Vertebrate Skull." Oxford Univ. Press, Oxford.

Deraniyagala, P. E. P. (1939). Testudinates and crocodilians. *In* "The Tetrapod Reptiles of Ceylon". Colombo Museum, Colombo, Ceylon.

Dieulafé, L. (1904–1905). Les fosses nasales des vertébrés (morphologie et embryologie). *J. Anat. Physiol., Paris.* **40**, 268–298 and 414–444 and **41**, 102–112, 300–318, 478–560 and 658–678.

Dohrer, J. (1912). Die Metamorphose der Mundrachenwand der Schildkröte "*Chelydra serpentina*". *Morph. Jb.* **44**, 661–705.

Dullemeijer, P. (1956). The functional morphology of the head of the common viper *Vipera berus* (L.). *Archs néerl. Zool.* **11**, 387–497.

Dullemeijer, P. (1959). A comparative functional-anatomical study of the heads of some Viperidae. *Morph. Jb.* **99**, 881–985.

Dunson, W. A. (1968). Salt gland secretion in the pelagic sea snake *Pelamis*. *Am. J. Physiol.* **215**, 1512–1517.

Dunson, W. A. and Taub, A. M. (1967). Extrarenal salt excretion in sea snakes (*Laticauda*). *Am. J. Physiol.* **213**, 975–982.

Eckart, H. (1922). Das Geruchsorgan einiger ceylonischer Eidechsen (Agamiden). (Fauna et Anatomia ceylonica, Bd. II, Nr. 1). *Jena Z. Naturw.* **58**, 271–318.

Engelbrecht, D. van Z. (1951). Contributions to the cranial morphology of the chamaeleon *Microsaura pumila* Daudin. *Annale Univ. Stellenbosch* (A)27, 3–31.

Eyal-Giladi, H. (1964). The development of the chondrocranium of *Agama stellio*. *Acta zool. Stockh.* 45, 139–165.

Fischer, E. (1900). Beiträge zur Kenntniss der Nasenhöhle und des Thränennasenganges der Amphisbaeniden. *Arch. mikrosk. Anat. EntwMech.* 55, 441–478.

Frank, G. H. (1951). Contributions to the cranial morphology of *Rhampholeon platyceps* Günther. *Annale Univ. Stellenbosch* (A)27, 33–67.

Franz, V. (1934). Vergleichende Anatomie des Wirbeltierauges. *In* "Handbuch der vergleichenden Anatomie der Wirbeltiere" (L. Bolk, E. Göppert, E. Kallius and W. Lubosch, eds), Vol. 2 (2), pp. 989–1292. Urban und Schwarzenberg, Berlin and Wien.

Fuchs, H. (1907). Untersuchungen über Ontogenie und Phylogenie der Gaumenbildugen bei den Wirbeltieren. Erste Mitteilung. Über den Gaumen der Schildkröten und seine Entwickelungsgeschichte. *Z. Morph. Anthrop.* 10, 409–463.

Fuchs, H. (1908). Untersuchungen über Ontogenie und Phylogenie der Gaumenbildungen bei den Wirbeltieren. Zweite Mitteilung. Über das Munddach der Rhynchocephalen, Saurier, Schlangen, Krokodile und Säuger und den Zusammenhang zwischen Mund- und Nasenhöhle bei diesen Tieren. *Z. Morph. Anthrop.* 11, 153–248.

Fuchs, H. (1911). Bemerkungen über das Munddach der Amnioten, insbesondere der Schildkröten und Schlangen. *Anat. Anz.* 38, 609–637.

Fuchs, H. (1915). Über den Bau und die Entwicklung des Schädels der *Chelone imbricata*. Ein Beitrag zur Entwicklungsgeschichte und vergleichenden Anatomie des Wirbeltierschädels. Erster Teil: Das Primordialskelett des Neurocraniums und des Kieferbogens. *In* "Reise in Ostafrika in den Jahren 1903–1905, Wissenschaftliche Ergebnisse" (A. Voeltzkow, ed.), Vol. 5, pp. 1–325. E. Schweizerbart, Stuttgart.

Gabe, M. and Saint Girons, H. (1964). "Contribution à l'Histologie de *Sphenodon punctatus* Gray." Centre National de la Recherche Scientifique, Paris.

Gaupp, E. (1888). Anatomische Untersuchungen über die Nervenversorgung der Mund- und Nasenhöhlendrüsen der Wirbelthiere. *Morph. Jb.* 14, 436–489.

Gegenbaur, C. (1873). Über die Nasenmuscheln der Vögel. *Jena Z. Naturw.* 7, 1–21.

Göppert, E. (1903). Die Bedeutung der Zunge für den sekundären Gaumen und den Ductus naso-pharyngeus. Beobachtungen an Reptilien und Vögeln. *Morph. Jb.* 31, 311–359.

Haas, G. (1937). The structure of the nasal cavity in *Chamaeleo chameleon* (Linnaeus). *J. Morph.* 61, 433–451.

Haas, G. (1947). Jacobson's organ in the chameleon. *J. Morph.* 81, 195–207.

Haas, G. (1959). Bemerkungen über die Anatomie des Kopfes und des Schädels der Leptotyphlopidae (Ophidia), speziell von *L. macrorhynchus* Jan. *Vjschr. naturf. Ges. Zürich* 104, 90–104.

Haas, G. (1964). Anatomical observations on the head of *Liotyphlops albirostris* (Typhlopidae, Ophidia). *Acta zool.* 45, 1–62.

Haas, G. (1968). Anatomical observations on the head of *Anomalepis aspinosus* (Typhlopidae, Ophidia). *Acta zool.* 49, 63–139.

Hafferl, A. (1921). Das knorpelige Neurocranium des Gecko (*Platydactylus annularis*). Ein Beitrag zur Entwicklungsgeschichte des Reptilienschädels. *Z. Anat. EntwGesch.* 62, 433–518.

Haller, Graf (1921). Über den Gaumen der amnioten Wirbeltiere. I. Teil. Über den Gaumen der Reptilien. *Z. Anat. EntwGesch.* 61, 283–311.

Hoffmann, C. K. (1879–1890). Reptilien. *In* "Klassen und Ordnungen des Thier-Reichs" (H. G. Bronn, ed.), Vol. 6, Pt. 3. 3 vols C. F. Winter'sche Verlagshandlung, Leipzig.

Hofmann, O. (1905). Das Munddach der Saurier. *Morph. Jb.* **33**, 3–38.

Hopkins, A. E. (1926). The olfactory receptors in vertebrates. *J. comp. Neurol.* **41**, 253–289.

Hoppe, G. (1934). Das Geruchsorgan von *Hatteria punctata*. *Z. Anat. EntwGesch.* **102**, 434–461.

Kathariner, L. (1900). Die Nase der im Wasser lebenden Schlangen als Luftweg und Geruchsorgan. *Zool. Jb., Abt. Syst.* **13**, 415–442.

Kolmer, W. (1927). Geruchsorgan. *In* "Handbuch der mikroskopischen Anatomie des Menschen" (W. von Möllendorff, ed.), Vol. 3 (1), pp. 192–249. J. Springer, Berlin.

Kolmer, W. (1928). Kapillaren im Epithel des Jacobson'schen Organs und einige andere Beziehungen von Gefässen zum Epithel. *Anat. Anz.* **65**, 321–327.

Krause, R. (1922). Vögel und Reptilien "Mikroskopische Anatomie der Wirbeltiere in Einzeldarstellungen." Vol. II, pp. 187–454. Walter de Gruyter, Berlin.

Kritzinger, C. C. (1946). The cranial anatomy and kinesis of the South African amphisbaenid *Monopeltis capensis* Smith. *S. Afr. J. Sci.* **42**, 175–204.

Kunkel, B. W. (1912). The development of the skull of *Emys lutaria*. *J. Morph.* **23**, 693–780.

Lakjer, T. (1927). Studien über die Gaumenregion bei Sauriern im Vergleich mit Anamniern und primitiven Sauropsiden. *Zool. Jb., Abt. Anat.* **49**, 57–356.

Lapage, E. O. (1928). The septomaxillary of the Amphibia Anura and of the Reptilia. II. *J. Morph.* **46**, 399–430.

Leydig, F. (1872a). "Die in Deutschland lebenden Arten der Saurier." Laupp'sche Buchhandlung, Tübingen.

Leydig, F. (1872b). Zur Kenntniss der Sinnesorgane der Schlangen. *Arch. mikrosk. Anat. EntwMech.* **8**, 317–357.

Leydig, F. (1873). Über die Kopfdrüsen einheimischer Ophidier. *Arch. mikrosk. Anat. EntwMech.* **9**, 598–652.

Loew, J. (1956). Beiträge zur Entwicklungsgeschichte des Jacobsonschen Organs bei *Emys europaea*. *Acta. zool. Stockh.* **37**, 61–85.

Loveridge, A. and Williams, E. E. (1957). Revision of the African tortoises and turtles of the suborder Cryptodira. *Bull. Mus. comp. Zool. Harvard* **115**, 161–557.

Macallum, A. B. (1883). The nasal region in *Eutaenia*. *Proc. Can. Inst.* (N.S.) **1**, 390–404.

Malan, M. E. (1946). Contributions to the comparative anatomy of the nasal capsule and the organ of Jacobson of the Lacertilia. *Annale Univ. Stellenbosch* (A)**24**, 69–137.

Matthes, E. (1934). Geruchsorgan. *In* "Handbuch der vergleichenden Anatomie der Wirbeltiere" (L. Bolk, E. Göppert, E. Kallius and W. Lubosch, eds), Vol. 2 (2), pp. 879–948. Urban und Schwarzenberg, Berlin and Wien.

McCotter, R. E. (1917). The vomero-nasal apparatus in *Chrysemys punctata* and *Rana catesbiana*. *Anat. Rec.* **13**, 51–67.

McDowell, S. B. and Bogert, C. M. (1954). The systematic position of *Lanthanotus* and the affinities of the anguinomorphan lizards. *Bull. Am. Mus. nat. Hist.* **105**, 1–142.

Meek, A. (1893). On the occurrence of a Jacobson's organ, with notes on the development of the nasal cavity, the lachrymal duct, and the Harderian gland in *Crocodilus porosus*. *J. Anat. Physiol.* **27**, 151–160.

Meek, A. (1911). On the morphogenesis of the head of the crocodile (*Crocodilus porosus*). *J. Anat. Physiol.* **45**, 357–377.

Merwe, N. J. van der (1940). Die skedelmorfologie van *Pelomedusa galeata* (Wagler). *Tydskr. Wet. Kuns.* **1**, 67–85.

Mihalkovics, V. von (1898). Nasenhöhle und Jacobsonsches Organ. Eine morphologische Studie. *Arb. anat. Inst., Wiesbaden (Anat. Hefte, Abt. I)* **11**, 1–107.

Müller, F. (1965). Zur Morphogenese des Ductus nasopharyngeus und des sekundären Gaumendaches bei den Crocodilia. *Revue suisse Zool.* 72, 647–652.

Müller, F. (1967). Zur embryonalen Kopfentwicklung von *Crocodylus cataphractus* Cuv. *Revue. suisse Zool.* 74, 189–294.

Müller, J. (1829). Über die Nasendrüse der Schlangen. *Meckel's Arch. Anat. Physiol.* 1829, 71–72 [not seen].

Navratil, D. von (1926). Über das Jacobsonsche Organ der Wirbeltiere. *Z. Anat. Entw-Gesch.* 81, 648–656.

Negus, V. (1958). "The Comparative Anatomy and Physiology of the Nose and Paranasal Sinuses." Livingstone, Edinburgh and London.

Nemours, P. R. (1930). Studies on the accessory nasal sinuses: the comparative morphology of the nasal cavities of reptiles and birds. *Ann. Otol. Rhinol. Lar.* 39, 1086–1108.

Nick, L. (1912). Das Kopfskelet von *Dermochelys coriacea* L. *Zool. Jb., Abt. Anat.* 33, 1–238.

Oelrich, T. M. (1956). The anatomy of the head of *Ctenosaura pectinata* (Iguanidae). *Misc. Publs Mus. Zool. Univ. Mich.* 94, 122 pp.

Oledzka-Slotwinska, H. (1961). Caractère histochimique de la sécrétion des glandes olfactives de Bowman chez les urodèles et les reptiles. *C. r. Ass. Anat.* 46, 876–889.

Olson, E. C. (1965). Relationships of *Seymouria*, *Diadectes*, and Chelonia. *Am. Zool.* 5, 295–307.

Osawa, G. (1898). Beiträge zur Lehre von den Sinnesorganen der *Hatteria punctata*. *Arch. mikrosk. Anat. EntwMech.* 52, 268–366.

Ostrom, J. H. (1961). Cranial morphology of the hadrosaurian dinosaurs of North America. *Bull. Am. Mus. nat. Hist.* 122, 33–186.

Parrington, F. R. (1958). The problem of the classification of reptiles. *J. Linn. Soc., Zool.* 44, 99–115.

Parsons, T. S. (1958). The choanal papillae of the Cheloniidae. *Breviora* 85, 5 pp.

Parsons, T. S. (1959a). Studies on the comparative embryology of the reptilian nose. *Bull. Mus. comp. Zool. Harvard* 120, 101–277.

Parsons, T. S. (1959b). Nasal anatomy and the phylogeny of reptiles. *Evolution, Lancaster, Pa.* 13, 175–187.

Parsons, T. S. (1960). The structure of the choanae of the Emydinae (Testudines, Testudinidae). *Bull. Mus. comp. Zool. Harvard* 123, 111–127.

Parsons, T. S. (1967). Evolution of the nasal structure in the lower tetrapods. *Am. Zool.* 7, 397–413.

Parsons, T. S. (1968). Variation in the choanal structure of Recent turtles. *Can. J. Zool.* 46, 1235–1263.

Parsons, T. S. and Stephens, S. M. (1968). The nasal anatomy of *Kinosternon* and *Sternotherus* (Testudines: Kinosternidae). *Can. J. Zool.* 46, 399–404.

Peter, K. (1900). Mittheilungen zur Entwicklungsgeschichte der Eidechse. I. Das Wachsthum des Riechgrübchens. Ein Beitrag zur Lehre vom embryonalen Wachsthum. *Arch mikrosk. Anat. EntwMech.* 55, 585–617.

Peter, K. (1906). Die Entwickelung des Geruchsorgans und Jakobson'schen Organs in der Reihe der Wirbeltiere. Bildung der äusseren Nase und des Gaumens. *In* "Handbuch der vergleichenden und experimentellen Entwickelungslehre der Wirbeltiere" (O. Hertwig, ed.), Vol. 2 (2), 1–82. Gustav Fischer, Jena.

Peyer, B. (1912). Die Entwicklung des Schädelskeletes von *Vipera aspis. Morph. Jb.* 44, 563–621.

Philpott, C. W. and Templeton, J. R. (1964). A comparative study of the histology and fine structure of the nasal salt secreting gland of the lizard, *Dipsosaurus. Anat. Rec.* 148, 394–395.

Plate, L. (1924). "Allgemeine Zoologie und Abstammungslehre. Zweiter Teil: Die Sinnesorgane der Tiere." Gustav Fischer, Jena.

Pratt, C. W. McE. (1948). The morphology of the ethmoidal region of *Sphenodon* and lizards. *Proc. zool. Soc. Lond.* **118**, 171–201.

Pringle, J. A. (1954). The cranial development of certain South African snakes and the relationship of these groups. *Proc. zool. Soc. Lond.* **123**, 813–865.

Rathke, H. (1839). "Entwickelungsgeschichte der Natter (*Coluber natrix*)." Gebrüder Bornträger, Königsberg.

Rathke, H. (1866). "Untersuchungen über die Entwickelung und den Körperbau der Krokodile" (W. von Wittich, ed.). F. Vieweg & Sohn, Braunschweig.

Reese, A. M. (1901). The nasal passages of the Florida alligator. *Proc. Acad. nat. Sci. Philad.* **53**, 457–464.

Reese, A. M. (1925). The cephalic glands of *Alligator mississippiensis*, Florida alligator, and of *Agkistrodon*, copperhead and moccasin. *Biologia gen.* **1**, 482–500.

Reese, T. S. (1965). Olfactory cilia in the frog. *J. Cell Biol.* **25**(2), 209–230.

Retzius, G. (1894). Die Riechzellen der Ophidier in der Riechschleimhaut und im Jacobson'schen Organ. *Biol. Unters.* (N.S.)**6**, 48–51.

Romer, A. S. (1956). "Osteology of the Reptiles." Univ. Chicago Press, Chicago.

Röse, C. (1893). Über die Nasendrüse und die Gaumendrüsen von *Crocodilus porosus*. *Anat. Anz.* **8**, 745–751.

Schauinsland, H. (1903). Beiträge zur Entwickelungsgeschichte und Anatomie der Wirbeltiere. I. *Sphenodon, Callorhynchus, Chamaeleo. Zoologica, Stuttg.* **16**, 1–98.

Seydel, O. (1895). Über die Nasenhöhle und das Jacobson'sche Organ der Amphibien. *Morph. Jb.* **23**, 453–543.

Seydel, O. (1896). Über die Nasenhöhle und das Jacobson'sche Organ der Land- und Sumpfschildkröten. "Festschrift 70 Geburtstag Gegenbaur". Vol. 2, pp. 385–486.

Seydel, O. (1899). Über Entwickelungsvorgänge an der Nasenhöhle und am Mund-höhlendache von *Echidna* nebst Beiträgen zur Morphologie des peripheren Geruchs-organs und des Gaumens der Wirbelthiere. *Denkschr. med.-Naturw. Ges. Jena* **6**, 445–532.

Shiino, K. (1914). Studien zur Kenntnis des Wirbeltierkopfes. I. Das Chondrocranium von *Crocodilus* mit Berücksichtigung der Gehirnnerven und der Kopfgefässe. *Arb. anat. Inst., Wiesbaden (Anat. Hefte, Abt. I)* **50**, 253–382.

Shrivastava, R. K. (1963). The structure and the development of the chondrocranium of *Varanus*. Part I. The development of the ethmoidal region. *Okajimas Folia anat. jap.* **39**, 55–83.

Smith, M. and Bellairs, A. d'A. (1947). The head glands of snakes, with remarks on the evolution of the parotid gland and teeth of the Opisthoglypha. *J. Linn. Soc. Zool.* **41**, 351–368.

Solger, B. (1876). Beiträge zur Kenntniss der Nasenwandung, und besonders der Nasen-muscheln der Reptilien. *Morph. Jb.* **1**, 467–494.

Stannius, H. (1848). Vergleichende Anatomie der Wirbelthiere. *In* "Lehrbuch der vergleichenden Anatomie" (C. T. von Siebold and H. Stannius), Pt. 2. Veit, Berlin.

Stebbins, R. C. (1943). Adaptations in the nasal passages for sand burrowing in the saurian genus *Uma. Am. Nat.* **77**, 38–52.

Stebbins, R. C. (1948). Nasal structure in lizards with reference to olfaction and con-ditioning of the inspired air. *Am. J. Anat.* **83**, 183–221.

Stimie, M. (1966). The cranial anatomy of the iguanid *Anolis carolinensis* (Cuvier). *Annale Univ. Stellenbosch* (A)**41**, 239–268.

Sülter, M. M. (1962). A contribution to the cranial morphology of *Causus rhombeatus* (Lichtenstein) with special reference to cranial kinesis. *Annale Univ. Stellenbosch* (A)37, 1–40.

Taub, A. M. (1966). Ophidian cephalic glands. *J. Morph.* 118, 529–541.

Taub, A. M. and Dunson, W. A. (1967). The salt gland in a sea snake (*Laticauda*). *Nature, Lond.* 215, 995–996.

Thäter, K. (1910). Das Munddach der Schlangen und Schildkröten. *Morph. Jb.* 41, 471–518.

Toerien, M. J. (1950). The cranial morphology of the Californian lizard—*Anniella pulchra* Gray. *S. Afr. J. Sci.* 46, 321–342.

Underwood, G. (1957). On lizards of the family Pygopodidae. A contribution to the morphology and phylogeny of the Squamata. *J. Morph.* 100, 207–268.

Voeltzkow, A. (1899). Beiträge zur Entwicklungsgeschichte der Reptilien. Biologie und Entwicklung der äusseren Körperform von *Crocodilus madagascariensis* Grand. *Abh. senckenb. naturforsch. Ges.* 26, 1–150.

Voeltzkow, A. (1903). Beiträge zur Entwicklungsgeschichte der Reptilien. VI. Gesichts-bildung und Entwicklung der äusseren Körperform bei *Chelone imbricata* Schweigg. *Abh. senckenb. naturforsch. Ges.* 27, 179–190.

Walker, W. F. (1959). Closure of the nostrils in the Atlantic loggerhead and other sea turtles. *Copeia* 1959, 257–259.

Watson, D. M. S. (1913). Further notes on the skull, brain, and organs of special sense of *Diademodon*. *Ann. Mag. nat. Hist.* (8)12, 217–228.

Webb, M. (1951). The cranial anatomy of the South African geckoes *Palmatogecko rangei* (Andersson), and *Oedura karroica* (Hewitt). *Annale Univ. Stellenbosch* (A)27, 131–165.

Weber, R. (1950). Transitorische Verschlüsse von Fernsinnesorganen in der Embryo-nalperiode bei Amnioten. *Revue suisse Zool.* 57, 19–108.

Wegner, R. N. (1958). Die Nebenhöhlen der Nase bei den Krokodilen (Studien über Nebenhöhlen des Schädels, 2 Teil). *Wiss. Z. Ernst Moritz Arndt-Univ. Greifswald* 7, 1–39.

Wettstein, O. von (1954). Sauropsida: Allgemeines—Reptilia. *In* "Handbuch der Zoologie. Eine Naturgeschichte der Stämme des Tierreiches" (W. Kükenthal, T. Krumbach, J. G. Helmcke and H. von Lengerken, eds), Vol. 7, (2), 321–424. de Gruyter, Berlin.

Willard, W. A. (1915). The cranial nerves of *Anolis carolinensis*. *Bull. Mus. comp. Zool. Harvard* 59, 15–116.

Wright, R. R. (1883). On the organ of Jacobson in Ophidia. *Zool. Anz.* 6, 389–393.

Zuckerkandl, E. (1910a). Über die Wechselbeziehung in der Ausbildung des Jacobson-schen Organs und des Riechlappens nebst Bemerkungen über das Jacobsonsche Organ der Amphibien. *Arb. anat. Inst., Wiesbaden* (*Anat. Hefte, Abt. I*) 41, 1–75.

Zuckerkandl, E. (1910b). Das Jacobsonsche Organ. *Ergebn. Anat. EntwGesch.* 18, 801–843.

CHAPTER 3

The Anatomy of the Reptilian Ear

IRWIN L. BAIRD

Department of Anatomy, The Milton S. Hershey Medical Center,
Pennsylvania State University, Hershey, Pennsylvania, U.S.A.

I. Introduction

Housed in the posterolateral region of the reptilian head, the ear is a structural complex which functions both in the maintenance of balance (equilibration) and in the reception of sound (audition). For descriptive purposes, this complex can be divided into three regions generally comparable to the external ear, middle ear, and internal ear of mammals. All of these regions are subject to variation within the Reptilia, and hence it is difficult to provide succinct universal definitions for them. In a general sense, however, the internal ear may be said to consist primarily of the otic capsule and its contents, and the middle ear may be defined as a region, largely lateral to the otic capsule, containing structures concerned with the transmission of vibrations to the internal ear. Although an external ear is lacking in many reptiles, the term can be applied, in a variety of forms, to the shallow depression or short air-filled passage extending from the lateral or posterolateral surface of the head to the tympanic membrane, which forms part of the lateral wall of the middle ear.

The literature includes relatively few reptilian otological studies. A great volume of peripheral work touches incidentally upon limited aspects of the auditory region and indicates great variation in the amount and type of information concerning each of the major divisions of the reptilian ear. The external ear has been largely treated as a feature of taxonomic interest and has received some consideration in phylogenetic discussions. The osteology of the middle ear is known in a considerable number of living and extinct forms, and papers pertaining to this topic constitute well over half of the total literature. Conversely, relatively little is known of the soft parts of the middle ear, and scant attention has been paid to its structural and functional relationships to hearing. Presumably because of technical problems, studies of the internal ear are sparse in the older literature, but publications appearing within the past decade have provided much valuable information on the structure and function of auditory parts. Adequate coverage of the vestibular system and development of the internal ear is wanting. Unfortunately, there is no recent comprehensive review of literature that includes both studies devoted to the reptilian ear and those that mention it incidentally, and none will be undertaken here. References to related peripheral literature (such as works on osteology, cranial morphology, aural histology and cytology, etc.) can be found in the major references cited below.

Recent advances in reptilian otology have emphasized the gaps in the literature and have indicated that the field is broader and more complex than previously supposed. Studies of the internal ear (Baird, 1960b; Hamilton, 1960, 1963b, 1964; Miller, 1966a, 1966b, 1968; Wever, 1965, 1967a, 1967b; and others) have shown obvious interfamilial and intergeneric aural specializations in lizards and snakes and suggest that similar specializations probably also exist in other reptiles. During the preparation of this report it has become evident that these specializations of the internal ear can be correlated, to some extent, with recorded differences in the structure of the middle ear. Thus, it is apparent that generalizations based on assumptions of anatomical uniformity throughout major groups are open to question, and that all phases of aural anatomy should be investigated within limited assemblages in order to achieve understanding of the field. In view of this, it has seemed advisable to emphasize certain morphological features and problems which are known to be of significance rather than to attempt a broader but more superficial coverage extending into equally interesting peripheral areas.

The general anatomy of the ear is probably best known in lizards, and relative structural similarity exists throughout numerous forms in a variety of groups. Thus, it will be useful to describe the "typical" anatomy of the lacertilian ear to provide a basis for the general discussion of reptilian aural anatomy, which follows. It should be noted that this approach is not intended to suggest that the ear of lizards constitutes a general reptilian type, since, as will be seen below, kinetic features of the diapsid skull and relationships of the tympanic membrane preclude such a consideration. The following description of "typical" conditions is based upon materials examined by the author (see Table I). It is not intended to be directly applicable to any particular group of lizards, but it could be referred, without significant modification, to representatives of several iguanid genera (e.g., *Iguana*, *Ctenosaura*, *Anolis*) and to some members of other families.

II. General Aural Anatomy of a "Typical" Lizard

A. THE EXTERNAL AND MIDDLE EAR

The external ear usually present in lizards hardly merits separate recognition, since it consists only of a slight depression at the posterolateral angle of the head and is formed largely by modification and attachment of the skin (Fig. 1). Anteriorly and dorsally the deeper fixed margin of this depression is formed by the curved posterior margin of the quadrate and associated parts of the mandibular adductor (levator) musculature. Posteriorly and ventrally, respectively, the depression is bounded by the anterior surface of the mandibular depressor and connective tissues attached to the mandibular articulation and retroarticular process. The skin adjacent to these boundaries is variably elevated to form one or more circumferential folds that mark the lateral limit of the external ear. From this external orifice the internal surface

FIG. 1. The external ear of *Crotaphytus collaris*. Note the shallow external meatus formed by folds of skin, the absence of scales on the tympanic membrane, and the central elevation of the membrane by the extrastapes.

of the bounding fold extends toward the margin of the tympanic membrane to which the skin is firmly attached. The scales lining this short "external acoustic meatus" usually exhibit progressive reduction in size as they approach the tympanic membrane, which is devoid of scales (see below). Thus, the usual form of the lacertilian external ear probably offers only slight protection to auditory structures; it shows little other basis for comparison to the elaborate structures in birds and mammals.

The major component of the "typical" lacertilian middle ear (Fig. 2) is a large, air-filled tympanic cavity. The central part of the cavity is situated medial to the tympanic membrane and lateral to the otic-occipital region of the skull, but anterior and posterior extensions frequently lie, respectively, lateral to the sphenoid region and lateral to the anterior cervical vertebrae and axial musculature. Variable in shape because of the constitution of its walls, the tympanic cavity is roofed by the paroccipital process and the

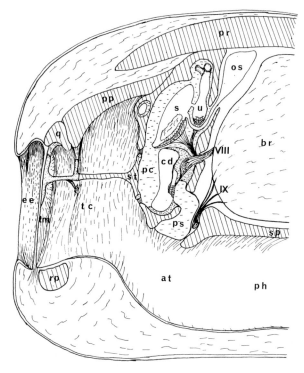

Fig. 2. Diagram of the auditory region of a "typical" lizard. at, Auditory tube; br, brain; cd, cochlear duct; ee, external ear; os, otic sac; pc, periotic cistern; ph, pharynx; pp, paroccipital process; pr, parietal; ps, periotic sac; q, quadrate; rp, retroarticular process; s, saccule; sp, sphenoid; st, stapes; tc, tympanic cavity; tm, tympanic membrane; u, utricle; VIII, vestibulo-cochlear nerve; IX, glossopharyngeal nerve. (Modified from Versluys, 1898.)

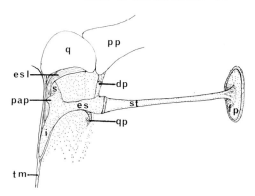

FIG. 4. Diagram of the columellar apparatus of a "typical" lizard. dp, Dorsal process; es, extra-stapes; esl, extrastapedial ligament; fp, footplate; i, pars inferior; pap, posterior accessory process; pp, paroccipital process; q, quadrate; qp, quadrate process; s, pars superior; st, stapes; tm, tympanic membrane.

consists of the extrastapes (extracolumella) and the stapes (columella auris). The extrastapes is short, lateral, cartilaginous, and complex in its form; the stapes extends from the medial extremity of the extrastapes to the otic capsule, is bony and is relatively simple in its shape.

Although the extrastapes varies considerably in reptiles with resultant questions concerning homologies (see de Beer, 1937), in the "typical" lacertilian it consists of a short central shaft to which are appended several processes or parts. At the lateral extremity of the shaft, the pars superior and

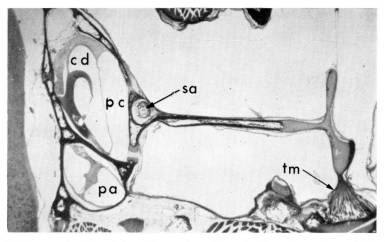

FIG. 5. Oblique section through the auditory region of the gecko *Teratoscincus scincus*. cd, Cochlear duct; pa, posterior ampulla; pc, periotic cistern; sa, stapedial artery in stapedial foramen; tm, tympanic muscle attaching to extrastapes.

the pars inferior form a platelike expansion embedded in the connective tissue of the upper half of the tympanic membrane. The pars superior extends posterodorsally from the shaft toward the junction of the tympanic crest and cephalic condyle of the quadrate (terms applied by Oelrich, 1956). Here it attaches by thickening and augmentation of the tympanic connective tissue in which it lies; this attachment, more strongly developed in some forms than in others, can be termed the extrastapedial (extracolumellar) ligament. The pars inferior extends anteroventrally from the shaft and tapers toward a termination near the center of the tympanic membrane; the pars inferior, also, may be encompassed by fibers of the extrastapedial ligament. Two small processes, the anterior accessory and the posterior accessory, frequently extend from the margins of the lateral expansion of the extrastapes and give it a cruciform appearance. The anterior process extends anterodorsally and is attached to the tympanic crest by a thickening of tympanic connective tissue. The posterior process, directed posteroventrally from the extrastapedial axis, is attached to a condensation of tympanic connective tissue which continues into the posterior marginal attachment of the membrane.

Just short of its medial extremity, the shaft of the extrastapes is slightly expanded and bears two additional processes for its attachment. These, frequently short and indistinct, are the dorsal process and the quadrate (internal) process; the former extends dorsally and attaches to the paroccipital process, while the latter projects anteroventrally and attaches to the posterior surface of the quadrate medial to its posterior crest. Both attach by short ligaments which lie within a fanlike sheet of collagenous connective tissue radiating anterodorsally from the extrastapedial shaft. Medial to these processes the rounded extremity of the extrastapes abuts against and, in a simple fibrous union, articulates with the small cartilaginous cap carried upon the lateral extremity of the stapedial shaft.

From its extrastapedial articulation, the slender elongate shaft of the stapes projects toward the vestibular window. The shaft expands, at first gradually then abruptly, as it terminates in the discoidal footplate which marks its medial extremity. The shaft is frequently indented, or in some forms pierced, by a stapedial notch or foramen just before it reaches the footplate. The footplate consists of a bony plate surrounded by a narrow tapered lip of cartilage. It lies within the cartilage-covered margins of the vestibular window and is usually positioned somewhat eccentrically toward the posterior and ventral borders of that opening. The annular ligament of the stapes, composed of fibrous and elastic connective tissue, extends from the marginal cartilage of the footplate to that of the vestibular window and completes the closure of the opening. Externally and internally extensions from the periosteum of the otic capsule continue across the annular ligament and blend with the stapedial periosteum to complete the articulation.

The middle ear is lined by a mucous membrane which is continuous with that of the auditory tube and pharynx. It consists, throughout the bulk of the cavity, of a low cuboidal and squamous epithelium with scattered mucous cells seated upon a delicate or indistinct basement membrane. Peripheral to the margins of the tympanic membrane, particularly dorsally, there is a zone of high cuboidal cells which grade abruptly into the exceedingly thin squamous epithelium lining the tympanic membrane itself. A second transition occurs more gradually where the epithelium lining the cavity grades into the ciliated columnar epithelium with sparse goblet cells of the auditory tube. The mucous membrane lining the tympanic cavity is closely adherent to underlying structures, particularly where those are bony; in reflecting over the columellar apparatus, however, the membrane typically forms two distinct folds. The larger and more constant of these is the columellar fold, which extends from the roof of the cavity to enclose the shafts of the stapes and extrastapes in its free margin. The second fold is formed by reflection of the mucous membrane over the quadrate process of the extrastapes and its ligament. It extends anteriorly from the columellar fold to the posterior surface of the quadrate, and typically contains the chorda tympani nerve.

B. The Internal Ear

1. General

Diverse origins of early literature, lack of communication between workers in mammalian otology and those studying the ear in lower vertebrates, and limited knowledge of sub-mammalian aural anatomy have resulted in some confusion and produced an extensive synonymy in the nomenclature of the internal ear. Additional problems in terminology have been presented by failure of presently "official" anatomical nomenclature (*Nomina Anatomica*, 1964) to recognize several terms widely used in otological literature. Thus, objections can be found to virtually any system of names applied to the internal ear of any vertebrate. Suggestions made in the interest of achieving a degree of standardization in nomenclature used for the reptilian internal ear (Baird, 1960b) have been rather well received. Those will, therefore, be incorporated into the terminology employed below. It should be pointed out that precise homologies have not been established for many reptilian aural structures, so certain of the terms have been applied on the basis of analogy. In the interest of improved communication, however, such usages seem justified until developmental studies test their validity.

The general organization of the reptilian internal ear corresponds to the typical vertebrate pattern. Within the otic capsule a series of interconnected bony cavities and canals constitute the osseus labyrinth. This contains complex, membranous, fluid-filled channels and sacs (the so-called membranous labyrinth) organized into the morphologically distinct otic and periotic labyrinths, one of which surrounds the other. The otic labyrinth is innermost, develops from the embryonic ectodermal otocyst, and contains otic fluid (endolymph). Interposed between the otic labyrinth and walls of the osseus labyrinth are highly organized and specialized connective tissues, differentiated from embryonic mesenchyme. These contribute to the support of the otic labyrinth and form well defined channels and sacs filled with periotic fluid (perilymph); this complex constitutes the periotic labyrinth. Although the otic and periotic labyrinths are primarily enclosed within the osseus labyrinth, one part of each extends outside and relates to other structures.

2. *Osseus Labyrinth*

In "typical" lizards the osseus labyrinth is primarily contained within prootic and opisthotic elements of the otic capsule, and consists of a large central cavity from which several smaller cavities and channels extend (Fig. 6). The major cavity, the vestibule, has the form of an irregular, medially-flattened ovoid and does not conform closely to the shapes of contained parts of the otic labyrinth. Ventrally the vestibule communicates freely with the cochlear recess, a deep space transversely narrowed and somewhat shorter than the vestibule; a ridge of bone, the inferior cisternal crest, frequently marks the junction of the two spaces laterally. The antero-ventral region of the cochlear recess is commonly termed its lagenar part.

Anteriorly and posteriorly, respectively, the vestibule communicates with the anterior and the posterior osseus ampulla. Anterolaterally, adjacent to the anterior ampulla, the lateral osseus ampulla extends from the central cavity. From the anterior ampulla, the anterior semicircular canal arches

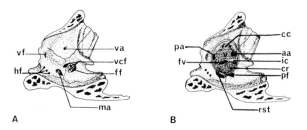

Fig. 6. Semidiagrammatic representation of the occipito-otic region of an iguanid lizard viewed from the medial aspect. A, Bones intact; B, bone removed to expose osseus labyrinth. aa, Anterior osseus ampulla; cc, osseus common crus with openings of anterior and posterior semicircular canals; cr, cochlear recess; ff, facial foramen; fv, vestibular window; hf, hypoglossal foramina; ic, inferior cisternal crest; ma, medial aperture of recessus scalae tympani; pa, posterior osseus ampulla; pf, lateral lip of periotic foramen (medial lip removed in dissection); rst, recessus scalae tympani; v, vestibule; va, vestibular aqueduct; vcf, anterior and posterior vestibulocochlear foramina; vf, vagus foramen.

dorsomedially to a point above the medial wall of the vestibule where it is met by the posterior semicircular canal arching dorsomedially from the posterior ampulla. The union of the two vertical canals forms the osseus common crus, a short, broad channel which extends ventrally and enters the dorsomedial aspect of the vestibule. The lateral semicircular canal originates from the lateral osseus ampulla, arches posteriorly within the lateral wall of the vestibule, and communicates posteriorly with that chamber dorsal to the posterior osseus ampulla. All of the osseus ampullae and semicircular canals contribute, to some extent, to external contours of the otic capsule.

Several openings pierce the walls of the osseus labyrinth. The vestibular window opens primarily in the lateral wall of the cochlear recess but usually shows some extension into the wall of the vestibule. Medially, at the level of junction of the vestibule and cochlear recess, two or three foramina for branches of the vestibulocochlear nerve open into the cranial cavity. Between these and the opening of the osseus common crus, the short vestibular aqueduct passes obliquely dorsomedially through the vestibular wall and communicates with the cranial cavity. One opening, the periotic foramen, pierces the ventromedial part of the posterior wall of the cochlear recess. By way of this foramen the cochlear recess communicates with the recessus scalae tympani, a poorly defined space which lies posteroventral to the otic capsule. As noted above, the recessus represents a remnant of part of the embryonic metotic fissure, has a medial aperture into the cranial cavity, and typically communicates with the tympanic cavity by means of a lateral aperture.

3. Otic Labyrinth
a. General

The otic labyrinth (Fig. 7) is composed of a series of epithelial sacs and tubes resting on and supported within connective tissues of the periotic labyrinth. Specific areas of the epithelium are specialized for reception of stimuli, and organized acellular structures lie over these within otic fluid contained throughout the system. Three major chambers, the utricle, the saccule and the cochlear duct, lie within the osseus labyrinth and can serve as a convenient basis for consideration of the system.

b. Utricle and Semicircular Ducts

The utricle is an elongate arched tube which occupies and extends through the medial region of the vestibule. Its anterior limb extends posterodorsally from the opening of the anterior osseus ampulla to the region below the orifice of the osseus common crus; from this area its posterior limb slopes posteroventrally to the opening of the posterior osseus ampulla. The major

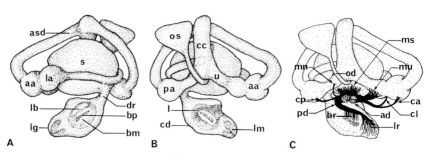

Fig. 7. The otic labyrinth of a "typical" lizard. A, Lateral view; B, medial view; C, medial view with vestibulocochlear nerve in position. aa, Anterior ampulla; ad, anterior division of vestibulo-cochlear nerve; asd, anterior semicircular duct; bm, basilar membrane; bp, basilar papilla; br, rami to basilar papilla; ca, anterior ampullary crest; cc, membranous common crus; cd, coch-lear duct; cl, ramus to lateral ampullary crest; cp, posterior ampullary crest; dr, reunient duct; l, limbus; la, lateral ampulla; lb, limbic bulge; lg, lagena; lm, lagenar macula; lr, rami to lagenar macula; mn, macula neglecta; ms, saccular macula; mu, utricular macula; od, otic duct; os, otic sac; pa, posterior ampulla; pd, posterior division of vestibulocochlear nerve; s, saccule; u, utricle.

utricular receptor, the utricular macula, forms part of the floor and adjacent wall of the anterior limb. A much smaller patch of sensory epithelium, the macula neglecta, lies posterolaterally in the floor of the utricular flexure. The utricular macula is supplied by a ramus of the anterior division of the vestibulocochlear nerve, and the macula neglecta receives a small branch from the posterior division of that nerve. The former is clearly an equilib-ratory receptor; the same may be true of the latter, but its function has not been firmly established.

Histologically, the bulk of the utricular wall consists of simple squamous cells resting on a thin membrana propria (basal lamina plus underlying connective tissue) formed by periotic connective tissue; here and elsewhere the membrana propria contains a few delicate blood vessels. Peripheral to each of the maculae in the utricle, both epithelium and connective tissue begin an increase in thickness which culminates at the receptor. Thickening of the membrana propria results simply from additional deposition and organization of tissue beneath the basal lamina, but, as the epithelium thickens toward the high cuboidal cells adjacent to the sensory area, several types of cells can be distinguished in it. Among these are darkly staining and rela-tively clear cuboidal cells and cells with broad bases and narrow apices bearing microvilli; the latter cells have been inadequately studied in reptiles and deserve additional consideration.

The sensory epithelia of the maculae (Fig. 8) are of a complex columnar type. Tall supporting cells with expanded bases rest upon the basal lamina and extend compressed apices to the utricular lumen. Supported between the supranuclear parts of these are columnar and flask-shaped hair cells, each of which has an apical cuticle bearing a tuft of sensory cilia. The cilia extend into the utricular lumen and are related to specialized acellular membranes possibly secreted by the macular and/or adjacent epithelium. Histochemical analyses are lacking for all such membranes in the reptilian ear, but histologically the membrane of the utricular macula resembles typical statoconic membranes of mammals. The reptilian structure is a thin, PAS-positive, gelatinous sheet with minute statoconia (calcareous granules) embedded in its luminal surface. The membrane's macular surface receives the tufts of sensory cilia into small depressions and, between these, is intimately related to the apices of supporting cells. The membranous covering of the macula neglecta is more delicate and less easily characterized than the statoconic membrane of the utricular macula. It, too, is PAS-positive and may have a few statoconia embedded in its luminal surface, but it is more fibrillar in appearance and less intimately related to the macular surface than is a typical statoconic membrane. Additionally, its macular surface is not clearly marked by depressions for the sensory cilia, and it frequently appears to be attached to the perimacular cells along one margin. Detailed histological and fine structural studies of this and other parts of the reptilian utricle are presently lacking.

Appended to the utricle are three semicircular ducts and the otic ampulla associated with each; these occupy and bear names equivalent to parts of the

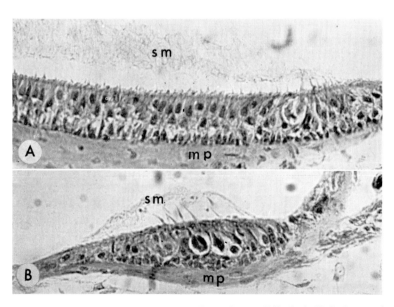

FIG. 8. Sensory epithelia of the utricle in *Anolis carolinensis* (410×). A, Utricular macula; B, macula neglecta. mp, Thick membrana propria; sm, statoconic membrane.

osseus labyrinth. Thus, at points adjacent to the orifices of the osseus ampullae, the utricle gives rise to posterior, anterior, and lateral otic ampullae. From these, semicircular ducts course onward through the semicircular canals. The anterior and posterior semicircular ducts terminate in the formation of the membranous common crus, a broad tubular channel which courses ventrally through the osseus common crus to blend with the apex of the utricular arch. The large size of the membranous common crus gives this union the form of an inverted "Y" and makes it difficult to establish boundaries of the joining parts. The lateral semicircular duct traverses its semicircular canal, enters the vestibule above the posterior ampulla, and courses dorsomedial to the posterior limb of the utricle to terminate in the membranous common crus as that structure joins the utricle.

The semicircular ducts are simple epithelial tubes approximately three-fourths the diameter of the canals they occupy and have no apparent innervation. Each otic ampulla, however, shows sensory specialization and receives a strong ramus from the vestibulocochlear nerve; anterior and lateral ampullae are supplied by the anterior division and the posterior ampulla by the posterior division of that nerve. Ampullary receptors are concerned with equilibration, but their function has been inadequately investigated in reptiles.

Histologically, the walls of the semicircular ducts and of approximately half of each ampulla are composed of thin squamous epithelium seated upon a membrana propria comparable to that of the general utricular wall; in contrast, the basal half of each otic ampulla is considerably specialized.

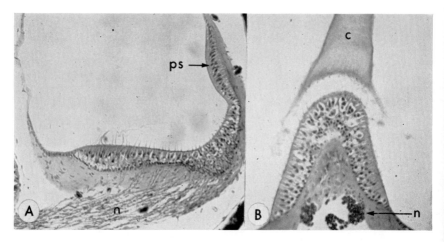

Fig. 9. Ampullary crest of *Anolis carolinensis*. A, Section slightly oblique to the long axis of the crest with only a few delicate strands of the cupula remaining (60×); B, section transverse to the above (180×). c, Cupula; n, nerve fibers; ps, planum semilunatum.

Approximately at right angles to a line connecting its orifices into the utricle and the semicircular duct, an evagination of the basal epithelium projects into the lumen of each ampulla. This ampullary crest (Fig. 9) contains a basally attached core of dense periotic connective tissue through which vessels and nerves course to the epithelium. A narrow zone of columnar sensory epithelium, generally comparable to that of the utricular macula except that its tufts of sensory cilia are significantly longer, obliquely crosses the ampullary crest. The sensory zone and crest are overlain by the cupula, a gelatinous mass into which the tufts of sensory cilia project. In fixed and sectioned material, the cupula may appear as an amorphous body of PAS-positive granular material or as dispersed granules in the ampullary lumen. High cuboidal epithelium borders the sensory epithelium on the slopes of the ampullary crest and in the adjacent sulci. The cuboidal epithelium is composed of lightly and darkly staining cells, many of which exhibit microvilli.

A planum semilunatum faces the ampullary crest from each wall between the ampullary orifices. Each of the two plana appears as an oval to crescentic area of tall columnar cells with lightly staining, faintly granular cytoplasm. Beyond them, the epithelium grades rapidly into squamous cells of the general ampullary wall. Electron microscopy has shown that the zone of cells between the sensory epithelium and the planum semilunatum is complex in lizards and contains microvillous cells with characteristics comparable to those of cells known to be concerned with fluid and ionic balance (Hamilton, 1965). Prebil (1966) has shown cytological differences in the plana semi-lunata of *Anolis* and *Leiolopisma*, and a report on electron microscopy of ampullary epithelia in those forms is presently being prepared by Prebil *et al.* These studies emphasize the need for additional cytological investigations.

c. Saccule and Otic Sac

The large ovoid saccule is suspended in the central part of the vestibule primarily by periotic attachments along its medial wall. Occupying a third or more of the vestibule, it lies lateral to the utricle, and a short utriculo-saccular duct joins the two structures. The duct leaves the lateral wall of the utricle posterior to the common crus, passes ventral to the vestibular part of the lateral semicircular duct, and then runs dorsolaterally to enter the upper part of the medial saccular wall; a valvular structure is frequently present at the saccular extremity of the duct (Hamilton, 1963b, 1964). Just anterior to the utriculosaccular duct, the otic (endolymphatic) duct joins the dorsomedial surface of the saccule. From this junction the duct passes ventromedially, hooks beneath the utricular flexure, and then enters the vestibular aqueduct. Beginning its expansion within the aqueduct, the otic duct terminates within the cranial cavity as the otic (endolymphatic) sac, an intrameningeal dilation of variable size which is intimately related to the choroid plexus of the fourth ventricle and the dorsal longitudinal venous sinus. The otic sac contains variable amounts of granular calcareous material of unknown significance but houses no obvious sensory structure. The saccule, however, has a third or more of its medial wall specialized to form the saccular macula, a sensory area which receives branches from both anterior and posterior (and intermediate, if present) divisions of the vestibulocochlear nerve. The function of the saccular macula has not been definitely shown in reptiles, but it is generally believed to serve in equilibration; morphological studies have suggested that it may have some auditory function.

The histology of the saccule resembles that of the utricle. The wall, excepting the macular and perimacular area, is formed by thin squamous and low cuboidal epithelium seated upon a thin periotic membrana propria. Thickening of both connective tissue and epithelium, with the appearance of several cell types in the latter, occurs in a perimacular transition zone surrounding the sensory epithelium. The size and shape of the sensory area is variable, but it typically forms the greater part of the ventromedial saccular

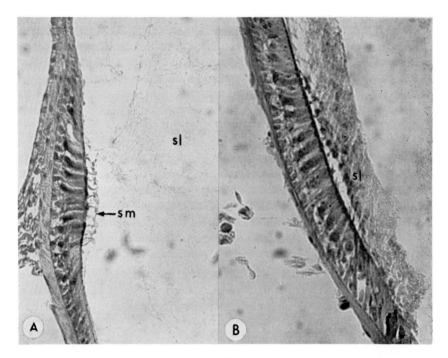

Fig. 10. Saccular macula of *Anolis carolinensis* (450×). A, Anterior region; B, posterior region of the same receptor. Lateral is to the right in both cases. sl, Cuticular matrix of statolith; sm, statoconic membrane.

wall, particularly toward the posterior extremity of the chamber. The cellular composition and organization of the saccular macula (Fig. 10) are comparable to those of the utricular macula, and tufts of short sensory cilia extend into depressions in a statoconic membrane. Adjacent to the wall, this membrane is similar to that of the utricular macula. To the luminal surface of the saccular statoconic membrane, however, is attached the saccular statolith; this consists of a delicate, gelatinous, PAS-positive matrix containing densely packed statoconia. The statolith is large and occupies the greater part of the saccular lumen.

Squamous and low cuboidal epithelia underlain by a delicate membrana propria characterize the vestibular part of the otic duct. Within the cochlear aqueduct the epithelium continues unchanged, but the surrounding connective tissue forms a dense meshwork firmly affixed to the bony walls. At the junction of the duct with the otic sac the epithelium changes abruptly. Tall simple columnar cells with randomly located nuclei and granular cytoplasm cover a large area of the medial wall of the sac; the luminal surface of this epithelium undulates and may be thrown into a valvelike fold at the orifice of the otic duct. The remaining mural epithelium is cuboidal, stains rather darkly, and has an indistinct luminal margin suggestive of the presence of microvilli. No detailed histological or cytological studies of the reptilian saccule or otic sac presently appear in the literature, but Kluge (1967) has recently summarized general information.

d. Cochlear Duct

Joined posteriorly to the posterior or posteromedial aspect of the saccule by a short reunient (sacculocochlear) duct of moderate diameter, the lacertilian cochlear duct typically forms an irregular, transversely narrow pyramid. The rounded apex of the pyramid, the lagena, projects anteroventrally into the lagenar part of the cochlear recess, and its base, the basilar (Retzius, 1884) or limbic (Miller, 1966a) part of the cochlear duct, occupies the dorsal and posterior parts of the recess. Variable areas of the walls and floor of the lagena are occupied by the large lagenar macula; the function of this receptor has not been experimentally demonstrated, but, in *Lacerta vivipara*, fibers from it traverse the cochlear ramus of the vestibulocochlear nerve and terminate in auditory areas of the brain (Hamilton, 1963a). Posterior to the lagena, the remaining part of the smoothly convex lateral wall of the cochlear duct faces a periotic compartment and constitutes the vestibular membrane. Dorsal and ventral walls are attached to dense periotic connective tissue and the medial wall is affixed to the limbus and basilar membrane, components of the periotic labyrinth described below. Centrally on the basilar membrane the epithelium of the cochlear duct is modified to form the basilar papilla, an oval or elongate receptor supplied by the cochlear ramus of the vestibulocochlear nerve and at least partially homologous to the mammalian organ of Corti. A tectorial membrane typically arises as a delicate intraluminal velum attached to cells dorsal to the basilar papilla and membrane; it extends ventrally, and its terminal part, variably specialized, overlies the basilar papilla. The tectorial membrane is relatively easily destroyed during the preparation of specimens for microscopy, but it has been sufficiently preserved in enough of the forms examined by the author to suggest that it is present in all lizards.

The histology of the cochlear duct shows similarities to that of the saccule and utricle but is somewhat more complex. The vestibular membrane is formed by cuboidal epithelium seated upon a thin membrana propria containing a few delicate blood vessels. Light microscopy discloses that the epithelium contains lightly staining cells and cells with basophilic inclusions and tufted apical microvilli. Where the vestibular membrane grades into the lateral wall of the lagena, the epithelium enters a perimacular transition zone comparable to those surrounding utricular and saccular maculae. Laterally this zone rests upon a membrana propria only slightly thicker than that of the vestibular membrane, but elsewhere periotic connective tissue beneath the basal lamina of the perimacular epithelium exhibits a progressive increase in thickness and density as it approaches the lagenar macula. The macula itself is formed of columnar epithelium in which the usual arrangement of hair cells and supporting cells can be recognized. The latter resemble supporting cells of the other maculae, but the former generally appear to be somewhat more expanded basally than are the hair cells of the saccule and utricle. The sensory epithelium is overlain by a statoconic membrane similar to that of the utricular macula.

Except for that covering the limbus and basilar membrane, the remaining epithelium of the cochlear duct is a simple cuboidal type and stains rather intensely with standard procedures (e.g., hematoxylin and eosin, Mallory methods). On the limbus surrounding the basilar membrane, the epithelium becomes columnar and consists of cells with poorly defined boundaries and randomly placed nuclei. The dorsal part of the tectorial membrane overlies the epithelium above the basilar membrane and appears to be attached to it by filamentous strands. At the margin of the basilar membrane, columnar cells give way to large cuboidal cells which show distinct boundaries but have nuclei and cytoplasm which stain very faintly; these cells extend over the basilar membrane to the margins of the basilar papilla. The papilla itself (Fig. 11) consists of columnar hair cells and supporting cells arranged as are those of other aural sensory epithelia, but this receptor typically exhibits larger, more clearly defined cells and greater organization than can be seen in maculae and cristae. The supporting cells rest upon a thin but distinct basal lamina and their broad nucleated basal regions are contiguous above it.

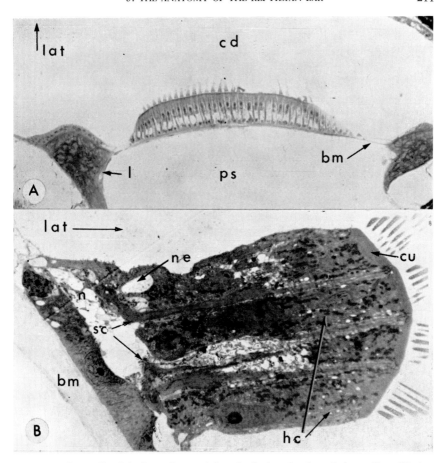

FIG. 11. Basilar papilla of *Anolis carolinensis*. A, Longitudinal section through the papilla and limbus (160×); B, transverse section through the papilla and basilar membrane (1,500×). bm, Basilar membrane; cd, cochlear duct; cu, cuticle; hc, hair cells; l, limbus; lat, lateral side of specimen; n, nerves entering dorsal margin of papilla; ne, nerve ending; ps, periotic sac; sc, supporting cells.

From the basal zone slender extensions of the cells project to the luminal surface of the papilla. These extensions are interrelated along their lateral surfaces and form continuous cellular walls around each hair cell and the outer limits of the papilla. Near the luminal surface, they are joined firmly to the hair cells by distinct junctional specializations. Deeper, where supporting cells form receptacles for the hair cells, a clear area occurs around the nucleated base of each of the latter; in suitable preparations nerve fibers can be seen coursing between supporting cells toward the clear area. The supra-nuclear cytoplasm of the hair cells is granular, and each has, apically, a biconvex cuticle surmounted by a tuft of sensory cilia of graded length.

H

Hair cells are typically arranged in staggered rows parallel to the long axis of the basilar papilla (Fig. 12); the number of rows can be relatively constant throughout the length of the papilla or may vary in an orderly fashion from one zone to another. Wever's (1965) report on the ear in thirteen species representing six families of lizards suggests that the pattern of distribution and total number of hair cells are rather constant in each species, but that they vary considerably between different forms. Information presently available suggests that "typical" lizards have 100 to 200 hair cells in the basilar papilla and others range from approximately 50 to 1600.

The lacertilian tectorial membrane is still insufficiently known to permit a detailed description of its structure. From its dorsal attachment to limbic epithelium, the membrane extends toward the basilar papilla as a delicate sheet of cuticular material. Its distal margin passes into relationship with

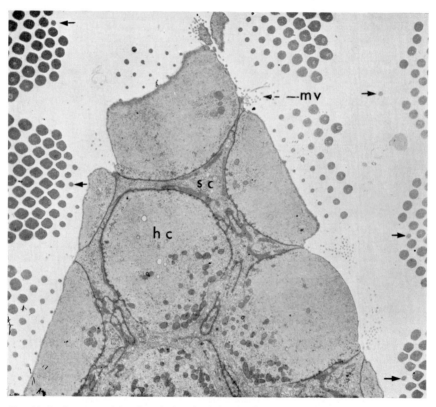

Fig. 12. Section tangential to the apical surface of the basilar papilla of *Anolis carolinensis* (4,000×). The longitudinal axis of the papilla is oriented vertically near the center of the micrograph; note the orientation of kinocilia (arrows) of the outer ciliary bundles toward that axis. hc, Cuticle of hair cell; mv, microvilli of supporting cell; sc, apical region of supporting cell.

sensory cilia of that receptor and is usually thickened and variously modified. Studies by Wever (1965, 1967a, 1967b) indicate that the form of the tectorial membrane and its type of relationship to papillar cilia can be classified, and that the latter feature varies interspecifically as well as regionally within a single form. Three general types of membrane and seven types of specialized ciliary relationships have been identified in twenty-one species representing eight lacertilian families. The structural patterns of both features correlate with the taxonomic assemblages investigated, and it is suggested that progressive specialization can probably be demonstrated in some of the ciliary specializations. Additional investigation of these delicate structures is certainly merited.

Fine structural studies of the reptilian cochlear duct have recently begun, but only brief preliminary reports have appeared in the literature (Baird and Winborn, 1966; Baird, 1966, 1967, 1969; Mulroy, 1968). These studies indicate greater cytological specialization than has previously been suggested, and more extensive investigations are now in progress. Detailed reports will appear elsewhere, but a few cytological features noted in the author's fine structural studies in lizards (Table I) are worthy of mention here. These studies are most advanced in *Anolis carolinensis* (Figs. 13–16), but the major characteristics given are present in other forms examined. The vestibular membrane and other parts of the mural epithelium contain several types of cells, some of which resemble basally infolded cells known to be concerned with fluid and ionic balance, while others may have a secretory function. Supporting cells of the basilar papilla concentrate their organelles in the basal region where adjacent cells are closely united by unusual junctions. Above this, the tapered supranuclear parts are loosely related one to another and to adjacent hair cells, and are densely packed with microtubules oriented parallel to the cellular axis; the luminal surfaces bear microvilli and, apicolaterally, typical intercellular junctions are made with adjacent cells.

In contrast to supporting cells, the hair cells show a concentration of organelles and scattered microtubules in the supranuclear region, while the infranuclear cytoplasm contains many vesicles and a few mitochondria. Adjacent to the basal and basolateral surfaces of each hair cell, numerous nerve endings intervene between sensory and supporting elements. Most of these make synaptic contact with the hair cells, but occasional relationships suggestive of synapses can be seen between nerve endings. All terminals thus far noted in functional relationship to sensory cells appear to be afferent; spheroidal, osmiophilic, synaptic bodies surrounded by vesicles frequently occur in hair cells adjacent to synaptic thickenings of the cell membrane, but intracellular structure typical of efferent synapses in auditory receptors of other vertebrates has not yet been found in lizards. The cuticle and tuft of sensory cilia at the apex of each hair cell are basically similar to those

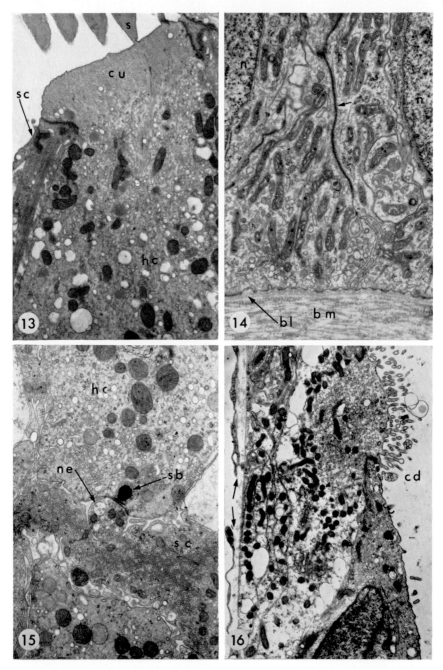

FIGS 13–16. Electron micrographs of parts of the cochlear duct of *Anolis carolinensis*. FIG. 13. Longitudinal section through marginal hair cell (hc) and adjacent supporting cell (sc) of the basilar papilla (15,500×); note junctional complexes between the cells and the dense filaments of stereo-

described in vestibular receptors and in auditory receptors of other sub-mammalian vertebrates. A variable number of stereocilia (e.g., 40 to 50 in *Anolis*, 35 to 45 in *Gekko*) extends from the cuticle in association with a single kinocilium projecting from the cytoplasm through an eccentrically placed cuticular hiatus. In all lizards examined the kinocilia have an orderly arrangement and an orientation that differs from the unidirectional one reported in auditory receptors of other vertebrates. Ciliary orientation differs in the species examined, and rather complete information is presently available only for *Anolis carolinensis*. Throughout the posterior part of the papilla, comprised of four staggered rows of hair cells, the kinocilia are oriented toward the longitudinal axis of those rows. The anterior part of the papilla is oval, five or six hair cells in width, and its elements are somewhat less regularly arranged. There, each kinocilium is oriented toward one of at least two axes that diverge as they extend from the major papillar axis; the tendency for orientation of cells in opposing pairs along these axes is evident, but it is less consistent than in the posterior region. The presence of membrane-bounded granular bodies and remnants of these between tufts of sensory cilia and the overlying granular tectorial membrane suggests secretion as a function of some papillar cells. The luminal ends of sensory cilia project into depressions in the tectorial membrane, where the extremities of the kinocilia become terminally enlarged, and all elements of the tuft are enmeshed in delicate filamentous material attached to the tectorial membrane.

4. Periotic Labyrinth

The labyrinthine channels and spaces in which the periotic fluid is contained are formed by specialized connective tissues classified regionally as: *internal periosteum*, the fibrous periosteal lining of the osseus labyrinth; *membrana propria*, the connective tissue intimately investing the epithelial otic labyrinth; and *periotic reticulum*, the trabecular and laminar connections which extend between the internal periosteum and membrana propria, lend support to the otic labyrinth, and complete the definition of periotic spaces and channels.

The internal periosteum consists of a thin layer of fibrous tissue closely

---

cilia (s) coursing through cuticle (cu) toward the cytoplasm. FIG. 14. Longitudinal section through the basal regions of two supporting cells (11,900×); note concentration of organelles and unusual junction between cells (arrow); bl, basal lamina; bm, basilar membrane; n, nucleus. FIG. 15. Transverse section through hair cell (hc), supporting cell (sc), and afferent nerve ending (ne) in synaptic relation to hair cell (12,600×); note thickening of membranes at the synapse, dense synaptic body (sb) with surrounding vesicles in the hair cell, and innumerable circular profiles of microtubules within the supporting cell. FIG. 16. Section through the vestibular membrane (5,700×); a basally infolded cell of the membrane directs its microvilli into the lumen of the cochlear duct (cd); on the opposite (periotic) surface, note the fine fibrillar layer and flattened fibroblasts which constitute the membrana propria (arrows).

attached to the walls of the osseus labyrinth; accumulations of pigment commonly occur within the layer, and flattened fibroblasts are numerous upon its luminal surface. The periotic reticulum is formed by fibers and fibroblasts comparable to those of the periosteal layer, but typically lacks deposits of pigment and varies through a relatively wide range of thickness and strength. The membrana propria lacks the histologic homogeneity of the periosteal and reticular parts of the labyrinth and shows several specializations. Most commonly, as on the thin walls of semicircular ducts and major otic compartments, the membrana propria consists of a delicate acellular layer of randomly oriented fibers situated between an extremely thin basal lamina beneath the otic epithelium and flattened fibroblasts on the surface toward the periotic spaces (Fig. 16). Where the membrana propria comes into relationship to cristae, maculae, perimacular areas, and the dorsal wall of the cochlear duct, it is thicker and composed of numerous fibroblasts interspersed among densely packed bundles of fibers; the basal lamina is slightly thicker in these areas and layering of fibroblasts toward periotic surfaces is less evident. Adjacent to the medial wall of the cochlear duct, the thick membrana propria of the dorsal wall and of the lagenar perimacular area grades into the tissue of the limbus; this bears a superficial resemblance to cartilage, but its histochemical responses and ultrastructure indicate that it cannot properly be classified as cartilage or usual fibrous connective tissue (Shute and Bellairs, 1953; Miller *et al.*, 1967). It consists of numerous irregular fibroblasts scattered in a matrix consisting of an amorphous ground substance containing predominately fine fibers. In the central part of the limbus, fibrillar material and ground substance are continuous into the basilar membrane, but fibroblasts do not occur within that structure. A basal lamina, continuous with that of the adjacent membrana propria, intervenes between overlying epithelia and the tissues of both the limbus and basilar membrane, while discontinuous flattened fibroblasts line the surfaces of both structures adjacent to periotic spaces.

The limbus (Fig. 17) essentially forms a base from which a major part of the periotic attachments radiate. Since attention was drawn to some of its significance and developmental features (Shute and Bellairs, 1953), a wide range of variation in reptilian limbic morphology has been demonstrated (Hamilton, 1963b, 1964; Miller, 1966a, 1966b), but basic features are well represented in "typical" lacertilians. The plate of limbic connective tissue, thicker dorsally than ventrally, is loosely attached to the posterior part of the medial wall of the cochlear recess; anterodorsally it overlaps the posterior foramen for the vestibulocochlear nerve and posteroventrally it overlies the periotic foramen. Adjacent to the latter opening the medial surface of the limbus is variably excavated, and part of the thin lamina remaining laterally at the depths of the excavation is modified to form the basilar membrane.

The transition from typical limbic tissue to modified tissue of the basilar membrane is striking, both grossly and microscopically; thus, despite embryonic and adult continuity between the two parts, the limbus is conventionally said to be "perforated" by an opening called the limbic hiatus and the basilar membrane is said to be stretched across the lateral margin of the opening. Dorsal to the hiatus and membrane the limbus medially accommodates part of the vestibulocochlear ganglion, from which nerve fibers radiate anteriorly through the limbus to the lagenar macula, ventrally to pierce the dorsal margin of the basilar membrane and supply the basilar papilla, and posteriorly toward the posterior ampulla. The presence of the ganglion and nerve fibers has prompted Miller (1966a) to designate the part above the basilar membrane as the neural limbus. The lateral surface of this region may bear a bulge or elaborate lip which indents the cochlear duct at the base of the tectorial membrane and provides an elevated point of attachment for that structure.

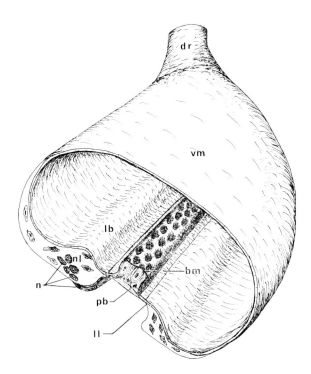

Fig. 17. Diagram of the cochlear duct of a "typical" lizard. bm, Basilar membrane; dr, reunient duct; lb, limbic bulge (from which tectorial membrane is suspended in most lizards); ll, lip of the ventral part of the limbus; n, rami of nerves coursing to basilar papilla and lagenar macula; nl, neural limbus; pb, basilar papilla; vm, vestibular membrane.

Delicate periotic reticulum attaches the limbus directly to much of the adjacent periosteum of the medial wall of the cochlear recess; the limbus receives additional anchorage, except laterally, through reticular attachments of the thick membrana propria with which it is continuous. The membrana propria of the dorsal surface of the cochlear duct typically blends with that of the adjacent part of the medial curvature of the saccule; from this union and from the membrana propria underlying the saccular and utricular maculae, periotic reticulum extends among ramifications of the vestibulo-cochlear nerve and attaches to the medial vestibular periosteum. Diffuse reticulum extends along the utricle and continues beyond it to anchor the otic ampullae and the semicircular ducts; attachments of the latter are particularly evident along their greater curvatures. A lamina of periotic reticulum, the cisternal septum, frequently extends laterally from the anterior part of the periotic tissue between the saccule and cochlear duct and attaches to the periosteum at the junction of the vestibule with the cochlear recess. In forms with a saccule of moderate size, a comparable lamina may attach the dorsal saccular membrana propria to the vestibular roof, but, in forms in which the saccule is large and expanded laterally, the dorsolateral wall of that structure may be closely attached to the adjacent vestibular periosteum by short strands of periotic reticulum.

Thus, coupled with parts of the otic labyrinth, the periotic connective tissues define a series of spaces occupied by periotic fluid (Fig. 18). Surrounding the utricle and semicircular ducts the fluid occupies a generalized space which is variably filled with periotic trabeculae and shows little evidence of delineated channels. Conversely, in areas lateral to the saccule and both lateral and medial to the cochlear duct, compartments and channels free of periotic reticulum occur. The largest of these, the periotic cistern, occupies space between the lateral surfaces of the saccule and cochlear duct and the opposing lateral walls of the vestibule and cochlear recess. The vestibular and cochlear parts of the cistern typically communicate freely as far anteriorly as the anterior limit of the vestibular window. More anteriorly, they frequently become constricted or totally separated by an inferior cisternal crest, a cisternal septum, or a combination of the two. When such an anterior division of the cistern is distinct, the ventral part extending adjacent to the anterior part of the vestibular membrane is termed the scala vestibuli. A diverticulum extending anteroventrally from the scala vestibuli (or comparable part of the periotic cistern) into relationship with the lagena is termed a scala lagenae, and one which may pass dorsomedially between the saccule and cochlear duct and expand beneath the saccular macula is called a scala sacculi.

Near the anterior extremity of the cochlear duct, the lateral periotic channel tapers and becomes constricted into a narrow duct, the helicotrema;

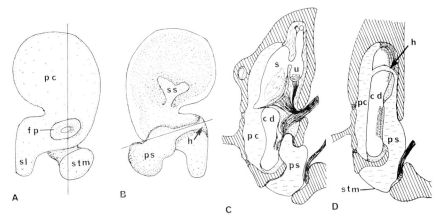

FIG. 18. Diagrams of the major periotic compartments of "typical" lizards. A, Lateral view of left periotic labyrinth with footplate superimposed; B, medial view of same; C, idealized section through internal ear at plane shown in A; D, same at plane shown in B. cd, Cochlear duct; fp, footplate of stapes; h, helicotrema; pc, periotic cistern; ps, periotic sac; s, saccule; sl, scala lagenae; ss, scala sacculi; stm, secondary tympanic membrane; u, utricle.

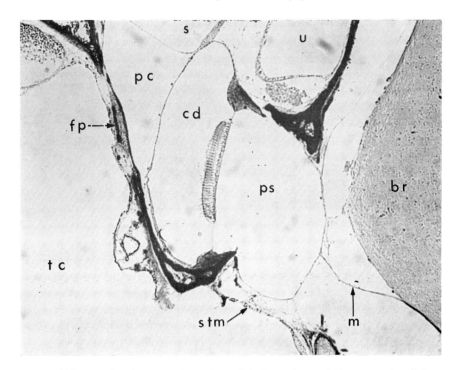

FIG. 19. Oblique section through the internal ear of *Anolis carolinensis* (100 ×). Note the relationships of the periotic sac to the meninges and secondary tympanic membrane. br, Brain; cd, cochlear duct; fp, footplate of stapes; m, meninges; pc, periotic cistern; ps, periotic sac; s, saccule; stm, secondary tympanic membrane; tc, tympanic cavity; u, utricle.

this channel is embedded in thick membrana propria, hooks medially around the anterior margin of the cochlear duct dorsal to the lagena and extends posteriorly to the limbus. There, depending upon the form of the limbic hiatus, the helicotrema either empties directly into a large periotic sac situated in the limbic hiatus in lateral contact with the basilar membrane, or expands into a tubular scala tympani related to the anterior part of the basilar membrane; in the latter case, the scala tympani communicates with a periotic sac that is restricted to the posterior part of the basilar membrane. In some forms, vermiform diverticula of the periotic sac extend into limbic recesses to achieve full contact with the basilar membrane; such a diverticulum constitutes an accessory scala tympani.

Opposite the basilar membrane, the periotic sac exits from the cochlear recess via the periotic foramen and extends into the recessus scalae tympani. This extracapsular extension of the sac derives its thin fibrous wall from contributions of periotic reticulum attached to the margin of the periotic foramen. At the medial aperture of the recess, immediately anterior to the ninth cranial nerve, the medial wall of the periotic sac is closely associated with the adjacent external surface of the cranial meninges (Fig. 19). Laterally, within or at the lateral aperture of the recessus scalae tympani, the periotic sac abuts against the tympanic mucous membrane and thus forms the secondary tympanic membrane; a thin layer of areolar connective tissue intervenes between the related parts and unites them.

III. The External and Middle Ear in Various Reptilian Groups

A. INTRODUCTION

Although literature touching upon the reptilian external and middle ear is vast, information concerning the regions in fossil forms is fragmentary, and there are no comprehensive comparative studies treating the morphology of these structures in Recent reptiles. Many of the references primarily concerned with taxonomy, embryology, and general cranial morphology are difficult to evaluate because only selected parts are considered and individual interpretations usually offer too little basis for accurate correlation. The classical works of Versluys (1898, 1903), Gaupp (1899, 1905), Goodrich (1915, 1930), Wyeth (1924), de Burlet (1934), de Beer (1937) and Smith (1938), plus more recent papers by Watson (1953, 1954), Earle (1961a, 1961b, 1961c, 1962), Toerien (1963), and Olson (1966) provide a valuable core of morphological and developmental information and bibliographies. These studies also make it apparent that detailed anatomical analyses are available for relatively few forms and that sampling of most groups has been extremely limited.

It is now generally accepted that certain fundamental morphological patterns characterize the middle ear in the major assemblages of reptiles. Despite unsettled questions concerning homologies of parts of the columellar apparatus (see recent comments of McDowell, 1967), considerable weight has been placed upon this premise in taxonomic and phylogenetic discussions. Yet, it is becoming increasingly apparent that the region is subject to adaptive change. In some instances (e.g., *Eremias, Chamaeleo*) such changes exist in forms known to have small basilar papillae and poor auditory sensitivity (see Miller, 1966a; Wever, 1965, 1968), but in others (e.g., *Acontias, Typhlosaurus*) alteration of the middle ear is not accompanied by correspondingly great change in the auditory receptor (see Miller, 1966a; Toerien, 1963). Somewhat similar associations may exist between the middle ear and variations in the external ear (see Wever, 1968), but these have not been extensively explored. Thus, the nature, extent, development and functional correlations of modifications in the external and middle ear are poorly understood and require further investigation. The increasing fund of information on the anatomy and physiology of the internal ear is presently increasing the feasibility and potential value of such study.

B. Squamata

The external ear in squamates shows a wide range of variation from the "typical" form described above. Snakes and amphisbaenians, presumably in association with specializations of the middle ear initially associated with burrowing (see, however, Berman and Regal, 1967), have no external evidence of aural structures, and lizards may show either accentuation or reduction of the external opening. Versluys' (1898) study, which has not been supplanted as the major source for general and relatively specific morphological information on the lacertilian external ear, indicates that differences in size, shape, and depth of the structure are prevalent in some families but do not occur in others. The majority of these differences are apparently related to altered bulk, form and relationships of the surrounding bony and muscular components of the mandibular articulation, to the site of attachment of the tympanic membrane, and/or to variations in cutaneous folds around the external opening. Such variations alter the amount of protection afforded the tympanic membrane and could influence hearing, and at least some of them appear to be more directly related to the auditory system than to other factors.

Reduction of the external ear and degrees of scalation of the tympanic membrane have been shown to occur in a variety of forms in which mobility of the columellar apparatus is reduced or altered (e.g., *Holbrookia, Phrynosoma, Chamaeleo, Lanthanotus*). The external ear is absent and extensive tympanic modifications occur in anniellids and some burrowing scincids (see below). The external ear is present and well defined in secretive limbless forms (pygopodids, except *Aprasia*; *Ophisaurus*) and in some semi-fossorial and fossorial scincids which have more "typical" middle ears. Conversely, the external ear is deep and the "external auditory meatus" is larger than the external orifice in numerous gekkonids and terrestrial scincids. In *Gekko* and *Mabuya*, both mentioned in this connection by Versluys (1898), en-largement of the "meatus" results in the formation of a sort of subsurface chamber, parts of the lateral walls of which are formed by bone and muscle as well as skin. Other genera show similar conditions and, in some gek-konids (e.g., *Pachydactylus*, *Thecadactylus*), slips of the sphincter muscle of the neck occupy the posterior part of the marginal cutaneous fold and may exert a sphincteric action on the external orifice ("Schliessmuskel" of Versluys, 1898). It is of interest that these elaborations are particularly noticeable in those forms having large basilar papillae (see Miller, 1966a). When viewed in their entirety, these various conditions indicate that there is reason to question implications of direct cause and effect in statements relating morphology of the external ear solely to a given habit or habitat.

On the basis of limited data available, it is frequently stated or implied that the organization of the middle ear in most terrestrial and arboreal lizards conforms generally to the "typical" lacertilian pattern described above. Within this conformity, however, major and minor variations in relative sizes, shapes, and relationships of most elements commonly occur. Some of these appear to form patterns throughout familial assemblages and to correlate with other features of the ear; others occur only in some mem-bers of comparable groups, show no clear association with available aural information, and may relate more directly to habits or habitats. Gekkonids and chamaeleonids provide reasonably well documented examples of the first case, although data are still insufficient to permit positive statements.

Morphologically based suggestions that geckoes have superior auditory abilities have recently been validated physiologically by Wever and his co-workers (1963, 1964, 1965, 1967). Several diverse gekkonid genera exhibit (1) a definitive "tympanic muscle" (Wever, 1965; presumably the equivalent of Versluys, 1898, "muscle of the extracolumella"), (2) a delicate and mobile columellar apparatus in which the stapedial artery passes through a stapedial foramen, (3) a secondary tympanic membrane characteristically placed deeply within the recessus scalae tympani and directed ventrally rather than laterally or ventrolaterally, and (4) an unusually large tympanic cavity and auditory tube. Minor intergeneric variations can be detected in most of these features, but those involving structures concerned with the transmission of sound appear to be correlated with the degree of development of auditory receptors and vocality. Posner and Chiasson (1966) provide a description of the middle ear of *Coleonyx*, and offer suggestions concerning auditory functions of the region.

An opposite pattern probably exists in chamaeleonids, in which Versluys (1898) noted attachment of the extrastapes to the quadrate and progressive reduction of the tympanic cavity and columellar apparatus. Toerien (1963) further indicated that alteration and reduction (to vestigial conditions in *Rhampholeon*) of middle ear structures is accompanied by reduction in the auditory receptor and alterations in the periotic sac (the latter deserve further elucidation). Miller (1966a) regards the chamaeleonid cochlear duct as "degenerate", and his measurements in *Chamaeleo* and *Brookesia* are not in conflict with Toerien's observations. Wever (1968) has recently shown that its quadrate attachment does not immobilize the columellar apparatus in at least two species of *Chamaeleo*, and that part of the pterygoid substitutes functionally for the missing tympanic membrane. His findings further indicate that the ear is reasonably functional in these animals, but is less sensitive than that of all save one of the lizards he has tested. Unfortunately, no physiological data are yet available for *Microsaura*, *Brookesia*, or *Rhampholeon*, but the morphological evidence now available suggests that they might be expected to have auditory sensitivities lower than that in *Chamaeleo*. Thus, progressive and associated reduction in the external, middle, and internal ear may well relate to reduction in auditory sensitivity within the group. There is no evidence that audition has had a negative selective value in these animals, and, in fact, the modification of the pterygoid and columellar relationships in *Chamaeleo* would seem to argue against that concept. It seems more probable that the process of selection for those characteristics advantageous to chamaeleonids has resulted in accentuation of an auditory apparatus that is relatively inefficient and poorly adapted to their habitat than that the auditory system has been selectively reduced.

In contrast to these cases, modifications of the middle ear which cannot be correlated with other aural information available occur in iguanids. In *Phrynosoma macalli* Norris and Lowe (1951) have shown reduction of the external ear and tympanic modifications that include attachment of the extrastapes to the quadrate, and have associated those changes with burrowing. Miller's (1966a) measurements indicate that the basilar papilla is indeed small in that species, but not remarkably smaller than in other forms of *Phrynosoma* lacking the modifications. Rather similar findings exist in sand lizards. Marked modification of the middle ear, including firm articulation of the extrastapes with the quadrate, occurs in *Holbrookia* and *Callisaurus* in association with the burrowing habit (Earle, 1961a, 1961b), but is not found in the related burrower *Uma* (Earle, 1962). Miller's (1966a) measurements in representatives of the three genera do not suggest significant differences in papillar size, although that author mentions that the basilar papilla is "relatively short and small" in *Holbrookia texana*. Thus, based upon information presently available, it can only be said that these tympanic modifications cannot now be correlated with marked change in the internal ear, and their influence upon hearing is not presently known from physiological studies. Even less is known concerning the auditory significance of other reported divergences of the middle ear, such as those in some agamids (Smith, 1938) and the unique condition in *Lanthanotus* (McDowell, 1967).

Sufficient attention has been accorded the middle ear in burrowing lizards to allow for speculative interpretation of changes, but information is still far from complete. Representatives of the scincids and anguids provide discontinuous series showing some parallelism in transitions from terrestrial to fossorial adaptations. In both groups, limbed terrestrial forms show conditions essentially similar to those in other lacertilians. Limbless terrestrial forms show only varying combinations of slight reduction in the size of the tympanic membrane, thickening of extrastapedial attachments, and minor enlargement of the footplate, but neither the secondary tympanic membrane nor the tympanic cavity show marked changes. In more fossorial forms (e.g., *Scelotes* and *Anguis*), external changes are accompanied by thickening and reduction of the tympanic membrane, further elaboration of extrastapedial ligaments, marked increase in size of the footplate, and reduction in the size of the tympanic cavity; a secondary tympanic membrane can be said to be present in both genera, but the mucous membrane and connective tissue layers of that structure are considerably thickened (Fig. 30). In the highly fossorial *Acontias* (de Villiers, 1939; Brock, 1941; van der Merwe, 1944; Toerien, 1963) the extrastapes is reportedly attached to a ligamentous tympanic membrane and, by a ligament, to the retroarticular process. *Typhlosaurus* (Toerien, 1963) shows a similar retroarticular attachment but lacks a tympanic membrane; the extrastapes is prolonged by a subcutaneous cartilage and ligament terminating in the upper lip. In both genera the footplate is greatly enlarged and the tympanic cavity and auditory tube are reported to be replaced by large lymph cavities; the lateral relationship of the periotic sac is not mentioned but merits investigation.

Touched upon most recently by Toerien (1963) and Hamilton (1963b), the middle ear in *Anniella* and representatives of the amphisbaenians shows similar extreme adaptations and interesting parallelism in the two squamate groups. In *Anniella* the extrastapes articulates firmly with the quadrate and otherwise attaches only to the short stapedial shaft. In most amphisbaenians the stapedial-extrastapedial articulation is loosely attached to the ventral aspect of the mandibular articulation; from this point an extrastapes, slender and sometimes cartilaginous, extends anteriorly along the lateral surface of the mandible and terminates with an attachment to the overlying skin. The trogonophid amphisbaenians (see Gans, 1960) depart from this pattern in that the extrastapes is short and may ossify as a plate attached to the skin lateral to the mandibular articulation; in the amphisbaenid *Rhineura*, the base of the extrastapes may also be ossified (Figs 20 and 21). Representatives of both anniellids and amphisbaenians lack a tympanic and a secondary tympanic membrane. Both exhibit a relatively immense stapedial footplate

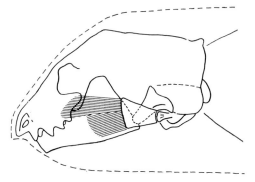

FIG. 20. Outline view of the head of *Diplometopon zarudnyi* showing the columellar apparatus. The stapes is evident in the posteroventral region of the skull. The extrastapes lies lateral to the mandibular articulation and is attached anteriorly to the skin of the upper and lower lips by bundles of dense connective tissue. (Courtesy of Dr. Carl Gans, with permission from the American Museum of Natural History.)

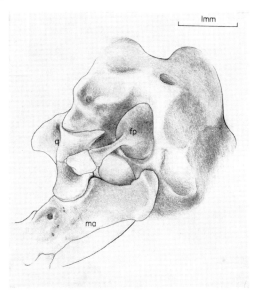

FIG. 21. Occipito-otic region of the skull of *Rhineura floridana*, viewed from a posteroventral position. Note the relatively huge stapedial footplate and the ossified base of the extrastapes adjacent to the mandibular articulation. (Courtesy of Dr. Carl Gans.) fp, Footplate of stapes; ma, mandible; q, quadrate.

overlain by loose areolar tissue containing large fluid spaces, and, in both, the periotic sac is related posteriorly to the glossopharyngeal nerve and its foramen, but does not extend into contact with the areolar tissue mentioned.

Other fossorial adaptations of the lacertilian middle ear are less well known, but they appear to follow the general patterns of the lizards and amphisbaenians mentioned. It seems significant that present data indicate that there is less correlation between the degree of tympanic modification and the size of the auditory receptor in fossorial forms than is found in terrestrial and arboreal lizards. Thus, it is probable that the auditory sense is of considerable value in fossorial existence. Burrowing modifications of the middle ear serve to reduce the width of the head and/or to strengthen cranial structure (see Norris and Lowe, 1951) while they usually maintain conditions reasonably suited to the reception and transmission of at least substratal vibrations. Additionally, Gans (1960) has demonstrated in some amphisbaenians that the semicircular canals are not reduced in the presence of considerable cranial modification. Thus, aural morphology may be of significant taxonomic value in well circumscribed groups of lizards, but, until it is more completely understood, its use in determining advances, degeneracy, and broad phylogenetic relationships must be limited to cases in which there is strong supporting data of other sorts.

The middle ear of snakes shows analogies to that in amphisbaenians and in some arboreal and fossorial lizards. The tympanic membrane, tympanic cavity and auditory tube are absent, and the region between the otic capsule and the quadrate is largely occupied by elements of the mandibular musculature. The lateral extremity of the columellar apparatus is typically joined to the quadrate at two points. The distal cartilaginous extremity of the stapes articulates, frequently diarthrodially, with a small cartilaginous element fused to the internal surface of the quadrate; just proximal to that joint, a small stapedial process attaches to the posteromedial surface of the quadrate by a short ligament. Homologies of the cartilaginous element and stapedial process are still in dispute and have recently been discussed by McDowell (1967).

Extending anteromedially from these articulations, the stapedial shaft terminates in a large oval footplate fixed in the vestibular window much as it is in lizards; the relationships of the lateral surface of the footplate are, however, considerably different. A ridge of bone, the circumfenestral crest (Baird, 1960a, 1960b) is elaborated by the otic capsule, encircles the vestibular window, and crosses the lateral aperture of the recessus scalae tympani, thus placing the window and footplate in the depths of a fossa (Fig. 22). The anterior part of the lateral aperture of the recessus opens into the posteroventral aspect of the fossa; this opening is traversed by an extension of the periotic sac, the juxtastapedial sinus (Baird, 1960a, 1960b) which occupies the fossa and abuts against the lateral surface of the footplate. The lateral wall of the sinus usually attaches to the lips of the circumfenestral crest and forms a thickened periotic membrane closing the fossa. Thus, although this periotic membrane represents part of a secondary tympanic membrane, it underlies mandibular musculature rather than the mucous membrane of a tympanic cavity and is traversed or indented by the shaft of the stapes.

Morphological alterations of the ophidian middle ear are poorly known, but some modifications, possibly adaptive, have been noted. In some forms exhibiting degrees of burrowing behavior (e.g., Aniliidae: *Uropeltis*, *Rhinophis*; Colubridae: *Calamelaps*, *Carphophis*, *Micrelaps*) the circumfenestral crest is greatly developed, overhangs the juxtastapedial fossa and correspondingly reduces the size of the periotic membrane closing the fossa. This condition reaches its greatest expression in typhlopids and leptotyphlopids,

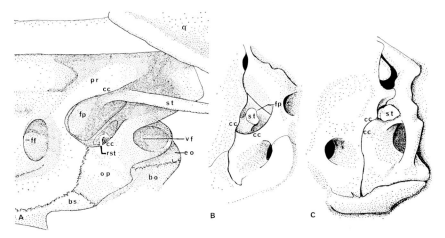

Fig. 22. Lateral views of the left otic region showing varying closure of the ophidian circumfenestral crest. A, *Thamnophis radix*; B, *Typhlops punctatus*; C, *Typhlops schlegelii*. bo, Basioccipital; bs, basisphenoid; cc, circumfenestral crest; eo, exoccipital; ff, facial foramen; fp, footplate; op, opisthotic; pr, prootic; q, quadrate; rst, recessus scalae tympani; st, stapedial shaft; vf, vagus foramen.

in which the crest closely surrounds the stapedial shaft, encloses the justastapedial sinus, and covers the lateral periotic membrane (Figs 23 and 24). Presumably, such elaboration of the crest strengthens the skull and affords additional protection to the fluid-filled labyrinths. It should be noted, however, that Miller's (1968) data and personal observations indicate that enlargement of the circumfenestral crest does occur in non-burrowing snakes.

A second modification is an enlargement of the stapedial footplate relative to the size of the cochlear duct and otic capsule; in some burrowing forms (e.g., typhlopids, leptotyphlopids, aniliids) and some viperids and elapids

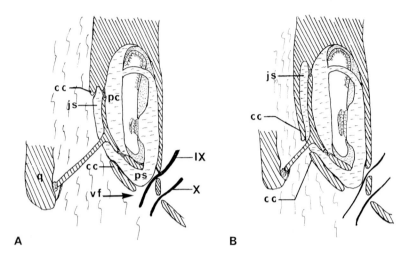

A   B

Fig. 23. Diagrams of idealized horizontal sections through the ophidian ear. A, Conditions typical of most terrestrial forms; B, relationships found in varying degrees in many burrowing snakes. In fossorial forms, the circumfenestral crest covers a significant part of the lateral surface of the juxtastapedial sinus, the footplate is relatively larger, and the stapedial shaft is relatively shorter than in terrestrial forms. cc, Circumfenestral crest; js, juxtastapedial sinus; pc, periotic cistern; ps, periotic sac; q, quadrate; vf, vagus foramen; IX, glossopharyngeal nerve; X, vagus nerve.

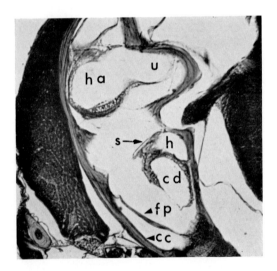

Fig. 24. Transverse section through the head of *Typhlops nigrescens* at the level of the lateral ampulla (60×). The brain and vestibulocochlear nerve lie to the right. Note that the footplate extends to this level and that, together with the adjacent juxtastapedial sinus, it is completely enclosed ventrolaterally by the circumfenestral crest. cc, Circumfenestral crest; cd, cochlear duct; fp, footplate of stapes; h, helicotrema; ha, lateral ampulla; s, saccule; u, utricle.

(e.g., *Echis, Naja*) the footplate forms significantly more than half or virtually all of the lateral wall of the cochlear recess and vestibule. Although analyses have not yet been made, it may be significant that enlargement of the footplate occurs in those groups in which Miller (1966b, 1968) notes relatively large basilar papillae. As in burrowing lizards, a given movement of the stapedial shaft would produce greater displacement of labyrinthine fluid through a large footplate than through a small one; thus, the relative efficiency of the transmitting apparatus may, here too, be directly related to the size of the primary auditory receptor and to total acoustic ability.

C. Rhynchocephalia

The tympanic region of *Sphenodon* is well known through works of, *inter alia*, Versluys (1903), Wyeth (1924) and de Beer (1937), and various interpretations have been suggested for the conditions shown. *Sphenodon* lacks an external ear, no tympanic cavity is present, and the tympanic membrane is degenerate (see, however, Gray, 1913; Tumarkin, 1955). Several features of the extrastapes are notable. The pars superior is joined to the dorsal process by a cartilaginous bar and the dorsal surface of this union is attached to the internal surface of the quadrate; the union results in the formation of a foramen of Huxley, which is traversed by the chorda tympani nerve as it passes dorsal to the extrastapes. Furthermore, an extrastapedial muscle passes between the pars superior and the paroccipital-quadrate union, and the internal surface of the pars inferior is fused with the cartilaginous

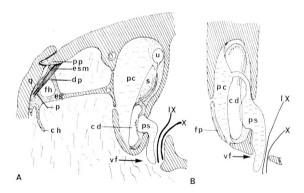

Fig. 25. Diagrams of idealized sections through the auditory region of *Sphenodon*. A, Transverse plane; B, horizontal plane. The periotic sac does not relate to a secondary tympanic membrane, but accompanies the glossopharyngeal and vagus nerves through the vagus foramen to end blindly in soft tissues of the suprapharyngeal region. cd, Cochlear duct; ch, ceratohyal; dp, dorsal process; es, extrastapes; esm, extrastapedial muscle; fh, foramen of Huxley; fp, footplate; p, pars superior; pc, periotic cistern; pp, paroccipital process; ps, periotic sac; q, quadrate; s, saccule; u, utricle; vf, vagus foramen; IX, glossopharyngeal nerve; X, vagus nerve.

ceratohyal. The stapes is notable for its stapedial foramen traversed by the stapedial artery, and the relatively large stapedial footplate articulates in a fenestra vestibuli confined almost entirely to the lateral vestibular wall rather than opening into the cochlear recess. No secondary tympanic membrane is present, for the periotic sac traverses the vagus foramen in company with glossopharyngeal and vagus nerves and ends blindly in the suprapharyngeal region (Fig. 25). Several of these conditions have been regarded as primitive, and there is little question that the auditory apparatus as a whole shows archaic features. Considering the extent to which the middle ear is modified in squamates, however, it seems probable that the majority of these tympanic conditions have arisen within the group.

D. Testudines

The general pattern of osteological modifications in the region of the middle ear of turtles has been well summarized by de Beer (1937) and Romer (1956), while Werner (1960) has clarified the osseous site of attachment of the tympanic membrane and McDowell (1961) has contributed to the understanding of certain foramina in the area. These items will, therefore, receive only passing attention here. The most significant difference is the great development of a vertical process of the quadrate which divides the region of the middle ear into a lateral tympanic cavity and a medial recessus cavi tympani. The latter contains the bulk of the structures normally associated with the tympanic cavity of other reptiles. The relative positions of most of these non-osseous structures are comparable to those in lizards, but incorporation of the anterior part of the recessus scalae tympani and glossopharyngeal nerve into the otic capsule (see de Beer, 1937; McDowell, 1961) results in an altered relationship between the nerve and the lateral aperture of the recess; the former enters the recessus cavi tympani through a foramen in the lateral wall of the otic capsule, and the latter is shifted posteriorly to the anterior part of the vagus foramen.

Aside from its superficial position (an external ear being absent), rather thick cutaneous layer, and more clearly circumscribed quadrate attachments (see Werner, 1960; Hadžiselimović and Anđelić, 1967), the structure of the tympanic membrane is basically similar to that in lizards. Except at the margins, however, this similarity is obscured because the tympanic parts of the extrastapes are expanded into a large, oval, cartilaginous plate which lies within the central part of the tympanic membrane and gives it the appearance of great thickness. Peripheral to the plate, the dorsal portion of the central lamina of connective tissue is thickened by collagenous bundles reminiscent of the lacertilian extrastapedial ligament. Posteroventrally the lamina contains a ligamentous band attached to retroarticular connective tissue, but elsewhere it is delicate. The external layer of the tympanic membrane is formed by the skin, although this is neither significantly thinned nor tightly attached; internally, the membrane is lined by the tympanic mucosa.

From its tympanic plate, the shaft of the extrastapes extends, free of processes and attachments, to join the tip of the stapedial shaft; this, in turn, passes posterior to (or through a foramen in) the vertical process of the quadrate, traverses the recessus cavi tympani, and expands into a vertically oval footplate articulated in the vestibular window (for some variations see McDowell, 1961). The lateral surface of the footplate is abutted by a fluid-filled sac, the paracapsular sinus (Fig. 26), discussed by de Burlet (1934) and Baird (1960b). The sinus, which is indented dorsally or traversed by the stapedial shaft, occupies the bulk of the recessus cavi tympani and, in all forms examined, the medial wall of its posterior part lies against the lateral surface of the periotic sac at the lateral aperture of the recessus scalae tympani. On the basis of its morphological relationships, Baird (1960b) suggested that the sinus represents a specialized derivative of the medial part of a typical reptilian tympanic cavity rather than part of the periotic labyrinth. This view has subsequently been supported by the observation that, particularly in young specimens, the paracapsular sinus is lined

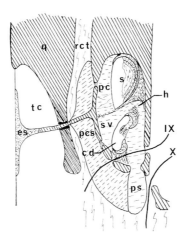

Fig. 26. Diagram of an idealized horizontal section through the auditory region of a turtle. The columellar apparatus passes behind or through the extended posterior process of the quadrate, which largely separates the tympanic cavity from the recessus cavi tympani. Note that the periotic sac abuts laterally against the paracapsular sinus but is not continuous with it, and that the saccule lies primarily anterior to the cochlear duct rather than dorsal to it. cd, Cochlear duct; es, extrastapes; h, helicotrema; pc, periotic cistern; pcs, paracapsular sinus; ps, periotic sac; q, quadrate; rct, recessus cavi tympani; s, saccule; sv, scala vestibuli; tc, tympanic cavity; IX, glossopharyngeal nerve; X, vagus nerve.

primarily by squamous epithelium with scattered patches of cuboidal and columnar cells. In adult specimens the areas of taller epithelia are relatively reduced and the epithelial lining is frequently obscured by staining characteristics of the fluid contents. The course of the auditory tube beneath the recessus cavi tympani and its termination in the floor of the air-filled tympanic cavity adjacent to the stapedial shaft can be explained by the osteological modifications of the region, and are compatible with this interpretation. Thus, although analogous to the juxtastapedial sinus of snakes and possibly to tympanic lymph spaces in some burrowing lizards (see above), the paracapsular sinus has no homology with either and represents a unique chelonian development.

E. CROCODILIA

The external ear of crocodilians (see Shute and Bellairs, 1955) is shallow, but it is specialized in that it consists primarily of two valvelike folds of skin which overlie and conceal the tympanic membrane. The ventral fold is the smaller of the two and its dorsal margin is overlapped by the dorsal fold. The latter contains a slender arcuate band of muscle attached anteriorly to the squamosal and posteriorly, primarily by fascia, to the mandibular depressor and dorsal axial musculature. Contraction of the muscular band accentuates the dorsal fold and firms its relationship to the ventral fold. Although it is undoubtedly a protective device, there have been no physiological studies of the valve, but its influence on hearing is mentioned by Wever and Vernon (1957).

Like that of turtles, the crocodilian middle ear exhibits complex osteological differences. Many of these are concisely presented by Romer (1956), and de Beer (1937) describes certain modifications of the otic capsule. Posterior closure of the otic notch by combined processes of the squamosal and opisthotic has altered the attachments of the tympanic membrane, and the tympanic cavities are complexly enlarged by extensive pneumatization of bone in the area. Of particular interest is the transverse passage between right and left tympanic cavities (reminiscent of a connection between paracapsular sinuses in embryonic turtles; Baird, 1960b) and the multiple communications of these spaces with the pharynx along the line of the basioccipital-basisphenoid suture (see van Beneden, 1882; Colbert, 1946). The tympanic cavities are more fully enclosed by bone, and structures traversing them show greater compartmentalization than is found in other reptiles. In part, these and other differences in the crocodilian middle ear may be interpreted as adaptations associated with habits and habitat, but that they have some relationship to the excellent auditory capacities within the group has been demonstrated by Wever and Vernon (1957).

The otic notch is closed (as it is in most turtles) and the tympanic membrane attaches to bone all along its periphery. At its margin and in its posterodorsal quadrant, the central lamina of connective tissue is thickened, but elsewhere the membrane is relatively thinner than that of lizards. Centrally the membrane receives the small lateral expansion of the cartilaginous extrastapes and, from that, a band of fibrous connective tissue, presumably a reduced extrastapedial ligament, can be traced dorsally. This ligament passes through the central lamina and its peripheral attachment and then turns medially on the internal surface of the quadrate; there, associated with a poorly defined cartilaginous element, it extends medially and blends with the short collagenous fibers attaching the dorsal process of the extrastapes to the tympanic roof. This association is considered to form a foramen of Huxley, which is traversed by the chorda tympani nerve.

Lateral to the base of the dorsal process, a second cartilaginous projection arches posterolaterally from the extrastapedial shaft and becomes embedded in the tympanic membrane. Covered medially by a fold of the tympanic mucous membrane, this projection, which is here accepted as the homolog of the lacertilian posterior accessory process, extends posteriorly to the peripheral thickening of the tympanic membrane. At this point it attaches to a ligament that unites with retroarticular connective tissue of the mandibular articulation; the ligament contains variable remnants of the embryonic epihyal, stylohyal, and Meckelian cartilages. A tympanic muscle, believed to be derived from the depressor mandibulae, inserts upon both tympanic ligaments of the extrastapes and into the thickened central lamina of the posterodorsal quadrant of the tympanic membrane encompassed between those ligaments.

From a synarthrodial union with the medial extremity of the short extrastapedial shaft, the bony stapes extends ventromedially and terminates in an elongate oval footplate articulated in a vestibular window oriented obliquely anteroventrally in the lateral wall of the otic capsule. Immediately adjacent to the vestibular window and facing anterodorsally into the tympanic cavity is the secondary tympanic membrane (Fig. 27). This conformation is produced by changes in the otic capsule, recessus scalae tympani, and periotic sac; these changes are discussed by de Beer (1937) and Baird (1960b). The most significant of them is the development of a subcapsular process; this derivative of a metotic cartilage extends the recessus scalae tympani laterally and, by its fusion with the otic capsule, produces a fenestra pseudorotunda across which the secondary tympanic membrane is stretched. This development, as well as others of the crocodilian auditory mechanism (particularly in the internal ear), is more closely comparable to conditions in birds than to those in other reptiles.

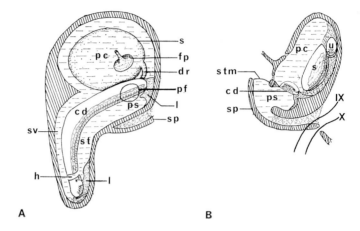

Fɪɢ. 27. Schematic representations of the ventral part of the crocodylid labyrinth. A, View from the lateral aspect with stapedial footplate and periotic foramen superimposed to show their relationships; B, transverse section through footplate and periotic foramen. cd, Cochlear duct; dr, reunient duct; fp, footplate; h, helicotrema; l, limbus; pc, periotic cistern; pf, periotic foramen; ps, periotic sac; s, saccule; sp, subcapsular process; st, scala tympani; stm, secondary tympanic membrane; sv, scala vestibuli; u, utricle; IX, glossopharyngeal nerve; X, vagus nerve.

F. Extinct Reptiles

The recent syntheses by Romer (1956) and Olson (1966) encompass salient features of present knowledge of the middle ear in fossil reptiles, and little can be added here. There are strong suggestions in the fossil record that adaptive modifications may have been at least as prevalent in the middle ear of extinct as of extant groups, but the fragmentary nature of the record and its lack of information concerning soft parts of both the middle and internal ear renders interpretation difficult. Parallelism and convergence in the tympanic regions of living reptiles are common, and only a few reptilian ears are yet known in detail. It is probable, therefore, that additional comprehensive study of Recent forms will provide a sounder basis for interpretation of fossil remains than is now available, particularly in the case of questions involving auditory abilities.

IV. The Internal Ear in Various Reptilian Groups

A. Introduction

Until recently, the structure of the internal ear had been investigated in relatively few reptiles, and the works of Retzius (1884) and de Burlet (1934) constituted the most comprehensive and authoritative sources available.

The quarter century following publication of de Burlet's (1934) work was marked by the appearance of significant contributions on limited topics, particularly those of Weston (1939) and Shute and Bellairs (1953), but it is only during the last decade that a major expansion of our knowledge has occurred. Coupled with the general treatment of Werner (1960) and numerous shorter reports, contributions of Baird (1960b), Hamilton (1960, 1963b, 1964), Wever (1965, 1967a, 1967b) and Miller (1966a, 1966b, 1968) have significantly increased the scope of information on reptilian auditory anatomy and physiology, and have begun to show the extent and complexity of specializations within the internal ear. They have also demonstrated the need for additional investigations, particularly on the embryology of the membranous labyrinth for which Fleissig's (1908) and Wyeth's (1924) studies must still serve as the major sources of information. Concentrated effort has, unfortunately, been directed almost entirely toward auditory mechanisms, so little is known of specializations which may occur in vestibular structures in various reptiles; there are, however, indications that such specializations do exist (e.g., Prebil, 1966), and it is to be hoped that future investigations may elucidate them.

Characteristic morphological patterns can be recognized in the internal ear throughout orders and families, and there are suggestions that constant features occur in genera and species as well. Within limitations of information presently available, it appears that certain of these patterns are well adapted to effective hearing over a rather wide range of frequencies while others are not (see, for example, Wever, 1965). This situation presents attractive opportunities for broad speculation upon questions concerning reptilian audition, phylogeny and taxonomy, but critical evaluation of present knowledge suggests that such speculation is as yet premature. In most instances, too little is known of reptilian natural history to determine the significance of audition as a selective factor in a given group, and there is still no firm basis for establishing more than the most general criteria for primitiveness in structures of the internal ear.

Thus, a burrowing lizard exhibiting morphological indications of lesser auditory capacities than related terrestrial forms might be interpreted as showing (1) degenerate, (2) specialized, or (3) primitive internal aural morphology. The first term would imply the assumption that the fossorial line was originally derived from stock in which the internal ear was essentially like that of present terrestrial forms, and that (presumably because hearing lost or acquired negative selective value) regressive changes have occurred during the fossorial evolution. Use of the second term would imply that the internal ear of the ancestral form was extremely primitive and that specialization for limited auditory range or acuity was of great selective value in the burrowing line. The third term also suggests relatively primitive conditions in the ancestral internal ear, but implies that there has been no net selection for audition in the fossorial line, although such selection has occurred in related terrestrial forms. It is possible that all three of these conditions can be found in the internal ear in diverse reptiles, but physiological studies (e.g., Wever, 1965, 1968) indicate that functional interpretation of isolated morphological parts of the ear can be quite misleading. Thus, designation of the "evolutionary state" of features of the internal ear must follow, rather than precede, comprehensive structural and functional studies of all parts of the ear in circumscribed groups well understood from other data.

B. RHYNCHOCEPHALIA

Basing judgments upon different combinations of features, Baird (1960b), Hamilton (1963b) and Miller (1966a) concur in interpreting the internal ear of *Sphenodon* as that least specialized among living reptiles. None of these evaluations incorporates consideration of the structure of the middle ear; they are based primarily upon comparisons of the internal ear of *Sphenodon* with that of other reptiles, and with the internal ear of amphibians. This premise should be re-examined when more is known of correlation between structures of the middle and internal ear, and if more information can be gained on the middle ear in extinct rhynchocephalians.

The internal ear of adult *Sphenodon* is basically comparable to that of a "typical" lizard, but the following differences seem particularly worthy of note. The vestibule is large and poorly separated from a shallow cochlear recess. The footplate is situated primarily in the lateral vestibular wall and faces the lateral wall of the saccule rather than that of the cochlear duct. The saccule lies largely ventral to the utricle rather than lateral to it. The reunient duct is large and attached to the medial saccular wall; it grades into a cochlear duct in which basilar and lagenar parts are of approximately the same size and distinctly delimited, one from the other, by a mural constriction (Fig. 28). The limbus is formed of tissue poorly differentiated from the adjacent thick membrana propria and is annular, rather than forming an excavated plate. Neither a limbic lip nor bulge is present, and the few specimens available for examination do not show a tectorial membrane in relationship to the elongate basilar papilla.

The periotic labyrinth of the adult animal (Fig. 25) resembles that of some lizards. Lateral to the saccule and basilar part of the cochlear duct, the periotic cistern forms a large chamber, the saccular and cochlear parts of which are not separated. Anteroventrally, a large scala lagenae is related to the lagenar part of the cochlear duct and, dorsal to this, a broad helicotrema tapers abruptly from the anterior limit of the cistern. The helicotrema arches medially and posteriorly, embedded in periotic connective tissue at the constricted part of the cochlear duct, and then expands abruptly into a large periotic sac medial to the basilar membrane. Medially, directly opposite the stapedial footplate, the periotic sac extends through a rather small periotic foramen and expands extrameningeally in the ventrolateral angle of the cranial cavity. The expansion extends primarily posteriorly into a groove, presumably a remnant of the anterior part of the metotic fissure, and then turns ventrolaterally through the vagus foramen, in which it is intimately related to the glossopharyngeal and vagus nerves. The sac terminates in suprapharyngeal tissues just external to the foramen. These extra-otic relationships of the periotic sac can be compared to those in both caudate and anuran amphibians, but they particularly resemble relationships in anurans (see de Burlet, 1934). They may well constitute a primitive feature, but it should be noted that similar relationships exist in several squamate forms exhibiting "atypical" morphology of the middle ear (see below).

C. SQUAMATA

1. Sauria

Recent investigations, cited above, have concentrated heavily upon the lacertilian internal ear and, more specifically, upon parts of the cochlear duct and periotic labyrinth believed to be concerned with transmission and reception of auditory stimuli. These studies have expanded and clarified knowledge of basic anatomy of the internal ear, but fundamental disagreements are evident among attempts to group and interpret morphological patterns that have been recognized (Hamilton, 1963b, 1964; Schmidt, 1964; Miller, 1966a, 1966b). In so far as sampled, representatives of all families show basic correspondence to the "typical" lacertilian pattern, but also exhibit familial characteristics. Only brief synopses are presented below.

a. Iguanidae

The saccule and cochlear duct are of approximately the same size; the latter (Fig. 28) is commonly pyramidal and shows some enlargement in *Anolis*. The limbus is ovoid to somewhat elongate (most marked in anoles) and, in some forms, there is a limbic bulge dorsal to the basilar membrane. The tectorial membrane in representatives of eight iguanid genera is broadly attached to the limbic bulge, but in limited relationship to hair cells (Wever, 1965, 1967a, 1967b). The basilar membrane is thin and relatively uniform in members of some genera, but in representatives of others (e.g., *Sauromalus*, *Sceloporus*), its central part is moderately thickened and forms a papillar bar (Miller, 1966a) or fundus (Wever, 1965); the former term seems preferable, since it is based upon a prior usage of Retzius (1884) and is more descriptive than the latter. The bar lies beneath the basilar papilla, is an intrinsic part of the basilar membrane, and is formed by the hyaline layer of fibers and ground substance extending from the margins of the limbic hiatus. The basal lamina and external layer of fibroblasts extend across the papillar bar with relationships unchanged from those in the surrounding un-modified parts of the basilar membrane. The basilar papilla varies from small and oval in genera in which tympanic modification occurs (e.g., *Phrynosoma*, *Holbrookia*), to rather elongate in *Anolis*. An additional otic modification occurs in at least some anoles; the otic sac may extend posteriorly out of the cranial cavity and into the anterior axial muscles adjacent to the tympanic region. The saccular and cochlear parts of the periotic cistern are only slightly separated, and the scala sacculi and scala lagenae are variably developed; relationships of the periotic sac are normal, but the secondary tympanic membrane varies considerably in thickness in different species.

b. Agamidae

In agamids in which it is now known, the internal ear resembles that of iguanids. The cochlear duct (Fig. 28) is short and broad, and the saccule is relatively small. The agamid limbus tends to have a more pronounced limbic bulge than does that of iguanids, and some forms show incipient lipping of the bulge. A papillar bar of varying thickness is present in most representa-tives examined by the author. The basilar papilla is of the same size range as that in iguanids, but it is typically elongate and wider posteriorly than anteriorly. Although some forms with tympanic modifications have small basilar papillae, agamids are not sufficiently well known to state that the relationship between such modifications and papillar size is consistent. Well defined cuticular material overlies the basilar papilla, but no intact tectorial membrane is evident in the material available. Periotic channels are "typical", but no scala sacculi has been noted, and the secondary tympanic membrane shows thickening in some forms (e.g., *Calotes*, *Uromastix*).

c. Chamaeleonidae

The internal ear has received limited attention in this group. The saccule is large, relative to the cochlear duct, and the reunient duct attaches to the ventral saccular wall rather than to its posterior or medial aspect. The cochlear duct (Fig. 28) is situated ventral to approximately the central third of the saccule; its general form is comparable to that in iguanids and agamids, but the limbus is thin and poorly differentiated from the surrounding thick membrana propria. The basilar membrane and papilla are circular to slightly ovoid, and show differences in size which apparently can be correlated with differing degrees of modification of the tympanic region. No papillar bar is evident in *Chamaeleo*, and hair cells of the basilar papilla are few and appear to be loosely ordered. Wever (1967a, 1967b) reports an unusual, fibrous tectorial membrane, which he terms a "dendritic type". The periotic cistern is undivided and shows poorly defined lagenar and saccular scalae extending from it. The remaining intracapsular periotic channels are rather "typical", but in *Chamaeleo*, the extracapsular part of the periotic sac follows an intracranial course and appears to exit through the vagus foramen (much as in *Sphenodon*) in the specimens examined. Wever (personal communication) suggests that there are two foramina, narrowly divided, in some species of *Chamaeleo*; in those, the sac exits through the anterior opening with the glossopharyngeal nerve. Toerien's (1963) figure of *Microsaura* indicates that relations of the periotic sac may differ in that genus, but he gives no detailed descriptions of the inner ear.

d. Gekkonidae

Although the internal ear has been studied in reasonable detail in a relatively large number of geckoes and shows some support for Underwood's (1954) taxonomic contentions, it cannot, at present, be said to confirm them. Certain striking features are remarkably constant throughout the family and variations appear to be quantitative rather than qualitative. Considered collectively, these features tend to show progressive development and are suggestive of long, independent and relatively intense aural specialization within the group.

The otic sac is, generally, tremendously large and irregular, occupies a larger part of the cranial cavity than in any other group, projects posteriorly into the axial musculature, and may invade the orbit (see Wiedersheim, 1875). Differences in the manner in which the sac exits from the cranial cavity, and differences in its calcareous content related to taxonomic grouping and sex, have recently been discussed by Kluge (1967). The relationship of the size of the saccule to that of the cochlear duct varies from conditions of approximate equivalence of the two (e.g., *Aristelliger*, *Sphaerodactylus*, *Thecadactylus*) to those of a small saccule coupled with a cochlear duct greatly elongated vertically or in an anteroventral-posterodorsal plane (e.g., *Coleonyx*, *Gymnodactylus*). The reunient duct varies from a broad flattened channel arising from the medial saccular wall (e.g., *Aristelliger*, *Thecadactylus*), through relatively "typical" morphology, to a condition of blending almost indistinguishably into the posterior walls of both parts (e.g., *Sphaerodactylus*). The limbus is heavy and posterodorsally elongated, and an elaborate limbic lip, usually described as awninglike, projects from the lateral surface of its neural part (Fig. 28). A tectorial membrane is suspended from the limbic lip and projects ventromedially to end in elaborate terminal specializations resting upon cilia of the basilar papilla (see Wever, 1967a, 1967b). The papilla is elongate, regionally variable in width as it tapers

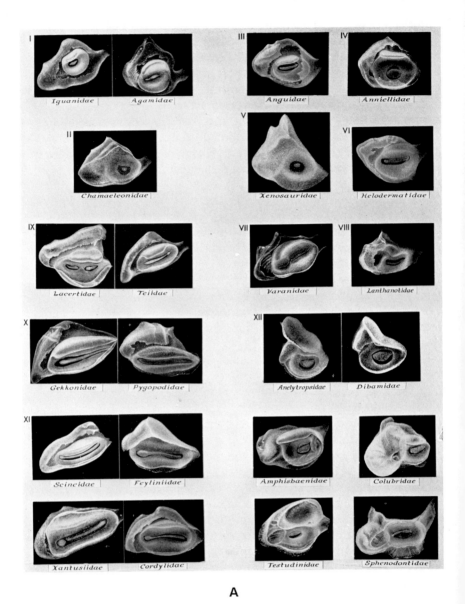

A

Fig. 28. Cochlear ducts from representatives of various reptilian families; the drawings are not to scale. A, Lateral views; B, medial views. (Courtesy of Dr. Malcolm R. Miller with permission of the California Academy of Sciences.)

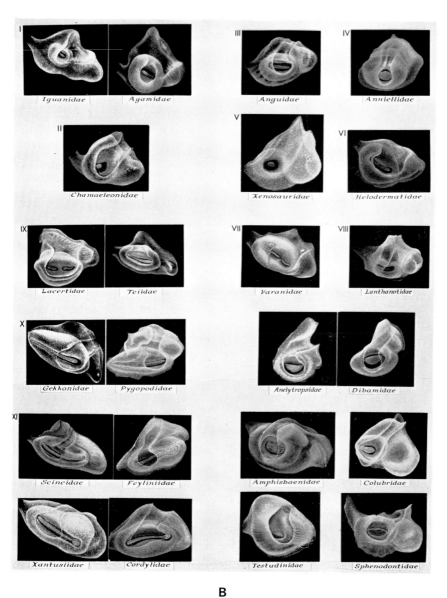

B

posterodorsally from its widest part, and is larger, relative to the size of the species, than that of other lizards. An extremely well developed papillar bar underlies the papilla in the basilar membrane and varies in thickness and width in different regions. The periotic cistern is typically divided by a cisternal septum and inferior cisternal crest; thus, a definitive scala vestibuli is characteristic, and clear cut lagenar and saccular scalae extend from it. The helicotrema is partially or entirely embedded in bone as it turns medially and terminates in the periotic sac, either directly or by way of a short scala tympani. A diverticulum of the periotic sac, the accessory scala tympani, extends posterodorsally into a limbic excavation and underlies the postero-dorsal part of the basilar membrane. The relative length of the accessory scala varies in different forms, but it is characteristically related to more than half of the basilar papilla. The extracapsular part of the periotic sac enters the recessus scalae tympani and exhibits "typical" medial meningeal relation-ships. In representatives of some genera (e.g., *Coleonyx*, *Sphaerodactylus*), the secondary tympanic membrane is placed at the lateral aperture of the recessus scalae tympani; in most gekkonids, however, the lateral aperture of the recess is altered by a development of the basioccipital crest, and the secondary tympanic membrane faces ventrally into the auditory tube from the depths of a distinct fossa.

e. Pygopodidae

Except in *Aprasia*, the structure of the internal ear in pygopodids (*Pygopus*, *Lialis*, *Delma*) is essentially like that of most gekkonids. The otic sac is similarly enlarged and the saccule is significantly smaller than the cochlear duct. The latter (Fig. 28) is markedly enlarged posterodorsally and projects dorsad into the vestibule behind a tubular reunient duct attached to the posterior saccular wall. The cochlear duct, limbus, basilar papilla and periotic channels resemble those of gekkonids. The secondary tympanic membrane faces directly into the tympanic cavity rather than being placed in a fossa.

Aprasia lacks a tympanic membrane, columellar apparatus and tympanic cavity, and its large fenestra vestibuli is occupied by a thin membrane of connective tissue. The saccule and cochlear duct approximately equal each other in size, and the limbus and basilar papilla are smaller than in other genera. Other characteristics of the cochlear duct and intracapsular periotic channels are essentially like those in other pygopodids and gekkonids. The extracapsular part of the periotic sac, however, extends from the periotic foramen into an intracranial groove, presumably derived from the anterior part of the metotic fissure, and terminates at the foramen for the vagus. Distinctive intracapsular features attest to *Aprasia*'s membership in the assemblage, but tympanic and periotic modifications are indicative of divergent, extreme, fossorial adaptation. Until more detail is available (morphological, physiological, causal factors), it seems unwise to speculate whether the ear in this genus is primitive, specialized, or degenerate.

f. Teiidae

The internal ear of teiids corresponds closely, in most features, to "typical" conditions. The saccule is slightly smaller than the cochlear duct, and the anterior part of the latter curves medially. The limbus is long and narrow, and its neural part bears a distinct limbic lip above the central part of the basilar papilla (Fig. 28); the lip is neither as highly developed nor as delicate as that of gekkonids. A distinct papillar bar underlies the basilar papilla. The latter tends to be bipartite; an elongate, fusiform, anterior part tapers posteriorly to a width of one to four cells and joins a short oval part forming the posterior extremity of the papilla. *Ameiva* shows a delicate tectorial membrane (Fig. 29), Hamilton (1963b) reports a membrane in *Tupinambis*, and Wever (1965, 1967a, 1967b) describes and figures an elaborate and regionally variable one suspended from the limbic lip in *Cnemidophorus*; therefore, a tectorial membrane is presumably present throughout the group. The periotic cistern is undivided, a saccular scala is present, and the periotic sac abuts against the medial surface of the basilar membrane; no accessory scalae are present and the extracapsular relationships of the periotic sac are "typical".

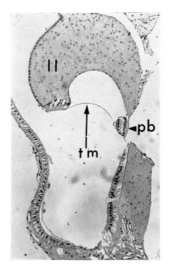

Fig. 29. Transverse section through the ventral part of the cochlear duct of *Ameiva ameiva* (210×). Note the heavy limbic lip (11), delicate tectorial membrane (tm), and papillar bar (pb) underlying the basilar papilla.

I

g. Scincidae

Like that of gekkonids, the internal ear of scincid lizards (and their feyliniid relatives) departs significantly from "typical" conditions, and shows diversification within the group. The otic sac is not particularly modified, and all forms apparently exhibit marked anteroventral excavation of the cochlear recess. In terrestrial species, the saccule is approximately as large or smaller than the cochlear duct, but the saccule is considerably larger than the cochlear duct in most burrowing forms. The duct is anteroventrally elongated and shows a tendency toward medial curvature or incipient spiraling (Fig. 28). The limbus is heavy and its neural part bulges slightly above the basilar membrane, but no evidence of lipping is present. A papillar bar underlies an elongate basilar papilla which tapers anteroventrally and terminates in an enlarged rounded patch of sensory cells; the range of thickness of the papillar bar and of the area of the basilar papilla is only slightly less than that of gekkonids. In *Eumeces*, Baird (1966) has shown a spheroidal tectorial body over the rounded anteroventral extremity of the basilar papilla and organized cuticular material related to more posterior papillar cells. Similar conditions are evident in representatives of other genera examined. In additional observations in *Eumeces*, Wever (1967a, 1967b) provides additional information and is continuing investigations in the genus. Both the basilar papilla and the cochlear duct are smaller in burrowing forms than in terrestrial skinks, but the basic morphological characteristics of these structures do not change with habitat (Miller, 1966a).

The periotic cistern is characteristically divided by a cisternal septum, so distinct lagenar and saccular scalae typically arise from a scala vestibuli. Medially in the cochlear recess, the periotic sac lies adjacent to the posterior extremity of the basilar membrane, and a vermiform accessory scala tympani extends anteroventrally into a limbic recess to abut against the long anterior part of the membrane. The accessory scala of scincids is presumably analogous to the posteriorly directed one of gekkonids and pygopodids. The periotic sac generally enters the recessus scalae tympani and forms a secondary tympanic membrane in the usual manner. The membrane may be thickened in some burrowers (e.g. *Scelotes*). Toerien (1963) infers that the periotic sac terminates within the cranial cavity in *Acontias*, but does not describe its relationships. Although *Anelytropsis* is usually assumed either to be a scincid or closely related to them, Miller (1966c) reports that its cochlear duct is "almost identical" to the cochlear duct of *Dibamus* (see below).

h. Xantusiidae

Although it differs in details, the internal ear of *Xantusia* is basically like that of scincids. The cochlear duct shows no medial curvature and tends to be tubular rather than pyramidal (Fig. 28). The basilar papilla is distinctly bipartite; its elongate, anteroventrally tapering, posterior part is separated by a finite space from a rounded anterior part. The papilla is underlain by a distinct papillar bar, and Hamilton (1963b) reports and figures part of a tectorial membrane in *Xantusia*. The periotic cistern is not divided, a scala sacculi is present, and an accessory scala tympani extends anteroventrally from the periotic sac; the accessory scala abuts against less than half of the basilar membrane as opposed to its coverage of more than half in scincids. Camp (1923) and Kluge (1967) differ concerning the presence of an extensive otic sac in the group.

i. Lacertidae

In some forms the saccule is laterally expanded and markedly larger than the cochlear duct, but in others the two structures are of approximately equal size. The cochlear duct (Fig. 28) is short and broad, and an oval limbus occupies somewhat less than two-thirds of its medial wall. The neural limbus has a limbic bulge which exhibits varying degrees of incipient lipping, and, in representatives of at least four genera (*Acanthodactylus*, *Eremias*, *Lacerta*, *Psammodromus*), a strip of limbic tissue separates the so-called limbic hiatus into approximately equal anterior and posterior halves (Miller, 1966a). This division, largely confined to the plane of the basilar membrane, also makes that membrane and the basilar papilla bipartite. Hamilton (1963b) reports continuity of supporting elements between anterior and posterior parts of the basilar papilla in material representing all of the above genera except *Eremias*, but other specimens of *Lacerta* and *Psammodromus* show complete separation of the two parts. Toerien (1963) mentions a tripartite papilla in *Eremias* (*Scaptira* of Toerien), so it is possible that the division may change both qualitatively and quantitatively within the family or even within genera. The anterior and posterior parts of the papilla in *Lacerta* and *Psammodromus* are of approximately equal size; both parts rest upon a distinct papillar bar, and sensory cilia of both parts are associated with cuticular material. A tectorial membrane is present only over the posterior division of the basilar papilla of *Eremias*, and the anterior division is capped by cuticular material that Wever terms a "true sallet" (Wever, 1965, 1967a, 1967b). The periotic channels are largely "typical"; the periotic cistern is variably divided, the scala sacculi is poorly defined, and no accessory scala tympani is present.

j. Cordylidae

The aural anatomy of cordylids is poorly known. Miller (1966a) describes gross features of the cochlear duct in *Gerrhosaurus* and *Cordylus*, but sectioned material has been studied only in *Cordylus* (Wever, unpublished; personal observations) and *Chamaesaura* (Hamilton, 1963b, 1964). Features of the last differ considerably from those of the other genera, which exhibit rather "typical" conditions. In the more normal forms, the saccule and cochlear duct are of approximately equal size and joined posteriorly by the reunient duct. The cochlear duct and limbus are elongate, and the neural part of the limbus shows a definite bulge above the basilar membrane (Fig. 28). The basilar papilla is long and similar in shape to that of scincids; it is seated upon a thin papillar bar and, at least in *Cordylus cataphractus*, is overlain by a definite tectorial membrane projecting from the limbic bulge to rest upon the sensory cilia. Wever (personal communication) states that the membrane has a peculiar form and never leaves the surface of the limbus in *C. vittifer*, *C. warreni*, and *Platysaurus minor*. Periotic channels are largely "typical", but short recesses of the periotic sac do extend into limbic tissue at both extremities of the basilar papilla; these hardly merit being termed accessory scalae because of their small size. A secondary tympanic membrane is formed at the lateral aperture of the recessus scalae tympani.

In *Chamaesaura* (as identified in de Burlet's material; Hamilton, personal communication), the saccule is extremely large and is joined to a small cochlear duct by a reunient duct attached to its medial wall (Hamilton, 1963b, 1964). The limbus is well developed and shows a limbic bulge, but the relatively large basilar membrane supports a small "buttonlike" basilar papilla. Hamilton does not mention a papillar bar and reports the absence of a tectorial membrane in the material. Intracapsular periotic channels are not remarkable, but, in the absence of a recessus scalae tympani, the periotic sac extends from the periotic foramen through the cranial cavity and vagus foramen and terminates without forming a secondary tympanic membrane. *Chamaesaura* has reduced limbs, but is known as a grass dweller rather than a fossorial form; its striking aural modifications suggest that further investigation within the genus is merited.

k. Dibamidae

Miller (1966a, 1966c) has examined the gross anatomy of the cochlear duct in two species of *Dibamus*; the aural anatomy of the group appears to be otherwise unknown. The cochlear duct (Fig. 28) shows a constriction between its basilar and lagenar parts, but this is less marked than that in *Sphenodon*. The limbus is thin, rounded, and carries a small oval basilar papilla upon a relatively large basilar membrane. The helicotrema appears to be broad and related to the cochlear duct in the usual manner, and the periotic sac slightly invades limbic tissue at the anterior and posterior extremities of the basilar papilla. Whether the sac terminates intracranially or at a secondary tympanic membrane is unknown. As noted above, Miller (1966c) states that the cochlear duct of *Dibamus* is "almost identical" to that of *Anelytropsis*.

l. Anguidae

Housed in the vestibule and poorly defined shallow cochlear recess, the saccule is significantly larger than the cochlear duct. The reunient duct arises from the posteroventral part of the medial saccular wall. The cochlear duct is short and blunt, and the oval, well developed limbus exhibits a distinct limbic bulge on the lateral surface of its neural part (Fig. 28). The basilar papilla is elongate but rather small, and tapers slightly from its posterior to its anterior extremity; a thin papillar bar underlies the papilla, and a delicate tectorial membrane projects from the limbic bulge to overlie it in the species examined. Wever (1967a, 1967b) describes a fibrous, plate-like, terminal specialization of the membrane in *Ophisaurus* and *Gerrhonotus*. The periotic cistern is poorly divided anteriorly and the scala sacculi is not

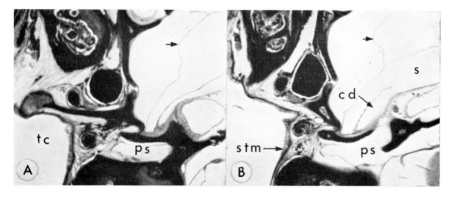

FIG. 30. Oblique sections (in the plane of the stapedial shaft) through the auditory region of *Anguis fragilis* (25×). A, At the level of the central part of the footplate and reunient duct; B, at the level of the anterior surface of the stapedial shaft. Note that the periotic sac (ps) does not course through the cranial cavity, but passes rather directly from relationship to the cochlear duct (cd) into the anterior region of the vagus foramen; it is separated from the tympanic cavity (tc) by varying thicknesses of tissue, but this relationship more closely resembles a thickened secondary tympanic membrane (stm) than it does the condition in *Sphenodon*. Arrows indicate internal periosteum separated from bone during processing; s, saccule.

distinct. Medially, the periotic sac abuts against the full length of the basilar membrane and excavates the limbus slightly at the anterior and posterior extremities of that structure; no definitive accessory scala tympani can be recognized. The sac is constricted as it traverses the periotic foramen and, in forms other than *Anguis*, extends to normal relationships within the recessus scalae tympani. In *Anguis* the sac projects slightly more posteriorly within the cranial cavity than in other forms and exits through a foramen in company with the glossopharyngeal and vagus nerves. Rather than ending blindly as indicated by de Burlet's (1934) figures, the sac extends ventrolaterally and terminates in the formation of a thick but recognizable secondary tympanic membrane (Fig. 30).

m. Anniellidae

In *Anniella* interrelationships of parts of the otic labyrinth are normal, but the saccule is expanded laterally and occupies virtually the entire vestibule; its ventromedial wall gives rise to the reunient duct, which joins a small rounded cochlear duct lying beneath the central region of the saccule. The limbus forms the greater part of the medial wall of the cochlear duct and exhibits a small but distinct limbic bulge considerably dorsal to the anterior part of the basilar membrane (Fig. 28). The oval basilar papilla occupies almost all of the basilar membrane and rests upon a thin but distinct papillar bar. No definitive tectorial membrane has been reported, but a well developed cuticular body rests upon the anterior part of the papilla and thin cuticular material is related to posterior hair cells. The periotic cistern is greatly restricted in the vestibule because of the saccular expansion; the ventrolateral part of the saccular wall forms the dorsal boundary of the cochlear part of the cistern or scala vestibuli. The latter continues into a helicotrema enclosed first in a bony canal, and then in a groove between the anterior part of the limbus and medial wall of the cochlear recess. The helicotrema terminates in the periotic sac, which expands medial to the basilar membrane and extends through the periotic foramen into the cranial cavity. Extrameningeally, it courses posteriorly in a groove and enters a foramen in company with the glossopharyngeal nerve. The sac terminates at the external margin of that foramen and abuts against loose areolar tissue which lies adjacent to the lateral wall of the otic capsule and stapedial footplate.

n. Xenosauridae

The internal ear of *Xenosaurus* has not been studied from sectioned material, but its cochlear duct seems to resemble that of *Anniella* (Miller, 1966a). The lagenar part of the cochlear duct is larger than the basilar part, and the two are distinguished by a slight constriction between them. The limbus is small and shows no modelling of its neural part; it carries an oval basilar membrane and small ovoid basilar papilla (Fig. 28). The presence or absence of a papillar bar and tectorial membrane has not been reported. The helicotrema is broad, and the periotic sac is in normal relationship to the basilar membrane, but other relationships of periotic channels have not been investigated.

o. Helodermatidae

The cochlear duct of *Heloderma* corresponds grossly to the "typical" pattern (Miller, 1966a; personal observation). The limbus is heavy and exhibits a distinct bulge (Fig. 28), and the basilar papilla is larger than that of iguanids and anguids; in the author's specimens, the papilla is somewhat wider anteriorly than posteriorly. The periotic sac slightly excavates the limbus at the posterior limit of the basilar membrane, but does not form an accessory scala tympani. The internal ear has not been reported from sectioned material, and details of periotic channels are not known.

p. Varanidae

The internal ear of varanids is relatively poorly known. Miller (1966a) reports on the gross morphology of the cochlear duct in four individuals representing *Varanus salvator nuchalis*, *V. bengalensis*, *V. salvator* and *V.* sp., and Wever (1967a, 1967b) deals with the tectorial membrane and basilar papilla in sectioned material of *V. bengalensis*. The author has examined sections of one poorly prepared late embryo of *V. niloticus* and of two adequate specimens of *V.* sp. Although the members of this sample agree in their basic aural anatomy, variations in the limbus and particularly the basilar papilla suggest that intensive study of varanids is needed.

The saccule and cochlear duct are of approximately equal size and are joined by a large laterally compressed reunient duct attached to the postero-medial saccular wall. The cochlear duct, anteroventrally elongate, is associated medially with a large and massive limbus (Fig. 28). Anteroventral to its midpoint, the long basilar membrane is either narrowed by opposing projections of the margins of the limbic hiatus or, in a manner similar to that noted in lacertids, divided by a strip of limbic tissue extending completely across the hiatus. It is not known whether narrowing, as opposed to bridging, is characteristic of given species or whether both conditions may be found in the same species. Correlated with this feature, the elongate basilar papilla may either form a continuous strip or be divided into two parts, the posterior of which is approximately twice as long as the anterior. The papilla rests upon a distinct papillar bar and is overlain by marginal specializations of a definitive tectorial membrane attached to the thickened but projection-free lateral surface of the neural limbus. Wever (1967a, 1967b) provides a detailed description of the membrane and papilla in *V. bengalensis*.

The periotic cistern is partially divided by a cisternal septum and inferior cisternal crest, and saccular and lagenar scalae project from it. The relationships of the remaining parts of the periotic labyrinth are "typical", except that a definitive accessory scala tympani projects posterodorsally from the periotic sac and invades the limbus to abut against the posterior third of the basilar membrane; the accessory scala is broader than that in other families.

q. Lanthanotidae

Known from a single specimen of *Lanthanotus*, the cochlear duct is strongly developed and resembles that of varanids (Miller, 1966c). The limbus is heavy and elongate. It does not show lipping or bulging of its neural part, but does house a posteriorly directed accessory scala tympani medial to the posterior part of the basilar membrane. The basilar papilla is rather long, narrow and of uniform width. No information is available concerning histological features of the cochlear duct, and the anatomy of other parts of the internal ear is unknown.

2. *Amphisbaenia*

The saccule of amphisbaenians is approximately three times as large as the cochlear duct, and the two structures are joined by a short reunient duct passing between their adjacent walls well anterior to their posterior limits. The cochlear duct, situated parallel to the ventral wall of the saccule, is elongate and rather tubular; the lagenar part is considerably smaller than the limbic region and is usually distinguished from that by a slight constriction (Fig. 28). The limbus is large but thin and its margins grade insensibly into surrounding thickened membrana propria; in transverse section this aggregation of periotic connective tissue is C-shaped, and the small vestibular membrane is supported between its anterolaterally projecting arms. Anteromedially, the neural part of the limbus bulges distinctly into the lumen of the cochlear duct, but this elevation does not extend into the usual position dorsal to the basilar membrane. The latter is small and irregular, lies in the curve of the posteromedial wall of the cochlear duct, and is almost completely occupied by an oval basilar papilla.

The basilar papilla faces anterolaterally into the cochlear duct and, examined by light microscopy, its organization resembles that in *Chamaeleo*. The sensory cells in *Bipes biporus* and *Amphisbaena caeca* are more loosely ordered than are those of any lizard yet examined electron microscopically, and supporting cells form a significant part of the surface area of the papilla. Preliminary cytological studies indicate that kinocilia of the sensory cells are unidirectionally oriented, and that the supporting cells are less highly specialized than those of lizards (Baird, 1969). In *Amphisbaena caeca*, *A. xera* and *Blanus cinereus*, formed cuticular specializations overlie the papilla and a thin papillar bar occupies the basilar membrane beneath it, but in other species and genera examined these have not been detected; they were either absent or the plane of section was unfavorable. No definitive tectorial membrane is evident in the specimens examined, but Wever (personal communication) states that one is present in *A. caeca* and *A. manni*.

The periotic cistern is in extensive contact with the saccule and is undivided; poorly defined lagenar and saccular scalae are present. The helicotrema is laterally related to the anterior part of the enlarged footplate, and is broad as it turns medially, anterior to the cochlear duct. It then narrows and courses posteriorly, occupying a channel formed between the medial wall of the cochlear recess and periotic tissue along the dorsomedial aspect of the cochlear duct. At the level of the periotic foramen this channel turns sharply ventrad and expands into the periotic sac adjacent to the posterior part of the basilar membrane. The anterior part of the sac invades limbic tissue to reach the anterior part of the basilar membrane and, although the extension of the sac is not vermiform, this arrangement appears to be analogous to an accessory scala tympani. The periotic sac exits posteriorly from the cochlear recess and expands within an unusual system of bony canals ventromedial to the otic capsule. Medially, a diverticulum of the sac extends into a short bony channel that houses anterior rootlets of the glossopharyngeal nerve; the sac extends anteriorly through that channel to make contact with the cranial meninges internal to the posterior part of the cochlear recess. Posteriorly, still enclosed in a canal, the sac extends to the external orifice of the vagus foramen and there terminates in relationship to the definitive ninth and tenth nerves. This arrangement apparently results from a unique enclosure of the anterior part of the metotic fissure and is not known to be duplicated in other reptiles.

3. *Ophidia*

There have been fewer recent studies of the internal ear in snakes than of that in lizards. The reports of Baird (1960a, 1960b, 1961, 1969) and those of Miller (1966a, 1968) have clarified some basic morphological features, have shown that a characteristic aural pattern is present in snakes, and have demonstrated that differences do exist within that pattern. Miller (1968) states that differences in the ophidian cochlear duct cannot be closely correlated with taxonomic groupings but can be related to specific habitat modifications. Personal observations indicate that the general anatomy of the internal ear does, indeed, show striking adaptive modifications in numerous snakes, but they do not yet fully confirm or deny the absence of good (although more subtle than those in lizards) taxonomic correlations. Both Miller's (1968) findings (see, for example, his figures 31–35) and my own indicate that there are many cases in which adaptive modification to a specific habitat cannot be clearly shown, and detailed anatomical studies of the ear have been done in relatively few species. Thus, information on the anatomy of the ophidian internal ear should still be regarded as being extremely limited and the area considered as worthy of extensive investigation.

Although much of the organization of the internal ear conforms to the general lacertilian pattern at gross and histological levels, obvious variations occur in the otic capsule and in the otic and periotic labyrinths. One of the more striking of these, modification of the lateral relationships of the vestibular window and recessus scalae tympani, has been described above (see also Baird, 1960a, 1960b; Miller, 1968). In conjunction with this, in all snakes investigated by the author, the stapedial footplate is relatively larger than that of most terrestrial lizards; it tends to be small in hydrophids but contributes significantly to the formation of the posterolateral wall of the vestibule and cochlear recess. In most fossorial snakes, as in fossorial lizards and amphisbaenians, the footplate is particularly large, and it forms the greater part of the lateral wall of the vestibule and cochlear recess, as well as the posterolateral wall of those cavities. The footplate is typically situated with its dorsal half directed toward the vestibule and its ventral half toward the shallow cochlear recess; thus it is more ventrally placed than in *Sphenodon* and extends farther dorsally than is usual in lizards. Other features of the osseus labyrinth show some modification, the most consistent of which appears to be posterior (as opposed to medial) positioning of the periotic foramen in the cochlear recess. This results in direct communication between the cochlear recess and the small recessus scalae tympani. The medial aperture of the recess is narrow; the lateral aperture, which is partially blocked and divided by the circumfenestral crest, opens anterodorsally into the juxtastapedial fossa and posteriorly toward the mouth of the vagus foramen.

The utricle and semicircular ducts constitute the larger part of the otic labyrinth, and the saccule is characteristically larger than the cochlear duct, but both of these features tend to be less pronounced in representatives of families commonly accepted as primitive (i.e., typhlopids, leptotyphlopids, aniliids). The saccule tapers posteriorly and grades into a short reunient duct which passes ventrally to join the posterior extremity of the cochlear duct. The latter extends anteriorly, its dorsal wall parallel and affixed to the ventromedial saccular wall by an intervening thick layer of periotic connective tissue. A cisternal septum usually extends laterally from this layer to blend with the internal periosteum; posteriorly the septal attachment follows the anterior half of the long axis of the footplate, and it continues anteriorly along a slight ridge marking the junction of the vestibule with the cochlear recess. The remaining attachments of the otic labyrinth are similar to those described in lizards.

The cochlear duct is characteristically shorter than the saccule and it expands slightly toward the anterior limit of its basilar or limbic part. Beyond that enlargement, the duct shows a constriction and then expands abruptly into its lagenar part. Miller (1966b) reported that the constriction is absent in "uropeltids", but he does not repeat that observation in his more recent study; he makes the generalization that ". . . the limbus and lagena are almost always constricted one from the other . . ." (Miller, 1968, p. 437), and remarks upon the small size of the lagena in "uropeltids". Marked constriction between parts of the cochlear duct does not occur in lizards (although some forms show suggestions of it; see Fig. 28), amphisbaenians show slight constrictions, and *Sphenodon* has an obvious constriction. No explanation for this feature can be offered at present, but it is of interest that it commonly occurs in forms showing modification of the middle ear. The relative sizes of the limbic and lagenar parts of the cochlear duct show considerable interfamilial and intrafamilial variation. Generally, the limbic part tends to be as large or larger than the lagenar part in typhlopids, lepto-typhlopids and aniliids, while in other families the lagenar region tends to be the larger of the two. Within boids, colubrids, elapids and viperids, there is a tendency for the limbic region to be relatively the larger in burrowing forms, but there are exceptions to this generalization (Miller, 1968; personal observations).

The size and shape of the limbus itself vary with the corresponding part of the cochlear duct. Limbic tissue is less clearly differentiated from the surrounding thick membrana propria than it is in "typical" lizards; this results from a somewhat greater thickness and organization of the membrana, coupled with somewhat less definitive organization of limbic tissue than occurs in lizards. Thus, except at the vestibular and basilar membranes, the ophidian cochlear duct frequently appears to be surrounded by dense periotic connective tissue, so the exact form of the limbus is difficult to ascertain. The medial part of the limbus underlies the medial cochlear epithelium of the limbic region and corresponds to a simple unmodified lacertilian limbus. The anterodorsal (neural) part of that plate, however, curves or projects laterally around the anterodorsal surface of the cochlear duct; there the limbus is embedded in the periotic connective tissue between the saccule and cochlear duct. These conditions (relatively poor differentiation of the limbus and lateral curvature of the neural limbus) resemble those found in turtles, described below. Depending upon its shape, the limbus supports an elongate, oval, or rounded basilar membrane; no evidence of a papillar bar has yet been found (Miller, 1968; personal observations). The cochlear ganglion is embedded in the neural limbus, and nerve fibers extend from it much as they do in lizards.

The shape of the ophidian basilar papilla does not show familial characteristics comparable to those noted in lizards. The papilla appears as a moderately long strip of neuroepithelium in typhlopids, leptotyphlopids and aniliids, varies from elongate to oval in boids, colubrids, viperids and elapids, and is oval or rounded in hydrophids (Fig. 31) (Miller, 1968; personal observations). Miller (1968) considers that the shape and size of the papilla (as well as those of the cochlear duct) may reflect adaptive modifications, and numerous such correlations can be made. Preliminary fine structural observations in typhlopids, colubrids and viperids suggest that supporting cells form a larger part of the surface area of the papilla than they do in lizards. Additionally, the number and distribution of cyto-skeletal microtubules in supporting cells of *Typhlops*, at least, approach conditions noted in lizards. Microtubules are significantly more numerous than in the amphisbaenians *Bipes* and *Amphisbaena* and in the turtles *Trionyx* and *Sternotherus*; their density approaches that in *Anolis*. This and other considerations (see Baird, 1969) suggest that supporting cells of the ophidian basilar papilla may be significantly more specialized than those in turtles. Within the matrix of supporting cells, hair cells tend to be arranged in non-compact (relative to lizards) rows lying oblique to the neural limbic margin of the basilar membrane. Sensory cilia are structurally similar to those described in lizards, kinocilia are apparently unidirectionally oriented (Mulroy, 1968; personal observations) and a well developed tectorial membrane with terminal specialization is apparent in most sectioned material. The membrane is typically attached basally to the epithelium lining the cochlear duct where it abuts anterodorsally against the lateral projection of the limbus. In general, the positional relationships of the tectorial membrane to the basilar papilla in snakes resemble those in lizards having moderate to strong development of a limbic bulge or lip. In some forms (e.g., typhlopids, leptotyphlopids) the membrane extends rather sharply medially toward the basilar papilla (Fig. 32), but considerable variation can be found among other forms examined. Strong development and curvature of the limbic projection are associated with medial inclination of the membrane, and relatively short uncurved limbic projections are associated with ventromedial inclination of the membrane.

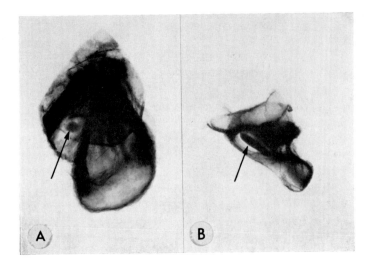

Fig. 31. Osmium-impregnated whole mounts of ophidian cochlear ducts (40×). A, *Laticauda* sp.; B, *Typhlops* sp. Note difference in size and form of the basilar papillae (arrows) in the two animals, and the relatively great size of the lagena in the marine animal (A).

Intracapsular periotic channels show considerable consistency throughout the group. The periotic cistern is typically divided by a cisternal septum, so a scala vestibuli is usually present. A bulge of the vestibular scala may abut against the lateral wall of the lagena, but neither definitive lagenar nor saccular scalae have been identified. Medially, the helicotrema continues into

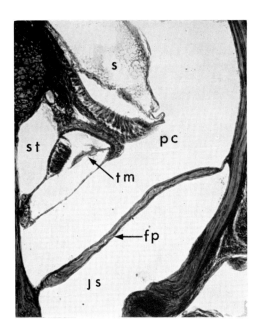

FIG. 32. Transverse section through the auditory region of *Typhlops nigrescens* (130×). Note the elaborate form of the tectorial membrane, which is attached to the arched lateral projection of the dorsal (neural) part of the limbus. fp, Footplate; js, juxtastapedial sinus; pc, periotic cistern; s, saccule containing matrix of statolith; st, scala tympani; tm, tectorial membrane.

an elongate scala tympani, which passes adjacent to the basilar membrane without great enlargement and exits through the periotic foramen. No definitive accessory scala tympani has been noted in snakes, although minor expansions of the scala tympani may slightly invade limbic tissue at the extremities of the basilar membrane in numerous forms. Upon traversing the periotic foramen, the scala enlarges slightly (least in hydrophids) into the periotic sac. Lying within the recessus scalae tympani, the sac is related medially to the meninges and glossopharyngeal nerve and, more posteriorly, to structures traversing the vagus foramen. Anterolaterally it extends into the juxtastapedial fossa and forms the juxtastapedial sinus, described above.

D. Testudines

Turtles have received little attention in recent investigations of the internal ear. Wever and Vernon (1956) mention certain gross features, Baird (1960b, 1964) covers aspects of the periotic and otic labyrinths in a few forms, and Miller (1966a) makes incidental mention of the cochlear duct, yet no comprehensive study of the chelonion internal ear has been added to classical works of Retzius (1884) and de Burlet (1934). Thus, it is currently unknown whether patterns of aural morphology characteristic of families occur within the group.

The vestibular part of the osseus labyrinth is somewhat simpler than, but basically similar to that of lizards. The cochlear recess, however, lies primarily posterior to the vestibule rather than ventral to it. In conjunction with this, the long axes of the vestibular window and stapedial footplate are almost vertical rather than approximately horizontal; the anterior two-thirds of the footplate face into the vestibule, while its posterior third faces the cochlear recess. The latter chamber is extended posteriorly by incorporation of the anterior part of the recessus scalae tympani into the otic capsule, and is marked in this region by medial and lateral foramina for the glossopharyngeal nerve. Thus, the posterior extremity of the cochlear recess, the small recessus scalae tympani posterior to it, and the periotic foramen joining the two cavities all represent developmental modifications of the anterior part of the metotic fissure and are, therefore, probably only analogous to structures of the same names in lizards (see de Beer, 1937; Baird, 1960b; McDowell, 1961).

The utricle and semicircular ducts conform closely to conditions described in lizards, but the saccule lies ventral to the utricle, a situation noted elsewhere in reptiles only in *Sphenodon*. Typically somewhat larger than the cochlear duct, the saccule is rounded in most forms, but in some its posteroventral part is extended posteriorly. In *Trionyx*, that region appears as a conical projection and reaches posteriorly into the anterolateral part of the cochlear recess. In addition to its typical medial attachments by heavy periotic reticulum, the ventral wall of the saccule is affixed to the vestibular floor, and some forms (notably *Trionyx*) exhibit strong reticular attachments between the membrana propria of the posterior part of the lateral saccular wall and the internal periosteum of the footplate; the significance of these attachments, first noted and termed stapedeo-saccular strands by Wever and Vernon (1956), is not understood.

The reunient duct, a short oval channel, leaves the posterodorsal aspect of the saccule and immediately joins the anterodorsal wall of the cochlear duct. The latter, inclining slightly medially, extends ventrad within the cochlear recess and enlarges slightly at its lagenar extremity (Figs 28 and 33).

Periotic reticulum of variable density unites the anterior wall of the cochlear duct with the posterior or posteromedial surface of the saccule, and, from this tissue, a cribrate lamina of periotic reticulum extends laterally to attach to the internal periosteum of the footplate in most forms examined; the lamina is least obvious in forms showing posterior extension of the saccule (e.g., *Trionyx*). This lamina, despite obvious structural differences, is probably homologous to the cisternal septum of other reptiles. In some forms it extends onto the posterior saccular wall and replaces definitive stapedeo-saccular strands in that area; in others it is restricted to the plane between the saccule and cochlear duct and seems only to help delimit the vestibule from the cochlear recess.

As in snakes, the limbus is not clearly differentiated from surrounding thick membrana propria; thus the entire medial wall of the cochlear duct is supported by dense periotic connective tissue, and in some forms this may extend into the area between the saccule and cochlear duct. In *Trionyx* the extension also grades laterally into thickened tissue underlying the saccular macula in the conical saccular projection mentioned above. In all forms investigated, a vertically oval basilar membrane lacking a papillar bar is

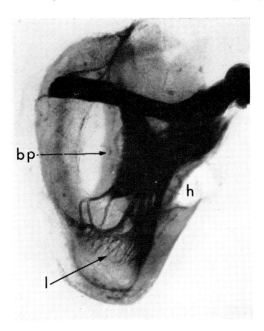

Fig. 33. Osmium-impregnated whole mount of the cochlear duct of an immature specimen (38 mm carapace length) of *Chelydra serpentina* (40×). The large basilar papilla lies along the anterior margin of the basilar membrane. bp, Basilar papilla; h, helicotrema; l, lagenar rami of vestibulocochlear nerve.

situated in the dorsal part of the medial wall of the cochlear duct. It underlies an oval to elongate basilar papilla positioned slightly eccentrically toward
its anterior margin; nerve fibers enter the papilla from the cochlear ganglion
situated in the neural limbus anterior to the basilar membrane. Preliminary
cytological observations indicate a general similarity of papillar components
to those of lizards, but the supporting cells comprise a relatively large part of
the surface area of the papilla and are considered to be least specialized
among those examined to date (see Baird, 1969). Hair cells in *Chelydra*,

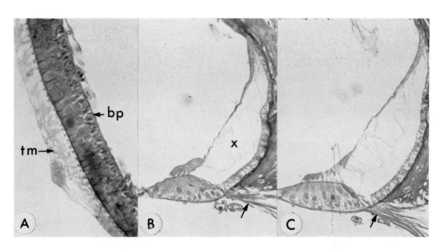

Fɪɢ. 34. Sections of the basilar papilla (bp) and tectorial membrane (tm) in turtles (290×). A,
Longitudinal section of the papilla in *Trionyx spinifer* (the complex structure of the tectorial membrane is rather similar and constant in trionychids examined); B, transverse section taken near the
lagenar extremity of the papilla in *Terrapene ornata*; C, section from mid-papillar region of the
same specimen. The form of the terminal specialization of the tectorial membrane differs in the
two regions, as does the morphology of the basilar papilla. Note the fine strands of cuticular material
(x) attaching the membrane to the facing epithelium, and the nerve fibers (arrows) entering the
anterior margin of the papilla.

Sternotherus and *Trionyx* are arranged in rather widely separated (relative
to conditions in lizards and snakes) rows lying oblique to the margin of the
neural limbus. The kinocilia of the usual ciliary bundles are unidirectionally
oriented (Mulroy, 1968; Baird, 1969). A definitive tectorial membrane
extends posteriorly from the neural limbus, becoming thicker and regionally
specialized over the sensory cilia (Fig. 34).

The periotic channels reflect the modifications of the saccule and cochlear
duct. A periotic cistern lies lateral to the dorsal parts of both elements and
medial to the dorsal part of the footplate. From this, the saccular part of the
cistern extends ventrally anterior to the cisternal septum, and the scala

vestibuli occupies a position lateral to the cochlear duct and posterior to the cisternal septum. The helicotrema extends anteromedially from the ventral extremity of the scala vestibuli, traverses the periotic connective tissue between the lagena and the ventral part of the saccule, and then arches posterodorsally to grade into a scala vestibuli adjacent to the medial surface of the limbus and basilar membrane. The scala courses posteriorly through periotic tissue in the posterior part of the cochlear recess, where it is crossed dorsally by the glossopharyngeal nerve; it then traverses the periotic foramen to enter the recessus scalae tympani and enlarges to form the periotic sac. The sac abuts medially against the cranial meninges and vagus nerve, and laterally against the posterior extremity of the paracapsular sinus described above.

E. CROCODILIA

Except for studies of the periotic labyrinth in crocodilians (de Burlet, 1934; Baird, 1960b), little has been added to the work of Retzius (1884) on the ear of *Alligator*, and no serious effort has apparently been made to verify his observations. Thus, despite the fact that the crocodilian ear is certainly among the most highly specialized within the Reptilia, it is not as well known as that of several other assemblages. Relatively thick (20–60μ) sections of several crocodilians available in de Burlet's and my own collections do not provide an adequate basis for detailed histological study, but do suggest that certain of the histological details indicated in Retzius' figures (e.g., Tafel XIV, Fig. 8) merit additional investigation. A general survey of comparative aural morphology and detailed histological and cytological studies are sorely needed for the Crocodilia.

The vestibule and semicircular canals of the osseus labyrinth exhibit relatively minor differences from those in other reptiles, but the cochlear recess is significantly altered. The posterior part of the recess forms a shallow groove in the lateral half of the floor of the vestibule. It continues anteriorly as a deep tubular fossa that projects ventrally from the anterior limit of that groove. The periotic foramen is situated in the posterolateral wall of the cochlear recess immediately ventral to the vestibular window, from which it is separated only by a slender strut of bone. Hidden by the subcapsular process (de Beer, 1937), the foramen opens into a narrow channel enclosed between the otic capsule and that process. This channel, representing an extension of the recessus scalae tympani, curves ventromedially to a point anterior to the internal orifice of the vagus foramen and terminates externally at the fenestra pseudorotunda, immediately anterodorsal to the periotic foramen.

The utricle and semicircular ducts occupy normal positions within the osseus labyrinth, but the saccule is relatively small and affixed to the ventro-medial vestibular wall ventral to the utricle. The narrow elliptical reunient duct leaves the posterior extremity of the saccule and curves ventrolaterally to join the posterior extremity of the cochlear duct. The latter is greatly elongate and composed of two limbs; the posterior of these slopes antero-ventrally in the groove forming the posterior part of the cochlear recess and, as its direct continuation, the anterior limb bends sharply ventrad and occupies the tubular part of the recess. The lagena comprises only a small terminal part of the anterior limb and lies at the depths of the recess. Throughout its length, the duct is affixed to the internal periosteum by marginal attachments of the limbus. Those of the posterior part of the duct occur along margins of the cochlear recess and, laterally, along the strut of bone separating the vestibular window and the periotic foramen. Within the tubular portion of the recess, limbic attachments are made to the medial and lateral walls of the fossa and to the thickened membrana propria attached to the bony wall posteroventral to the lagena. The medial part of the limbus, although without a limbic bulge or lip, is heavier than the lateral; since it houses the cochlear ganglion and its peripheral ramuli, it constitutes the neural limbus. The basilar membrane, contained within the bent and narrow rim of limbic tissue, is somewhat thickened centrally but it shows no evidence of a papillar bar. The sectioned material available for study neither fully supports nor disproves the cellular and fibrillar organization of the membrane shown in Retzius' (1884; Tafel XIV) figures.

The basilar papilla is wide posteriorly, greatly elongate, and tapers toward its anterior extremity. It is not centered upon the basilar membrane, but lies adjacent to its neural limbic attachment and, particularly posteriorly, extends to overlie the neural limbus slightly. In the sections available, it is impossible to verify either the sharp differentiation of inner and outer hair cells recorded by Retzius (1884) or the patterns of distribution he has shown. Supporting cells appear to be generally similar to those noted elsewhere, and to be related to the hair cells much as in other forms. The sensory cilia are overlain by a thick tectorial membrane, which bears some similarity to that in turtles and projects laterally from an attachment to the epithelium lining the neural limbus. Opposite these structures, facing essentially dorsally into the vestibular recess and anteriorly within the tubular part of the cochlear recess, the vestibular membrane is somewhat thicker and more highly vascularized than that of other reptiles; the "tegmentum vasculosum" does not appear to form as clearly differentiated a structure as indicated by Retzius (1884) and should be investigated more fully.

The periotic cistern occupies the vestibule lateral to the saccule and dorsal to the cochlear duct, and is impinged upon laterally by the stapedial foot-plate. At its anteroventral extremity the cistern projects into the anterior part of the cochlear recess as the scala vestibuli. A small lagenar scala extends the channel containing periotic fluid into contact with the lagena at the depths of the recess. In the same area a narrow helicotrema arches laterally around the cochlear duct just dorsal to the lagena and communicates with the scala tympani housed in the posterior part of the recess. The homology of the crocodilian helicotrema has been questioned (Baird, 1960b) and is not yet fully established. The scala tympani extends dorsally and, ventral to the posterior part of the cochlear duct, expands into the periotic sac. Thus, the basilar membrane of the anterior limb of the cochlear duct abuts against the scala tympani, and the membrane of the posterior limb rests against the periotic sac; small periotic diverticula comparable to short accessory tympanic scalae invade the limbus at both its anterior and posterior extremities. Posterolaterally, the periotic sac extends through the periotic foramen and lies within the extended recessus scalae tympani formed by the subcapsular process. The sac extends slightly anterodorsally and fuses with the tympanic mucous membrane to form a secondary tympanic membrane at the fenestra pseudorotunda. Ventromedially the sac evaginates, forms a channel partially occluded by periotic reticulum, and curves medially to reach the cranial meninges at the point of exit of the glossopharyngeal nerve. The latter extension and its relationships bear strong resemblances to the periotic (perilymphatic) duct of mammals.

V. Summary

A rather highly structured ear, consisting of both equilibratory and auditory systems, is present in all reptiles. The equilibratory system shows relatively little morphological variation throughout the group and resembles that of other vertebrates. At present, there seems to be no reason to question the homologies of that system or its parts, despite the fact that it has been inadequately studied in reptiles and probably shows at least histological and cytological variations. Here, as in other vertebrates, least information is available concerning the macula neglecta. The auditory system is better known, varies rather extensively within the class, and has been shown to provide some degree of hearing in all reptiles that have been tested physiologically. It is probable that most of its structural differences relate to differences in auditory sensitivity, but the reasons for structural changes are obscure in most cases, and the homologies of most of the parts of the system are still in question. Thus, both the nomenclature of the reptilian auditory system and generalized comparisons of the system with that of other vertebrates are based heavily upon analogy, and are open to challenge.

An external ear, consisting of a shallow depression or a short passage variably protected by folds of skin, is found in many lizards and in crocodilians, but is absent in turtles and in reptiles lacking a tympanic cavity and/or membrane. Thus, it apparently protects the tympanic membrane and deeper parts of the auditory mechanism, but its possible relationships to sound gathering and localization have not been specifically investigated. The structure of the reptilian external ear does not lend itself to meaningful comparison with that of the analogous region in other vertebrates.

Variability in the reptilian middle ear, evidenced both in the fossil record and in living forms, has resulted in controversy concerning the evolution of the middle ear and its parts. Recent studies have indicated that audition is maintained in even rather extreme modifications of the region (e.g., snakes, amphisbaenians), but they have contributed little toward settling the many disputed homologies in the area. In crocodilians and most lizards the middle ear is analogous to that in birds and mammals. A tympanic membrane, columellar apparatus and secondary tympanic membrane are related to a tympanic cavity connected to the pharynx by way of an auditory tube, and these parts function much as they do in the higher forms. In turtles, some of the same structural and functional characteristics are evident, but the medial part of the tympanic cavity is partially isolated by bone and contains a unique, fluid-filled, dampening mechanism, the paracapsular sinus. In *Sphenodon*, snakes, amphisbaenians, and some fossorial and arboreal lizards, the tympanic cavity and/or membrane are absent, the columellar apparatus is altered or reduced, and the dampening mechanism is different. In general, these forms show emphasis of a quadrate attachment of the extrastapes and other parts of that element are altered or absent; the dampening mechanism ranges from a slightly thickened secondary tympanic membrane, to intracranial termination of the periotic sac (reminiscent of a condition in amphibians), and the unique juxtastapedial sinus in snakes. In some forms (e.g., amphisbaenians, some iguanid lizards) rather convincing evidence indicates that cranial modifications associated with the burrowing habit may be causally related to changes in the middle ear. In others (e.g., chameleons) causality has not been established, but there is presently no evidence that audition has had negative selective value in any form.

Investigations of recent years have clarified numerous aspects of the anatomy of the reptilian internal ear, and have indicated that there is considerable correlation between aural morphology and established taxonomic assemblages. They have also revealed unexpected sophistication and adaptability in structures once thought to be simple and generally similar throughout the group. Although the auditory part of the internal ear shows more variation than the vestibular part, it is, relatively, the most conservative portion of the auditory mechanism. The general anatomy of the cochlear duct and associated periotic labyrinth in some reptiles (e.g., *Sphenodon*, some fossorial and arboreal lizards) shows similarities to that in amphibians

(particularly anurans), and the rather highly developed structures in crocodilians can be meaningfully compared to those in birds and monotremes. It is
generally accepted that the basilar papilla and lagenar macula are at least
partially homologous throughout these forms; the homologies of other parts
of the cochlear duct and of the periotic labyrinth have not been established,
but plausible suggestions have been made. The early reports of fine structural studies of the basilar papilla have shown a basic consistency in its
organization and points of comparison with the auditory receptors of
amphibians, birds and mammals, but they have also indicated cytological
specializations within the Reptilia. It is now apparent that, in different
groups of reptiles, there are differences in the structure and arrangement of
hair cells and supporting cells within the receptor, and that lizards differ
from turtles, snakes and amphisbaenians in the orientation and (probably)
the innervation of papillar hair cells.

   Although significant progress has been made toward an understanding of
the structure and function of the reptilian ear, recent studies have emphasized
deficiencies in the information available and underscore the need for additional investigations, both surveys and detailed studies in sharply circumscribed groups. For example, histological and cytological knowledge of the
parts of the internal ear is extremely limited; patterns of innervation within
otic receptors are virtually unknown; only the most general information is
available concerning the central connections of the reptilian vestibulocochlear nerve; the functional significance of the macula neglecta, saccular
macula, and lagenar macula are poorly understood; relatively few structural
and functional correlations have been attempted in reptiles showing highly
modified auditory mechanisms; and knowledge of vestibular structure and
aural embryology is limited to a few forms and to special features. In short,
the opportunities for productive investigation of the ear have few limits
within a group so large and diversified as the Class Reptilia.

VI. Acknowledgements

   The author's debt of gratitude is great, for colleagues, friends, and, in some
cases, complete strangers have contributed to this work in various ways.
Dr. David W. Hamilton, Harvard Medical School, and Dr. Malcolm R.
Miller, University of California School of Medicine, have provided suggestions, criticisms and information concerning their work, and have loaned
materials freely. Dr. E. E. Williams, Harvard University, has loaned
numerous specimens for anatomical study and has provided access to
reptilian material in the Museum of Comparative Zoology. Dr. C. C. D.
Shute, Cambridge University, made available facilities for study of his
personal collection of sectioned reptilian material, and similar courtesies

were extended by Professor A. G. de Wilde, State University at Gröningen, The Netherlands, for study of de Burlet's materials. Dr. Carl Gans, State University of New York at Buffalo, has contributed most extensively to the author's personal collection, but thanks are due to more individuals than can be mentioned for assisting in procuring certain types of specimens over the past several years. For her patience and unusually competent technical assistance, I am particularly grateful to Mrs. Richard E. Rome, The University of Tennessee Medical Units; to Dr. J. F. Reger, University of Tennessee Medical Units, Dr. W. B. Winborn, University of South Texas Medical School, and Dr. D. E. Bockman, Medical College of Ohio at Toledo, I owe thanks for introducing me to the field of electron microscopy. This work has been partially supported by Research Grants NB 04993 and NB 07860 from the National Institute for Neurological Diseases and Blindness.

VII. Lists of Materials

The following lists encompass the bulk of living reptiles in which the anatomy of the ear, as such, has received attention in the literature or has been investigated by the author. Table I indicates the species and types of material seen personally. The serial sections include those studied in other laboratories as well as my own, and consist, almost entirely, of sections through the otic region in intact heads or halves of heads; the fine structural studies indicated have concentrated primarily upon the basilar papilla, and only the work on *Anolis carolinensis* is nearing completion. In the generic list that follows, value judgement has figured strongly in the omission of forms in which sharply limited observations have been made or in which features of the auditory region have been considered only in a taxonomic or phylogenetic context. Such omission is not intended to reflect questions concerning the validity of work done, but rather to restrict the list to forms in which at least a minimal level of information on auditory anatomy has been achieved. On the other hand, it should be noted that comprehensive studies of the ear have been done in relatively few representatives of the genera listed.

The classification used is, in almost all cases, that of Romer (1956). This has, in numerous instances, been challenged by more recent workers; see, for example, the comments of Maderson (this volume) on the genera of boids.

TABLE I

List of Materials Examined

Form	Serial Sections	Dissection	Skull	Fine Structure
TESTUDINES				
Chelydridae				
Chelydra serpentina	4	×	×	×
Kinosternon flavescens	2			
Sternotherus odoratus	4	×	×	×
Testudinidae				
Chrysemys picta	4	×	×	×
Chrysemys picta marginata	2	×		
Clemmys insculpta	1	×		
Clemmys marmorata	1			
Emydoidea blandingii	2			
Gopherus agassizii		×		
Graptemys pseudogeographica	2	×		×
Pseudemys scripta	2	×		×
Terrapene carolina	4	×		
Terrapene ornata	2	×		
Testudo sp.	1			
Trionychidae				
Lissemys punctata		×		×
Trionyx spinifer	6	×		×
Trionyx triunguis	1	×		×
Pelomedusidae				
Podocnemis unifilis	2			
RHYNCHOCEPHALIA				
Sphenodontidae				
Sphenodon punctatus	2		×	
SQUAMATA				
	Sauria			
Iguanidae				
Anolis carolinensis	15	×	×	×
Anolis lineatropus	1			
Callisaurus draconoides	2	×		
Crotaphytus collaris	2	×	×	
Ctenosaura pectinata	1	×	×	
Dipsosaurus dorsalis	1			
Holbrookia maculata	1	×		
Holbrookia texana	1			
Iguana iguana	2	×		
Phrynosoma cornutum	2	×		

TABLE I—*continued*

Form	Serial Sections	Dissection	Skull	Fine Structure
Iguanidae—*cont.*				
Phrynosoma douglassii	2	×	×	
Sauromalus obesus	2	×		
Sceloporus graciosus	2			
Sceloporus olivaceus	2			
Sceloporus scalaris	1			
Sceloporus undulatus	4			
Uma notata	2			
Uta stansburiana	1	×		
Xiphocercus valencienni	1			
Agamidae				
Agama agilis	2	×		
Agama atricollis	1			
Agama sp.	1			
Calotes versicolor	1			
Uromastix hardwickii	1			
Chamaeleonidae				
Chamaeleo chamaeleon	2			
Microsaura pumila	1			
Gekkonidae				
Aristelliger praesignis	2			
Coleonyx variegatus	2	×		×
Diplodactylus strophurus	1			
Diplodactylus vittatus	1			
Eublepharis maculatus	1			
Gehyra variegata	1			
Gekko gecko	2	×		×
Gonatodes albogularis fuscus	1			
Gymnodactylus milii	1			
Hemidactylus fasciatus	1			
Hemidactylus mabouia	1			
Heteronotia binoei	1			
Lepidoblepharis microlepis	1			
Pachydactylus sp.		×		
Phyllodactylus marmoratus	1			
Ptenopus garrulus	1			
Sphaerodactylus macrolepis	2			
Stenodactylus orientalis	1			
Teratoscincus scincus	1	×		
Thecadactylus rapicauda	2			
Pygopodidae				
Aprasia repens	3			
Delma fraseri	2			
Lialis burtonis	2			
Pygopus lepidopodus	1			

TABLE I—*continued*

Form	Serial Sections	Dissection	Skull	Fine Structure
Xantusiidae				
Xantusia henshawi	1			
Xantusia vigilis	2	×		
Teiidae				
Ameiva ameiva	2	×		
Cnemidophorus gularis	2	×		
Cnemidophorus sexlineatus	4	×		
Cnemidophorus tessellatus	2	×		
Cnemidophorus tigris	1	×		
Tupinambis teguixin	2	×		
Scincidae				
Acontias meleagris		×		
Chalcides chalcides striatus	1			
Chalcides ocellatus	2	×		
Eumeces fasciatus	4	×	×	×
Eumeces inexpectatus	2			
Eumeces obsoletus	4	×		
Eumeces schneiderii	2			
Eumeces taeniolatus	3			
Leiolopisma laterale	10	×		×
Leiolopisma pretiosum	1			
Leiolopisma trilineatum	1			
Lygosoma quoyii	2	×		
Lygosoma weeksae	1			
Mabuya megalura	1			
Mabuya multifasciata	1			
Scelotes sp.		×		
Lacertidae				
Acanthodactylus erythrurus	1			
Eremias guttulata	4			
Lacerta muralis	2			
Lacerta vivipara	2			
Lacerta sp.	1			
Psammodromus algirus	1			
Cordylidae				
Cordylus cataphractus	2			
Anguidae				
Anguis fragilis	3			
Gerrhonotus coeruleus	2	×		
Ophisaurus ventralis	2	×	×	
Anniellidae				
Anniella pulchra	2			
Helodermatidae				
Heloderma suspectum		×		

TABLE I—*continued*

Form	Serial Sections	Dissection	Skull	Fine Structure
Varanidae				
Varanus niloticus	1			
Varanus sp.	2			
Amphisbaenia				
Amphisbaenidae				
Amphisbaena caeca	4	×		×
Amphisbaena camura	2			
Amphisbaena manni	2	×		×
Amphisbaena xera	2			
Amphisbaena sp.	1			
Anops kingii	1			
Bipes biporus	2	×		×
Blanus cinereus	2			
Monopeltis capensis	2	×		
Rhineura floridana	2			
Trogonophidae				
Diplometopon zarudnyi	1			
Trogonophis wiegmanni	1			
Ophidia				
Typhlopidae				
Typhlops braminus	2			
Typhlops kenti	1			
Typhlops lumbricalis	2			
Typhlops nigrescens	9			
Typhlops platycephalus	2			
Typhlops punctatus	2		×	
Typhlops richardii	2			
Typhlops rostellatus	2			
Typhlops schlegelii	2		×	
Typhlops torresianus	2			
Typhlops sp.	1	×		×
Leptotyphlopidae				
Leptotyphlops humilis	4			
Aniliidae				
Anilius scytale	1		×	
Cylindrophis rufus			×	
Loxocemus bicolor			×	
Rhinophis oxyrhynchus			×	
Rhinophis sp.	1			
Uropeltis sp.	1		×	
Xenopeltis unicolor	2		×	

TABLE I—*continued*

Form	Serial Sections	Dissection	Skull	Fine Structure
Boidae				
Boa canina	1		×	
Charina bottae	1		×	
Constrictor constrictor	1		×	
Eryx johnii			×	
Liasis childreni			×	
Python molurus			×	
Python sp.	1			
Trachyboa sp.	1			
Colubridae				
Acrochordus granulatus			×	
Arizona elegans	1	×		
Calamelaps sp.	1			
Carphophis amoena	6	×	×	
Coluber constrictor	4	×		
Coluber melanurus	1			
Dasypeltis scabra			×	
Dendrelaphis caudolineatus	1			
Diadophis punctatus	6	×	×	
Elaphe obsoleta	2	×	×	
Geophis caninus			×	
Homalopsis buccata	1		×	
Lampropeltis calligaster	2	×		
Lampropeltis getulus	2	×		
Micrelaps muelleri	1			
Natrix rhombifera	1		×	
Natrix sipedon	1		×	
Opheodrys aestivus	1			
Oxybelis sp.			×	
Pituophis catenifer	1			
Tantilla gracilis	2	×	×	
Tantilla nigriceps			×	
Thamnophis radix	1		×	
Thamnophis sirtalis	4	×	×	
Trimorphodon lyrophanes			×	
Elapidae				
Bungarus fasciatus			×	
Bungarus sp.	1			
Micrurus sp.			×	
Naja haje			×	
Naja naja	1			
Naja sp.	1			
Ophiophagus hannah			×	
Hydrophiidae				
Hydrophis fasciatus			×	

TABLE I—*continued*

Form	Serial Sections	Dissection	Skull	Fine Structure
Hydrophidae—*cont.*				
Hydrophis ornatus			×	
Hydrophis sp.	1			
Laticauda colubrina	1		×	
Laticauda sp.	1	×		
Thalassophis sp.	1			
Viperidae				
Agkistrodon contortrix	2	×	×	×
Atractaspis bibronii			×	
Bitis arietans			×	
Bitis gabonica			×	
Causus rhombeatus			×	
Crotalus atrox	2	×	×	×
Crotalus horridus	1	×		
Echis carinatus	3		×	
Sistrurus catenatus	1		×	
Trimeresurus gramineus	1			
CROCODILIA				
Crocodylidae				
Alligator mississippiensis	3	×	×	
Caiman crocodilus	1	×		
Caiman sp.	1			
Crocodylus sp.	1			

LIST OF GENERA STUDIED

TESTUDINES

Chelydridae: *Chelydra, Kinosternon, Sternotherus*
Testudinidae: *Chrysemys, Clemmys, Emydoidea, Gopherus, Graptemys, Pseudemys, Terrapene, Testudo*
Cheloniidae: *Chelonia*
Dermochelyidae: *Dermochelys*
Trionychidae: *Lissemys, Trionyx*
Pelomedusidae: *Podocnemis*
Chelidae: *Chelodina*

RHYNCHOCEPHALIA

Sphenodontidae: *Sphenodon*

SQUAMATA, SAURIA

Iguanidae: *Amblyrhynchus, Anolis, Basiliscus, Brachylophus, Callisaurus, Chalarodon, Corytophanes, Crotaphytus, Ctenosaura, Dipsosaurus, Holbrookia,*

Hoplocercus, Iguana, Leiocephalus, Liolaemus, Mariguana, Norops, Oplurus, Phrynosoma, Plica, Polychrus, Sauromalus, Sceloporus, Tropidurus, Uma, Urostrophus, Uta, Xiphocercus

Agamidae: *Agama, Amphibolurus, Aphaniotis, Calotes, Ceratophora, Clamydosaurus, Cophotis, Draco, Goniocephalus, Japalura, Lophura, Lyriocephalus, Phrynocephalus, Sitana, Tympanocryptis, Uromastix*

Chamaeleonidae: *Brookesia, Chamaeleo, Microsaura, Rhampholeon*

Gekkonidae: *Aristelliger, Bavayia, Cnemaspis, Coleonyx, Cosymbotus, Eublepharis, Gehyra, Gekko, Gonatodes, Gymnodactylus, Hemidactylus, Heteronotia, Hoplodactylus, Lepidoblepharis, Lepidodactylus, Microgecko, Oedura, Pachydactylus, Phelsuma, Phyllodactylus, Phyllurus, Ptenopus, Ptychozoon, Ptyodactylus, Sphaerodactylus, Stenodactylus, Tarentola, Teratoscincus, Thecadactylus, Uroplatus*

Pygopodidae: *Aprasia, Delma, Lialis, Pygopus*

Xantusiidae: *Klauberina, Lepidophyma, Xantusia*

Teiidae: *Ameiva, Anadia, Bachia, Cnemidophorus, Dicrodon, Kentropyx, Neusticurus, Pantodactylus, Proctoporus, Tupinambis*

Scincidae: *Ablepharus, Acontias, Anelytropsis, Aulacoplax, Brachymeles, Chalcides, Dasia, Egernia, Emoia, Eumeces, Feylinia, Leiolopisma, Lygosoma, Mabuya, Nessia, Ophiomorus, Otosaurus, Rhodona, Riopa, Scelotes, Scincus, Tiliqua, Tribolonotus, Tropidophorus, Typhlosaurus*

Lacertidae: *Acanthodactylus, Eremias, Lacerta, Psammodromus, Takydromus*

Cordylidae: *Chamaesaura, Cordylus, Gerrhosaurus*

Dibamidae: *Dibamus*

Anguidae: *Anguis, Diploglossus, Gerrhonotus, Ophisaurus*

Anniellidae: *Anniella*

Xenosauridae: *Xenosaurus*

Helodermatidae: *Heloderma*

Varanidae: *Varanus*

Lanthanotidae: *Lanthanotus*

SQUAMATA, AMPHISBAENIA

Amphisbaenidae: *Amphisbaena, Anops, Bipes, Blanus, Monopeltis, Rhineura*

Trogonophidae: *Diplometopon, Trogonophis*

SQUAMATA, OPHIDIA

Typhlopidae: *Liotyphlops, Typhlops*

Leptotyphlopidae: *Leptotyphlops*

Aniliidae: *Anilius, Cylindrophis, Loxocemus, Platypectrurus, Plectrurus, Rhinophis, Uropeltis, Xenopeltis*

Boidae: *Calabaria, Charina, Chondropython, Constrictor, Enygrus, Epicrates, Eryx, Eunectes, Liasis, Lichanura, Python, Trachyboa, Tropidophis*

Colubridae: *Abastor, Acrochordus, Ahaetulla, Alsophis, Aparallactus, Aplopeltura, Arizona, Boiga, Calamaria, Calamelaps, Carphophis, Cemo-*

*phora, Cerberus, Chilomeniscus, Chionactis, Chrysopelea, Coluber, Conio-
phanes, Contia, Coronella, Crotaphopeltis, Cyclocorus, Dasypeltis, Den-
drelaphis, Diadophis, Dispholidus, Dromicus, Dryadophis, Drymarchon,
Drymobius, Duberria, Elaphe, Enhydris, Erpeton, Farancia, Ficimia,
Geophis, Haldea, Helicops, Heterodon, Hologerrhum, Homalopsis, Hypsi-
glena, Imantodes, Lampropeltis, Leioheterodon, Leptodeira, Leptophis,
Liodytes, Liophis, Lycodon, Lycophidion, Lytorhynchus, Macrocalamus,
Malpolon, Micrelaps, Mimophis, Natrix, Neusterophis, Ninia, Oligodon,
Opheodrys, Oxybelis, Oxyrhabdium, Pareas, Philodryas, Philothamnus,
Phyllorhynchus, Pituophis, Pliocercus, Psammodynastes, Psammophis,
Psammophylax, Pseudoboa, Pseudorabdion, Ptyas, Rhadinaea, Rhinocheilus,
Salvadora, Sibon, Sibynomorphus, Sibynophis, Sonora, Stegonotus, Stilo-
soma, Storeria, Tachymenis, Tantilla, Thamnophis, Thelotornis, Trachis-
chium, Trimorphodon, Xenelaphis, Xenodon, Zaocys*

Elapidae: *Acanthophis, Aspidomorphus, Brachyurophis, Bungarus, Calliophis,
Demansia, Dendroaspis, Denisonia, Elaps, Hemachatus, Hoplocephalus,
Maticora, Micruroides, Micrurus, Naja, Notechis, Ophiophagus, Pseuda-
pistocalamus, Pseudechis, Rhynchoelaps, Vermicella, Walterinnesia*

Hydrophiidae: *Aipysurus, Enhydrina, Hydrophis, Lapemis, Laticauda,
Microcephalophis, Pelamis, Thalassophis*

Viperidae: *Agkistrodon, Atheris, Atractaspis, Bitis, Causus, Cerastes, Crotalus,
Echis, Eristicophis, Lachesis, Sistrurus, Trimeresurus, Vipera*

CROCODILIA
Crocodylidae: *Alligator, Caiman, Crocodylus*

References

Baird, I. L. (1960a). Observations on the auditory apparatus in typhlopid snakes. *Anat. Rec.* 138, 332.

Baird, I. L. (1960b). A survey of the periotic labyrinth in some representative recent reptiles. *Kans. Univ. Sci. Bull.* 41, 891–981.

Baird, I. L. (1961). Sensory areas of the saccule and cochlea in certain burrowing snakes. *Anat. Rec.* 139, 204.

Baird, I. L. (1964). Some features of the aural anatomy of the turtle, *Trionyx spiniferus*. *Am. Zool.* 4, 396.

Baird, I. L. (1966). Discussion of the reptilian ear. *Am. Zool.* 6, 431–436.

Baird, I. L. (1967). Some histological and cytological features of the basilar papilla in the lizard, *Anolis carolinensis*. *Anat. Rec.* 157, 208–209.

Baird, I. L. (1969). Some findings of comparative fine structural studies of the basilar papilla in certain reptiles. *Anat. Rec.* 163, 149.

Baird, I. L. and Winborn, W. B. (1966). A preliminary report on some aspects of the fine structure of the cochlear duct in certain reptiles. *Anat. Rec.* 154, 449.

de Beer, G. R. (1937). "The Development of the Vertebrate Skull." Oxford University Press, London.

van Beneden, E. (1882). Recherches sur l'oreille moyenne des crocodiliens et ses communications multiples avec le pharynx. *Archs Biol.*, *Paris* **3**, 497–560.

Berman, D. S. and Regal, P. J. (1967). The loss of the ophidian middle ear. *Evolution*, *Lancaster*, *Pa.* **21**, 641–643.

Brock, G. T. (1941). The skull of *Acontias meleagris*, with a study of the affinities between lizards and snakes. *J. Linn. Soc.*, *Zool.* **44**, 71–88.

de Burlet, H. M. (1934). Vergleichenden Anatomie des stato-akustischen Organs. a. Die innere Ohrsphäre. b. Die mittlere Ohrsphäre. *In* "Handbuch der vergleichenden Anatomie der Wirbeltiere" (L. Bolk, E. Göppert, E. Kallius and W. Lubosch, eds). Urban und Schwarzenberg, Berlin and Wien. **2**, 1293–1432.

Camp, C. L. (1923). Classification of the lizards. *Bull. Am. Mus. nat. Hist.* **48**, 289–481.

Colbert, E. H. (1946). The Eustachian tubes in the Crocodilia. *Copeia* **1946**, 12–14.

Earle, A. M. (1961a). The middle ear of *Holbrookia maculata maculata*, the northern earless lizard. *Copeia* **1961**, 68–74.

Earle, A. M. (1961b). An additional note on the ear of *Holbrookia maculata*. *Copeia* **1961**, 355.

Earle, A. M. (1961c). The middle ear of *Holbrookia* and *Callisaurus*. *Copeia* **1961**, 405–410.

Earle, A. M. (1962). The middle ear of the genus *Uma* compared to those of other sand lizards. *Copeia* **1962**, 185–188.

Fleissig, J. (1908). Die Entwicklung des Geckolabyrinthes. *Arb. anat. Inst.*, *Wiesbaden* (*Anat. Hefte, Abt. I*) **37**, 1–116.

Gans, C. (1960). Studies on amphisbaenids (Amphisbaenia, Reptilia). 1. A taxonomic revision of the Trogonophinae, and a functional interpretation of the amphisbaenid adaptive pattern. *Bull. Am. Mus. nat. Hist.* **119**, 129–204.

Gaupp, E. (1899). Ontogenese und Phylogenese des schalleitenden Apparates bei den Wirbeltieren. *Ergebn. Anat. EntwGesch.* **8**, 990–1149.

Gaupp, E. (1905). Das Hyobranchialskelet der Wirbeltiere. *Ergebn. Anat. EntwGesch.* **14**, 808–1048.

Goodrich, E. S. (1915). The chorda tympani and middle ear in reptiles, birds and mammals. *Q. Jl microsc. Sci.* **61**, 137–160.

Goodrich, E. S. (1930). "Studies on the Structure and Development of Vertebrates." Macmillan, London.

Gray, A. A. (1913). Notes on the comparative anatomy of the middle ear. *J. Anat. Physiol.*, *Lond.* **47**, 391–413.

Hadžiselmović, H. and Anđelić, M. (1967). Contribution to the knowledge of the ear in the sea turtle. *Acta anat.* **66**, 460–477.

Hamilton, D. W. (1960). Observations on the morphology of the inner ear in certain gekkonid lizards. *Kans. Univ. Sci. Bull.* **41**, 983–1024.

Hamilton, D. W. (1963a). Posterior division of the eighth cranial nerve in *Lacerta vivipara*. *Nature, Lond.* **200**, 705–706.

Hamilton, D. W. (1963b). "Structure and evolution of the lizard inner ear." Doctoral Dissertation, Univ. of Cambridge.

Hamilton, D. W. (1964). The inner ear of lizards. I. Gross structure. *J. Morph.* **115**, 255–271.

Hamilton, D. W. (1965). Microvillous cells in ampullae of the lizard inner ear. *J. Morph.* **116**, 339–356.

Kluge, A. G. (1967). Higher taxonomic categories of gekkonid lizards and their evolution. *Bull. Am. Mus. nat. Hist.* **135**, 1–59.

McDowell, S. B., Jr. (1961). On the major arterial canals in the ear-region of testudinoid turtles and the classification of the Testudinoidea. *Bull. Mus. comp. Zool. Harvard* **125**, 23–39.

McDowell, S. B., Jr. (1967). The extracolumella and tympanic cavity of the "earless" monitor lizard, *Lanthanotus borneensis. Copeia* **1967**, 154–159.

van der Merwe, N. J. (1944). Die skedelmorfologie van *Acontias meleagris* (Linn.). *Tydskr. Wet. Kuns.* **5**, 59–88.

Miller, M. R. (1966a). The cochlear duct of lizards. *Proc. Calif. Acad. Sci.* **33**, 255–359.

Miller, M. R. (1966b). The cochlear duct of lizards and snakes. *Am. Zool.* **6**, 421–429.

Miller, M. R. (1966c). The cochlear ducts of *Lanthanotus* and *Anelytropsis* with remarks on the familial relationship between *Anelytropsis* and *Dibamus. Occ. Pap. Calif. Acad. Sci.* **60**, 1–15.

Miller, M. R. (1968). The cochlear duct of snakes. *Proc. Calif. Acad. Sci.* **35**, 425–475.

Miller, M. R., Kasahara, M. and Mulroy, M. (1967). Observations on the structure of the cochlear duct limbus of reptiles. *Proc. Calif. Acad. Sci.* **35**, 37–51.

Mulroy, M. (1968). Orientation of hair cells in the reptilian auditory papilla. *Anat. Rec.* **160**, 397.

Norris, K. S. and Lowe, C. H., Jr. (1951). A study of the osteology and musculature of *Phrynosoma m'callii* pertinent to its systematic status. *Bull. Chicago Acad. Sci.* **9**, 117–125.

Oelrich, T. M. (1956). The anatomy of the head of *Ctenosaura pectinata* (Iguanidae). *Misc. Publs Mus. Zool. Univ. Mich.* **94**, 1–122.

Olson, E. C. (1966). The middle ear—morphological types in amphibians and reptiles. *Am. Zool.* **6**, 399–419.

Posner, R. B. and Chiasson, R. B. (1966). The middle ear of *Coleonyx variegatus. Copeia* **1966**, 520–524.

Prebil, K. J. (1966). Some cytological features of the planum semilunatum in two lizards, *Anolis carolinensis* and *Leiolopisma laterale. Anat. Rec.* **154**, 404–405.

Retzius, G. (1884). "Das Gehörorgan der Wirbelthiere. II. Das Gehörorgan der Reptilien, der Vögel und der Säugethiere." Samson and Wallin, Stockholm.

Romer, A. S. (1956). "Osteology of the Reptiles." Univ. Chicago Press, Chicago.

Schmidt, R. S. (1964). Phylogenetic significance of the lizard cochlea. *Copeia* **1964**, 542–549.

Shute, C. C. D. and Bellairs, A. d'A. (1953). The cochlear apparatus of Gekkonidae and Pygopodidae and its bearing on the affinities of these groups of lizards. *Proc. zool. Soc. Lond.* **123**, 695–709.

Shute, C. C. D. and Bellairs, A. d'A. (1955). The external ear in Crocodilia. *Proc. zool. Soc. Lond.* **124**, 741–749.

Smith, M. A. (1938). Evolutionary changes in the middle ear of certain agamid and iguanid lizards. *Proc. zool. Soc. Lond.* (B) **108**, 544–549.

Toerien, M. J. (1963). The sound-conducting systems of lizards without tympanic membranes. *Evolution, Lancaster, Pa.* **17**, 540–547.

Tumarkin, A. (1955). On the evolution of the auditory conducting apparatus: A new theory based on functional considerations. *Evolution, Lancaster, Pa.* **9**, 221–243.

Underwood, G. (1954). On the classification and evolution of geckos. *Proc. zool. Soc. Lond.* **124**, 469–492.

Versluys, J. (1898). Die mittlere und äussere Ohrsphäre der Lacertilia und Rhynchocephalia. *Zool. Jb., Abt. Anat.* **12**, 161–406.

Versluys, J. (1903). Entwicklung der Columella auris bei den Lacertiliern. Ein Beitrag zur Kenntniss der schalleitenden Apparate und des Zungenbeinbogens bei den Sauropsiden. *Zool. Jb., Abt. Anat.* **19**, 107–188.

de Villiers, C. G. S. (1939). Über den Schädel des Südafrikanischen schlangenartigen Scinciden *Acontias meleagris. Anat. Anz.* **88**, 320–347.

Watson, D. M. S. (1953). Evolution of the mammalian ear. *Evolution, Lancaster, Pa.* **7**, 159–177.

Watson, D. M. S. (1954). On *Bolosaurus* and the origin and classification of reptiles. *Bull. Mus. comp. Zool. Harvard* **111**, 297–449.

Werner, C. F. (1960). "Das Gehörorgan der Wirbeltiere und des Menschen." Georg Thieme, Leipzig.

Weston, J. K. (1939). Notes on the comparative anatomy of the sensory areas of the vertebrate inner ear. *J. comp. Neurol.* **70**, 355–394.

Wever, E. G. (1965). Structure and function of the lizard ear. *J. Auditory Res.* **5**, 331–371.

Wever, E. G. (1967a). The tectorial membrane of the lizard ear: Types of structure. *J. Morph.* **122**, 307–320.

Wever, E. G. (1967b). The tectorial membrane of the lizard ear: Species variations. *J. Morph.* **123**, 355–372.

Wever, E. G. (1968). The ear of the chameleon: *Chamaeleo senegalensis* and *Chamaeleo quilensis. J. exp. Zool.* **168**, 423–436.

Wever, E. G. and Hepp-Reymond, M.-C. (1967). Auditory sensitivity in the fan-toed gecko, *Ptyodactylus hasselquistii puiseuxi* Boutan. *Proc. natn. Acad. Sci. U.S.A.* **57**, 681–687.

Wever, E. G. and Vernon, J. A. (1956). Sound transmission in the turtle's ear. *Proc. natn. Acad. Sci. U.S.A.* **42**, 292–299.

Wever, E. G. and Vernon, J. A. (1957). Auditory responses in the spectacled caiman. *J. cell. comp. Physiol.* **50**, 333–339.

Wever, E. G., Peterson, E. A., Crowley, D. E. and Vernon, J. A. (1964). Further studies of hearing in the gekkonid lizards. *Proc. natn. Acad. Sci. U.S.A.* **51**, 561–567.

Wever, E. G., Vernon, J. A., Crowley, D. E. and Peterson, E. A. (1965). Electrical output of lizard ear: Relation to hair-cell population. *Science, N.Y.* **150**, 1172–1174.

Wever, E. G., Vernon, J. A., Peterson, E. A. and Crowley, D. E. (1963). Auditory responses in the Tokay gecko. *Proc. natn. Acad. Sci. U.S.A.* **50**, 806–811.

Wiedersheim, R. (1875). Zur Anatomie und Physiologie des *Phyllodactylus europaeus*, mit besonderer Berücksichtigung des Aquaeductus Vestibuli der Ascaloboten im Allgemeinen. *Morph. Jb.* **3**, 495–534.

Wyeth, F. J. (1924). The development of the auditory apparatus in *Sphenodon punctatus*, with an account of the visceral pouches, aortic arches and other accessory structures. *Phil. Trans. R. Soc.* (B) **212**, 259–366.

K

CHAPTER 4

The Pit Organs of Snakes

ROBERT BARRETT

*Department of Zoology, University of California at Los Angeles,
Los Angeles, California, U.S.A.*

with appendices by

P. F. A. MADERSON

*Department of Biology,
Brooklyn College of the City University of New York, New York, U.S.A.*

and

RICHARD M. MESZLER*

*Department of Anatomy, School of Medicine
University of Louisville, Louisville, Kentucky, U.S.A.*

I. Introduction

Heat and cold are obvious aspects of the environment, and the level and availability of thermal energy affect almost all biological processes. It is not surprising, therefore, that organisms have evolved a spectrum of behavioral, physiological, and structural adaptations for effective response to the thermal states of their environments.

It is now well established that reptiles maintain rather constant temperature levels; their sensitivity is very high in behavioral situations involving sunning and shading, burrowing, and locomotion, and their thermal preference range is narrow. For example, a sidewinder (*Crotalus cerastes*) has been observed to maintain its body state within the narrow limits of 31° and 32° C, even when relatively inactive (Cowles and Bogert, 1944). A slow moving desert species such as a horned lizard (*Phrynosoma*) has very precise control (Heath, 1965). Desert iguanas (*Dipsosaurus dorsalis*) have been shown to maintain body temperature at a 38·5° level, and their orientation to the sun, positions on the substrate, and movements through their natural en-

*Present Address: Department of Anatomy, Albert Einstein College of Medicine, New York, U.S.A.

vironments all indicate a high degree of sensitivity to spatial and temporal distributions of temperature (DeWitt, 1963). Saint Girons and Saint Girons (1956) have reviewed behavioral thermoregulation in reptiles.

These narrow ranges of optimal temperatures are effected not only by thermoregulatory behavior, but undoubtedly also by physiological compensations, both of which are links in the chain of events by which an organism responds to temperature changes. This chapter considers a highly specialized sensing of the environmental state, the receptor mechanisms by means of which certain reptiles detect external thermal stimuli emitted by their prey. Two groups of snakes possess what appear to be the most sensitive and specialized thermal receptors known: the facial pits of the Crotalinae, a subfamily of the family Viperidae, and the labial scales of some snakes of the family Boidae. Both detect infra-red radiation of relatively long wavelengths, and have special morphological and functional properties which make them remarkably sensitive to changes in their thermal environment. The structure and functions of these mechanisms are dealt with here. Maderson, in an appendix to this chapter, lists the numbers and locations of pit organs in the Boidae and Meszler in a second appendix provides more recent information on ultrastructure and function.

II. Diffused Temperature Receptors

Temperature receptors are known to exist at many phylogenetic levels (see the comprehensive reviews of Murray, 1962a, 1962b), but until recently most physiological studies had utilized homoiotherms. In man, heat receptors are distributed in a punctate fashion over the body in varying degrees of density (Zotterman, 1959). These receptors appear to be morphologically unspecialized tapered free nerve endings abundant in both the epidermis and dermis, having lower thresholds for temperature changes than other nerve fibers and possibly for steady state temperatures as well.

A recent neuroanatomical study of the cutaneous innervation of lizards (Miller and Kasahara, 1967) indicates that the tapered free nerve endings so common in the epidermis of man occur in the dermis, but only infrequently enter the epidermis. Small to medium sized myelinated fibers with "expanded-tip" endings are most numerous in the epidermis and are found over the whole body. The authors conclude that "this type of epidermal innervation is unique to the reptiles," thus corroborating earlier work (Jaburek, 1926). It is possible that some of these may be involved in temperature reception.

The fact that the reptilian epidermis lacks the type of free nerve ending most often associated with thermal reception in mammals is hardly evidence that reptiles are insensitive to temperature over large areas of the body. Thermal receptors may exist, perhaps in a different form. The skin of most reptiles possesses specialized sensory "pores" or "plaques" (Miller and

Kasahara, 1967; "pits" or "tubercles" of Underwood, 1967) located on scales of both head and body. Miller and Kasahara (1967) describe the living epidermal cells in these areas as taller than in the non-specialized areas and very well innervated by the expanded tip nerve terminals. The keratinized layers of skin are either thicker or thinner than in the surrounding skin and take on a "lenslike" appearance (Miller and Kasahara, 1967). They tentatively postulate that "this area might be sensitive to some type of radiant energy" (p. 559). Regions of concentrated and specialized cells in the epidermis of *Sphenodon* resembling the ocelli of insects, although dissimilar from those described by Miller and Kasahara (1967), lead Maderson (1968) to a similar suggestion. Underwood distinguishes two kinds of "scale organs" on the basis of size and shape, "pits" and "tubercles". He finds tubercles on all snakes, with pits confined to Caenophidia. Many snakes have these tubercles widely distributed on the head and body. Tubercles are slightly convex "scale organs" with refractive edges, while the larger pits have slight depressions, thinner cuticle and no refractive outline. He says that "their distribution on the heads of colubrids suggests that perhaps the tubercles are tactile and the pits radiant receptors" (p. 42).

Nevertheless, substantive physiological evidence as to the function of these specialized structures is lacking. Functional data is also absent concerning the presence of non-specialized heat receptors spread over the body walls. Bullock and Diecke (1956), who recorded from the cutaneous nerves of the ventral skin of crotalids and colubrids, did not obtain responses to temperature changes. Bullock and Barrett (1968) found that the cutaneous nerves on the side of the body wall of boid snakes had touch rather than heat sensitive fibers. They concluded that "there may be a group of small diameter fibers mediating this modality [heat], but . . . these must be scarce since small bundles show no discharge to warmth" (p. 25). Bullock has observed no behavioral avoidance when solar rays were focused on the skin of crotalids over periods of time much longer than permitted by his own pain threshold (personal communication).

There is some evidence that the reptilian brain monitors blood temperature. Correlations have been established between reptilian brain temperatures and circulatory responses (Robard et al., 1950), between head temperatures and thermoregulatory behavior (Heath, 1964), and between brain temperatures and general thermoregulatory behavior (Hammel et al., 1967). A recent and provocative study points to the existence of "warm" and "cold" neurons in the reptilian brain, which may be possible antecedents to the mammalian hypothalamic thermostat (Cabanac et al., 1967). The possible role of the pineal in temperature detection is as yet unclear.

Thus, there still exists the question of how most reptiles, for whom ambient temperatures are critical and who maintain an activity temperature within very narrow limits, detect temperature changes. Problems of body temperature regulation and control, that is, the compensating thermoregulatory mechanisms developed for producing, conserving, or dissipating body heat, are beyond the scope of this chapter.

III. Radiant Heat Receptors

A. THE FACIAL PITS OF THE CROTALINAE

1. *Introduction*

The "pit vipers," of the subfamily Crotalinae are so-called because they bear a pit on each side of the face between the nostril and the eye. The Old World vipers (Viperinae) lack these facial pits, although Lynn (1935) describes "nasal sacs" under the supranasal scale of some viperines (*Pseudocerastes, Bitis,* and *Causus*) very similar to the facial pit. The Crotalinae range throughout Southern Asia, the adjacent Indo-Australian archipelago, and North and South America.

The existence of a facial depression as a unique character of certain vipers has long been known, since they were first dissected by Tyson in 1682. In 1824 Desmoulins observed that the pits were richly innervated and was the first to emphasize their probably sensory nature. West (1900) first provided a comprehensive anatomical account of the pits.

Lynn (1931) reviewed these and other early studies (see also Klauber, 1956), and was the first to use fresh specimens. He examined the copperhead (*Agkistrodon contortrix*) and identified the nerve terminals in the membrane of the pit as cell bodies, rather than axonal swellings. Noble (1934) and Noble and Schmidt (1937) were the first to characterize the "small knob-like enlargements" widely distributed in the epidermis of the pit membrane as nerve terminals. Bullock and Fox (1957) made an extensive histological examination of the pit membrane, using light microscopy and demonstrating the presence of an unusual concentration of free nerve endings in the membrane.

Lynn (1931) also summarized seven early hypotheses regarding the function of the facial pit and added an eighth—that they serve to detect air vibrations. Behavioral observations by Noble and Schmidt (1937) suggested a function in the detection of air temperature (as well as air vibrations). Not until Bullock and Cowles (1952) and Bullock and Diecke (1956) presented electrophysiological evidence was it demonstrated that the facial pit was a highly specialized receptor of infra-red radiation.

2. *Anatomy of the Facial Pit*

The facial pits are prominently located on either side of the broad face of the crotalines, between the eye and nostril (Fig. 1). Although their position varies slightly in different species, the pits always face forwards and their

FIG. 1. View of the head of black-tailed rattlesnake, *Crotalus molossus*, to show right pit in oblique view and tongue fully extended. (San Diego Zoo Photo by Ron Garrison).

anterior edge is scalloped so that both are visible in anterior view. The cavity is not limited to the skin, but occupies a corresponding depression of the maxillary bone (Dullemeijer, 1959). The pit is about 5 mm deep in snakes about 1·5 m long, and its base is much wider than its opening. A membrane about 10 μ thick effectively divides the cavity into two chambers (Fig. 2). The membrane is broken by a small pore, so that the inner cavity is connected to the outer near its posteromedial edge. This pore is hidden under the edge of the lower preocular scale and may be controlled by a sphincter muscle (Lynn, 1931).

The membrane represents the sensory component of the facial pit. In this thin tissue is concentrated almost the total nerve supply of two of the main divisions (ophthalmic and maxillary) of the Vth (trigeminal) cranial nerve.

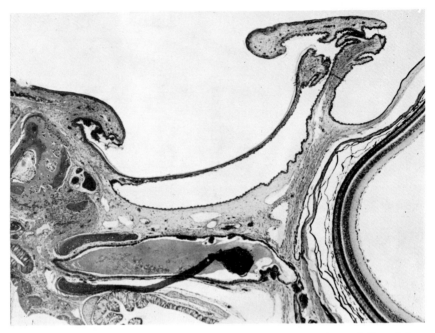

FIG. 2. Cross section of facial pit of *Agkistrodon contortrix* showing membrane dividing pit into anterior and posterior chambers (from Cordier, 1964).

The membrane is bounded on either side by cornified 0·5 to 1·5 μ thick epidermal layers (Bullock and Fox, 1957). A dermal connective tissue layer of about the same thickness lies beneath each epidermal layer. In the middle is the thickest layer, often called "parenchymal" as it contains nucleate cells with a granular cytoplasm. Cordier (1964), on the basis of light microscopy, describes these parenchyma cells as modified dermal cells, resembling histiocytes. This central layer also shows a high concentration of vascular beds and rich innervation. The density of this neural investment, associated with heavy vascularization in a 10 μ thick tissue, becomes surprising when we realize that the red blood cells of reptiles are generally greater in diameter than are those of mammals, which themselves average 7·7 μ.

The nerve endings themselves present the most remarkable picture of all. The pit is supplied from the major portion of the trigeminal nerve, apart from the mandibular branch. Bullock and Fox (1957) showed by degeneration studies that each branch supplied a different area of the membrane. The axons (Fig. 3) fan out, lose their myelin sheaths, taper to 1 or 2 μ, and then each "suddenly expands into a very broad palmate structure from which 3 to 7, usually 5 or 6, processes spring to branch repeatedly and end as

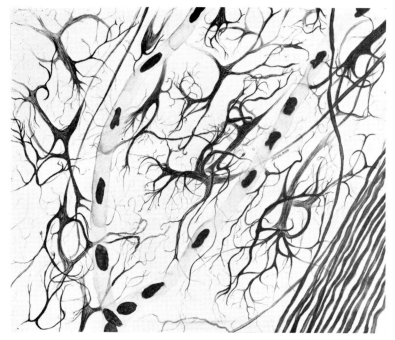

FIG. 3. Silver stained whole mount of the membrane from the facial pit of *Crotalus viridis* showing nerve endings (from Bullock and Fox, 1957).

exceedingly fine, free endings" (p. 224). The branching is irregular, there is little overlap of adjacent "palms," and neither "palms" nor their branches appear to anastomose.

The unique geometrical pattern may allow the nerve fibers to fire after very small changes in temperature. These free nerve endings are the site of generator potentials (Terashima *et al.*, 1968) which are subthreshold and graded. The spatial configuration of the endings, by allowing these potentials to propagate decrementally without interfering with each other, could facilitate the summation of these generator potentials at the axon-palm junction leading to the production of an all-or-none action potential.

The dense packing of free nerve endings has recently attracted the interest of electron microscopists, beginning with Bleichmar and de Robertis (1962). These authors have confirmed much of Bullock and Fox's (1957) work, and gave additional details on the ultrastructure of the membrane (Fig. 4). The basic subdivisions of two epithelial layers and the connective tissue between them is confirmed. The "outer and inner connective layers" are distinguished from the rest of the connective tissue filling the membrane on the basis of a higher concentration of collagen fibers; this may explain Bullock and Fox's

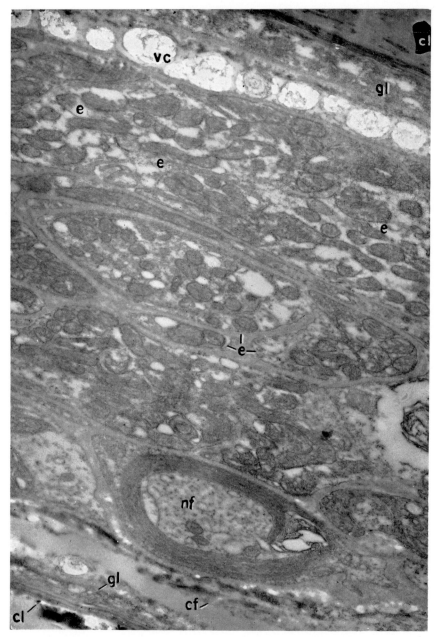

FIG. 4. Electronmicrograph of a section across the whole thickness of the sensory membrane of *Crotalus durissus terrificus*. cf, Collagen fibers; cl, corneal layer; e, nerve endings; gl, germinative layer; nf, nerve fiber; vc, vcauolar cell. 24,500 × (from Bleichmar and de Robertis, 1962).

report that this stratum stains differently. A layer of vacuolar cells lies between the outer connective layer and the nerve endings, in contact with the collagen of the outer layers. Bleichmar and de Robertis (1962) also observed the rich supply, to the membrane, of nerve fibers that are grouped into trunks and gradually taper down to the palmate endings.

There is hence not the "total discrepancy" between light and electron microscopic observations claimed by Cordier (1964), although the higher resolution of the electron microscope does force some revision of our descriptions. Bleichmar and de Robertis (1962) show that the "parenchyma cells" of light microscopists are really masses of free nerve endings with extremely dense concentrations of mitochondria. The "cytoplasm" of the cells actually consists of some of the branches of palmate endings filled with mitochondria, while the "nuclei" are the small vacuolated cells lying beneath the outer epithelium. It is furthermore shown that the nerve endings are even more compactly organized than originally thought and comprise at least half the total thickness of the membrane.

It might still be postulated, however, that the vacuolated cells noted by Bleichmar and de Robertis (1962) and the parenchyma cells reported by Bullock and Fox (1957) are the same, leaving even less discrepancy between light and electron microscopic results.

Further details are available from studies (Terashima, 1968) on two Asiatic pit vipers, *Trimeresurus f. flavoviridis* and *T. okinavensis*. The nerve endings in the membrane seem to have three distinct parts—the myelinated nerve fiber, the nonmyelinated palmate structure, and the "terminal nerve mass." This latter complex, about 15 μ in diameter, is composed of fine branchlets surrounding Schwann cell bodies. The branchlets also contain very high concentrations of mitochondria. Those branchlets, which are on the surface of the nerve mass, are free from the Schwann cytoplasm which otherwise meshes with the endings, and can thus be directly exposed to infrared radiation impinging on the membrane. Terashima also interprets the so-called "parenchyma cells" as sections of the terminal nerve mass.

The thinness of the sensory membrane and the closeness of nerve endings to the surface (possibly as close as 2 μ) would tend to increase the sensitivity of the organ to stimuli. In man, for comparison, the temperature receptors lie at a depth of 300 μ. In addition, the overhang of the pit, resulting from the diameter of its opening being less than half that of the membrane, confers by its geometry the possibility of detecting directionality of the stimulus. Sharply defined cones of reception occur and their boundaries overlap directly ahead of the animal (Bullock and Diecke, 1956).

3. *Physiology of the Crotaline Facial Pit*

Data on the function of the pits initially derived primarily from behavioral observation. Noble (1934), Noble and Schmidt (1937), and Noble (1945) demonstrated that when the pits were the only cephalic sensory organs remaining functional, snakes could still distinguish between moving electric light bulbs of different temperatures and could use the sensory input to aim a strike. Measuring air temperatures near the bulb, the authors found that the animal could discriminate temperature differences of less than 0·2° C. Since the behavioral threshold was determined by whether or not the animal made a strike, it is possible that the animal recognized the warm object at even lower levels of stimulation.

Noble and Schmidt (1937) concluded that the pits "serve to detect the body temperature of the snakes' prey," and also that "they have the additional function of detecting air vibrations" (p. 263). They came close to a correct statement, but since they referred only to air temperature and not *radiant* heat energy, they were unable to explain how body temperature was detected. The pit receptors of snakes cannot measure body temperatures, but rather respond to changes in the *surface* temperatures of the sensory background being examined.

This thermal receptor has been shown to be one of the most sensitive possessed by any animal (Bullock and Cowles, 1952; Bullock and Diecke, 1956); it can respond to changes in temperature (of water flowing on the membrane) of 0·003° C. To be detected, a stimulus need only be warmer or colder than the background temperatures, where background refers to the dominant, integrated radiating sources in the field of view. These are usually solid objects whose surfaces are radiators acting as black bodies. The response is independent of the absolute or relative level of the ambient *or* body temperatures. A positive response, i.e., an increase in the frequency of firing, occurs when the stimulus is warmer than the background or than the surface temperatures most recently sensed in the field of view. Inhibition of the discharge occurs when the stimulus is cooler than the background. No response at all is obtained from sound, odor, vibration of the substratum, or heat-filtered light, and only secondary minor response to touch and air movement.

An unusual feature of the nerve fibers is that they are all warm receptors, increasing the frequency of their response when temperatures are raised. This is in contrast to mammalian cutaneous nerves, in which warm fibers are much scarcer than cold units. The physiological properties of these fibers differ in several other respects from those of heat receptors studied in other animals (see Table I). Spontaneous discharge, that is a continuous activity without any known stimulus, is consistently observed (Bullock and Diecke, 1956) and is irregular and fluctuating. Such spontaneous discharge is characteristic of many peripheral sensory systems (Granit, 1955), and is also present in the labial pits of boas (see below). It may be advantageous in enhancing sensitivity and conferring two-way detection since the nerve is responsive to both warming and cooling. Yet it is difficult to explain the adaptive value of the irregular, nonrhythmic feature, since lack of rhythmicity may affect the sensitivity of the warm receptors and interfere with the central system's analysis of input. Spontaneous discharge must increase sensitivity but irregularity must decrease temporal resolution of brief or successive stimuli unless very complex integrative processes are employed by the central nervous system (Bullock, 1956).

The responses to heat stimuli are mainly phasic: the frequency of neural impulses returns toward the original level in spite of a maintained stimulus (adaptation). The rate of adaptation depends on the intensity of the stimuli; it is rapid to a weak stimulus and very slow to a strong one. There is little change in the maintained steady state discharge when the receptor organ is stimulated by different constant temperatures. The opposite is true in mammalian fibers, and a steady state response is probably one of their principal features (Hensel, 1966). But in the snakes, although the receptor is much more sensitive to small changes in temperature, it is much less sensitive to *maintained* temperatures.

The preceding work was done on specimens of *Crotalus viridis*, *C. ruber*, *C. mitchelli*, *C. cerastes*, *C. atrox*, *C. horridus*, *C. adamanteus*, and *Agkistrodon piscivorus*, all New World species (Bullock and Diecke, 1956). Our knowledge of the facial pit has been widened by the work of Goris and Nomoto (1967) on the Oriental crotalines, *Trimeresurus f. flavoviridis*, *T. okinavensis*, and *Agkistrodon halys*. All showed response to infra-red radiant stimuli, even though these species are widely separated ecologically. This suggests that the facial pits function similarly in all members of the Crotalinae.

Generator or receptor potentials have been recorded from a number of sense organs in recent years. These potentials are distinguished from self-propagating and "all-or-none" action potentials in being confined to the terminals, in representing actual changes in the trans-membrane potential of the nerve endings, and in being graded and non-propagating. They are local excitations which reflect the transduction of various forms of energy to an electrical change, and are a sort of go-between between the stimulus and the resulting action potential.

Until recently, no one had recorded generator potentials from temperature receptors. In what must certainly be described as a technical tour de force, generator potentials have now been recorded from the terminal nerve ramifications in the sensory membrane of the facial pits of Oriental crotalines (Terashima *et al.*, 1968).

In order to record the potentials the external cornified layer of the thin membrane had to be carefully stripped. This exposed the central layer in which the neural endings lay, but compounded the recording difficulties, since the cornified layers contribute rigidity to the membrane. In addition, the combined neural and vascular layers are less than 10 μ thick, and the micro-electrodes had to be inserted at an acute angle to effect penetration. The generator potentials appeared as slow potential changes, normally in a negative direction, with a maximum amplitude of 500 microvolts in extra-cellular recordings. Terashima *et al.* (1968) found that the potentials were strongest at the center of the membrane, weaker towards its edges, and absent where it was shadowed by the overhanging lips of the pits.

Very little is known of the mechanisms by which one form of energy, in this case heat, is transduced to another, here the electrical nerve impulse. We are closest to answers in the study of vision. The photochemical steps in the breakdown of visual pigment have been elucidated, and an "early receptor potential," which is a direct consequence of the photochemical molecular event, has been recorded in response to brief high intensity flashes (Brown *et al.*, 1965). As the authors state (p. 480): "It seems to be the first case where an essentially instantaneous end-product of a biological chemo-electric trans-duction has been detected and identified."

In the case of infra-red heat receptors, photochemistry can hardly be ex-pected to play a role, since the low amount of energy in the longer infra-red wavelengths is insufficient to account for transduction to electrical energy. The nerves of the pit may respond to temperature change of the tissue due to its general absorption of radiant energy rather than, as in the eye, to specific wavelengths (Bullock and Diecke, 1956).

Bleichmar and de Robertis (1962) present a provocative hypothesis as to the significance of the large concentration of mitochondria present in the nerve endings. Since no morphologically specialized sensory elements exist at the nerve ending, the mitochondria themselves may be involved in the transduction of temperature change to electrical neural activity. Such a transducing mechanism could provide the energy required, perhaps by enzymatic changes (see Appendix II).

In an initial histochemical analysis of the pit membrane, Meszler and Webster (1968) have demonstrated the presence of some enzymes that could function as transducers. These include succinic dehydrogenase and ATPase, both of which are, like the mitochondria, concentrated in the center of the membrane and could supply the extra metabolic energy required for de-polarization of the nerve ending. Lactic dehydrogenase, a key glycolytic agent, and the enzyme acetylcholine esterase are also present.

The facial pit offers great potential for further exploration of the sensory transduction mechanism, and reptiles may well provide the experimental material that will permit students of sensory physiology and anatomy to answer some of these problems.

B. Labial Pits (Boidae)

1. *Introduction*

Integumentary areas on the face of snakes of the family Boidae* have been shown to be sensitive to radiant heat (Bullock and Barrett, 1968; Warren and Proske, 1968). This sensitivity is concentrated on the labial scales in areas innervated by the trigeminal nerve. Some members of this family have pits on certain of the labial scales (Figs 5 and 6), and these attracted the attention of early observers. Owen (1866), Gadow (1901), and Ditmars (1910) all commented on the presence of these pits and speculated on their function. Lynn (1931) briefly described the histological structure, and Ros (1935) and Noble and Schmidt (1937) presented behavioral evidence as to their function. Bullock and Barrett (1968) and Warren and Proske (1968) presented electrophysiological evidence of their function as radiant heat receptors. Bullock and Barrett (1968) also surveyed three other snake families for the presence or absence of such localized sensitivity, and reported that the presence of sensitivity to heat is not dependent on the existence of pits, since reception of infra-red radiant heat was demonstrated in species of boids completely lacking them.

2. *Anatomy and Innervation of the Labial Pits*

Like the crotaline facial pit, the boid labial pits are innervated by the trigeminal nerve complex with its three main branches: ophthalmic, maxillary, and mandibular. The location of pits on the scales of those snakes possessing them varies (Lynn, 1931). Some genera have pits on all labial, supralabial, infralabial, and the rostral scales; in others the pits either are reduced in number and/or in size or are absent (see Appendix I). The rostral pit is typically innervated by the ophthalmic branch (Lynn, 1931); however, the rostral pit of *Morelia argus* is innervated by the maxillary branch which also innervates the pits of the upper labial while the mandibular branch goes to the infralabial scales (Warren and Proske, 1968).

Labial pits are shallow depressions and lack the thin membrane of the facial pit. In fact, according to Ros (1935), the only feature distinguishing the lining of the bottom of the pit from the rest of the animal's skin is a capillary net deep to the epidermis. Noble and Schmidt (1937) state that the nerve supply of the pit is far richer, that there is greater vascularity, and that the epidermis is thinner than in the surrounding areas. There is no abrupt transition between the connective tissue and the epidermis, as is common in the skin outside the pit (Bullock and Barrett, 1968).

---

*For an explanation of the Latin names used here, see the second paragraph of Appendix I (p.301)

A.

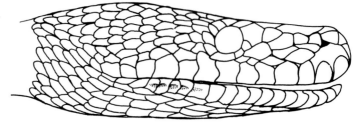

B.

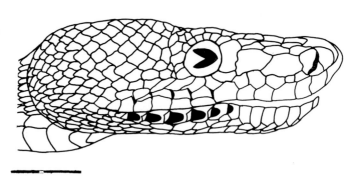

C.

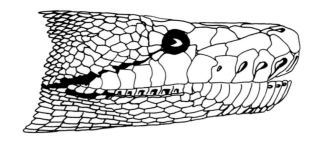

D.

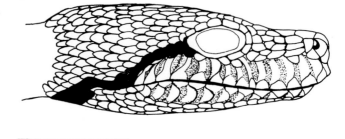

Filaments arise from preterminal axonal "globose swellings" about 20 μ in diameter and extend into the outermost regions of skin at the bottom of the pit (Warren and Proske, 1968). These filaments then also expand and in turn give rise to fine filaments, which lie in the a-layer of the skin (see Maderson, 1964, for description of various layers of reptilian skin). No such axonal swellings occur outside of the pits.

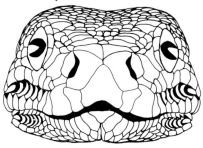

FIG. 6. Anterior view of *Corallus enydris cookii* to show how the two sets of labial pits face forward. The line measures 1 cm to scale. (Sketch by Marjorie Parmenter, courtesy V. C. Hutchison.)

The important question as to how far the nerve endings invade the epidermis is still unanswered. Noble and Schmidt (1937), using modified Gros silver nitrate techniques, stained many of the fibers "completely," yet failed to state how closely the nerve endings approached the external surface of the epithelium. Bullock and Barrett (1968), using light microscopy, observed that the nerve fibers invaded the epidermal layers to within 25 μ of the external surface, and electron microscopy now places them "immediately below the cornified surface" (Meszler, Appendix II to this chapter).

Examination of crotaline embryos (Noble and Schmidt, 1937) revealed that each facial pit arises from two invaginations very similar to boid labial pits, the intervening wall between them becoming the facial pit membrane. They refer to "many similarities", neural, anatomical, and ontogenetic, between the crotalid facial pit and the boid labial pit. This is at some variance with Lynn's (1931) earlier view that the only anatomical point of similarity between the two structures is the source of innervation.

3. *Physiology of the Boid Labial Pits*

Knowledge of the function of the labial pits stemmed initially from the behavioral observations of Ros (1935) and Noble and Schmidt (1937). Ros concluded that the pits on the scales of a single specimen of *Python sebae* re-

FIG. 5. Sketches showing various placements of labial pits in members of the Boidae (compare with Appendix I). Each line measures 1 cm to scale. A, *Python sebae*; B, *Corallus enydris cookii*; C, *Python reticulatus*; D, *Sanzinia madagascariensis*, note interscalar pit placement. (Sketches by Marjorie Parmenter, courtesy V. C. Hutchison.)

sponded to heat waves and air vibrations. Noble and Schmidt (1937) repeated their facial pit experiments on boids and showed that these animals could also distinguish bodies of different temperatures by the pits alone; they concluded that the pit functioned mainly to detect warm objects in motion. Again, they did not conceive of this as a radiant heat response, but rather as a receptivity to air temperatures.

Bullock and Barrett (1968) have now extended these behavioral findings and have shown a remarkable similarity in electrophysiological responses between the labial scales and the facial pits. The labial scales also respond primarily to radiant heat in the intermediate to long infra-red wavelengths, and are only about four times less sensitive than the crotaline pits expressed in terms of changes in calorific flux: $1\cdot3 \times 10^{-3}$ calories/cm²/sec⁻¹ (labial), compared to $3\cdot15 \times 10^{-4}$ (facial). Neither organ responds to light, sounds, vibration, odors, or gentle air movement without temperature change. Neither body temperatures of the snake nor air temperatures have significant effects on the response. An effective stimulus is one that is warmer than the general environmental background.

There are other close physiological similarities with the facial pit. The spontaneous or "resting" discharge is again irregular, and at the same time has within the arhythmicity a slow cyclic fluctuation, which is unrelated to heart beat or respiration (Fig. 7). This slow cycle is more evident in the labial scale than in the facial pit (Bullock and Barrett, 1968). Those boid scales with pits possess a directional receptivity, although it is not as sharply defined and lacks the frontal overlap noted in crotalines. Warren and Proske (1968) believe that since the pits in *Morelia argus* have a wider distribution on the face with a greater angle than do those of crotalines (there are rostral as well as upper and lower labial pits), they may have a greater radiant background to which to respond. Almost all the fibers in the branches innervating the pits are temperature receptors, with only a small number of tactile fibers; they are almost entirely heat receptors, being inhibited by cold. Close parallels can also be drawn, quantitatively and qualitatively, between the two types of pits regarding the various phases of excitability which can be recorded.

Thus these two sensory organs, from widely separated families of snakes,

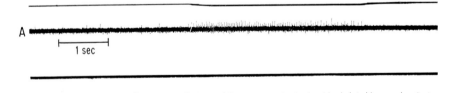

A

|— 1 sec —|

B

Fig. 7. A comparison of spontaneous discharge and stimulated discharge in a typical labial pit preparation of *Corallus enydris cookii*.

differ more in their anatomy and topography than in their physiology. Both are innervated by the trigeminal complex, and the differences result from the presence of the thin membrane in the facial pit. Its shape, depth, and location probably account for some of the relatively small physiological differences (e.g., greater sensitivity and directionality in crotalines).

The function of the labial pits has also been studied by Warren and Proske (1968) who recorded responses from the labial pits (*not* "facial pits") of the python *Morelia argus*. Their results confirm that the labial scales detect radiant heat.

The work on labial pit receptors summarized above has been limited to recording from peripheral neural elements in one or another of the three main branches of the trigeminal complex. A preliminary investigation of responses recorded from the midbrain of boids (*Corallus enydris cookii*) reveals that the integrative processes of the central nervous system confer increased sensitivity to duration, distance, and movement of target (Barrett, unpublished). Evoked potentials vary in wave form, amplitude, and latency depending upon the angle of the thermal stimulus in relation to the pits, on what side of the face it appears, and in what direction it is moving.

4. *Role of the Labial Pits*

It is curious and interesting that species of boids *without* pits are still sensitive to radiant heat (Bullock and Barrett, 1968) although *Eunectes murinus*, the anaconda, which lacks pits, has fewer warm units and more tactile units than do boids with labial pits. The function of the pits is probably to increase directional sensitivity to stimuli. The larger concentrations of nerve endings in the pits may also confer increased sensitivity by lowering the response threshold through summation from a spatially limited zone.

C. COMPARISON OF THE TWO SENSORY ORGANS WITH OTHER THERMAL RECEPTORS

A comparison is made in Table I of some of the principal vertebrate thermal receptors that have been examined electrophysiologically. Many of the general responses to stimulation are much the same in the different receptors, but there are some important differences. While the heat receptors of homoiotherms show a steady (tonic) discharge at a frequency which is dependent on absolute temperatures (Hensel and Zotterman, 1951; Dodt and Zotterman, 1952; Hensel et al., 1960), the response of snakes is primarily phasic, soon returning to its original "resting" discharge. The steady state discharge to a constant absolute temperature so prominent in the cat's tongue, for example, is reduced or lacking. In the cat there is paradoxical discharge upon a sudden cooling of warm fibers or a sudden warming of cold fibers. This does not appear in the response of the labial or facial pits.

TABLE I

Comparison of Some Vertebrate Thermal Receptors

Receptor Site	Fiber Type	Specificity	Type of Response	Sensitivity to Rapid Change	Innervation	Authority
Facial Pit (crotalines)	A (myelinated)	warm fibers only; touch secondary	Phasic: fast adaptation to weak stimuli; slow to strong	$0 \cdot 003°C (3 \cdot 15 \times 10^{-4}$ cal/cm²/sec⁻¹)	Trigeminal (ophthalmic and maxillary branches)	Bullock and Diecke (1956)
Labial Pit (boids)	A	warm fibers only; touch secondary	Phasic: fast adaptation to weak stimuli; slow to strong	approximately $0 \cdot 026°C (1 \cdot 3 \times 10^{-3}$ cal/cm²/sec⁻¹)	Trigeminal (ophthalmic, maxillary, and mandibular branches)	Bullock and Barrett (1968); Warren and Proske (1968)
Tongue (cat)	A	separate warm and cold fibers; mostly cold	Tonic mainly (cold fibers); phasic in warm fibers	$1°C$	Trigeminal (lingual nerve of mandibular branch)	Zotterman (1936); Hensel and Zotterman (1951); Dodt and Zotterman (1952)
Skin of leg (cat)	C (unmyelinated)	cold and warm fibers	Tonic mainly (cold fibers); phasic in warm fibers	$0 \cdot 2°C$	Saphenous	Hensel, Iggo, and Witt (1960); Iriuchijima and Zotterman (1960)
Skin of hand (man)	A	cold; cold-pressure; no warm fibers	Tonic	−5 impulses/sec/°C ("dynamic sensitivity")	Radial	Hensel and Bowman (1960)
Cornea (cat)	A and C	specific warm and cold fibers; touch and pain	Phasic	$0 \cdot 058°C-7 \cdot 47°C$	Trigeminal (ciliary nerve of ophthalmic branch)	Dawson (1963)
Skin of face (hibernating hamster)	A and C	cold and pressure fibers	Tonic	−4·2 impulses/sec/°C ("dynamic sensitivity")	Trigeminal (infra-orbital nerve)	Raths et al. (1964)

D. FUNCTIONAL SIGNIFICANCE OF THE FACIAL PIT AND LABIAL PITS

Representative species from the snake families and subfamilies Colubridae, Hydrophidae, and Viperinae were surveyed for heat reception via the

TABLE II

Presence or Absence of Sensitivity to Radiant Heat in
Trigeminally Innervated Receptors in the Skin of the Face
(After Bullock and Barrett, 1968)

Family and Species	Response Present (+) or Absent (0)	Pits Present (+) or Absent (0)	Authority
BOIDAE			
Boa constrictor	+	0	Bullock and Barrett (1968)
Corallus annulata	+	+	Bullock and Barrett (1968)
C. caninus	+	+	Bullock and Barrett (1968)
C. enydris enydris	+	+	Bullock and Barrett (1968)
C. enydris cookii	+	+	Bullock and Barrett (1968)
Eunectes murinus	+	0	Bullock and Barrett (1968)
Lichanura roseofusca	+	0	Bullock and Barrett (1968)
Liasis amethistinus	+	+	Bullock and Barrett (1968)
Morelia argus	+	+	Warren and Proske (1968)
COLUBRIDAE			
Pseustes poecilonotus	0	0	Bullock and Barrett (1968)
Elaphe obsoleta	0	0	Bullock and Barrett (1968)
E. guttata	0	0	Bullock and Barrett (1968)
Lampropeltis getulus	0	0	Bullock and Barrett (1968)
Thamnophis sp.	0	0	Bullock and Barrett (1968)
Pituophis catenifer	0	0	Bullock and Barrett (1968)
CROTALINAE			
Agkistrodon halys	+	+	Goris and Nomoto (1967)
A. piscivorus	+	+	Bullock and Diecke (1956)
Crotalus adamanteus	+	+	Bullock and Diecke (1956)
C. atrox	+	+	Bullock and Diecke (1956)
C. cerastes	+	+	Bullock and Diecke (1956)
C. horridus	+	+	Bullock and Diecke (1956)
C. mitchelli	+	+	Bullock and Diecke (1956)
C. ruber	+	+	Bullock and Diecke (1956)
C. viridis	+	+	Bullock and Diecke (1956)
Trimeresurus f. flavoviridis	+	+	Goris and Nomoto (1967)
T. okinavensis	+	+	Goris and Nomoto (1967)
VIPERINAE			
Echis carinatus	0	0	Bullock and Barrett (1968)
HYDROPHIDAE			
Hydrophis major	0	0	Bullock and Barrett (1968)

trigeminal nerve complex (Bullock and Barrett, 1968). While all members of the Crotalinae and Boidae studied display sensitivity to radiant heat, no other snake has been found to possess it. The results (Table II) are unequivocal: the sensitivity is either definitely present or absent. This raises the problem of the selective advantage that accrues to those species that possess this sensitivity.

Both types of pits can function at any temperature in the range at which the snakes are active and are *capable* of directionally detecting prey or predators as well as other environmental features hotter or colder than the general background.

The possession of any thermal receptivity would confer an advantage on snakes that take a significant fraction of warm-blooded prey. The advantage might even exist in seeking certain kinds of ectothermal prey, since reptiles often seem to operate at temperatures slightly different from those of their thermal background, controlling their temperature by utilization of heat sources and sinks. Any sensitivity to infra-red radiation may permit the snake to recognize the existence of prey even when visual or olfactory cues are undetectable or non-diagnostic. Nocturnal or crepuscular species and those that hunt in trees and bushes immediately come to mind. Once the capacity exists it appears obvious to refine the information yield, first by increasing the sensitivity and secondly by assuring symmetry so that left-right differentials may be compared. The first change increases the recognition distance; the second permits the snake to aim its strike.

From observations of the feeding behaviour of rattlesnakes (*Crotalus ruber*), Dullemeijer (1961) believes that the facial pits control the strike. When the prey is dead (thermoneutral) or the pits are covered, there is no strike and the snake approaches the prey and touches it with its tongue. It is significant that the great majority of snakes having these sense organs feed on warm blooded prey and that the boid *Eunectes*, in which minimal sensitivity is found, is an aquatic snake much of whose prey is cold blooded.

A secondary advantage would, of course, result from the use of the pits as aiming devices for defensive strikes, but pits should presumably be regarded primarily as food-getting mechanisms. Another possible role is as detectors of thermal habitats. They might be suitable for detecting breezes of different temperatures and scanning other elements in the habitat such as stones, logs, sunny and shady spots, or holes (Bullock and Barrett, 1968). Some such scanning capacity has been reported for *Trimeresurus flavoviridis* (Goris and Nomoto, 1967). The usefulness of the receptors for controlling body temperature must be limited, however, since a sense organ which is so phasic (i.e., adapts so rapidly) would only be effective very briefly. Furthermore, responses to identical stimuli vary considerably. This would, at the very least, make the information conveyed to the central nervous system rather gross.

In any case, present behavioral evidence is insufficient to warrant definitive statements as to the ethological significance or actual, normal function of these sense organs.

IV. Unanswered Question Requiring Further Research

Advances in the field of reptilian temperature reception have been made in recent years, yet a number of substantive problems remain. For example, one critical, but largely unanswered, question is how do snakes, whose relatively accurate body and habitat temperature requirements are well known, actually sense these conditions in order to act upon the information effectively? Facial and labial pits occur in only 5% of snakes, and it seems doubtful that the trigeminal sensitivity even in these species is actually useful in tonic body or habitat temperature estimation. Thus temperature sensitive structures, whether in skin or deeper, e.g., in the hypothalamic area of the brain, should be sought in all snakes and in other reptiles as well. This search would involve studies of circulatory-nervous relations, particularly in the head region.

The few colubrids with pits similar to the crotalids and boids would also bear examination; for example, *Elachistodon*, an egg-eating snake from India, has a large pit in the posterior part of each nasal scale (Gans and Williams, 1954). Old World vipers (Viperinae) have a structure very similar to the facial pit of the crotalines and the labial pit of the boas (Lynn, 1935). This "supranasal sac" is a sac-like invagination under the supranasal scale, innervated by the ophthalmic branch of the trigeminal nerve, in *Pseudocerastes*, *Bitis*, and *Causus*, and is especially well developed in species of *Bitis*. The physiology of this structure awaits electrophysical investigation.

Ethological observations, represent an obvious path for further research, leading to more definitive behavioral-physiological correlations.

The facial pit is an attractive preparation for further electron microscopic examination of free nerve endings, which might be vital in association with new electrophysiological studies of transduction mechanisms. Nerve degeneration studies using electron microscopy are also germane.

Comparison of the crotaline facial pit with the labial scale pit organs of boas still leaves unanswered the question of their analogy or homology. The physiological profile shared by the two is a striking one, and physiological similarities, especially if they are complex and particular, may be reliable evidence in taxonomic problems (Simpson, 1961). Also their anatomy presents many similarities. In addition to a common source of innervation, the ontogeny of the facial pit indicates that it evolved by a fusion of two invaginations very much like the individual labial pits of boids, with the intervening wall forming the membrane (Noble and Schmidt, 1937). Despite the isolated occurrence of the pits, it is by no means certain that they are only functional analogues. If they are, they represent remarkable examples of convergence; if not, they carry implications for the evolutionary history of snakes. In any case, such speculation deserves further examination, anatomical, physiological, and developmental.

References

Bleichmar, H. and De Robertis, E. (1962). Submicroscopic morphology of the infrared receptor of pit vipers. *Z. Zellforsch. mikrosk. Anat.* **56**, 748–761.

Brown, K. T., Watanabe, K. and Murakami, M. (1965). The early and late receptor potentials of monkey cones and rods. *Cold Spring Harb. Symp. quant. Biol.* **30**, 457–482.

Bullock, T. H. (1956). Neuronal integrative mechanisms. *In* "Recent Advances in Invertebrate Physiology", (B. T. Scheer, ed.). Oregon University Press, Corvallis, **6**, 1–20.

Bullock, T. H. and Barrett, R. (1968). Radiant heat reception in snakes. *Communications in Behavioral Biology*, Part A, **1**, 19–29.

Bullock, T. H. and Cowles, R. B. (1952). Physiology of an infrared receptor: The facial pit of pit vipers. *Science, N.Y.* **115**, 541–543.

Bullock, T. H. and Diecke, F. P. J. (1956). Properties of an infrared receptor. *J. Physiol.* **134**, 47–87.

Bullock, T. H. and Fox, W. (1957). The anatomy of the infrared sense organ in the facial pit of pit vipers. *Q. Jl microsc. Sci.* **98**, 219–234.

Cabanac, M., Hammel, T. and Hardy, J. D. (1967). *Tiliqua scincoides*: Temperature-sensitive units in lizard brain. *Science, N.Y.* **158** (3804), 1050–1051.

Cordier, R. (1964). Sensory cells. *In* "The Cell". (Jean Brachet and Alfred Mirsky, eds) Academic Press, New York, **6** (5), 313–386.

Cowles, R. B. and Bogert, C. M. (1944). A preliminary study of the thermal requirements of desert reptiles. *Bull. Am. Mus. nat. Hist,* **83** (5), 265–296.

Dawson, W. W. (1963). The thermal excitation of afferent neurones in the mammalian cornea and iris. *In* "Temperature: Its Measurement and Control", (C. M. Herzfield, ed.) Reinhold, New York, **3** (3), 199–210.

Desmoulins, A. (1824). Mémoire sur le système nerveux et l'appareil lacrymal des serpents à sonnettes, des trigonocéphales, et de quelques autres serpents. *Magendie J. Phys. exp. Path.* **4**, 264–284.

DeWitt, C. B. (1963). "Behavioral Thermoregulation in the Iguanid Lizard, *Dipsosaurus dorsalis*". University Microfilms, Inc., Ann Arbor, Michigan.

Ditmars, R. L. (1910). "Reptiles of the World". Macmillan, New York.

Dodt, E. and Zotterman, Y. (1952). Mode of action of warm receptors. *Acta physiol. scand.* **26**, 345–357.

Dullemeijer, P. (1959). A comparative functional-anatomical study of the heads of some Viperidae. *Morph. Jb.* **99** (4), 881–985.

Dullemeijer, P. (1961). Some remarks on the feeding behavior of rattlesnakes. *Proc. Acad. Wetensch. Amsterdam*, Ser. C. **64**, 383–396.

Gadow, H. (1901). "Amphibia and Reptiles". The Cambridge Natural History, Macmillan, London. Vol. 8.

Gans, C. and Williams, E. (1954). Present knowledge of the snake *Elachistodon westermanni* Reinhardt. *Breviora* (36), 1–17.

Goris, R. C. and Nomoto, M. (1967). Infrared reception in oriental crotaline snakes. *Comp. Biochem. Physiol.* **23**, 879–892.

Granit, R. (1955). "Receptors and Sensory Perception". Yale University Press, New Haven.

Hammel, H. T. Caldwell, F. T., Jr. and Abrams, A. M. (1967). Regulation of body temperature in the blue-tongued lizard. *Science, N.Y.* **156** (3779), 1260–1262.

Heath, J. (1964). Head-body temperature differences in horned lizards. *Physiol. Zoöl.* **37** (3), 273–279.

Heath, J. (1965). Temperature regulation and diurnal activity in horned lizards. *Univ. Calif. Publs Zool.* **64** (3), 97–136.

Hensel, H. (1966). Classes of receptor units predominantly related to thermal stimuli. *In* "Touch, Heat and Pain". Ciba Foundation Symposium. (A. V. S. de Reuck and J. Knight, eds). Little, Brown & Co., Boston, pp. 275–288.

Hensel, H. and Bowman, K. (1960). Afferent impulses in cutaneous sensory nerves in human subjects. *J.Neurophysiol.* **23**, 564–578.

Hensel, H., Iggo, A. and Witt, I. (1960). A quantitative study of sensitive cutaneous thermoreceptors with C afferent fibres. *J. Physiol.* **153**, 113–126.

Hensel, H. and Zotterman, Y. (1951). The response of mechanoreceptors to thermal stimulation. *J. Physiol.* **115**, 16–24.

Iriuchijima, J. and Zotter man, Y. (1960). The specificity of afferent cutaneous C fibres in mammals. *Acta physiol. scand.* **49**, 267–278.

Jaburek, L. (1926). Über Nervenendigungen in der Epidermis der Reptilien. *Z. mikroskanat. Forsch.* **10**, 1–49.

Klauber, L. M. (1956). "Rattlesnakes". Vol. 1, Univ. California Press, Berkeley.

Lynn, W. G. (1931). The structure and function of the facial pit of the pit vipers. *Am. J. Anat.* **49**, 97–139.

Lynn, W. G. (1935). On the supranasal sac of the Viperinae. *Copeia* **1935**, 9–12.

Maderson, P. F. A. (1964). The skin of lizards and snakes. *Br. J. Herpet.* **3**, 151–154.

Maderson, P. F. A. (1968). Observations on the epidermis of the tuatara (*Sphenodon punctatus*). *J. Anat.* **103**, 311–320.

Meszler, R. M. and Webster, D. B. (1968). Histochemistry of the rattlesnake facial pit. *Copeia* **1968**, 722–728.

Miller, M. R. and Kasahara, M. (1967). Studies on the cutaneous innervation of lizards. *Proc. Calif. Acad. Sci.* **34**, 549–568.

Murray, R. W. (1962a). Temperature receptors in animals. *Symp. Soc. exp. Biol.* **10**, 245–266.

Murray, R. W. (1962b). Temperature receptors. *Adv. Comp. Physiol. Biochem.* **1**, 117–175.

Noble, G. K. (1934). The structure of the facial pit of the pit vipers and its probable function. *Anat. Rec.* **58** (Supp. to no. 2), 4.

Noble, G. K. and Schmidt, A. (1937). The structure and function of the facial and labial pits of snakes. *Proc. Am. phil. Soc.* **77**, 263–288.

Noble, R. C. (1945). "The Nature of the Beast". Garden City Press, New York.

Owen, R. (1866). "On the Anatomy of Vertebrates". Vol. 1. Fishes and Reptiles. Longman, Green, and Co., London.

Raths, P., Witt, I. and Hensel, H. (1964). Thermoreceptoren bei Winterschlafern. *Pflügers Arch. ges. Physiol.* **281**, 73.

Rodbard, S., Samson, F. and Ferguson, D. (1950). Thermosensitivity of the turtle brain as manifested by blood pressure changes. *Am. J. Physiol.* **160**, 402–408.

Ros, M. (1935). Die Lippengruben der Pythonen als Temperaturorgane. *Jena Z. Naturw.* (N.F.) **70**, 1–32.

Saint-Girons, H. and Saint-Girons, M. (1956). Cycle d'activité et thermorégulation chez les reptiles (lézards et serpentes). *Vie Milieu.* **7**, 133–226.

Simpson, G. G. (1961). "Principles of Animal Taxonomy." Columbia University Press, New York.

Terashima, S. I. (1968). Warm fiber terminal structure in the viper pit membrane. (In manuscript).

Terashima, S. I., Goris, R. C. and Katsuki, Y. (1968). Generator potential of crotaline snake infrared receptor. *J.Neurophysiol.* 31, 682–688.

Tyson, E. (1682). Vipera Caudisona Americana, or the anatomy of a rattlesnake, *Phil. Trans. R. Soc.* 13, 25–58.

Underwood, G. (1967). "A Contribution to the Classification of Snakes." British Museum (Nat. Hist.), London.

Warren, J. W., and Proske, U. (1968). Infrared receptors in the facial pits of the Australian python *Morelia spilotes. Science, N.Y.* 159, 439–441.

West, G. S. (1900). On the sensory pit of the Crotalinae. *Q. Jl. microsc. Sci.* 43, 49–59.

Zotterman, Y. (1936). Specific action potentials in the lingual nerve of cat. *Scand. Arch. Physiol.* 75, 106–119.

Zotterman, Y. (1959). Thermal Sensations. *In* "Handbook of Physiology". Vol. 1. Neurophysiology. (I. J. Field, ed.). American Physiological Society, Washington D.C.

The Distribution of Specialized Labial Scales in the Boidae

P. F. A. MADERSON

Although the literature contains a few specific works and many general statements regarding specialized sensory pits in the labial scales of boid snakes, there is apparently no general review of this material. Two major problems are to be found: first, there is some doubt as to the validity of many of the ascribed genera; second, identification of specialized integumentary derivatives in snakes and lizards often depends on microscopic observation, and gross appearances may be misleading. This appendix provides a general impression of the presence or absence of apparently specialized labial scales in boids based on an examination of the collections at the American Museum of Natural History. Further data on the morphology of such scales will be presented elsewhere.

The generic assignations used here follow those of Underwood (1967) and Stimson (1969). They hence differ in five respects from those of Romer (1956). *Boa* refers only to the "boa constrictor". *Corallus* refers to all the forms called "*Boa*" by Romer *excepting* the "boa constrictor". *Candoia* is used instead of *Enygrus*. *Lococemus* is accepted as a member of the family Boidae. *Morelia* is accepted as a separate genus and is not included within *Python* (contra Romer, 1956).

Thirteen genera represented in the collection of the American Museum show no apparent gross signs of specialized labial scales: *Aspidites*, *Acrantophis*, *Boa* (Dr. Underwood, personal communication, was kind enough to indicate to me that the format of p. 78 of his 1967 paper erroneously implies that *Boa*, referring to the boa constrictor, has labial pits), *Calabaria*, *Candoia*, *Charina*, *Eryx*, *Eunectes*, *Lichanura*, *Loxocemus*, *Trachyboa*, *Tropidophis*, and *Ungaliophis*. Three other boid genera, *Bolyeria*, *Casarea*, and *Exiliboa*, also lack specialized labial scales (Underwood, 1967; Bogert, 1968).

According to Underwood's (1967) classification, 9 genera show specialized labial scales. Identification is based on scale shape, degree of pigmentation, shape of a definitive "pit", and presence of an apparent groove housing the scales; all of these may be open to subjective interpretation without micro-scropic examination. The scales are, therefore, described genus by genus, with such notation as appears necessary.

Pits are found on the medial scales of the upper (= rostral) and lower jaw (= mental) and on the supralabials and infralabials along the margins of the upper and lower jaws respectively.

Bothrochilus: *B. boa* (A.M.N.H. Nos. 82325, 85666, 44002). The three to five most posterior scales of the infralabials bear large pigmented depres-sions.

Chondropython: *C. viridis* (A.M.N.H. Nos. 41620, 43874, 62629, 72777, 85667, 85671). The upper rostral bears paired slits, one on either side of the mid-line. The first three supralabials are similarly slitted, with the posterior slits being much smaller than the most anterior. The six posterior infra-labials have distinct pits. In all cases, the specialized areas appear to lie within the limits of the outer surface of single scales (see below).

Corallus: All species examined show specializations of the labial scales to-wards the posterior margins of both jaws, with each "sensory area" lying "between" two adjacent scales and being recognized by its pigmentation. All the specialized scales, both supralabials and infralabials, tend to lie in a groove, which gets deeper posteriorly.

C. annulatus (A.M.N.H. Nos. 75048, 74785). The last 10 to 14 supralabials and the first eight to nine infralabials bear pits.

C. annulatus colombianus (A.M.N.H. No. 61754). The last eight (specimen damaged) supralabials and eight to 11 infralabials bear pits.

C. caninus (A.M.N.H. Nos. 75167, 74837). The last 10 to 13 supralabials and nine to 10 infralabials bear pits.

C. enydris (A.M.N.H. Nos. 27352, 8660, 9027, 73831). The last five to 10 supralabials and five to seven infralabials bear pits. The shape and degree of pigmentation of the specialized regions varies greatly, which makes their identification difficult in this form.

Epicrates: The specialized areas may or may not occur. In the former case their distribution is the same as in *Corallus.*

E. angulifer (A.M.N.H. No. 77766—two others checked). The last 12 to 13 supralabials and 12 to 13 infralabials bear pits.

E. cenchria (A.M.N.H. Nos. 98186, 87940). The upper jaw has six to ten, and the lower jaw 11 to 12 pits.

E. inornatus fordii (A.M.N.H. Nos. 70137, 99155) and

E. striatus (A.M.N.H. Nos 73506, 50465, several others checked). There are no indications of specializations.

Liasis: There is considerable variation in the number and distribution of specialized scales in this genus.

L. f. fuscus (A.M.N.H. Nos. 82439, 82440, 69334). There are four or five modified infralabials on the posterior margin of the lower jaw, but only the first supralabial bears a slit.

L. fuscus albertisii (A.M.N.H. Nos. 101073, 98861). There are six pitted posterior infralabial scales. These lie in a pronounced groove, and the fourth and fifth pits are especially conspicuous.

L. childreni (A.M.N.H. Nos. 86209, 86215, 86214, 86210). There are three or four such scales in a similar position, but the groove is less pronounced.

L. olivaceus (A.M.N.H. No. 101074). The lower jaw resembles that of *L. childreni*, but in addition the first three supralabials bear slits; the first slit is especially pronounced, and the third much less so.

L. amethistinus (A.M.N.H. Nos. 82435 and 82436). There are six or seven pitted infralabials in a small groove on the posterior margin of the lower jaw, and four anterior slitted supralabials (similar to those in *L. olivaceus*). In addition, there is a conspicuous modification of the upper rostral which appears to bear an obliquely oriented slit, but the specialized area definitely involves a pair of tiny, possibly suprarostral, scales.

Morelia: *M. argus* (A.M.N.H. Nos. 8361, 8114, 8113, 7296) and *M. argus variegata* (A.M.N.H. Nos. 59880, 57831). The four anterior supralabials and seven posterior infralabials are conspicuously modified. The first three supralabials are distinctly slitted, while the fourth has a pit. In the lower pitted series, which lies in a small groove, the first and seventh are much smaller than the others. There is also a conspicuously modified upper rostral with twin slits which may involve lateral units as described above for *Liasis amethistinus*.

Python: All species resemble, in general, *Morelia*, but the shape and number of the specialized scales are somewhat different. The upper rostral always bears, on either side on the midline, two squarish slits, associated with two tiny dorsolaterally placed scales (suprarostrals?). All the other modified scales bear distinct, squarish pits.

P. molurus (A.M.N.H. Nos. 85533, 2190, 73226, 102281, 44527). There are pits in the first two supralabials, and the last four infralabials, although the fourth is much smaller than the others.

P. m. bivittatus (A.M.N.H. Nos. 27810, 27807, 27809, 27806). This species is essentially similar to *P. molurus*, but the pit in the fourth infralabial is much more obvious, and all the pits occupy a small groove.

P. regius (A.M.N.H. Nos. 73157, 31709, 31702, 73364, 73363, 31910, 32383, 31731, 32325, 33000). This resembles *P. molurus*, but has the first four (in one specimen, also a trace on the fifth) infralabial scales specialized.

P. sebae (A.M.N.H. Nos. 11689, 11685, 31652, 32588, 51796, 11690). This form is exactly like *P. molurus*.

P. curtus (A.M.N.H. Nos. 50993, 73829, 75333). Two specimens have badly damaged heads, but the general distribution is identical to that in other species: the first two supralabials and the last four infralabials bear pits.

P. anchietae (A.M.N.H. No. 50501). The first five supralabials and last four infralabials have pits.

P. reticulatus (A.M.N.H. Nos. 44517, 73828, 71541). The first three or four supralabials bear pits which may lie between, rather than on, individual scales. The last six or seven infralabials are distinctly pitted and lie in a fairly well-developed groove.

Sanzinia: *S. madagascariensis* (A.M.N.H. Nos. 71501, 2231). Both the upper and lower rostral scales, although neither are pitted or slit-bearing as in other genera, *may* be specialized. All 13 supralabial and 14 infralabial scales show "between-scale" specializations similar to those seen in *Corallus*. Underwood (personal communication) notes that, in *Sanzinia*, both anterior and posterior scale edges surrounding the specialized regions are equally "scooped", whereas in *Corallus*, and to a less noticeable degree in *Epicrates*, the anterior half-scale is slightly raised, while the posterior is definitely depressed.

Xenoboa: *X. cropanii* (A.M.N.H. No. 92997). All 10 or 11 supralabial scales bear fairly well-developed pits. The seven or eight posterior infralabials are similarly modified.

Acknowledgements

I wish to thank Dr. R. G. Zweifel of the American Museum of Natural History for making the collections available to me. Thanks are also due to Drs. G. Underwood and G. Zug for their comments on an early version of the ms. This work was supported in part by N. I. H. Grant CA-10844.

References

Bogert, C. M. (1968). A new genus and species of dwarf boa from Southern Mexico. *Am. Mus. Novit.* (2354), 1–38.

Romer, A. S. (1956). "Osteology of the Reptiles". Univ. Chicago Press, Chicago.

Stimson, A. F. (1969). Liste der rezenten Amphibien und Reptilien. Boidae (Boinae + Bolyeriinae + Loxoceminae + Pythoninae). *Tierreich* 89, i-xi, 1–49.

Underwood, G. (1967). "A Contribution to the Classification of Snakes." British Museum (Nat. Hist.), London.

Correlation of Ultrastructure and Function*

RICHARD M. MESZLER

The rattlesnake *Crotalus durissus terrificus* is the only species for which data concerning the ultrastructure of the radiant heat receptor have been published (Bleichmar and De Robertis, 1962). The following summary abstracts more recent work (Meszler and Gennaro, in preparation) on specimens of *Agkistrodon p. piscivorus*, *Python reticulatus*, and *Corallus enydris cookii*. It also presents evidence on some functional changes in the organ's ultrastructure during stimulation.

I. Structure

Electron microscopy of the receptor membranes of the cottonmouth moccasin (*Agkistrodon p. piscivorus*) reveals that they contain receptor nerve terminals that are free, nonmyelinated, and characteristically packed with mitochondria (Fig. 1A). Groups of these nerve endings are embedded in Schwann cells, thus forming a layer of small clumps approximately 5–15 micra thick and lying approximately 7–10 micra from the surface, subjacent to the outer epidermal layer (Fig. 1B). The cornified surface of the epidermis is quite smooth (Fig. 1C) and the epidermal layer is approximately 5 micra thick. The smooth surface of the membrane presumably permits passage of the stimulus to the nerve endings with a minimum of distortion.

The labial pits of the reticulated python (*Python reticulatus*) lack suspended sensory membranes, but show a concentration of nerve endings in the skin on the floor of each pit (Fig. 2A). The otherwise unmodified epidermis is somewhat thinner than that of the adjacent skin. A distinct basement membrane closely follows the tortuous boundary between the epidermis and

*This work was carried out in the Department of Anatomy, University of Louisville School of Medicine in collaboration with Dr. Joseph F. Gennaro, Jr., Department of Biology, New York University and supported by United States Public Health Service Training Grant No. 5 TO1 GM1356–04 and by Health, Education and Welfare Grant No. 5 RO1 DS00006.

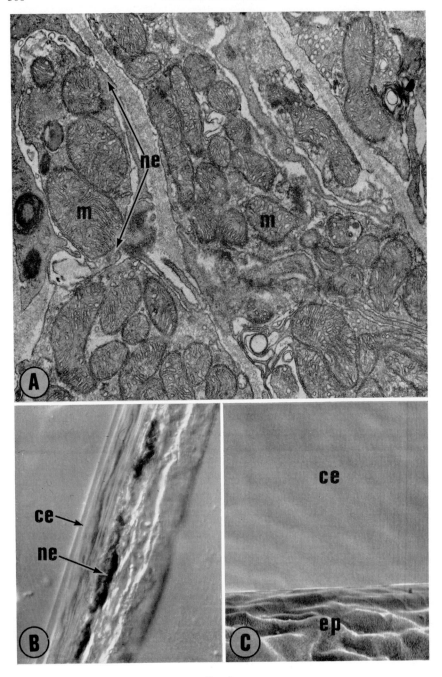

Fig. 1

the underlying connective tissue (Fig. 2B). Numerous nonmyelinated, mito-chondria-packed nerve fibers may be found adjacent to the basement mem-brane. These may be preterminal swellings similar to those described by Warren and Proske (1968) in *Morelia argus*. Nerve fibers of smaller diameter may be found closer to the surface between the epithelial cells (Fig. 2C). These are the nonmyelinated, mitochondria-packed nerve endings which extend toward the surface from the underlying neural network.

The labial pits of *C. e. cookii* are similar to those of the python, as the re-ceptor endings lie in the skin at the floor of the pit; however, the epidermis is only one cell thick (Fig. 3A). The bases of the epithelial cells seem to be separated by insertion of nonmyelinated, mitochondria-packed nerve terminals (Fig. 3B). The nerve fibers come from deeper regions and course outward between the branches of a capillary network to end immediately below the cornified surface.

II. Correlation of Structure and Function

The ultrastructure shows that the radiant heat receptors of these different species possess a common sensory element which may be characterized as a mitochondria-packed, free, nonmyelinated nerve terminal. Its primary ultrastructural response to infra-red radiation is a change in the configura-tion of the mitochondria in the nerve endings. The unstimulated nerve end-ings have (1) condensed mitochondria with densely stained matrices between compressed parallel cristal membranes (Fig. 4A), (2) twisted tubular mito-chondria with light matrices and nonparallel tubular cristae (Fig. 4B), and (3) mitochondria with characteristics that appear to be intermediate between the preceding configurations (Figs. 4C and 4D). Mitochondria with-in an individual nerve terminal usually have the same or closely allied con-figurations. If the heat receptor is excised and fixed during exposure to

FIG. 1. A. Electron micrograph of pit membrane of *Agkistrodon p. piscivorus*. m, Mitochondria; ne, one of several mitochondria-packed nerve endings in a Schwann cell. Fixed 3% glutaraldehyde, postfixed 1% osmium tetroxide, and stained with uranyl acetate and lead citrate. 23,600 ×.
B. Phase contrast light micrograph of a cross section of pit membrane of *Agkistrodon p. piscivorus*, stained for succinic dehydrogenase activity. ce, Outer cornified epidermis; ne, group of nerve end-ing showing strong reaction for succinic dehydrogenase activity. Clumping is the result of many nerve endings being embedded in a Schwann cell. 630 ×.
C. Scanning electron micrograph of the facial pit of *Agkistrodon p. piscivorus*. ce, Smooth surface of the cornified epidermis of the pit membrane; ep, surface of the deep epithelial cells of the skin at the border of the pit. These cells were revealed by removal of the outer epithelium of this skin. (Photo-graph taken on Cambridge Stereoscan Electron Microscope at Engis Equipment Company, Morton Grove, Illinois). 580 ×.

L

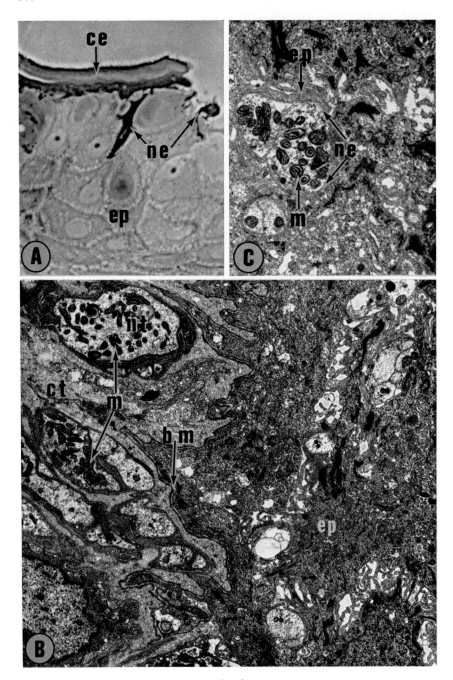

Fig. 2

various stimuli, one observes consistent and characteristic configurations of the mitochondria in the nerve endings (Figs 4 and 5, see pp. 312 and 314). The patterns observed can be correlated with the neurophysiological responses obtained from similarly stimulated snake infra-red receptors (Table I).

TABLE I

Configuration of Nerve Ending Mitochondria in
Relation to Type of Stimulus and Nerve Response

Stimulus	Configuration of Nerve Ending Mitochondria	Characteristics of Nerve Response*
None, ambient conditions	All possible configurations	Spontaneous, arhythmic impulses
High intensity infra-red radiation	All condensed	Strong burst of impulses followed by complete silence
Moderate intensity radiant heat	Majority condensed, or intermediate-condensed	Increasing firing of impulses
Infra-red stimulated Allowed to recover	All possible configurations	Return to spontaneous, arhythmic impulses
Cold source	Majority twisted-tubular, or intermediate-twisted tubular	No impulses

*Bullock and Diecke, 1956; Goris and Nomoto, 1968; Bullock and Barrett, 1968.

Fig. 2. A. Phase contrast light micrograph of section of floor of the labial pit of *Python reticulatus*. ce, Cornified epidermis; ep, epithelial cells of epidermis; ne, nerve endings. Epon embedded, 1 micron thick section stained with acid fuchsin-toluidine blue. 800 ×.
B. Electron micrograph of floor of the labial pit of *Python reticulatus*. bm, Basement membrane underlying epidermis; ct, connective tissue; ep, epithelial cell of epidermis; m, mitochondria; nt, mitochondria-packed nerve preterminals in dermis. Fixed 3% glutaraldehyde, postfixed 1% osmium tetroxide, and stained with uranyl acetate and lead citrate. 6900 ×.
C. Electron micrograph of floor of the labial pit of *Python reticulatus* showing a nerve ending in the epidermis. ep, Epithelial cell of epidermis with cell processes that closely invest the nerve ending; m, mitochondria; ne, mitochondria-packed nonmyelinated nerve ending. Fixed 3% glutaraldehyde, postfixed 1% osmium tetroxide, and stained with uranyl acetate and lead citrate. 11,000 ×.
L*

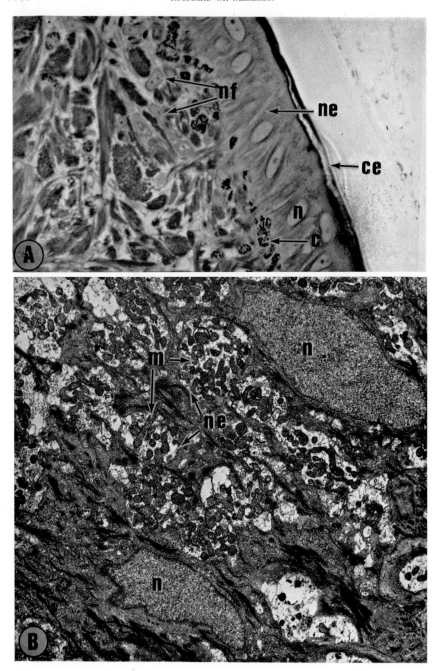

Fig. 3

These different mitochondrial configurations appear to indicate the physiological state of the mitochondria at the time of fixation. Similar configurational changes have been demonstrated in isolated beef heart mitochondria by Harris *et al.* (1968), Penniston *et al.* (1968), and Green *et al.* (1968), and were related by these authors to the state of the energy conservation system. These workers identified three configurational states which they termed nonenergized (membranes compressed, dense matrix), energized (membranes separated by a lighter matrix), and energized twisted (tubular cristae). They suggest that the latter two configurations contain energized cristal membrane subunits which consequently had a certain amount of stored energy that could be used to support cellular work processes. As this energy supply is depleted, the mitochondria revert to the nonenergized configuration until the supply is restored.

Changes in mitochondrial configuration have been correlated with variations in the rate of active transport of sodium ions in toad bladder (Saladino and Bentley, 1969). Acceleration of sodium transport resulted in an increased oxygen consumption and an increased number of discharged (condensed) mitochondria. Conversely, inhibition of sodium transport decreased oxygen consumption concomitant with an increase in the number of mitochondria in the energized configuration.

As in a variety of other receptors (Diamond *et al.*, 1958; Nakajima and Takahashi, 1966; Smith and Stell, 1968), the metabolic energy in the nerve ending is probably applied to the active transport of sodium ions, resulting in an ion gradient across the nerve ending membrane. The influx of ions during depolarization would be expected to accelerate the sodium pump. Since the frequency of nerve impulses increases, within limits, with an increase in the intensity of the stimulus (Bullock and Diecke, 1956; Goris and Nomoto, 1968; Bullock and Barrett, 1968), the energy drain produced by accelerated ion transport would also be expected to increase. Thus, nerve activity as a function of the energy drain is reflected in the number of nerve terminals containing discharged mitochondria. Conversely, the absence of nerve activity, for instance after introduction of a cold object into the field of

---

FIG. 3. A. Phase contrast light micrograph of floor of labial pit of *Corallus enydris cookii*. c, Capillary of vascular network in floor of pit; ce, thin cornified epidermis; n, nucleus of epithelial cell of epidermis; ne, nerve ending in epidermis; nf, myelinated nerve fiber coursing toward surface. Epon embedded, 1 micron thick section stained with acid fuchsin-toluidine blue. 1100 ×.

B. Electron micrograph of section of floor of pit of *C. e. cookii*. m, Mitochondria; n, nucleus of epithelial cell of epidermis; ne, mitochondria-packed, nonmyelinated nerve ending in epidermis. Fixed 3% glutaraldehyde, post-fixed 1% osmium tetroxide, and stained with uranyl acetate and lead citrate. 7100 ×

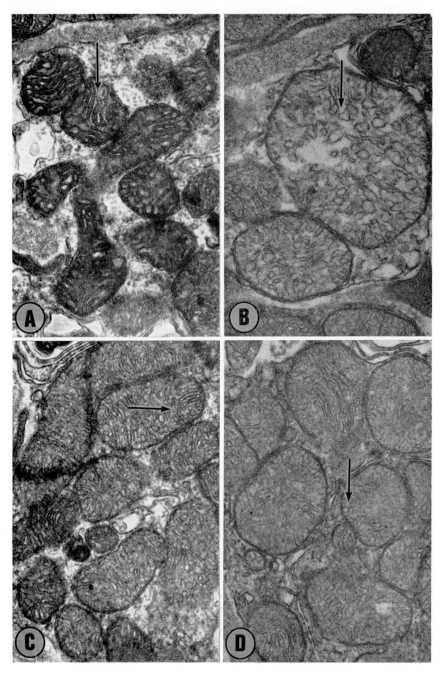

FIG. 4

reception (Bullock and Diecke, 1956; Goris and Nomoto, 1968; Bullock and Barrett, 1968), is characterized by the presence of a majority of energized mitochondria, reflecting a decrease in sodium ion transport. It is apparent, therefore, that the functional state of the radiant heat receptor can be inferred from the ultrastructural state of the mitochondrial population.

References
(Not cited in main chapter)

Diamond, J., Gray, J. A. B. and Inman, D. R. (1958). The relation between receptor potentials and the concentration of sodium ions. *J. Physiol.* **142**, 382–394.

Green, D. E., Asai, J., Harris, R. A. and Penniston, J. T. (1968). Conformational basis of energy transformations in membrane systems. III. Configurational changes in the mitochondrial inner membrane induced by changes in functional states. *Archs. Biochem. Biophys.* **125**, 684–705.

Harris, R. A., Penniston, J. T., Asai, J. and Green, D. E. (1968). The conformational basis of energy conservation in membrane systems. II. Correlation between conformational change and functional states. *Proc. natn. Acad. Sci. U.S.A.* **59**, 830–837.

Nakajima, S. and Takahashi, K. (1966). Post-tetanic hyperpolarization and electrogenic Na pump in stretch receptor neurone of crayfish. *J. Physiol.* **187**, 105–127.

Penniston, J. T., Harris, R. A., Asai, J. and Green, D. E. (1968). The conformational basis of energy transformations in membrane systems. I. Conformational changes in mitochondria. *Proc. natn. Acad. Sci. U.S.A.* **59**, 624–631.

Saladino, A. J. and Bentley, P. J. (1969). Correlation of mitochondrial structure and respiratory control in intact toad bladder epithelium. *Fed. Proc. Fedn. Am. Socs. exp. Biol.* **28**, 894.

Smith, T. G. and Stell, W. K. (1968). A role for the sodium pump in photoreception in *Limulus*. *Science, N.Y.* **162**, 456–458.

Fig. 4. Electron micrographs showing the variety of configurations of mitochondria in radiant heat receptor nerve endings fixed under ambient conditions. All taken from a single section of the pit membrane of *Agkistrodon p. piscivorus*. Fixed 3% glutaraldehyde, post-fixed 1% osmium tetroxide, and stained with uranyl acetate and lead citrate.

A. Condensed (discharged) configuration, exhibiting compressed, parallel cristal membranes and dense matrix (arrow). 30,300 ×.

B. Twisted tubular (energized) configuration, larger in size, exhibiting tubular cristae that give circular profiles in cross section (arrow). 30,300 ×.

C. Intermediate-condensed configuration exhibiting denser matrix than those in Fig. 4D and some compressed, parallel cristal membranes (arrow). 30,300 ×.

D. Intermediate-twisted tubular configuration exhibiting lighter matrix than those in Fig. 4C and some tubular cristae (arrow). 30,300 ×.

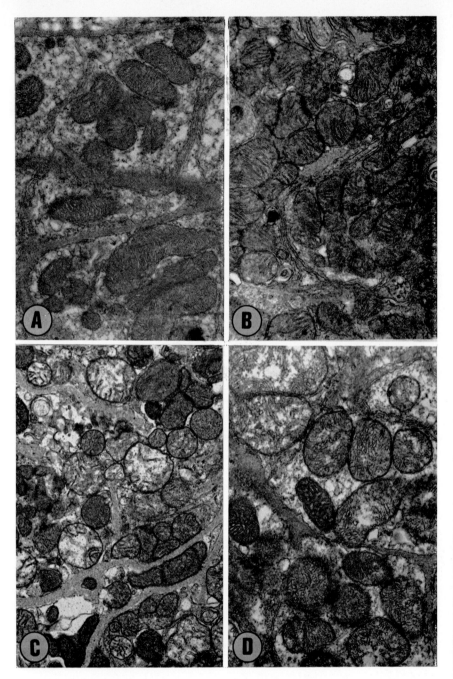

Fig. 5. Electron micrographs showing patterns of configuration of nerve ending mitochondria fixed during exposure to various stimuli. Fixed 3% glutaraldehyde, postfixed 1% osmium tetroxide, and stained with uranyl acetate and lead citrate.

A. High intensity infra-red—all condensed. 18,000 ×.

B. Moderate intensity radiant heat—condensed and intermediate-condensed. 18,000 ×.

C. One minute after exposure to high intensity infra-red to permit recovery—presence of energized and discharged configurations similar to pattern during ambient conditions. 14,900 ×.

D. Cold source—majority twisted tubular and intermediate twisted tubular. 18,000 ×.

CHAPTER 5

Taxonomic Literature on Reptiles

CARL GANS

Department of Biology, State University of New York at Buffalo, Buffalo, New York, U.S.A.

and

THOMAS S. PARSONS

Department of Zoology, University of Toronto, Toronto, Ontario, Canada.

I. Introduction

The Biology of the Reptilia is not intended to answer taxonomic questions, although the data presented may, indeed, be useful to taxonomists. These volumes are instead intended to supply a detailed statement of the structural or functional solutions that have evolved in this vertebrate group. It is hoped that they will interest not only herpetologists, but also specialists in subject matter. Some of the latter may require a brief guide to the literature on reptilian classification. We here attempt to provide this.

Consideration of the taxonomic literature has presumably the aim of insuring reproducibility of results. The need is for appropriate identification of specimens, assurance that series are not mixed, and application of the currently valid name in its appropriate form. Much of the older anatomical, embryological, physiological, and even ecological literature reflects failings in one or more of these criteria.

Then there are the names given in many of the very old papers. Even when it may be assumed that the identifications were correct, the names sometimes reflect usages so far out of date that current reference materials are of little use. The catalogues prepared by G. A. Boulenger (1885a, 1885b, 1887, 1889, 1893, 1894, 1896), supposedly for the reptiles in the British Museum but actually for all forms then known, form an invaluable source of more appropriate names. The names given by Boulenger will almost always be noted in modern synonymies.

Such problems have increased rather than diminished now that rare, exotic and highly interesting animals are often available from pet shops and department stores four or five steps removed from the original collector and quite generally without any indication of source and often with fanciful vernacular names attached. Yet one often meets senior investigators who accept the names offered by the dealer without further check.

II. Assistance of Specialists

Utilization of simple keys and textbooks designed for undergraduate students is generally insufficient for the identification of specimens to be used in research. While the Peterson Series Field Guides to reptiles and amphibians (Conant, 1958; Stebbins, 1966) offer reasonable coverage of the animals of the United States and Canada, there are no equivalent treatments for the reptiles of other continents.

Yet many groups of reptiles have been reviewed or are currently under review. Curators of major museums, or "The Naturalists' Directory" (Anonymous, 1968) may inform the investigator of individuals who are both knowledgeable and willing to identify specimens that have been used or are to form the basis for a research project. As important, these individuals are apt to be most cognizant of recent discoveries in the group of their specialization. They are often able to suggest appropriate species for experimental procedures and to warn of cases in which the recent discovery of cryptic species or taxonomic problems are apt to lead to subsequent difficulties.

There are some additional ways in which an experimental investigator may utilize our knowledge of biological variation to minimize subsequent confusion about identifications. Whenever possible, one should utilize locally collected animals, since this is likely to increase the probability that the entire sample stems from a particular area, and to limit the effect of geographical variation on sample composition. The locality at which the experimental animals have been collected should always be specified in the Materials section of the paper, as this makes it simpler to spot past errors and assign the report to the appropriate taxonomic category.

It is also useful to deposit one or more specimens of each experimental series in a natural history museum and to cite in the paper the number assigned to them in the museum's catalog. Assuming that the series was homogenous, this will maintain the utility of the original study even if subsequent taxonomic discoveries force changes in the nomenclature of the group. The effort invested in such simple steps is apt to be far outweighed in increased reliability and utility of the resulting report.

III. The Nature of the Taxonomic Literature

To workers trained in experimental disciplines, taxonomic studies often appear to be poorly organized. This results from the process by which specimens, the raw materials of taxonomy, tend to be assembled, or better yet, accumulated, and it may be useful here to digress in order to explain this point.

The earliest samplings from any region are likely to derive from the travels of naturalists or from collections sent in to a major museum after more or less random assembly by workers residing in a region. While these workers often do yeoman service, they are unlikely to be specialists for the group in question. The animals thus assembled are described and discussed in studies reporting on the results of such expeditions or on short or long term accumulations in particular museums.

Animals are hence described as they happen to be collected and discovered. Rarely has there been a concerted effort by a large number of investigators to search out, collect and describe the entire fauna of a region. In the past, the extraordinary cost in terms of funds and energy needed for such projects has been justified only under special circumstances such as the flooding of an area, the digging of a canal, or the waging of a war.

This gradual process of specimen accumulation forces the taxonomist to utilize the method of successive approximations. Preliminary reports memorialize the collector and document the accumulation of data. Temporary check-lists and studies of regional faunas permit the next generation of collectors to identify newly assembled animals. Specimens whose characteristics suggest that they represent undescribed taxa or that previous approaches are insufficient, then serve as a stimulus to the next level of analysis. Specialists tend periodically to assemble all material of a particular group and to re-examine its classification on the basis of more current data. New forms may be recognized for the first time during such a review of previously "identified" material. The review process often serves as the starting point of a new cycle of analysis, during which organized collecting is combined with ecological and other biological studies. It is at this level that the nomenclature approaches stability, and subsequent name changes result mainly from biological discoveries.

Taxonomic papers are often quite long and their utility to the specialist requires the inclusion of much tabular and historical material. Since they are generally considered to be but interim progress reports on a continuous process of re-evaluation, they tend to emphasize small and particularly aberrant samples. Most such papers are printed in various museum series that are apt to be distributed primarily to other museums and do not reach many libraries associated with medical schools and smaller universities. We have, therefore, emphasized mainly those studies that may be useful to workers who are not primarily interested in the taxonomic process.

IV. Literature Reviews and Special Journals

Taxonomic and systematic studies as well as those dealing with ecological topics are very poorly covered and worse indexed in the *Biological Abstracts*. Consequently these have in the past been inadequate sources for animal rather than subject oriented information. Somewhat better, but still of limited use for taxonomic papers, is the *Referativnii Zhurnal* (Section Biology, I. Vertebrate Zoology) published in Moscow. The *Bulletin Signaletique* (16, Biologie et Physiologie, Animals) is also of some use.

Much more useful has been the *Zoological Record* published by The Zoological Society of London (Regent's Park, London N.W.1, England). This breaks down the literature by taxonomic group. Papers published during a given year are listed alphabetically by authors, followed by three cross indexes, one to the species mentioned (classified under major groups), the second to geographical area, and the third to subject (such as osteology, vision and mating behavior). The section on reptiles costs about $5.00 a year and seems essential to any laboratory in which reptilian studies are carried out.

While the *Zoological Record* provides by far the most useful breakdown of the literature, there is normally at least a two year gap between publication of a paper and its inclusion. This gap is now being reduced by a new project, the *Herpetological Information Search System*, which is located at the American Museum of Natural History in New York City (address Dr. H. G. Dowling). Various techniques are used to scan the current literature and lists of titles (organized by authors) are published several times a year as a computer print out in the *Herpetological Review*. Delay between receipt of an article and its appearance in print is thus reduced to three months. The preparation of taxonomic, geographic, and subject indexes is now under way. An information retrieval system is also planned.

Some dozen societies publish journals that regularly include reports on reptilian biology. Three of these societies publish journals devoted entirely to amphibians and reptiles or to these and fishes, journals that include significant fractions of taxonomic materials. The first of these is the American Society of Ichthyologists and Herpetologists (membership including subscription is $10. per year in the U.S., Canada, and Mexico and $8. per year in other areas and for students), whose journal *Copeia* includes a review section. *Copeia*, published since 1913, is now produced from the Division of Reptiles and Amphibians of the U.S. National Museum (Washington, D.C.

20560). The Herpetologists League (membership including subscription is $5. per year payable to the Secretary-Treasurer, Frederick B. Turner, Laboratory of Nuclear Medicine and Radiation Biology, University of California, Los Angeles, California 90024) publishes *Herpetologica* founded in 1936. The Society for the Study of Amphibians and Reptiles (membership which includes receipt of the publication is $6. in the U.S. and Canada and $5. in other countries; application is to the Secretary-Treasurer, Joseph T. Collins, Museum of Natural History, University of Kansas, Lawrence, Kansas 66044) was founded in 1967 and now publishes the *Journal of Herpetology* devoted primarily to research papers and the *Herpetological Review* providing new reviews of the literature and the above-mentioned print-out of *Current Herpetological Titles*.

V. Listing by Groups

There is as yet no single summary of the classification of reptiles; its absence is one of the reasons why the present guide seems necessary. The closest semblance thereto is in the appendix to A. S. Romer's (1956) "*Osteology of the Reptiles*" where is presented the scheme followed, for the most part, in these volumes. Romer's classification goes down to the generic level and lists all primary synonyms (i.e. past erroneous usages). Subfamilies and higher categories are defined, primarily on osteological characteristics. Partial synonyms are listed only once. Aspects of Romer's classification of higher categories have been questioned by many workers who argue that on the familial and suprafamilial levels he recognizes too few categories for Recent forms (cf. Underwood, 1967, for an extreme example). Kuhn (1967) has listed names of subfamilies and higher taxa, including all synonyms.

More detailed check-lists of appropriate names and synonyms are available down to the species and subspecies levels of certain orders and families. Notable is the list of Wermuth and Mertens (1961) for the turtles and crocodilians, since it includes illustrations for most of the species; unfortunately it also contains a number of fiat decisions not accepted by many authors. Pritchard's (1967) popular book on turtles contains many illustrations, as does the authoritative pamphlet on turtle care by Gijzen and Wermuth (1958). Kimura (1966) provides a popular, well illustrated treatment of crocodilians.

The Squamata form the largest and most diverse assemblage and their literature poses the greatest problems. The Amphisbaenia have been reviewed by Gans (1967), the sea snakes by M. A. Smith (1926, but still useful), the poisonous snakes in general by Klemmer (1963; see also the recent U.S. Navy Manual, Minton *et al.*, 1968, and the 1968 papers of Klemmer, Broadley, and Leviton), and Wermuth is currently soliciting chapters for a complete catalog of check-lists, published within the framework of *Das Tierreich* and covering all reptiles (and amphibians). Sections that have already appeared are:

SAURIA: Gekkonidae, Pygopodidae, Xantusiidae (Wermuth, 1965). Chamaeleonidae (Mertens, 1966). Helodermatidae, Varanidae, Lanthanotidae (Mertens, 1963). Cordylidae (incl. Gerrhosaurinae) (Wermuth, 1968). Agamidae (Wermuth, 1967). Anguidae, Anniellidae, Xenosauridae (Wermuth, 1969).

SERPENTES: Uropeltidae (Gans, 1966). Boidae (Boinae, Bolyeriinae, Loxoceminae, Pythoninae) (Stimson, 1969). Colubridae (Dipsadinae) (Peters, 1965).

Some of these are lists prepared on the basis of compilations from the literature rather than reviews; they are consequently uneven in the reliability of the information presented.

Recently, there have appeared a few well-illustrated atlases, notably those of Schmidt and Inger (1957) and Mertens (1960), as well as Klingelhöffer's (1955–1959) four volume "Terrarienkunde." Such volumes may be of some use to those who wish to make preliminary identifications by scanning a series of pictures prior to consulting more detailed treatments. Yet, secondary consultation is absolutely essential. Not only are the illustrations in such volumes identified with varying reliability, but the differences between species, and even between families, may not be apparent, even in properly identified photographs. It is finally appropriate here to refer to the chapter on reptiles in Darlington's (1957) "Zoogeography" which discusses the distribution of the Recent groups and provides a bibliography also including some of the older papers.

VI. Regional Listings

It is sometimes possible to obtain preliminary identifications of specimens by the use of various kinds of books and papers dealing with reptiles of geographically restricted regions. Even a scanning of the list of such productions here provided will indicate drastic differences in the professional aim, in the audience to which these are addressed, and consequently in the reliability of the classification presented therein. Yet, if these limitations are kept in mind, the following listing may have some utility. It includes only fairly recent accounts, those that are larger, and those that may facilitate the sorting out of large collections. Papers on small collections, listings without discussion and reports on local regions or restricted groups are ordinarily omitted.

Two major geographically oriented projects may ultimately be of considerable utility to those studying reptiles. The first is the *Catalogue of American Amphibians and Reptiles* published by the American Society of

Ichthyologists and Herpetologists (Riemer, ed., 1963 *et seq.*) as a successor to the sixth edition of an older checklist (Schmidt, 1953). It is furnished in looseleaf form, with individual accounts presented by different authors, and summarizes taxonomic as well as distributional and much other biological information on each North American species and genus (for subscriptions, address the Herpetological Catalog Committee at the American Museum of Natural History, New York, N.Y. 10024, U.S.A.). Common names used here have been standardized according to the list of *Common Names for North American Amphibians and Reptiles* (Conant *et al.*, 1956). The catalogue is becoming the critical reference for studies of the herpetofauna of North America.

Also important, though less detailed, is the *Catalog of the Neotropical Squamata*, incorporating keys and synonymies, being compiled at the U. S. National Museum under the supervision of James A. Peters and B. Orejas Miranda. The latter project, much of which derives from the literature rather than a review of specimens, is obviously intended as a stimulus to further work, rather than a definitive statement. Certainly the fauna of South America is still extremely poorly understood and literally dozens of reptilian species and numerous genera remain to be discovered.

The following account, organized by geographical regions, should serve as a guide, indicating the most recent adequate reviews of various faunas.

AMERICA: General: Crocodilians (Medem and Marx, 1955, a brief key). CANADA: General (Logier and Toner, 1961, check-list with range maps only). Eastern (Bleakney, 1958, a restricted but more detailed account). UNITED STATES: General (Riemer, ed., 1963, see above). Western North America (Stebbins, 1966, contains illustrations, keys and range maps; also Stebbins, 1954). Eastern North America (Conant, 1958, contains illustrations, keys and range maps). Turtles (Carr, 1952, a handbook with detailed discussions of all species, illustrations). Lizards (H. Smith, 1946, parallels Carr, 1952). Snakes (Wright and Wright, 1957 and 1962, parallels Carr, 1952). There are also multiple regional listings and handbooks of the herpetofauna of the several states referred to in the volumes just cited. MEXICO: Lizards and turtles (H. Smith and Taylor, 1950, check-list that includes keys). Snakes (H. Smith and Taylor, 1945, check-list that includes keys). GUATEMALA: General (Stuart, 1963, check-list that includes keys). EL SALVADOR: General (Mertens, 1952a, expanded trip report). COSTA RICA: General (Taylor, 1954a, 1955, 1958; these and the following papers review much new material). Lizards (Taylor, 1956). Snakes (Taylor, 1951, 1954b). CARIBBEAN: General (Underwood, 1962, detailed discussions of Caribbean reptiles, including keys and organized both by species and by islands, unfortunately bereft of any literature citations; Barbour, 1937, an out dated check-list with references to the older literature). CUBA: General (Barbour and Ramsden, 1919, very dated but has excellent figures as well as keys). HISPANIOLA: General (Cochran, 1941, keys, descriptions and figures). JAMAICA: General (Grant, 1940, descriptions but no keys).

SOUTH AMERICA: Check-list and key to the reptiles of South America (Peters, see above). Lizards (Burt and Burt, 1933, check-list, now out of date). Snakes (Amaral, 1929, check-list now quite out of date). Neotropical Crotalinae (Hoge, 1965, check-list incorporating new descriptions, maps and illustrations). BRITISH GUIANA: Lizards (Crawford, 1931, an old and somewhat dated key). VENEZUELA: Lizards (Donoso-Barros, 1968, check-list and keys from the literature). Snakes (Roze, 1966, detailed description based on much original work). ECUADOR: Lizards (Peters, 1967, check-list and key). Snakes (Peters, 1960, check-list and key). GALAPAGOS: Turtles (van Denburgh, 1914). Lizards (van Denburgh, 1912b; van Denburgh and Slevin, 1913). Snakes (van Denburgh, 1912a). COLOMBIA: General (Dunn, 1957, collected papers dealing mainly with the fauna of the more northern regions). BRAZIL: Lizards-Gekkonidae (Vanzolini, 1968). Amazonian lizards (da Cunha, 1961, mainly based on the collections in the Museo Goeldi). CHILE: General (Donoso-Barros, 1966, extensive, illustrated).

EUROPE: General (Mertens and Wermuth, 1960, check-list and keys with sketches, authoritative; Schreiber, 1912, antique, but with much biological information; also Frommhold, 1959 on central Europe; Hellmich, 1962, popular illustrated treatment; Dottrens and Aellen, 1963, popular, well illustrated, contains keys). SWEDEN: General (Gislèn and Kauri, 1959). DENMARK: General (Hvass, 1936). ENGLAND: General (M. Smith, 1951, detailed treatment of limited fauna, well illustrated). HOLLAND: General (Bund, 1964). BELGIUM: General (de Witte, 1948). FRANCE: General (Angel, 1946, detailed, illustrated). ITALY: General (Tortonese and Lanza, 1968, brief, popular). POLAND: General (Młynarski, 1966; Berger et al., 1969), BALKANS: Snakes (Radovanović and Martino, 1950). JUGOSLAVIA: General (Radovanović, 1951; Pozzi, 1966). ROMANIA: General (Fuhn and Vançea, 1961, good treatment). BULGARIA: General (Beskov and Beron, 1964). GREECE and the AEGEAN: General (Werner, 1938; Wettstein, 1953, 1957, listings; Ontria, 1966). U.S.S.R.: General (Terent'ev and Chernov, 1949, keys, descriptions, illustrations and range maps; now being revised by P. V. Terent'ev and I. S. Darevsky). Regional works are also available (cf. Chernov, 1959, for Tadjikskoi SSR; Bogdanov, 1960, for Uzbekstan; Paraskiv, 1956, for Kazakstan-Alma-Ata; Taratschuk, 1959, for the Ukraine; Shcherbak, 1966, for the Crimea; and Bogdanov, 1962, for Turkmenia).

ASIA: TURKEY: General (Mertens, 1952b, 1953). ISRAEL: General (Barash and Hoofien, 1956, keys, sketches and descriptions). IRAQ: General (Khalaf, 1959, keys, sketches and descriptions). ARABIA: (Haas, 1957, collection report with photographs; Leviton and Anderson, 1967). IRAN: (Anderson, 1963, collection report; also Anderson, 1968). AFGHANISTAN: General (Leviton, 1959; Leviton and Anderson, 1961, 1963, reports on collections; Clark *et al.*, 1969). INDIA: Turtles and 'Crocodilians (M. Smith, 1931). Lizards (M. Smith, 1935). Snakes (M. Smith, 1943, still the standard for this subcontinent; Deoras, 1965, incomplete, but more recent with keys and color photographs). NEPAL: (Swan and Leviton, 1962). WEST PAKISTAN: General (Minton, 1962, annotated, well illustrated key; Minton, 1966, detailed descriptions and discussions; Mertens, 1969, numerous addenda to previous report). CEYLON: Turtles and Crocodilians (Deraniyagala, 1939, an interesting, broadly biological treatment; also Deraniyagala, 1953, which repeats part of the earlier discussion). Lizards (Deraniyagala, 1953, numerous colored illustrations; Taylor, 1953, several keys and taxonomic revisions). Snakes (Deraniyagala, 1955, keys and numerous colored illustrations). THAILAND: Lizards (Taylor, 1963, keys, descriptions and illustrations). Snakes (Taylor, 1965, keys, descriptions and illustrations). "INDOCHINA": Turtles (Bourret, 1941, separate keys to skulls, shells, heads and external patterns, descriptions and illustrations – useful though outdated). Lizards (Bourret, 1943, keys only). Snakes (Bourret, 1936, keys, detailed discussions). MALAYSIA: General (M. A. Smith, 1930, somewhat outdated). Snakes (Tweedie, 1961, keys, descriptions and figures). INDONESIA: General (Mertens, 1930, lists and descriptions, but no keys). Turtles, Crocodilians and Lizards (de Rooij, 1915, detailed, but somewhat dated account). Snakes (de Rooij, 1917, detailed, but somewhat dated account; de Haas, 1950, check-list and range notes). JAVA: Snakes (van Hoesel, 1959, keys, illustrations, descriptions in Indonesian and English).

PHILIPPINE ISLANDS: Turtles (Taylor, 1920, 1921). Lizards (Taylor, 1922, out of date, but still the only reference). Snakes (Leviton, 1961, 1963a and b, 1964a,b,c,d, 1965a,b,c,d, 1968a, a detailed review, with keys, published in parts). CHINA: (Pope, 1935, out of date but still the only general treatment). TAIWAN: Reptiles (Wang and Wang, 1956). Snakes (Kuntz, 1963, colored photographs of all species). JAPAN: General (Nakamura and Ueno, 1963; Goris, 1966, in Japanese, semipopular account with colored photographs). Snakes (Maki, 1931, an extensive, beautifully illustrated account). Lizards (Okada, 1936, 1937, 1939). PACIFIC AREA: General (Loveridge, 1946, a general account that is still the only comprehensive treatment). Snakes (Oshima, 1943, descriptions and useful list of snakes by islands of the southwestern Pacific; Werler and Keegan, 1963, well illustrated account of the poisonous snakes). NEW GUINEA: General (Loveridge, 1948, lists, some descriptions, but no keys). Snakes (Slater, 1968; see also Worrell, 1961). Turtles (see Goode, 1967). AUSTRALIA: General (Worrell, 1963, keys, descriptions, and illustrations, but nomenclature not up to date). Turtles (Goode, 1967, a good review incorporating many illustrations and keys). Snakes

(Worrell, 1961, a popular treatment of the poisonous forms; Kinghorn, 1964, numerous colored illustrations). South Australia (Waite, 1929). NEW ZEALAND: General (Sharell, 1966, a semipopular account with colored photographs). Lizards (McCann, 1955). HAWAII: General (Oliver and Shaw, 1953).

AFRICA: Turtles (Loveridge and Williams, 1957, detailed analysis). Lizards-Gekkonidae (Loveridge, 1947; this author has also published numerous other generic and familial revisions, as well as expedition reports in the Bulletin of the Museum of Comparative Zoology). Snakes (Bogert, 1940, descriptions but no keys). EGYPT: (Marx, 1968, keys and descriptions). SOMALI REPUBLIC: (Gans *et al.*, 1965, partial coverage of fauna, contains complete bibliography for region; fauna now being revised by B. Lanza, Ist. Zool., Florence). Lizards (Parker, 1942, keys and descriptions for species, but not for genera, few illustrations). Snakes (Parker, 1949, includes keys to the species of some genera). KENYA-TANZANIA-UGANDA: (Loveridge, 1957, check-list only, with numerous taxonomic comments). UGANDA: Snakes (Pitman, 1938, a beautifully prepared but now slightly dated account with colored plates and tabulations; now being revised). RHODESIA: General (see lists and papers in *Journal of the Herpetological Association of Africa* available from the Umtali Museum, Rhodesia). Lizards (D. G. Broadley, in process). Snakes (Broadley, 1959, keys and taxonomic discussions). MADAGASCAR: Lizards (Angel, 1942, a beautiful study). Snakes (Guibé, 1958, keys, descriptions, illustrations). SOUTHERN AFRICA: Snakes (FitzSimmons, 1962, a monographic treatment with keys, maps, descriptions and numerous colored plates; FitzSimons, 1966, check-list with keys). Lizards (FitzSimons, 1943, keys, descriptions and discussion). KRUGER PARK: General (Pienaar, 1966, keys, range maps and many photographs). S. W. AFRICA: (Mertens, 1955, a revision with keys, descriptions, illustrations and taxonomic discussions). ANGOLA: (Laurent, 1964, discussion of several extensive collections). CONGO: General (Laurent, 1956, 1960, 1965, major contributions toward an important fauna, with keys to small groups, but lacking a summary). Snakes (de Witte, 1962, keys to the genera and lists of the species, well illustrated). WEST AFRICA: Turtles and crocodilians (Villiers, 1958, keys, descriptions and numerous illustrations). Snakes (Cansdale, 1961, a popular account with numerous colored pictures; Villiers, 1963, keys, descriptions and illustrations). NIGERIA: (Note various papers by G. T. Dunger in recent issues of *The Nigerian Field*). GHANA: Snakes (Leeson, 1950, general account, with figures; Hughes, in press, checklist and key). IVORY COAST: Snakes (Doucet, 1963, keys and excellent illustrations of various anatomical features). MAROC: General (Pasteur and Bons, 1960, check-list with some descriptive material). Lizards (Bons, 1959).

Acknowledgements

Comments were received from I. S. Darevsky, C. O. Diefenbach, H. G. Dowling, I. Gilboa, Alan E. Leviton, C. J. McCoy, Robert Mertens, Sherman Minton, Phil Regal, Heinz Wermuth, and R. G. Zweifel. We are grateful to these friends who took the time to review an early version of this manuscript. Not only did their advice permit us to rectify inadvertent omissions, but they also indicated the extent to which some older papers were still being used. The decision to include or omit, as well as the annotations, are entirely the responsibility of the authors. The work of Gans is supported by N. S. F. Grant GB 6521X.

References

Amaral, A. do (1929). Estudos sobre ophidios neotropicos. XVIII – Lista remissiva dos ophidios da Região Neotropica. *Mems. Inst. Butantan* 4, 129–271.

Anderson, S. C. (1963). Amphibians and reptiles from Iran. *Proc. Calif. Acad. Sci.* (4), 31 (16), 417–498.

Anderson, S. C. (1968). Zoogeographic analysis of the lizard fauna of Iran. *In* "The Cambridge History of Iran. I. The Land of Iran." (W. B. Fisher, ed.) Cambridge University Press, Cambridge.

Angel, F. (1942). Les lézards de Madagascar. *Mém. Acad. malgache* (36) 1–193.

Angel, F. (1946). Reptiles et amphibiens. *Faune Fr.* (45) 1–204.

Anonymous. (1968). "The Naturalists' Directory (International). 40th Edition – 1968–9." PCL Publications, South Orange, New Jersey.

Barash, A. and Hoofien, J. H. (1956). "Reptiles of Israel" (in Hebrew). Hakibutz Hameuchad Ltd., Tel Aviv.

Barbour, T. (1937). Third list of Antillean reptiles and amphibians. *Bull. Mus. comp. Zool. Harvard* 82, 77–166.

Barbour, T. and Ramsden, C. T. (1919). The herpetology of Cuba. *Mem. Mus. comp. Zool. Harvard.* 47, 69–214.

Berger, L., Jaskowska, J. and Młynarski, M. (1969). Płazy i gady (Amphibia et Reptilia). *Kat. Fauny polski (Catalogus Faunae Poloniae)* 39, 1–73.

Beskov, V. and Beron, P. (1964). "Catalogue et Bibliographie des Amphibiens et des Reptiles en Bulgarie." Acad. Bulgare Sci., Sofia.

Bleakney, J. S. (1958). A zoogeographical study of the amphibians and reptiles of eastern Canada. *Bull. natn. Mus. Can.* (155) 1–119.

Bogdanov, O. P. (1960). Amphibians and reptiles. (in Russian). *Fauna Usbeskej SSR* 1–260.

Bogdanov, O. P. (1962). "Reptiles of Turkmenia" (in Russian). Akad. Nauk Turkmenskoi SSR, Ashgabat.

Bogert, C. M. (1940). Herpetological results of the Vernay Angola Expedition. With notes on African reptiles in other collections. I. Snakes, including an arrangement of African Colubridae. *Bull. Am. Mus. nat. Hist.* 77(1), 1–107.

Bons, J. (1959). Les lacertiliens du sud-ouest Marocain. *Trav. Inst. scient. chérif.*, Sér. Zool. (18) 1–130.

Boulenger, G. A. (1885a). "Catalogue of the Lizards in the British Museum (Natural History). Second Edition. Volume I." British Museum (Nat. Hist.), London. (reprinted 1966).

Boulenger, G. A. (1885b). "Catalogue of the Lizards in the British Museum (Natural History). Second Edition. Volume II." British Museum (Nat. Hist.), London. (reprinted 1966).

Boulenger, G. A. (1887). "Catalogue of the Lizards in the British Museum (Natural History). Second Edition. Volume III." British Museum (Nat. Hist.), London. (reprinted 1966).

Boulenger, G. A. (1889). "Catalogue of the Chelonians, Rhynchocephalians, and Crocodiles in the British Museum (Natural History)." British Museum (Nat. Hist.), London. (reprinted 1966).

Boulenger, G. A. (1893). "Catalogue of the Snakes in the British Museum (Natural History). Volume I." British Museum (Nat. Hist.), London. (reprinted 1961).

Boulenger, G. A. (1894). "Catalogue of the Snakes in the British Museum (Natural History). Volume II." British Museum (Nat. Hist.), London. (reprinted 1961).

Boulenger, G. A. (1896). "Catalogue of the Snakes in the British Museum (Natural History). Volume III." British Museum (Nat. Hist.), London. (reprinted 1961).

Bourret, R. (1936). "Les Serpents de l'Indochine." 2 vols. Henri Basuyau, Toulouse.

Bourret, R. (1941). Les tortues de l'Indochine. *Publ. Inst. Oceanogr. Indochine Nhatrang* (38) 1–235.

Bourret, R. (1943). "Comment Déterminer un Lézard d'Indochine." Trung-Bac Tan-Van, Hanoi.

Broadley, D. G. (1959). The herpetology of Southern Rhodesia. Part I. Snakes. *Bull. Mus. comp. Zool. Harvard* **129**(1), 1–100.

Broadley, D. G. (1968). The venomous snakes of Central and South Africa. *In* "Venomous Animals and Their Venoms. Volume I." (W. Bücherl, E. Buckley, and V. Deulofeu, eds). Academic Press, New York.

Bund, C. F. van de (1964). De verspreiding van de reptilien en amphibieen in Nederland. *Lacerta* **22**(4–5), 1–72.

Burt, C. E. and Burt, M. D. (1933). A preliminary check-list of the lizards of South America. *Trans. Acad. Sci. St. Louis* **28**(1–2), 1–104.

Cansdale, G. S. (1961). "West African Snakes." Longman, London.

Carr, A. (1952). "Handbook of Turtles. The Turtles of the United States, Canada, and Baja California." Cornell University Press, Ithaca. (reprinted 1966).

Chernov, S. A. (1959). Reptiles. (in Russian). *Fauna Tajikskoi SSR* (18) 1–204.

Clark, R. J., Clark, E. D., Anderson, S. C. and Leviton, A. E. (1969). Report on a collection of amphibians and reptiles from Afghanistan. *Proc. Calif. Acad. Sci.* (4), **36**, 279–316.

Cochran, D. M. (1941). The herpetology of Hispaniola. *Bull. U.S. natn. Mus.* 177, 1–398.

Conant, R. (1958). "A Field Guide to Reptiles and Amphibians of the United States and Canada East of the 100th Meridian." Houghton Mifflin, Boston. (a new edition is in preparation).

Conant, R. *et al.* (1956). Common names for North American amphibians and reptiles. *Copeia* **1956**, 172–185.

Crawford, S. C. (1931). Field keys to the lizards and amphibians of British Guiana. *Ann. Carneg. Mus.* **21**, 11–42.

Cunha, O. R. da (1961). II. Lacertilios da Amazonia. *Bolm. Mus. para. "Emilio Goeldi" (Zool.)* (N.S.), (39) 1–189.

Darlington, P. J., Jr. (1957). "Zoogeography: The Geographic Distribution of Animals." John Wiley, New York.

Denburgh, J. van (1912a). The snakes of the Galapagos Islands. *Proc. Calif. Acad. Sci.* (4), **1**, 323–374.

Denburgh, J. van (1912b). The geckos of the Galapagos Archipelago. *Proc. Calif. Acad. Sci.* (4), 1, 405–430.

Denburgh, J. van (1914). The gigantic land tortoises of the Galapagos Archipelago. *Proc. Calif. Acad. Sci.* (4), 2(1), 203–374.

Denburgh, J. van and Slevin, J. R. (1913). The Galapagos lizards of the genus *Tropidurus*; with notes on the iguanas of the genera *Conolophus* and *Amblyrhynchus*. *Proc. Calif. Acad. Sci.* (4), 2, 133–202.

Deoras, P. J. (1965). "Snakes of India." National Book Trust, New Delhi.

Deraniyagala, P. E. P. (1939). "The Tetrapod Reptiles of Ceylon. Volume I. Testudinates and Crocodilians." Colombo Museum, Colombo.

Deraniyagala, P. E. P. (1953). Tetrapod Reptilia. *In* "A Coloured Atlas of Some Vertebrates from Ceylon." Vol. 2. Government Press, Ceylon.

Deraniyagala, P. E. P. (1955). Serpentoid Reptilia. *In* "A Coloured Atlas of Some Vertebrates from Ceylon." Vol. 3. Government Press, Ceylon.

Donoso Barros, R. (1966). "Reptiles de Chile." University of Chile, Santiago de Chile.

Donoso Barros, R. (1968). Lizards of Venezuela. *Carrib. J. Sci.* 8(304), 105–122.

Dottrens, E. and Aellen, V. (1963). "Batraciens et Reptiles d'Europe." Delachaux et Niestlé, Neuchatel.

Doucet, J. (1963). Les serpents de la République de Côte d'Ivoire. *Acta trop.* 20, 201–340.

Dunn, E. R. (1957). "Contributions to the Herpetology of Colombia. 1943–1946." Reprinted from the Revista de la Academia Colombiana de Ciencias Exactas, Físicas y Naturales and from Caldasia Boletín del Institutto de Ciencias Naturales de la Universidad Nacional de Colombia-Bogotá. Privately printed.

FitzSimons, V. F. M. (1943). The lizards of South Africa. *Transv. Mus. Mem.* 1, i–xvi + 1–528.

FitzSimons, V. F. M. (1962). "Snakes of Southern Africa." Macdonald, London.

FitzSimons, V. F. M. (1966). A check-list, with synoptic keys, to the snakes of Southern Africa. *Ann. Transv. Mus.* 25(3), 35–79.

Frommhold, E. (1959). "Wir Bestimmen Lurche und Kriechtiere Mitteleuropas." Neumann Verlag, Radebeul.

Fuhn, I. E. and Vançea, S. (1961). Reptilia (Ţestoase, şopîrle, şerpi). *In* "Fauna Republicii Populare Romîne." Acad. Rep. Pop. Romîne, Bucharest.

Gans, C. (1966). Liste der rezenten Amphibien und Reptilien. Uropeltidae. *Tierreich* (84) 1–29.

Gans, C. (1967). A check-list of recent amphisbaenians (Amphisbaenia, Reptilia). *Bull. Am. Mus. nat. Hist.* 135(2), 6–105.

Gans, C., Laurent, R. F. and Pandit, H. (1965). Notes on a herpetological collection from the Somali Republic. *Annls. Mus. r. Afr. cent. (Sci. Zool.)* (8°), (134), 1–93.

Gijzen, A. and Wermuth, H. (1958). Schildkröten-Pflege in öffentlichen Schau-Aquarien nach biologischen Gesichtspunkten. *Bull. Soc. r. Zool. Anvers* (6) 1–65.

Gislén, T. and Kauri, H. (1959). Zoogeography of the Swedish amphibians and reptiles with notes on their growth and ecology. *Acta Vert.* 1(3), 197–397.

Goode, J. (1967). "Freshwater Tortoises of Australia and New Guinea (in the Family Chelidae)." Landsowne Printery Ltd., Melbourne.

Goris, R. C. (1966). "Reptiles of Japan" (in Japanese). Shogakkan, Tokyo.

Grant, C. (1940). The herpetology of Jamaica. II. The reptiles. *Bull. Inst. Jamaica Sci. Ser.* 1, 61–148.

Guibé, J. (1958). Les serpents de Madagascar. *Mém. Inst. scient. Madagascar* (A), 12, 189–260.

Haas, C. P. J. de (1950). Check-list of the snakes of the Indo-Australian Archipelago (Reptiles, Ophidia). *Treubia* **20**(3), 511–625.

Haas, G. (1957). Some amphibians and reptiles from Arabia. *Proc. Calif. Acad. Sci.* (4), **29**, 47–86.

Hellmich, W. (1962). "Reptiles and Amphibians of Europe." Blandford Press, Ltd., London.

Hoesel, J. K. P. van (1959). "Ophidia Javanica." Museum Zoologicum Bogoriense, Bogor.

Hoge, A. R. (1965). Preliminary account on neotropical Crotalinae (Serpentes, Viperidae). *Mems. Inst. Butantan* **32**, 109–184.

Hughes, B. (in press). A check-list and key to the snakes of Ghana. *Bull. Inst. Fond. Afrique Noire.*

Hvass, H. (1936). "Danmarks Padder og Krybdyr." G. E. C. Gads Forlag, Copenhagen.

Khalaf, K. T. (1959). "Reptiles of Iraq, With Some Notes on the Amphibians." Ar-Rabitta Press, Baghdad.

Kimura, W. (1966). "Crocodilians of the World" (in Japanese). Atagawa Alligator Gardens, Atagawa Higashi Riu, Shizuoka.

Kinghorn, J. R. (1964). "The Snakes of Australia." 2nd edition. Angus and Robertson, Sydney.

Klemmer, K. (1963). Liste der rezenten Giftschlangen. Elapidae, Hydropheidae, Viperidae und Crotalidae. *In* "Die Giftschlangen der Erde." N. G. Elwert Univ. und Verlagsbuchhandlung, Marburg/Lahn.

Klemmer, K. (1968). Classification and distribution of European, North African, and North and West Asiatic venomous snakes. *In* "Venomous Animals and Their Venoms. Volume I." (W. Bücherl, E. Buckley and V. Deulofeu, eds.). Academic Press, New York.

Klingelhöffer, W. (1955–1959). "Terrarienkunde." 2nd edition. Revised by C. Scherpner. 4 vols. A. Kernen, Stuttgart.

Kuhn, O. (1967). "Amphibien und Reptilien. Katalog der Subfamilien und Höheren Taxa mit Nachweis des Ersten Auftretens." Gustav Fischer, Stuttgart.

Kuntz, R. E. (1963). Snakes of Taiwan. *Q. Jl. Taiwan Mus.* **16**(1–2), 1–80. (reprinted, U. S. Navy Med. Res. Unit No. 2).

Laurent, R. F. (1956). Contribution à l'herpétologie de la région des Grands Lacs de l'Afrique centrale. *Annls. Mus. r. Congo belge (Sci. Zool.)* (8°), **48**, 1–390.

Laurent, R. F. (1960). Notes complémentaires sur les chéloniens et les ophidiens du Congo oriental. *Annls. Mus. r. Congo belge (Sci. Zool.)* (8°), **84**, 1–86.

Laurent, R. F. (1964). Reptiles et amphibiens de l'Angola (Troisième contribution). *Mus. Dundo Publ. Culturais* (67) 1–165.

Laurent, R. F. (1965). Contribution à l'histoire de l'herpétologie congolaise et bibliographie générale. *Koninkl. Acad. Overz. Wetensch., Kl. Nat. Geneesk. Wetensch.* (N.S.), **16**(3), 1–53.

Leeson, F. (1950). "Identification of Snakes of the Gold Coast." Crown Agents for the Colonies, London.

Leviton, A. E. (1959). Report on a collection of reptiles from Afghanistan. *Proc. Calif. Acad. Sci.* (4), **29**, 445–463.

Leviton, A. E. (1961). Keys to the dangerously venomous terrestrial snakes of the Philippine Islands. *Silliman J.* **8**(2), 98–106.

Leviton, A. E. (1963a). Remarks on the zoogeography of Philippine terrestrial snakes. *Proc. Calif. Acad. Sci.* (4), **31**(15), 369–416.

Leviton, A. E. (1963b). Contributions to a review of Philippine snakes, I. The snakes of the genus *Oligodon*. *Philipp. J. Sci.* **91**(4), 459–484.

Leviton, A. E. (1964a). Contributions to a review of Philippine snakes, II. The snakes of the genera *Liopeltis* and *Sibynophis*. *Philipp. J. Sci.* 92(3), 367–379.

Leviton, A. E. (1964b). Contributions to a review of Philippine snakes, III. The snakes of the genera *Maticora* and *Calliophis*. *Philipp. J. Sci.* 92(4), 523–550.

Leviton, A. E. (1964c). Contributions to a review of Philippine snakes, IV. The snakes of the genera *Chrysopelea* and *Dryophiops*. *Philipp. J. Sci.* 93(1), 131–145.

Leviton, A. E. (1964d). Contributions to a review of Philippine snakes, V. The snakes of the genus *Trimeresurus*. *Philipp. J. Sci.* 93(2), 251–276.

Leviton, A. E. (1965a). Contributions to a review of Philippine snakes, VI. The snakes of the genus *Oxyrhabdium*. *Philipp. J. Sci.* 93(3), 407–422.

Leviton, A. E. (1965b). Contributions to a review of Philippine snakes, VII. The snakes of the genera *Naja and Ophiophagus*. *Philipp. J. Sci.* 93(4), 531–550.

Leviton, A. E. (1965c). Contributions to a review of Philippine snakes, VIII. The snakes of the genus *Lycodon* H. Boie. *Philipp. J. Sci.* 94(1), 117–140.

Leviton, A. E. (1965d). Contributions to a review of Philippine snakes, IX. The snakes of the genus *Cyclocorus*. *Philipp. J. Sci.* 94(4), 519–523.

Leviton, A. E. (1968a). Contributions to a review of Philippine snakes, X. The snakes of the genus *Ahaetulla*. *Philipp. J. Sci.* 96(1), 73–90.

Leviton, A. E. (1968b). The venomous terrestrial snakes of East Asia, India, Malaya, and Indonesia. *In* "Venomous Animals and Their Venoms. Volume I." (W. Bücherl, E. Buckley and V. Deulofeu, eds.). Academic Press, New York.

Leviton, A. E. and Anderson, S. C. (1961). Further remarks on the amphibians and reptiles of Afghanistan. *Wasmann J. Biol.* 19, 269–276.

Leviton, A. E. and Anderson, S. C. (1963). Third contribution to the herpetology of Afghanistan. *Proc. Calif. Acad. Sci.* (4), 31(12), 329–339.

Leviton, A. E. and Anderson, S. C. (1967). Survey of the reptiles of the Sheikhdom of Abu Dhabi, Arabian Peninsula. Part II. Systematic account of the collection of reptiles made in the Sheikhdom of Abu Dhabi by John Gasperetti. *Proc. Calif. Acad. Sci.* (4), 35, 157–192.

Logier, E. B. S. and Toner, G. C. (1961). Check-list of the amphibians and reptiles of Canada and Alaska. A revision of Contribution No. 41. *Contr. Life Sci. Div. R. Ont. Mus.* (53) 1–92.

Loveridge, A. (1946). "Reptiles of the Pacific World." Macmillan, New York.

Loveridge, A. (1947). Revision of the African lizards of the family Gekkonidae. *Bull. Mus. comp. Zool. Harvard* 98, 1–469.

Loveridge, A. (1948). New Guinean reptiles and amphibians in the Museum of Comparative Zoölogy and United States National Museum. *Bull. Mus. comp. Zool. Harvard* 101(2), 305–430.

Loveridge, A. (1957). Check-list of the reptiles and amphibians of East Africa (Uganda; Kenya; Tanganyika; Zanzibar). *Bull. Mus. comp. Zool. Harvard* 117(2), 153–362 + i–xxxvi.

Loveridge, A. and Williams, E. E. (1957). Revision of the African tortoises and turtles of the suborder Cryptodira. *Bull. Mus. comp. Zool. Harvard* 115(6), 161–557.

Maki, M. (1931). "A Monograph of the Snakes of Japan." 3 vols. Dai-Ichi Shobo, Tokyo.

Marx, H. (1968). Check-list of the reptiles and amphibians of Egypt. *Spec. Publs. U. S. Naval Med. Res. Unit No.* 3, Cairo, 1–91.

McCann, C. (1955). The lizards of New Zealand. *Dom. Mus. Bull.* (17), i–viii + 1–127.

Medem, F. and Marx, H. (1955). An artificial key to the New-World species of crocodilians. *Copeia* 1955, 1–2.

Mertens, R. (1930). Die Amphibien und Reptilien der Inseln Bali, Lombok, Sumbawa und Flores (Beitrag zur Fauna der Kleinen Sunda-Inseln I). *Abh. senckenb. Naturforsch. Ges.* **42**(3), 117–342.

Mertens, R. (1952a). Die Amphibien und Reptilien von El Salvador auf Grund der Reisen von R. Mertens und A. Zilch. *Abh. senckenb. naturforsch. Ges.* (487) 1–120.

Mertens, R. (1952b). Turkiye amfibi ve reptilleri hakkinda. Amphibien und Reptilien aus der Türkei. *Rev. Fac. Sci. Univ. Istanbul* (B), **17**(1), 41–75.

Mertens, R. (1953). Anadolu herpetofaunasi hakkinda. Weiteres zur Kenntnis der Herpeto-fauna der asiatischen Türkei. *Rev. Fac. Sci. Univ. Istanbul* (B), **18**(3–4), 373–375.

Mertens, R. (1955). Die Amphibien und Reptilien Sudwestafrikas. Aus den Ergebnissen einer im Jahr 1952 ausgeführten Reise. *Abh. senckenb. naturforsch. Ges.* (490) 1–172.

Mertens, R. (1960). "The World of Amphibians and Reptiles." McGraw-Hill, New York.

Mertens, R. (1963). Liste der rezenten Amphibien und Reptilien. Helodermatidae, Varanidae, Lanthanotidae. *Tierreich* (79) i–x + 1–26.

Mertens, R. (1966). Liste der rezenten Amphibien und Reptilien. Chamaeleonidae. *Tierreich* (83) i–x + 1–37.

Mertens, R. (1969). Die Amphibien und Reptilien West-Pakistans. *Stuttg. Beitr. Naturk* (in press).

Mertens, R. and Wermuth, H. (1960). "Die Amphibien und Reptilien Europas." Walde-mar Kramer, Frankfurt.

Minton, S. A. (1962). An annotated key to the amphibians and reptiles of Sind and Las Bela, West Pakistan. *Am. Mus. Novit.* (2081) 1–60.

Minton, S. A. (1966). A contribution to the herpetology of West Pakistan. *Bull. Am. Mus. nat. Hist.* **134**(2), 31–184.

Minton, S. A., Dowling, H. G. and Russell, F. E. (1968). "Poisonous Snakes of the World. A Manual for Use by U. S. Amphibious Forces." NAVMED P-5099. U. S. Govern-ment Printing Office, Washington.

Młynarski, M. (1966). "Płazy i gady Polski." Panstwowe Zaklady Wydawnicts Szkolnych, Warszawa.

Nakamura, K. and Ueno, S. (1963). "Reptiles and Amphibians of Japan" (in Japanese). Hoiku Co., Osaka.

Okada, Y. (1936). Studies on the lizards of Japan. Contribution I. Gekkonidae. *Sci. Rep. Tokyo Bunrika Daig.* **2**(42), 233–289.

Okada, Y. (1937). Studies on the lizards of Japan. Contribution II. Agamidae. *Sci. Rep. Tokyo Bunrika Daig.* **3**(51), 83–94.

Okada, Y. (1939). Studies on the lizards of Japan. Contribution III. Scincidae. *Sci. Rep. Tokyo Bunrika Daig.* **4**(73), 159–214.

Oliver, J. A. and Shaw, C. E. (1953). The amphibians and reptiles of the Hawaiian Islands. *Zoologica, N. Y.* **38**(5), 65–95.

Ontria, J. J. (1966). "Recent Amphibians and Reptiles of Greece" (in Greek).

Oshima, M. (1943). "Descriptions of the Poisonous Snakes of the Greater East Asia Co-Prosperity Sphere" (in Japanese). Hoku Riu Kan, Tokyo.

Paraskiv, K. P. (1956). "Reptiles of Kazakhstan" (in Russian). Akad. Nauk Kazakhskoi SSR, Alma-Alta.

Parker, H. W. (1942). The lizards of British Somaliland. *Bull. Mus. comp. Zool. Harvard* **91**(1), 1–101.

Parker, H. W. (1949). The snakes of Somaliland and the Sokotra Islands. *Zool. Verh.*, Leiden (6) 1–115.

Pasteur, G. and Bons, J. (1960). Catalogue des reptiles actuels du Maroc. Révision de formes d'Afrique, d'Europe et d'Asie. *Trav. Inst. scient. chérif., Sér. Zool.* (21) 1–132.

Peters, J. A. (1960). The snakes of Ecuador. *Bull. Mus. comp. Zool. Harvard* **122**(9), 491–541.

Peters, J. A. (1965). Liste der rezenten Amphibien und Reptilien. Colubridae (Dipsadinae). *Tierreich* (81), i–viii + 1–19.

Peters, J. A. (1967). The lizards of Ecuador, a check-list and key. *Proc. U. S. natn. Mus.* **119**(3545), 1–49.

Pienaar, U. de V. (1966). "The Reptiles of the Kruger National Park." National Parks Board of Trustees, Pretoria.

Pitman, C. R. S. (1938). "A Guide to the Snakes of Uganda." The Uganda Society, Kampala.

Pope, C. H. (1935). "Natural History of Central Asia. Volume 10. The Reptiles of China." American Museum of Natural History, New York.

Pozzi, A. (1966). Geonemia e catalogo ragionato degli anfibi e dei rettili della Jugoslavia. *Natura, Milano* **57**, 5–55.

Pritchard, P. C. H. (1967). "Living Turtles of the World." T. F. H. Publications, Jersey City.

Radovanović, M. (1951). "Vodozemci i Gmizavci nase Zemlje" (with a German summary: "Amphibien und Reptilien Jugoslaviens.") Belgrade.

Radovanović, M. and Martino, K. (1950). The snakes of the Balkan Peninsula. (in Serbian). *Nauehno-Popularni Spisi Srpska Akad. Nauka* **1**, 1–75.

Riemer, W. J., ed. (1963–). "Catalogue of American Amphibians and Reptiles." American Society of Ichthyologists and Herpetologists.

Romer, A. S. (1956). "Osteology of the Reptiles." Univ. Chigago Press, Chicago.

Rooij, N. de (1915). "The Reptiles of the Indo-Australian Archipelago. I. Lacertilia, Chelonia, Emydosauria." E. J. Brill, Leiden.

Rooij, N. de (1917). "The Reptiles of the Indo-Australian Archipelago. II. Ophidia." E. J. Brill, Leiden.

Roze, J. A. (1966)."La Taxonomia y Zoogeografia de los Ofidios de Venezuela." Univ. Central de Venezuela, Caracas. (reviewed by J. A. Peters, *Copeia*, **1967**, 496–498).

Schmidt, K. P. (1953). "A Check List of North American Amphibians and Reptiles." 6th edition. American Society of Ichthyologists and Herpetologists, Chicago.

Schmidt, K. P. and Inger, R. F. (1957). "Living Reptiles of the World." Hanover House, Garden City.

Schreiber, E. (1912). "Herpetologia Europaea (Eine Systematische Bearbeitung der Amphibien und Reptilien, Welche Bisher in Europa Aufgefunden Sind)." 2nd edition. Gustav Fischer, Jena.

Sharell, R. (1966). "The Tuatara, Lizards and Frogs of New Zealand." Collins, London.

Shcherbak, N. N. (1966). "Herpetologia Taurica" (in Russian). Akad. Nauk Ukrainskio SSR, Kiev.

Slater, K. (1968). "Guide to the Dangerous Snakes of Papua (Including Sections on First-Aid Treatment of Snake Bite by C. H. Campbell)." Government Printer, Port Moresby.

Smith, H. M. (1946). "Handbook of Lizards." Comstock Publishing Co., Ithaca.

Smith, H. M. and Taylor, E. H. (1945). An annotated check-list and key to the snakes of Mexico. *Bull. U. S. natn. Mus.* (187) 1–239. (Reprinted 1966).

Smith, H. M. and Taylor, E. H. (1950). An annotated check-list and key to the reptiles of Mexico exclusive of the snakes. *Bull. U. S. natn. Mus.* (199) 1–253. (Reprinted 1966.)

Smith, M. A. (1926). "Monograph of the Sea-snakes (Hydrophiidae)." British Museum (Nat. Hist.), London.

Smith, M. A. (1930). The Reptilia and Amphibia of the Malay Peninsula. *Bull. Raffles Mus.* **3**, i–xviii + 1–149.

Smith, M. A. (1931). "The Fauna of British India, Including Ceylon and Burma. Reptilia and Amphibia. Volume I. Loricata, Testudines." Taylor and Francis, London.

Smith, M. A. (1935). "The Fauna of British India, Including Ceylon and Burma. Reptilia and Amphibia. Volume II. Sauria." Taylor and Francis, London.

Smith, M. A. (1943). "The Fauna of British India, Ceylon and Burma, Including the Whole of the Indo-Chinese Sub-Region. Reptilia and Amphibia. Volume III. Serpentes." Taylor and Francis, London.

Smith, M. A. (1951). "The British Amphibians and Reptiles." Collins, London.

Stebbins, R. C. (1954). "Amphibians and Reptiles of Western North America." McGraw-Hill, New York.

Stebbins, R. C. (1966). "A Field Guide to Western Reptiles and Amphibians." Houghton Mifflin, Boston.

Stimson, A. F. (1969). Liste der rezenten Amphibien und Reptilien. Boidae (Boinae + Bolyeriinae + Loxoceminae + Pythoninae). *Tierreich* (89) i–xi, 1–49.

Stuart, L. C. (1963). A check-list of the herpetofauna of Guatemala. *Misc. Publs. Mus. Zool. Univ. Mich.* (122) 1–150.

Swan, L. W. and Leviton, A. E. (1962). The herpetology of Nepal: A history, check-list, and zoogeographical analysis of the herpetofauna. *Proc. Calif. Acad. Sci.* (4), **32**, 103–147.

Taratschuk, W. J. (1959). Amphibians and reptiles. (in Russian). *Fauna Ukrainy* (7) 1–247.

Taylor, E. H. (1920). Philippine turtles. *Philipp. J. Sci.* **16**(2), 111–144.

Taylor, E. H. (1921). "Amphibians and Turtles of the Philippine Islands." Bureau of Printing, Manila.

Taylor, E. H. (1922). The lizards of the Philippine Islands. *Philipp. Bur. Sci., Manila, Monogr.* (17), 1–269.

Taylor, E. H. (1951). A brief review of the snakes of Costa Rica. *Kans. Univ. Sci. Bull.* **34**(1), 3–188.

Taylor, E. H. (1953). A review of the lizards of Ceylon. *Kans. Univ. Sci. Bull.* **35**(12), 1525–1585.

Taylor, E. H. (1954a). Additions to the known herpetological fauna of Costa Rica with comments on other species. No. I. *Kans. Univ. Sci. Bull.* **36**(9), 587–639.

Taylor, E. H. (1954b). Further studies on the serpents of Costa Rica. *Kans. Univ. Sci. Bull.* **36**(11), 673–801.

Taylor, E. H. (1955). Additions to the known herpetological fauna of Costa Rica with comments on other species. No. II. *Kans. Univ. Sci. Bull.* **37**(13), 499–575.

Taylor, E. H. (1956). A review of the lizards of Costa Rica. *Kans. Univ. Sci. Bull.* **38**(1), 1–322.

Taylor, E. H. (1958). Additions to the known herpetological fauna of Costa Rica with comments on other species. No. III. *Kans. Univ. Sci. Bull.* **39**(1), 3–40.

Taylor, E. H. (1963). The lizards of Thailand. *Kans. Univ. Sci. Bull.* **44**(14), 687–1077.

Taylor, E. H. (1965). The serpents of Thailand and adjacent waters. *Kans. Univ. Sci. Bull.* **45**(9), 609–1096.

Terent'ev, P. V. and Chernov, S. A. (1949). "Opredelitel Presmykaiu Schikhsia i Zemno-vodnykh." Gosudarstvennoe Izdatel'stvo "Vyshaya shkola", Moskva. (translation: 1965, "Key to Amphibians and Reptiles", Israel Program for Scientific Translations, Jerusalem).

Tortonese, E. and Lanza, B. (1968). "Pesci, Anfibi e Rettili." Aldo Martello, Milano.

Tweedie, M. W. F. (1961). "The Snakes of Malaya." Reprinted edition. Government Printing Office, Singapore.

Underwood, G. (1962). Caribbean affairs—Reptiles of the eastern Caribbean. *Dept. Extra-Mural Stud., Univ. West Indies* (N.S.), (1), 1–192.

Underwood, G. (1967). "A Contribution to the Classification of Snakes." British Museum (Nat. Hist.), London.

Vanzolini, P. E. (1968). Lagartos brasileiros da família Gekkonidae (Sauria). *Archos. Zool. Est. S. Paulo* **17**, 1–84.

Villiers, A. (1958). Tortues et crocodiles de l'Afrique Noire Francaise. *Init. afr. Inst. Franç. Afr. Noire* (15) 1–354.

Villiers, A. (1963). Les serpentes de l'ouest Africain. *Init. afr. Inst. Franç. Afr. Noire* (2, 2nd edition), 1–190.

Waite, E. R. (1929). "The Reptiles and Amphibians of South Australia." Harrison Weir, Government Printer, Adelaide.

Wang, C.-S. and Wang, Y. M. (1956). The reptile [sic!] of Taiwan. *Q. Jl. Taiwan Mus.* **9**, 1–86.

Werler, J. E. and Keegan, H. L. (1963). Venomous snakes of the Pacific area. *In* "Venomous and Poisonous Animals and Noxious Plants of the Pacific Region." (H. L. Keegan, ed.). Macmillan, New York.

Wermuth, H. (1965). Liste der rezenten Amphibien und Reptilien. Gekkonidae, Pygopodidae, Xantusiidae. *Tierreich* (80), i–xxii + 1–246.

Wermuth, H. (1967). Liste der rezenten Amphibien und Reptilien. Agamidae. *Tierreich* (86), i–xiv + 1–127.

Wermuth, H. (1968). Liste der rezenten Amphibien und Reptilien. Cordylidae (Cordylinae + Gerrhosaurinae). *Tierreich* (87), i–x + 1–30.

Wermuth, H. (1969). Liste der rezenten Amphibien und Reptilien. Anguidae, Anniellidae, Xenosauridae. *Tierreich* (90), i–xii, 1–42.

Wermuth, H. and Mertens, R. (1961). "Schildkröten, Krokodile, Brückenechsen." Gustav Fischer Verlag, Jena.

Werner, F. (1938). Die Amphibien und Reptilien Griechenlands. *Zoologica, Stuttg.* (84) 1–117.

Wettstein, O. (1953). Herpetologia Aegaea. *Sber. österr. Akad. Wiss., Math.-naturw. Kl.,* Abt. I **162**(9–10), 651–833.

Wettstein, O. (1957). Nachtrag zu meiner Herpetologia Aegaea. *Sber. österr. Akad. Wiss., Math.-naturw. Kl.,* Abt. I **166**(3–4), 123–164.

Witte, G.-F. de (1948). "Fauna Belgique. Amphibiens et Reptiles." 2nd edition. Mus. Roy. Hist. Nat. Belgique, Bruxelles.

Witte, G.-F. de (1962). Genera des serpentes du Congo et du Ruanda-Urundi. *Annls. Mus. r. Afr. cent. (Sci. Zool.)* (8°), **104**, 1–203.

Worrell, E. (1961). "Dangerous Snakes of Australia and New Guinea." 4th edition. Angus and Robertson, Sydney.

Worrell, E. (1963). "Reptiles of Australia." Angus and Robertson, Sydney.

Wright, A. H. and Wright, A. A. (1957). "Handbook of Snakes of the United States and Canada." Volumes I and II. Cornell University Press, Ithaca.

Wright, A. H. and Wright, A. A. (1962). "Handbook of Snakes of the United States and Canada." Volume III. A. H. and A. A. Wright, Ithaca.

Author Index

The numbers in *italics* indicate the pages on which names are mentioned in the reference lists.

A

Abel, J. H., 67, *93*, 176, 185
Abelsdorff, G., 72, *95*
Abrams, A. M., 279, *299*
Aellen, V., 322, *327*
Allison, A. C., 156, 157, 158, 162, 174, 175, *186*
Amaral, A. do, 322, *325*
Andelic, M., 230, *273*
Anderson, S. C., 322, 323, *325*, *326*, *329*
Angel, F., 322, 324, 325
Anonymous, 316, *325*
Armstrong, J. A., 33, 53, *93*, 119, 164, *185*
Asai, J., 311, *313*

B

Baird, I. L., 194, 201, 213, 226, 230, 231, 232, 233, 235, 236, 244, 250, 251, 254, 256, 258, 259, 261, *272*
Bannister, L. H., 162, *185*
Barash, A., 322, *325*
Barbour, T., 321, *325*
Barge, J. A. J., 137, *185*
Barrett, R., 279, 237, 289, 291, 292, 293, 294, 295, 296, *298*, 309, 311, 313
Barrows, S., 27, 31, *93*
Barry, T. H., 119, 178, *185*
Baumeister, L., 54, *93*, 120, 126, 179, 182, 185
Beard, J., 161, 162, 164, *185*
Beecker, A., 119, 120, 121, 126, 137, 164, *185*
Beer, G. R., de, 102, 103, 117, *186*, 197, 199, 220, 229, 230, 232, 233, 256, 259, *272*
Beer, T., 75, *93*
Bellairs, A. d'A., 13, 14, 15, 49, 63, *93*, 116, 119, 120, 121, 125, 126, 127, 137, 139, 140, 141, 143, 145, 146, 159, 168, 172, 176, 177, 178, 179, *185*, *190*, 216, 232, 235, *274*
Beneden, E. van, 232, *273*
Benson, G. K., 176, *185*
Bentley, P. J., 311, *313*
Berger, L., 322, *325*
Berman, D. S., 221, 273
Beron, P., 322, *325*
Bertau, M., 144, 145, 146, 148, 149, 150, 151, 152, 154, 159, 169, 173, 174, 177, 179, *185*
Beskov, V., 322, *325*
Bleakney, J. S., 321, 325
Bleichmar, H., 283, 284, 285, 288, *298*, 305
Bloom, G., 153, *186*
Bogdanov, O. P., 322, *325*
Bogert, C. M., 14, 83, *93*, *95*, 140, *188*, 277, *298*, 301, *304*, 324, *325*
Bonin, J. J., 24, 87, *94*
Bons, J., 324, *325*, *330*
Born, G., 119, 120, 121, 162, 164, 165, 168, 169, *186*
Boulenger, G. A., 315, *325*, *326*
Bourret, R., 323, *326*
Bowman, K., 294, *299*
Boycott, B. B., 39, 61, *94*
Boyd, J. D., 14, 15, 49, 63, *93*, 116, 119, 120, 121, 125, 127, 137, 139, 140, 141, 143, 168, 172, *185*
Brink, A. S., 153, *186*
Broadley, D. G., 319, 324, *326*
Brock, G. T., 142, *186*, 224, *273*
Broman, I., 120, 121, 141, 143, 161, 164, *186*
Broom, R., 116, 118, *186*
Brown, K. T., 288, *298*
Brühl, C. B., 144, *186*
Bruner, H. L., 50, *94*, 129, 145, *186*

335

Subject Index

A

Abastor
  ear, 271
  eye, 55, 61
Abducens foramen, 8
Abducens nerve, 7, 11, 49, 50, 67, 74
Ablepharus
  ear, 271
  eye, 14, 27, 30
  nose, 120, 140
Absteigender Schenkel des Choanen-
  ganges, *see* Choanal tube
Acanthodactylus
  ear, 245, 267, 271
  eye, 27, 30
Acanthophis
  ear, 272
  eye, 55, 62
Accessory member of double cell, 3
Accessory nerve, 197
Accessory olfactory bulb, 104, 114, 142, 152
Accessory scala tympani, 220, 242, 243, 244, 245, 246, 249, 250, 251, 255, 261
Accommodation of eye, 22, 52, 71, 72, 75, 79, 81, 82–83, 84, 86, 91
Acetylcholine esterase, 288
Achalinus, eye, 49
Acid mucopolysaccharide, 158, 175
Acidophilic granules, 180
Acontias
  ear, 221, 224, 244, 267, 271
  eye, 13
  nose, 120, 140
Acrantophis, pit organs, 301
Acrochordus
  ear, 269, 271
  eye, 83
  nose, 121, 122, 136, 159, 174
Action potential, 287
Adaptation to stimuli, 287

ATPase, 288
Adnexae of eye, 6–15, 48–50, 63–64, 66–67, 73–75
Aegean, 322
Aeluroscalabotes, eye, 14, 29
Afghanistan, 323
Africa, 324
Agama
  ear, 266, 271
  eye, 27, 41
  nose, 119, 129, 178
Agamidae
  ear, 224, 238, 240, 241, 266, 271
  eye, 20, 25, 27, 28, 30, 31, 89
  nose, 119, 128, 131, 135, 139, 140, 142, 143, 154, 156, 158, 178
  taxonomic literature, 320
Agamodon, eye, 24, 25
Agkistrodon
  ear, 270, 272
  eye, 61
  nose, 179
  pit organs, 280, 282, 287, 295, 305, 306, 312
Ahaetulla
  ear, 271
  eye, 54, 55, 63
  nose, 179
Ailuronyx, eye, 26, 31
Aipysurus, ear, 272
Alligator
  ear, 259, 270, 272
  eye, 5, 76, 77, 78
  nose, 144, 145, 146, 148, 149, 150, 160, 165, 167, 168, 173, 179
Allometric growth, 144, 148
Alsophis, ear, 271
Amacrine cells, 34, 39, 61
Amblyrhynchus
  ear, 270
  eye, 82

F

Lampropeltis (*contd*)
  pit organs, 295
Lamprophis
  eye, 63
  nose, 121, 135
Landolt's club, 36, 38
Lanthanotidae
  ear, 240, 241, 249–250, 271
  eye, 27
  nose, 140
  taxonomic literature, 320
Lanthanotus
  ear, 221, 224, 249, 271
  eye, 14, 27, 32, 83
  nose, 122, 140
Lapemis, ear, 272
Large single cone, *see* Type A cone
  see also Type A₁ cone
Lateral ampulla, 204, 206, 228
Lateral ampullary crest, 204
Lateral branch of ramus ethmoidalis, *see*
  Ramus lateralis nasi of ethmoidal nerve
Lateral cephalic vein, 50, 197
Lateral choanal fissure, 126, 134, 137, 138,
  140
Lateral ethmoid nerve, *see* Ramus lateralis
  nasi of ethmoidal nerve
Lateral Grenzfalte, 105, 106, 107, 108, 109,
  110, 111, 169, 177, 183
Lateral head vein, *see* Lateral cephalic vein
Lateral nasal gland, *see* External nasal gland
Lateral nasal gland of Müller, *see* External
  nasal gland
Lateral nasal process, 166, 168, 171
Lateral osseus ampulla, 202, 203
Lateral ramus of the ethmoidal nerve, *see*
  Ramus lateralis nasi of ethmoidal
  nerve
Lateral recess, 136
  see also Extraconchal space
Lateral recess of nasal sac, *see* Subconchal
  recess
Lateral semicircular canal, 203, 206
Lateral semicircular duct, 206, 207
Lateral sulcus, 105, 106, 109, 110, 155
Laterale Grenzleiste, *see* Lateral Grenzfalte
Laterale Nasendrüse, *see* External nasal
  gland
Lateraler Nasenfortsatz, *see* Lateral nasal
  process

Laticauda
  ear, 254, 270, 272
  nose, 121, 122, 130, 136, 174
Leiocephalus, ear, 271
Leioheterodon, ear, 272
Leiolepis, eye, 25, 27
Leiolopisma, ear, 207, 267, 271
Leiosaurus, nose, 119, 128
Lens, 2, 6, 18, 19, 20, 21, 22, 23, 24, 25, 33,
  52, 64, 65, 69, 70, 71, 72, 75, 82, 83
Lens aperture, 83
Lens capsule 4, 25, 64, 69, 70
Lens fibres, 4, 19, 25, 52
Lens sutures, 52, 75
Lens vesicle, 4
Lepidoblepharis, ear, 266, 271
Lepidodactylus
  ear, 271
  nose, 120
Lepidophyma
  ear, 271
  eye, 26, 30, 31
Lepidosauria, eye, 86–92
Leposternon, nose, 122
Leptodeira
  ear, 272
  eye, 62, 91
Leptoglossa, nose, 127, 139
Leptophis, ear, 272
Leptotyphlopidae
  ear, 227, 252, 253, 254, 268, 271
  eye, 54
  nose, 120
Leptotyphlops
  ear, 268, 271
  eye, 50, 51, 52, 54, 55
  nose, 120
Levator bulbi muscle, 7, 9, 11, 12, 13, 14,
  49, 67
Levator palpebralis superior muscle, 74
Levator vomeris muscle, 49
Lialis
  ear, 242, 266, 271
  eye, 15, 20, 26, 42, 43
  nose, 120, 127, 132, 178
Liasis
  ear, 269, 271
  pit organs, 295, 302, 303
Lichanura
  ear, 271

SUBJECT INDEX

Trachyboa (contd)
  pit organs, 301
Tränenkanal, *see* Lachrymal duct
Tränennasengang, *see* Lachrymal duct
Transduction, 288
Transmission of sound, *see* Middle ear
Transversalis muscle, 5, 17, 18, 19, 22, 41,
  52, 70, 75, 82
Tribolonotus, ear, 271
Trigeminal nerve, 11, 41, 50, 74, 75, 177,
  180, 281, 282, 289, 293, 294, 295, 296,
  297
Trimeresurus
  ear, 270, 272
  pit organs, 285, 287, 295, 296
Trimorphodon
  ear, 269, 272
  eye, 55, 63
Trinacromerum, eye, 80
Trionychidae
  ear, 265, 270
  nose, 106, 114
Trionychoidea, eye, 67
Trionyx
  ear, 254, 256, 257, 258, 265, 270
  eye, 68, 72
  nose, 104, 107, 108, 110, 113, 114, 178,
  180, 181
Triple cells, 35, 43, 44
Trochlear nerve, 7, 11, 49, 50
Trogonophidae
  ear, 224, 268, 271
  nose, 120
Trogonophis
  ear, 268, 271
  eye, 24, 43, 46, 48
  nose, 120, 127, 140, 143
Tropidonotus, *see Natrix*
Tropidophis
  ear, 271
  eye, 51, 54, 55, 56
  pit organs, 301
Tropidophorus, ear, 271
Tropidurinae, eye, 31
Tropidurus
  ear, 271
  nose, 119
True nasal cavity, *see* Cavum nasi proprium
"True sallet", 245
Tupinambis

  ear, 243, 267, 271
  eye, 20, 27
  nose, 120
Turbinal, *see* Concha
Turkey, 322
Turkmenia, 322
Twin cells, 42, 44, 45, 46, 48, 62
Two-tier pattern, 62, 85, 91
Tympanic cavity, 196, 197, 198, 201, 203,
  219, 222, 223, 224, 226, 229, 230, 231,
  232, 233, 242, 247, 262
Tympanic crest of quadrate, 198, 200
Tympanic lymph cavities, 224, 232
Tympanic membrane, 193, 194, 195, 196,
  197, 198, 199, 200, 201, 221, 223, 224,
  225, 226, 229, 230, 231, 232, 233, 242,
  262
Tympanic muscle, 199, 222, 233
Tympanic plate of extrastapes, 231
Tympanocryptis, ear, 271
Type A cone, 44, 56, 58, 60, 61, 62, 63, 86
Type A_1 cone, 34, 35, 36, 40, 41, 42, 45, 46
Type A_2 cone, 34, 35, 36, 40, 41, 42, 46
Type A twin cell, 91
Type B cone, 63
Type B double cell, 3, 34, 42, 43, 44, 45, 46,
  56, 60, 77, 91
Type C cone, 54, 56, 60, 61, 62, 63
Type C double cell, 3, 35, 42, 43, 44, 45, 46, 88
Type C' cell, *see* Type D rod
Type D rod, 54, 56, 63
Typhlacontias, eye, 14
Typhlopidae
  ear, 227, 252, 253, 254, 268, 271
  eye, 54
  nose, 120
Typhlops
  ear, 227, 228, 253, 254, 255, 268, 271
  eye, 24, 50, 51, 52, 54, 55, 87
  nose, 120, 122, 136
Typhlosaurus
  ear, 221, 224, 271
  nose, 140

U

Uganda, 324
Ukraine, 322
Uma
  ear, 223, 266, 271